European Demography and Economic Growth

First published in 1979, *European Demography and Economic Growth* presents a collection of essays on the demographic development of individual European economies like Austria, Hungary, Germany, France, Italy, Norway, Portugal etc. It provides a comparative analysis to clarify many crucial issues connected with the growth in European population from mid-eighteenth century. It looks at the suitable criteria for assessing the applicability of general theory to the experience of individual nations. It showcases the over-riding contrast between substantial economic variations on a national and regional level and the existence of common underlying demographic trends.

This book will be useful for scholars and researchers of economic history, political economy, European history, population geography and economics in general.

T0292883

European Demography and Economic Growth

Edited by W. R. Lee

Routledge
Taylor & Francis Group

First published in 1979
by Croom Helm Ltd

This edition first published in 2021 by Routledge
2 Park Square, Milton Park, Abingdon, Oxon, OX14 4RN
and by Routledge
605 Third Avenue, New York, NY 10017

Routledge is an imprint of the Taylor & Francis Group, an informa business

Publisher's Note
The publisher has gone to great lengths to ensure the quality of this reprint but points
out that some imperfections in the original copies may be apparent.

Disclaimer
The publisher has made every effort to trace copyright holders and welcomes
correspondence from those they have been unable to contact.

A Library of Congress record exists under LCCN:79305185

ISBN 13: 978-0-367-68687-1 (hbk)
ISBN 13: 978-1-003-13862-4 (ebk)
ISBN 13: 978-0-367-68690-1 (pbk)

European Demography and Economic Growth

Edited by W. R. LEE

CROOM HELM LONDON

© 1979 W.R. Lee
Croom Helm Ltd, 2-10 St John's Road, London SW11

British Library Cataloguing in Publication Data

European demography and economic growth.
   1. Europe — Population — History
   I. Lee, W R
   301. 32'9'4   HB3581

ISBN 0-85664-492-7

CONTENTS

For Liz, Henry, Pat, Tony, Susan, Richard and Vecha

PREFACE

The present collection of essays on the demographic development of individual European economies stems from an increasing awareness of three important trends. In the first place there has been a significant extension of studies in historical demography to a wide variety of individual European countries, following the early initiative in this field shown by France, and to a lesser extent, the United Kingdom. Secondly, a great deal of local research continues to remain relatively inaccessible to a wider international audience on account of a number of factors, including language barriers and the local journals in which a great deal of important field work is inevitably reported. Thirdly, demographic history as a discipline has never succeeded in establishing a unified methodology and still runs the risk of failing to concentrate on the inherent relationship between population growth and economic and social variables. Naturally a new direction will not be achieved overnight, but this series of individual studies will hopefully provide some indication of the present state of research in individual European countries and highlight the future directions which new research could take. Furthermore a comparative analysis should also help to clarify many of the crucial problems connected with the growth in European population from the mid-eighteenth century onwards and provide a suitable criterion for assessing the applicability of general theory to the experience of individual nation-states. I am of course tremendously grateful to the individual contributors, without whose constant co-operation this work would never have assumed a tangible form.

Liverpool   Robert Lee
September, 1977

INTRODUCTION: POPULATION GROWTH, ECONOMIC DEVELOPMENT AND SOCIAL CHANGE IN EUROPE, 1750-1970

Robert Lee

The role of the population variable in the process of economic growth from the mid-eighteenth century onwards has frequently been recognised as having been of crucial importance. According to Lörsch, 'changes in population are among the main causes of economic changes',[1] and the pattern of 'great waves' created by population growth has been compared in its effect to the impact of great wars. Certainly the overall magnitude of the increase in European population during the period under consideration cannot be doubted. Total population in Europe (including Russia) rose from 144 millions in 1750 to 274 millions (1850), 423 millions (1900) and to 506 millions by 1949.[2] The present set of individual essays attempts to deal with this unique phenomenon not from the point of view of what might be termed 'demographic accounting',[3] but in a more analytical fashion, with the emphasis placed largely on an examination not only of the causative mechanism behind population growth over time, but also of the intrinsic inter-relationship between the registered increase in total population and the coterminous process of economic development and social change. The geographical range of the countries included in this collection is itself considerable, ranging from the Scandinavian states of Norway, Sweden and Denmark, to Central Europe (Germany and Austria-Hungary), the Mediterranean economies of Italy and Portugal, the Low Countries, and finally France. Given the significant changes in territorial boundaries during this period, with the formal secession of Belgium from the Dutch Crown in 1839 and the transformation of the dual monarchy of Austria-Hungary after 1918-19 into a number of independent successor states, the present collection of essays effectively covers thirteen individual countries.[4] Although the coverage cannot be comprehensive, the selection is hopefully sufficiently wideranging to enable some tentative conclusions to be drawn on the general process of demographic change in Europe in the two centuries since 1750, which witnessed in every case the various stages of the demographic transition and the gradual shift from comparatively high birth and death rates, to comparatively low levels of both natality and mortality.

Naturally the precise emphasis of the individual contributions has been determined both by the quality of extant archival material and the historical development of demography as an academic discipline. France, of course, has benefited enormously from the stimulus of the INED (the National Institute for Demographic Studies), whereas political abuse of historical demography in Germany in the 1930s hindered the overall development of research in this important field. At the same time the technique of family reconstitution is already well advanced in certain countries (France, Sweden and Denmark), but still at an initial developmental stage in other European states (Austria, Germany and Portugal). The problems of implementing a uniform analysis of the central role of demographic change within the context of European economic development and social change are further compounded by substantial differences in the quality, extent and coverage of archival sources, at a national, regional and local level. Although many individual European states began an irregular compilation of census statistics during the eighteenth century,[5] which were increasingly devoted to purely demographic and not fiscal purposes, other countries were relatively slow in developing an interest in this subject. In Italy national statistics were not compiled until the post-unification period and in Austria-Hungary the legal basis for the holding of a regular census was only established in 1869. Furthermore the quality of the data frequently militates against a refined analysis of many aspects of the demographic variable. Official information on both internal and external migration in Italy does not become available until 1901 and in the case of Denmark not until 1929. Similarly much of the contemporary discussion on changes in illegitimacy rates and their general sociological significance must rest on the 'illegitimacy ratio' (the number of illegitimate births per 100 live births), rather than a more refined index which would relate illegitimacy to the specific age groups of unmarried women. The inherent problems of analysis are aggravated by inaccurate data and bureaucratic errors. At a national level census techniques in the late eighteenth century frequently left a great deal to be desired. The Dachsberg census of 1771 in Bavaria, for example, was not finally finished until 1781 and its value was further impaired by procedural faults.[6] The quality of aggregate data based on local compilations is invariably dependent on the conscientious fulfilment of registration duties on the part of parish clergy. In parts of Denmark there may well have been a 10 per cent under-registration of births in the 1770s and the mechanism of compiling population statistics in a number of European states, at least in the earlier decades of the period under examination, would have allowed considerable scope for error. However, many of these individual contributions provide a useful survey of present research into the reliability of both national and local data, and this factor should clearly be taken into consideration in any general analysis of comparative trends in the demographic variable.

What immediately emerges from this collection of essays is the over-riding contrast between substantial socio-economic variations on a national and regional level, and the existence of common underlying demographic trends. The economic development of the various European states followed a variegated pattern. If the onset of the 'agricultural revolution' is taken as an approximate index of general economic development during the early part of this period, almost an entire century separated the significant rise in primary sector output in France (1750-6), from an equivalent increase in Austria, Italy and Sweden (1820-30).[7] Indeed no matter what specific criterion is employed, whether based on the sectoral structure of employment, or per capita growth in GNP, it is abundantly clear that the economic development of Belgium was significantly divergent from that of Portugal. Belgium was the first continental state to adopt on a large scale the pattern of industrial production initially developed in the United Kingdom, whereas substantial economic change was only evident in Portugal after 1945, despite the fact that the protectionist policies of the *condicionamento industrial* in the inter-war years had contributed to a gradual movement away from total dependence on the primary sector. Regional differences of a social and economic nature were also all-pervasive in a number of nation-states and no more so than in the heterogeneous territories incorporated into the Austro-Hungarian Monarchy. In Sweden, for example, the original subdivision of the country into three separate zones (north, east and west) by Gustaf Sundbärg in the mid-nineteenth century has been confirmed as an accurate portrayal of differing regional patterns in fertility, nuptiality and mortality (Gunnar Fridlizius). Italy, throughout the modern period, has been characterised by a marked dualism between the north and the south, which permeated both demographic and economic variables and gave rise to two distinct demographic regimes; one essentially of a Mediterranean character, and the other mirroring the Northwestern European pattern. Equally significant regional differences emerge in the case of Germany between the agricultural eastern provinces and the nascent industrial complex of the Ruhr, as well as in the Low Countries, where the two least accessible provinces of Friesland and Zeeland registered changes in the major demographic variables at variance with national trends. Consistent differences in fertility and in the rate of fertility decline also existed between Flanders and the various Walloon provinces.

Inevitably variations in the economic structure and development of the different national and local regions within continental Europe directly impinged on the general process of demographic development. At the same time, however, irrespective of the severity of these underlying differences, all the states examined in this collection of essays did in fact undergo the various stages of the demographic transition during this period, although its precise chronology varied from one country to another. The secular decline in fertility in France preceded the general European trend by almost a complete century. However, both the birth and death rates in Norway had been approximately halved between the 1760s and the 1960s, and this pattern of demographic development was equally operative in more backward European economies, such as Portugal. Indeed the secular decline in fertility from the turn of the nineteenth century onwards also meant that the age structure of the European population as a whole became increasingly homogeneous. The earlier fall in age-specific mortality had affected all age groups to a varying extent, and had therefore failed to produce a noticeable restructuring of the population pyramid. The secular decline in fertility, on the other hand, by reducing the relative importance of the younger age groups, had a direct and immediate effect on both the population structure and the dependency ratio.[8] In Italy, for example, this process led to a general ageing of total population and a 'thinning out' of the younger age groups. Similarly in Portugal, if the age group 0-19 had constituted over 43 per cent of the total population at the beginning of this century, by 1970 the proportion had fallen to under 36 per cent. Indeed the common strands in the nature of European demographic experience during this period from the mid-eighteenth century onwards are equally visible in a number of other important areas examined in this collection of essays, such as the extent and chronology of both external and internal migration (with only France as a possible exception in this context), as well as the gradual cessation of significant yearly fluctuations in basic demographic indices and particularly in the death rate, which had been a general aspect of the earlier pre-industrial demographic regime. The extent of this common element in European demographic experience during this period, however, has an important bearing on any assessment of the precise inter-relationship between demographic development and economic growth, particularly as underlying structural differences in individual states were exacerbated by multifarious religious and ethnic groupings, which were particularly acute in the case of the Austro-Hungarian Monarchy.

One of the major concerns of demographic historians has of course been the causative mechanism behind population growth during this period and discussion of this theme continues unabated. Various separate hypotheses have been put forward to explain this phenomenon, with a fundamental distinction existing between those interpretations that place a primary emphasis on movements in fertility and nuptiality, and hypotheses based on secular changes in the death rate. The central argument in the first case assumes that the rate of growth of the labour force and of total population is essentially a function of the real wage. It is further assumed on a Malthusian basis that labour supply is perfectly elastic at a certain real wage corresponding to standard subsistence requirements. Economic growth under these conditions would directly stimulate an increase in population. An increase in the relative demand for labour, for example, generated by economic development would operate on fertility through a number of important mechanisms, all of which would contribute to a resultant rise in total population. The second basic hypothesis, on the other hand, envisages an independent growth in population facilitated by secular changes in general mortality, which may have been partly influenced by underlying economic changes, but were essentially exogenous in their operation. To this extent the growth in European population during the period under examination was not dependent on the process of nascent industrialisation, but may have played an important contributory role in the development of individual national economies.

As far as the present set of contributions is concerned, little evidence emerges which would provide any substantive support for the first, essentially Malthusian, hypothesis. The significant decline in the death rate throughout Western Europe, which in many cases cut right across national territorial boundaries, was almost certainly the major causative factor behind the secular growth in total population. In Sweden, for example, the fall in the death rate was marked by a significant regional conformity in all the mortality series. Similarly in the Netherlands the crude death rate (per 1,000) fell from 26.6 (1840-49) to 15.7 (1900-09), and in most German states the levels of mortality already achieved by the beginning of the nineteenth century would have undoubtedly contributed to a significant increase in total population.

However, the isolation of the major causative mechanism behind the secular growth in European population is only the preliminary step in a complicated problem. A wide range of possible explanatory hypotheses have been developed to account for the fall in mortality and are discussed at length in the present collection of essays:

A. The Malthusian hypothesis, or what has been termed the 'nutrition factor' attributes the fall in age-specific mortality to a per capita increase in food supplies, facilitated by structural reform in the primary sector and accompanied by the introduction of new crops (in particular the potato). An improved availability of 'protective' food also led to an increase in the supply of vitamin C and a general improvement in resistance to disease. Indeed Mckeown has consistently argued that this was the major cause behind the fall in mortality and as a mechanism was specifically operative in England, Sweden, France, Ireland and Hungary, as well as other European countries.[9]

B. The medical hypothesis, which argues that advances in medical science and an expansion in medical facilities played a crucial role in accounting for the decline in mortality. This hypothesis, in turn, has a number of separate component parts, including the introduction of smallpox inoculation, which was made compulsory in a number of European states, and state quarantine measures designed to reduce mortality from both typhus and dysentery. Finally improved personal hygiene, including an increased use of soap and cotton underwear, may well have facilitated a fall in mortality by reducing the danger of infection.

C. The disease-specific hypothesis, which envisages an exogenous change in either the virulence of specific diseases, or the latent immunity of the human host. In this context changes in climate could have played an important role, particularly as the two centuries under consideration are known to have been characterised by long-term shifts in climatic conditions.

The picture that emerges from the present collection of essays to a large extent mirrors the inherent complexity of these separate hypotheses. By and large, however, the medical hypothesis carries little weight, although in Germany increased institutional medicalisation probably prevented any deterioration in mortality at a time when population was rising at a considerable rate. In the majority of cases, however, improvements in hygiene were not evident until the second half of the nineteenth century and the major breakthroughs in medical science invariably postdated the initial fall in European mortality. It is equally clear in a number of cases, particularly in Norway, Sweden and Germany, that the introduction of smallpox inoculation did not positively affect indigenous levels of mortality. In Norway, for example, in the late eighteenth century smallpox only accounted for approximately 8 per cent of total deaths and in most German states the age group 0-1 which stood to benefit most substantially from inoculation continued to be decimated by a wide variety of other illnesses and diseases. At the same time it is generally agreed that the impact of quarantine measures on the incidence of other major diseases is difficult to quantify and their overall impact must remain open to considerable doubt.

However, if a certain degree of unanimity is evident in the case of the medical hypothesis, this quickly disintegrates in relation to the postulated contribution of increased agricultural output to the recorded trend in overall mortality. In Denmark, for example, grain production rose two-fold between 1770 and 1800 and was accompanied by important structural changes in the system of land holding. These factors apparently contributed to a significant fall in mortality. On the other hand the positive influence of new crops and particularly the increasing cultivation of the potato, at least in the case of both Norway and Sweden, cannot be taken for granted. In the former country, even if smallpox inoculation accounted for up to 30 per cent of the registered mortality decline (which in view of the earlier evidence was highly unlikely), potato cultivation would only have contributed to a 13 per cent reduction in total deaths. Indeed if a general coincidence existed between both the grain and potato harvests, then the new crop would have failed to provide a more continuous and uninterrupted level of food supply. Furthermore within the later German Empire, those regions with a high level of increased output from the primary sector, particularly the eastern provinces of Prussia, continued to register above-average death rates. Indeed a number of the present contributions cast considerable doubt on the general applicability of this particular hypothesis. Its protagonists have frequently failed to examine the cost side of an attempt to raise agricultural output, and the net benefits of such a development were almost certainly dependent in the short term on a number of important factors, including the additional cost of further inputs of both capital and labour, the structure of land-holding, the size of the market and the contemporary movement in the price indices for agricultural produce. Indeed this hypothesis assumes a narrow Malthusian connection between mortality and relative standards of nutrition, which has still to be confirmed or disproved for many parts of Europe during the late eighteenth and early nineteenth centuries.

However, the disease-specific hypothesis cannot be uniformly accepted because of a continuing lack of adequate information on long-term changes in immunological components and the relative balance between infectious micro-organisms and the human host. Clearly only further research will provide the basis for an effective assessment of the causal mechanism behind the secular fall in mortality, although the general tenor of the arguments advanced in this collection of essays would seem to indicate that there was no simple monocausal factor which could explain both the extent and chronology of the mortality decline.

An important contribution to this debate, however, is provided by an analysis of both the age-specific trends in mortality, together with the chronological shifts over time in the major causes of death. The extensive series on age-specific mortality in Sweden is almost certainly unique, and it can only be hoped that ongoing research in other countries will eventually enable similar calculations to be made for other parts of Europe. By and large the main beneficiaries of the decline in mortality were the younger age groups. In Sweden, for example, the decline in age-specific mortality for the age group 1-5 years was not only more rapid than for other age groups, but preceded the general trend. However during the 1850s there was an accelerated decline in mortality for the age group 25-50. Similarly in the case of Germany mortality declined most markedly in the age groups 0-1, 1-2, 2-3, 10-19 and 20-29, and this pattern was common to most European states in the first half of the nineteenth century. The changes in infant mortality, on the other hand, were relatively more complex, and in view of its role in determining the level of overall mortality this subject deserves special consideration. In France infant mortality fell by one third between 1789 and 1829, whereas in most other European states the early nineteenth century was characterised by a marginal rise in this important index. This was the case in many individual German states, as well as in Denmark between 1850 and 1900, and in the Low Countries in the period 1871-95. High infant mortality was frequently linked with the practice of artificial feeding, which was more an expression of traditional custom than any other socio-economic factor, and to this extent would not have been influenced by the process of agricultural reform and increased levels of primary sector output. At the same time it is interesting to compare the experience of France and Southern Italy in this context. Whereas the early fall

in infant mortality in the former case almost certainly contributed to
an equivalent decline in marital fertility as a precursor of a general
European trend, the continuing high rates of infant mortality in
Southern Italy contributed to the maintenance of high marital fertility
levels and therefore to a retardation of economic development.

An equally crucial role as far as the general causes of death were
concerned was played by tuberculosis. In Austria-Hungary, for example,
tuberculosis, together with infectious diseases and 'inborn debility',
were consistently the major causes of death throughout the nineteenth
century. Tuberculosis mortality in Paris in the 1880s was 'unusually
high', and in many German states tended to reach a noticeable peak in
the period 1877-81. Indeed high rates of tuberculosis mortality were
evident not only in industrialising areas of Europe, but also in agrarian
regions such as Sweden, where mortality from this particular cause
rose from 200 (1751-70) to 266 (1801-30) per 100,000 inhabitants.[10]
Although there was a significant shift in the disease-specific pattern
of mortality during the twentieth century, with tuberculosis being
increasingly replaced in its role by malignant neoplasms, this change
was largely initiated by further important advances in medical science
and a relatively rapid diffusion of new medical techniques from the
1880s onwards. Indeed these developments to some extent account
for the further fall in overall mortality in a number of European states
which became increasingly apparent towards the very end of the
nineteenth century and the beginning of the twentieth century.
However it is clear that in view of the pronounced importance both
of tuberculosis as a cause of death, and of infant mortality as a major
component of the overall death rate throughout the nineteenth
century, that further research could profitably be directed into these
two areas in the hope of providing clarification on the exact causal
mechanism behind the secular decline in mortality and the precise
relationship between this general phenomenon and the underlying
socio-economic structure of individual European states.

In total contrast, many facets of nuptiality remained relatively
stable throughout the period under consideration. In France, for
example, the proportion married was almost static over a 200-year
period. In Norway the mean age at marriage (for both brides and
grooms) showed little change between the 1840s and 1950s, and this
was equally the case in Sweden, both at a national level and in the
different regional zones. In Italy the stability in the nuptiality rate has
been attributed to the operation of traditional social norms governing
the selection of a spouse and the relative lack of any significant change

in the country's occupational structure at least until the early twentieth century. It is important to note, however, that average age at first marriage tended to remain fairly high throughout the nineteenth century and in Italy underwent a marginal rise. This, in turn, indicates that the distinctive marriage pattern of Western Europe, which separates European experience from that of developing contemporary economies,[11] was retained for much of this period, irrespective of the countervailing pressures generated by the process of economic development and embodied in the gradual expansion of the secondary sector in many individual European states.

The secular decline in fertility from the late nineteenth century onwards, on the other hand, marked a distinct break with earlier pre-industrial fertility patterns. This phenomenon has also generated a great deal of debate and discussion, particularly as France in this particular context foreshadowed a general European trend by almost an entire century. Naturally enough a variety of different explanations has been offered, including in the case of the Low Countries, such factors as the agricultural depression of the post-1873 period, and religious and economic reasons. Improved levels of educational attainment, increased industrialisation, and a significant decline in infant mortality may also have played a decisive role and most of these possible factors are examined by the individual contributors to this publication. However two important facets of this secular decline in fertility deserve special emphasis. First, the phenomenon was common to many different areas of Europe. Although in the case of Italy the fertility decline was retarded in the South, which exacerbated regional differences in general fertility levels, and an equivalent fall did not take place in Portugal until the inter-war years, most European states registered a decline in fertility from the late nineteenth century onwards. In Denmark, for example, the changes in the fertility pattern were first apparent in the cities, but became increasingly obvious in rural areas after 1900. In the Low Countries there was a general fall in fertility from 1880-84 onwards, with only the province of Drenthe (in the Netherlands) diverging noticeably from the general trend. In Germany the first decline in fertility on a regional level by at least 10 per cent was recorded in 1879, with the last areas to undergo this transition registering an equivalent decline by 1914. In this context the general fall in fertility levels cut across national boundaries and regional economic differences, although a significant degree of economic backwardness, as in the case of Southern Italy, could clearly retard the general process. Secondly, the transition to lower levels of fertility took place over a very limited space of time. Once the secular decline had been initiated, the adoption of the new pattern of fertility was quickly assimilated at a national level and once again the rapidity of the transition was a phenomenon common to many areas and states of Europe.

At the same time the present contributions also provide important evidence of family limitation in the pre-decline period. It has been frequently surmised that a conscious limitation of family size was practised at certain times in various parts of Europe both in the eighteenth and early nineteenth centuries.[12] Although further research at a local level is clearly necessary to establish the precise pattern of family limitation and the factors which induced a voluntary control of fertility within marriage, the marital fertility curves in the case of France provide incontrovertible evidence of such a practice at a comparatively early date. Moreover similar evidence can be found in late eighteenth- and early nineteenth-century Germany, in such areas as Bavaria, Saxony and Mecklenburg. Even in Catholic Italy family limitation was practised in the first half of the nineteenth century by certain sectors of the population. Finally in the case of Sweden the strong links between annual harvests and marital fertility is 'evidence of a planned birth control' (Gunnar Fridlizius), which was particularly noticeable in relation to freehold peasants.

This collection of essays, however, is equally concerned with the complex inter-relationship between population growth on both a national and regional level, and the process of economic development and social change. Certainly the two centuries from 1750 onwards were characterised by dramatic changes in European social structures, which constitute an integral part of any examination of the mechanism of population growth. Given that behaviour patterns were often directly influenced by the specific social means of production, economic development during this period inevitably generated long-term repercussions. The processes at work were indeed considerable, including significant shifts in sectoral employment, extensive urbanisation and the increasing spread of wage labour to include in the course of the early twentieth century a rising number of women. All these factors, in turn, had an immediate impact in the demographic sphere, influencing such key variables as the average age at first marriage, average family size and relative population mobility. New light is also cast on the marked rise in illegitimacy in many parts of Europe during the early nineteenth century, which has frequently been taken by the practitioners of the 'new social history' as an inevitable accompaniment of significant changes in sexual relationships induced by the interaction of population growth and economic change. However, in almost every contribution where this topic is examined the available evidence provides little support for the posited emergence of a new morality or a radically different attitude to sexuality. In Norway, for example, there was 'no change in the acceptability of pre-marital cohabitation, but rather a growing inability to find the economic wherewithal for an official marriage' (Michael Drake), and in Sweden rising illegitimacy rates were not linked at all with the development of a new morality, but ironically reflected the continued resilience of traditional social values at a time when marriage opportunities were effectively reduced by contemporary economic factors. Equally in many German states, and particularly in Bavaria where the growth in illegitimacy was probably most acute, this phenomenon did not constitute a 'sexual revolution', as conceptions out of wedlock did not conflict with indigenous peasant codes of behaviour. To a large extent rising illegitimacy rates simply reflected the influence of external factors, such as changes in the legal code and fluctuations in real wages, rather than the impact of 'modernisation' on traditional codes of moral and sexual behaviour.

It is, however, in the context of the inter-relationship between population growth and economic development that these individual essays contribute to a better understanding of the mechanism of European economic expansion in the two centuries from 1750 onwards. A largely independent or exogenous growth in population during this period would have had important economic ramifications, both in relation to the supply of labour, and through shifts in the age structure of the indigenous population, on aggregate demand. The demand factor in the process of industrialisation was touched upon during the 1930s, when it became increasingly clear that fixed and stable levels of consumption would scarcely provide a fertile soil for economic growth. On this basis the high rates of growth in total population, particularly in the opening decades of the nineteenth century, would have positively influenced aggregate demand. In Italy, for example, the increase in population was most pronounced in the period 1821-31 and led to revival in the number of registered marriages. In the territories later incorporated into the German Empire the peak rates of annual population growth for the whole of the nineteenth century were recorded in the period 1816-20 at 1.43 per cent, and this unprecedented level of population growth undoubtedly had a dramatic effect on the level of internal demand. Furthermore, in

Sweden the pattern of the rise in population had a 'shock effect' on the economy (Gunnar Fridlizius), with the massive wave of births in the 1820s producing a further wave in the 1850s, which would only have been absorbed into the labour market by the early 1880s. Indeed it must be remembered that this remarkable rate of population growth frequently occurred in European economies which were still essentially agrarian. The burst in population growth in the case of Norway between 1815 and 1865, for example, was registered in a state which was only to undergo industrialisation approximately one hundred years after the industrial revolution in England. Equally important in the context of the long-term effect of population growth on demand, was the role of increased levels of internal population mobility, which was evident in almost all European countries during the late nineteenth and early twentieth centuries. By facilitating a growth in household formation, increased mobility had a direct impact on aggregate spending, which in areas of substantial in-migration, such as the Ruhr industrial base in Germany, and the expanding urban complexes in the Low Countries, helped to sustain and prolong the nascent process of economic expansion. Households which benefited through internal migration from new employment and improved income opportunities generated a multiplier effect throughout the economy and contributed to an increase in general levels of consumer expenditure.[13] Indeed this was even more the case where internal migration effectively reallocated the available supply of labour from low income employment, as in the agricultural eastern provinces of Germany, to areas, such as the industrial Rhineland and Westphalia, where average earnings were considerably higher.

As far as the impact of population growth on the size and composition of the work force was concerned, however, the impact of a decline in mortality on the overall constitution of the labour force depended on whether the relative gains in life expectancy were primarily felt in the younger or in the adult age groups. The ramifications of a decline in infant mortality, for example, would only have been long term, as an improvement in the death rate for this specific group would only have influenced the level of labour supply when the new generation eventually entered the work force. An improvement in life expectancy for teenagers and adult age groups, on the other hand, would have been accompanied by an immediate fall in the dependency ratio and a proportional rise in the active age group in the total population of individual European states. Due to the actual nature of the age-specific decline in mortality, there was a

significant growth in the proportion of active individuals in European
society. In Sweden, for example, the age group 20-25 expanded by
over 50 per cent during the early nineteenth century. There was a
similar increase in the age groups 20-24, 30-34 in the Netherlands
between 1830 and 1849, and in Prussia there was an increase of
46.68 per cent in the proportional importance of the age group 20-39
between 1816 and 1840. This sudden increase in the total size of the
available labour force, accompanied by an equally dramatic reduction
in the dependency ratio, facilitated continuous economic development
in a number of European economies through ensuring an increased
supply of labour at zero or marginal opportunity costs, particularly if
it is accepted that there was no perceptible improvement in real wage
levels during the initial stages of European industrialisation. An
independent fall in age-specific mortality under these conditions
would have produced an immediate increase in the labour force and a
corresponding effect on levels of consumer demand.[14] Indeed the
pattern of economic growth in certain European states in the early
nineteenth century was later reflected again in the case of Portugal
during the early twentieth century. It was precisely the high rates of
population increase in the inter-war years which enabled the Salazar
regime to implement restrictive controls both over trade union
activities and the level of wages, and thereby encouraged the growth
of industrial entrepreneurship.

There are in addition two further areas where the rate and pattern
of European population growth contributed to the nature of economic
development. First, population growth created its own independent
momentum, as the wave-like pattern of Swedish population movements
in the nineteenth century has already shown. This was reinforced by
the fact that private long-run expenditure decisions tend to cluster,
dependent on both the frequency of marriage and the birth rate. A
sudden increase in total population, accompanied by a corresponding
rise in the total number of marriages (but not necessarily in the
marriage rate itself) would have stimulated economic growth by
increasing the level of indigenous demand for such items as houses
and consumer goods.[15] Indeed in the case of Sweden, for example,
'a long-swing expansion in population growth. . .may explain the long
swings in residential construction and railroad construction'.[16] It is
equally possible, in view of the evidence now provided on the pattern
of population growth, that the initially high rates of population
increase to be found in various parts of Europe in the early decades of
the nineteenth century contributed to long-run cyclical movements in

aggregate demand, which, in turn, may have influenced the gradual emergence of distinctive business cycles in the different European economies. The intrinsic rhythm of European population growth was common to many individual countries, as it reflected to a large extent a general response to a secular decline in mortality. At the same time these individual states were becoming increasingly involved through the mechanism of international trade in the nascent structure of capitalist production. Economic growth and demographic development in this context would have been closely intertwined.

Secondly, the high rates of initial population expansion encouraged by necessity a further development in rural industries and domestic craft production, as employment possibilities in the primary sector no longer fully catered for the available supply of local labour. Increasingly individuals were forced to seek sources of income in non-agricultural pursuits; rural industries, and particularly textile manufacture, provided an immediate means of absorbing the registered increase in total population. Significantly many areas of Europe during this period, including the Low Countries, parts of Germany and Switzerland, witnessed an expansion in 'proto-industrial' production, as a direct response to rising population pressure. Furthermore the operation of the 'self-exploitation mechanism', as postulated by Chayanov,[17] in the context of rural industrial production would have influenced not only the differential rate of profitability of secondary sector development, but would have also accelerated the process of capital accumulation on the part of the entrepreneurial class, which was an important factor affecting long-term economic growth.

It is hoped that the present collection of essays may serve to promote the future development of European historical demography, not only by providing a survey of recent research findings on a national basis, but also by highlighting the directions which new research might profitably take. There are clearly important differences in demographic development both between and within individual European economies and countries. At the same time, however, many of the basic changes in the demographic variable during the period from the mid-eighteenth century onwards appear to have had a common basis. Regional differences were gradually eroded, and local peculiarities in demographic structure were increasingly subsumed into a more clearly recognisable national or even international pattern. It is precisely in this context that a comparative analysis of the demographic history of a series of European countries may help to shed some fresh light on the inherent similarities and dissimilarities in the process of population development and at the same time to facilitate the isolation of specific causative factors operative during this period of significant economic and social change. It is to be hoped that this collection of essays will generate renewed research interest into many of the fundamental problems connected with the specific inter-relationship between European population growth, economic development and social change in the modern period.

Notes

1. A Lörsch, 'Population Cycles as a Cause of Business Cycles', *Quarterly Journal of Economics*, vol.LI, 1937, p.649.
2. B.R. Mitchell, 'Statistical Appendix', in C.M. Cipolla (ed.), *The Fontana Economic History of Europe*, vol.4,2, *The Emergence of Industrial Societies*, London, 1973, p.747.
3. T. Hollingsworth, 'Relationships between Historical Sciences and Historical Demography', International Population Conference, Liège, 1973, vol.3, p.89.
4. The individual states included, range from Norway, Sweden, Denmark, Germany, Austria, Hungary, Czechoslovakia, Holland, Luxembourg, Belgium, France, to Portugal, and Italy.
5. A census was held, for example, in Austria in 1753-4, in Prussia in 1725, 1740, 1744, 1748-56, in Mecklenburg in 1756 and 1776, in Denmark in 1735 and in a number of following years. E. Keyser, *Die Bevölkerungsgeschichte Deutschlands*, Leipzig, 1943, p.399.
6. H. Schorer, 'Die Vornahme der kurbayerischen Volkszählung', *Archivalische Zeitschrift*, 1904, p.168.
7. P. Bairoch, 'Agriculture and the Industrial Revolution 1700-1914', in C.M. Cipolla, *The Fontana Economic History of Europe*, vol.3, *The Industrial Revolution*, London, 1973, p.460.
8. The 'dependency ratio' represents the proportion of total population aged 15 years and less and 65 years and over in relation to the size of the 'active' age group between 15 and 65 years of age.
9. T. Mckeown, R.G. Brown and R.G. Record, 'An Interpretation of the Modern Rise of Population in Europe', *Population Studies*, vol.26, 1972, pp.345-82.
10. A.G. Sundbärg, 'Mortalité par tuberculose en Suède, pendant les années 1751-1830', in S.E. Henschen (ed.), *La Lutte contre la Tuberculose en Suède*, Uppsala, 1905, p.189.
11. J. Hajnal, 'European Marriage Patterns in Historical Perspective', in D.E.C. Eversley and D.V. Glass, *Population in History, Essays in Historical Demography*, London, 1965, pp.101-43.
12. E.A. Wrigley, 'Family limitation in Pre-Industrial England', *Economic History Review*, vol.XIX, 1966, pp.82-109; W.R. Lee, 'Zur Bevölkerungsgeschichte Bayerns 1750-1850: Britische Forschungsergebnisse', *Vierteljahrschrift für Sozial- und Wirtschaftsgeschichte*, Bd.62, Heft 3, 1975, pp.323-9.
13. R.A. Easterlin, 'Population, Labour Force and Long Swings in Economic Growth', *The American Experience*, New York, 1968, p.49.
14. H. Belshaw, *Population Growth and Levels of Consumption, with special reference to Countries in Asia*, London, 1956, p.89.
15. R.A. Easterlin, 'Economic and Demographic Interactions: Long Swings

in Economic Growth', *American Economic Review*, 1966, pp.1063-104.

16. M. Wilkinson, 'Long Swings in Swedish Population', *Journal of Economic History*, vol.XXVII, 1967, p.37.

17. A.V. Chayanov, *The Theory of Peasant Economy*, edited and introduced by B. Kerblay, D. Thorner and R.E.F. Smith, Homewood Illinois, 1966, *passim*; P. Kriedte, H. Medick and J. Schlumbohm, *Industrialisierung vor der Industrialisierung*, Göttingen, 1977, pp.95-6.

1 AUSTRIA-HUNGARY*

Heimold Helczmanovszki

Preliminary Notes on Historical and Methodological Aspects

The 'Austrian-Hungarian' Monarchy, or 'Austria-Hungary' for short, is the name given to that state which constitutionally speaking was created on 8 February 1867 by the so-called 'Compromise', and which ceased to exist on 11 November 1918 after the defeat of the First World War and following the renunciation on the part of the Emperor of Austria and King of Hungary, Charles I, of the right of government. On the scale of world history, this state which only existed for a bare fifty years, would not normally be worthy of much attention. There are, however, several reasons which entitle it to be regarded as one of the most noteworthy of states ever to be created and there are a number of reasons which make this particular state of great interest to the demographer.

First of all some reference must be made to its physical dimensions and to its overall population size. Its surface area amounted to 676,615 sq.km., and at the end of 1910 it contained 51.4 million inhabitants. Austria-Hungary was a comparatively large state for its period; its surface area meant that it was the second largest state in Europe, after the European part of the Russian Empire, and it boasted the third largest population, after European Russia and the German Empire (Appendix Table 1.1).

Of even greater importance, however, is the fact that a large part of the territory which was subsequently integrated into the dual monarchy had belonged to the domain of the House of Hapsburg for almost 400 years, from 1526 onwards. Admittedly the Turks had ruled a large part of Hungary for more than 160 years and had greatly harassed Vienna in 1529 and 1683, but after a series of successful campaigns the Hapsburgs were able to secure the southeastern border of their Empire from the Danube and Sava rivers to the Iron Gate through the peace treaties of Karlowitz (1699) and Passarowitz (1718). The reign of Maria Theresa (1740-80) witnessed a similar process of consolidation along the northern and eastern borders. On the occasion

---

*The Editor is grateful for the assistance of Mr L. Austin, BA, of Birkenhead School in the translation of this contribution.

of the first partition of Poland, Galicia and Lodermeria (Vladimir) were incorporated into the Empire in 1772, and shortly afterwards the same happened to Bukovina in 1775 as a result of a treaty with Turkey. Although Austria's participation in the partition of Poland has been viewed by at least one notable historian as 'one of the most infamous acts in the politics of the Great Powers in the eighteenth century',[1] it must also be recognised that the reforms conceived and carried out under Maria Theresa, Joseph II (1780-90) and later under Franz-Joseph I (1848-1916), were in principle beneficial for all the provinces. Bukovina, which is to be found in the extreme northeast of the Monarchy between the Carpathian Mountains and the Dniestr river, provides a good example. 'After decades of intensive work the Austrian administration finally succeeded in creating from what had been a sparsely populated and completely neglected territory a model province within the Monarchy.'[2] Having secured its far-flung borders, Austria-Hungary was now able to provide the basis for the development of effective exchanges between many mutually complementary economic areas and at the same time to facilitate communication between peoples of essentially different characteristics, culture and vitality. Internal colonisation within the unified state succeeded in bringing about a systematic transformation of areas laid waste by the Turkish onslaught into productive arable land. The state therefore presented its youth with real challenges within its own territory. Indeed this was all the more remarkable, as Austria-Hungary was the only Great Power in Europe which refrained from the acquisition of overseas colonies, although it did belong to the ranks of the naval powers.

Finally, attention must be drawn to the following aspects of the Austro-Hungarian monarchy from the point of view of historical demography. Alongside the concept of common interest, which was guaranteed by the ruling dynasty and if need be was defended even at great cost, the salient feature of this state was its inner diversity. Within the borders of the state peoples who historically were still in a state of feudalism were brought face to face with the new requirements of the industrial age; here a wide variety of different mentalities met together, Roman Catholic, Protestant, Greek Orthodox, Jewish and Islamic. Individual nationalities of between one and twelve million people were domiciled within the monarchy and forced to get on with one another for decades or even for centuries, either peaceably or in irreconcilable antagonism.

Although now something approaching a generation stands between us and the final disintegration of the monarchy, it still remains a rewarding topic of research for the historical demographer. This was shown only recently by Paul Demeny in his interesting study on the early decline in the birth rate in Austria-Hungary.[3]

A number of characteristics make the now long-defunct Habsburg Empire of special interest as a demographic test tube for students of the fertility transition. Two of these characteristics should be stressed here. The first is the population's exceptional diversity. The Habsburg lands lacked many things, but were rich in ethnic, cultural and economic heterogeneity. . .The potential usefulness of such heterogeneity in aiding demographic research should be obvious. Moreover, this potential can be realized because large masses of statistics of good quality and of easy comparability are available — an asset, unlike diversity, which was largely lost after 1918.

Of course the government of this state which had become so substantial in size, endeavoured to compile both uniform and reliable statistical data on population.[4] The 'charter of souls' ordered by Maria Theresa can be seen as a forerunner of the modern census. The charters were carried out every three years by ecclesiastical and secular authorities and their explicit purpose was to record the total effective population. However the charters which were actually drawn up in the Austrian lands in 1754 and 1762 did not prove to be very reliable. Following a reorganisation in 1769 of the army on the basis of the principle of compulsory military service, these surveys, which initially were only implemented in a majority of the Austrian lands, were used predominantly for the purpose of recruitment (as 'conscriptions'). It was not until 1785 that the conscriptions were extended to include both Hungary and its neighbouring territories. Official opinion on the Hungarian side later came to the following conclusion concerning the conscriptions: 'The success [of these measures] was spoilt by the fact that the census was carried out unconstitutionally, without consultation with or the agreement of Parliament, indeed in the face of emphatic opposition from the nation as a whole.'[5] However, as Bokor emphasises, it was above all an opposition on the part of the Hungarian nobility, who did not consider universal conscription as being compatible with their privileges. As far as Hungary and its neighbouring territories were concerned, however, except for the 'military border' the results of this survey together with the later amendments of 1786 and 1787 provide the only available basis for a

continuous assessment of population figures, albeit along ecclesiastical
guidelines, until the mid-nineteenth century. The continued
implementation of conscriptions of the entire population, however, was
only possible in the Austrian Crown lands and in the 'military border'
in the southeastern part of the Empire, which was under strict military
organisation. Not until 1850 and 1857 did population surveys take
place again for the Empire as a whole.

Only in the period after the establishment of the dual monarchy,
however, is it possible to speak of a regular census system in the
modern sense. In 1869 the legal basis for implementing a census was
established in both halves of the Empire. A census was to be taken
regularly every ten years, and in accordance with this a census was
carried out in 1869, 1880, 1890, 1900 and 1910 – the appointed day
being in each case 31 December. The extensive volumes of tables, in
most cases accompanied by a textual commentary, provide a very rich
source of data. However, the information is not presented in a uniform
way for both halves of the Empire. The biggest difficulty in any
comparative analysis of the two data sources arises from the fact that
the tables for the Austrian half of the Empire are based predominantly
on the total population present, whereas those for the Hungarian half
are only based on the civil population present. Following the occupation
of Bosnia-Hercegovina a census was also taken in this region on 15 June
1879, 1 May 1885, 22 April 1895 and on the 10 October 1910. In the
1879 census only the civil population present was recorded, although
in the subsequent surveys a register was made of the effective
population as a whole. A statistical analysis of the natural process of
development in the Empire as a whole, however, is made possible on
the basis of church registers. As early as the eighteenth century the
state had been active in introducing an important element of
systematisation in the compilation of these registers, and from then
onwards church records of births, deaths and marriages effectively
took on the function of state registers. As a result of the obligation
of parishes to produce specific tables on an annual basis and to submit
these to the nearest state officials, it was possible to keep a continuous
record of births, deaths and marriages at a national level. There is,
however, some divergence in the initial dates at which comparable
statistics are available, depending on the individual parts of the Empire.

For the purpose of this study, however, which is also intended to
examine the question of regional differences in the structure and
process of population development, it was necessary to decide upon
an appropriate division of the territory encompassed by the state into

individual parts (Figure 1.1). In the case of the Austrian half of the
Empire the natural choice was the traditional *Länder* (administrative
regions), of which there were fifteen, if Trieste and the area around it,
Gorizia, Gradiska and Istria are taken together as a unified 'maritime
region'. They were normally arranged together on a geographical basis,
which gave rise to the following grouping: the seven 'Alpine regions'
(Lower and Upper Austria, Salzburg, Styria, Carinthia, the Tyrol and
the Vorarlberg); the three 'Sudeten regions' (Bohemia, Moravia and
Silesia); the two 'Carpathian regions' (Galicia, Bukovina) and the three
'Karst regions' (Carniola, the maritime region and Dalmatia). In the
Hungarian half of the Empire official statistics following the
publication of the results of the 1890 census also made use of an
official grouping of the traditional municipalities, including the 71
comitates (Hungarian administrative district) and the 30 towns of
municipal status into nine distinct regional divisions. The sequence
chosen was such that the first three of these units can be grouped
together into the 'trans-Danube area' and the Alföld area,[6] that is to
say Hungary in the restricted sense of the word (the right bank of the
Danube, the plain between the Danube and Tisza rivers, and the left
bank of the Tisza). Two of them can be grouped into 'Northern
Hungary', which corresponds approximately to present-day Slovakia
(the left bank of the Danube and the right bank of the Tisza). There
then follows 'Siebenbürgen',[7] the Tisza-Mures plain (known as the
'Temeser Banat'), Fiume (now Rijeka) and its surrounding area, and
finally Croatia-Slavonia. Where possible data has been taken directly
from official sources. In relation to the Hungarian part of the
monarchy, however, profitable use was also made of figures published
in the compilation edited by Kovacsics Jozsef, which includes
population figures reconstructed and edited in an exemplary fashion
by Papai Bela and Thirring Lajos.[8] In addition a great help was
provided in the interpretation of the data by the thoughtful
commentaries made by Heinrich Rauchberg on the results of the 1890
census[9] and those of Alois Kovacs[10] on the Hungarian census of 1900.

Population Development prior to the 'Compromise' (1786-1867)

In 1786, at the time of Emperor Joseph II, 11.5 million people lived
in the Austrian Crown Lands and a further 9.1 million in the kingdom
of Hungary. The total population of the monarchy therefore stood at
20.6 million.[11] In the 71 years up to 1857 the population increased
on average by 55 per cent, to 32.0 million, although the relative
increase in the Austrian Crown Lands was slightly greater at 58 per cent,

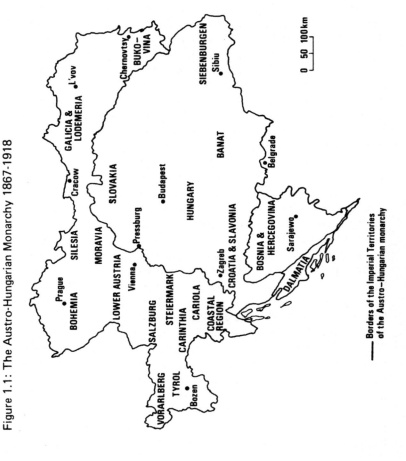

Figure 1.1: The Austro-Hungarian Monarchy 1867-1918

as the population rose to 18.2 million. In the kingdom of Hungary, however, the growth rate was comparatively smaller, with population only rising by 51 per cent, to 13.8 million (Appendix Table 1.2). The process of development, however, was not constant, as the times were frequently unsettled. During the period 1792 to 1814 population development in the Alpine regions of Austria, for example, was severely hampered by the wars with France and by the epidemics which broke out in their wake. Further setbacks were occasioned by the cholera epidemic of 1855 and by the wars of 1859 and 1866. The colonisation of the southern areas of Hungary, which had been launched systematically and with great success under Maria Theresa, also tailed off in the first half of the nineteenth century, as the result of a flagging interest on the part of the authorities after the French wars. The numerical increase in population during these decades was therefore primarily dependent on natural growth.

Papai Bela[12] published the following data on the natural

Year	Births		Deaths		Preponderance of births	
	Austria	Hungary	Austria	Hungary	Austria	Hungary
1777	—	55.1	—	40.8	—	14.3
1823	39.9	32.1	29.0	24.3	10.9	7.8
1830	38.1	32.0	30.4	31.0	7.7	1.0
1831	35.4	30.6	42.0	50.6	− 6.6	−20.0[a]
1838	38.2	35.4	28.4	28.1	9.8	7.3
1840	38.7	35.2	30.5	27.8	8.2	7.4
1842	41.5	36.2	31.0	29.0	10.5	7.2
1843	39.5	35.8	31.6	27.8	7.9	8.0

a. This strongly negative figure was largely due to the cholera epidemic.

development of population in Hungary (per thousand) for the years between 1777 and 1843, although the information is supplemented in this case by Austrian figures for the same years.

It can be seen from Table 1.2 that the dynamics of population development within such a large Empire varied greatly during this period, when the economy was still dominated by the primary sector. Bohemia, with a growth rate of 71.4 per cent in the period 1786 to 1857 clearly lay above the average figure of population growth in the Empire as a whole, and this can be attributed to the fact that although agriculture enjoyed favourable conditions during this period, industry also benefited from early development. Lower Austria, which included Vienna as the capital of the Empire and the seat of the royal court, also recorded an above average rate of growth of 67.9 per cent, which was largely due to the favourable factors affecting agriculture and promoting the early development of industry. The same was true of the region of the 'military border' in the southeastern part of the

Empire (63.8 per cent), which was organised and developed on a systematic basis along strict military lines. The rate of population growth during the same period in Galicia and Bukovina (54.2 per cent), as well as in Siebenbürgen (53.4 per cent) was only marginally below the average for the Empire, and the performance of these areas can be largely attributed to their high state of fertility. Some of the Austrian Crown Lands, however, had a strikingly low rate of increase: Carniola (9.6 per cent), Carinthia (13.0 per cent). Upper Austria and Salzburg (23.6 per cent), the Tyrol and Vorarlberg (24.8 per cent), and Styria (29.0 per cent). It is significant that these were largely Alpine regions, where there was apparently little chance of population growth due to the conditions prevalent at that time.

Population Development in Austria-Hungary (1867-1918)

In 1869 on the occasion of the first census after the 'compromise' the monarchy had a total population of 35.9 million, including 20.4 million in the Austrian Crown Lands and 15.5 million in Hungary, or 56.8 per cent and 43.2 per cent respectively of the combined total. Growth in the Austrian sector of the Empire (+ 40.1 per cent) clearly outstripped that in the Hungarian sector (+ 34.7 per cent), and the balance in the following years was to tip even more in Austria's favour. Before the outbreak of the First World War the Austrian Crown Lands with a population of 28.6 million inhabitants, constituted 57.8 per cent of the total population in the Empire as a whole: Hungary's share, with a population of 20.9 million, had dropped to 42.2 per cent. Bosnia and Hercegovina, however, which had been occupied in 1878, had a population of 1.2 million, as shown in the first census of 1879. By 1910, after their constitutional annexation, this figure had grown to 1.9 million. At the time of the last census to be carried out in the Monarchy the total number of inhabitants amounted to 51,390,223.

The extent of population growth within the territory of the monarchy, however, varied greatly. The following classification can be made of the various territories, based on the percentage growth rate in population in the years between 1869 and 1910 (two sets of figures are also included here which facilitate an examination of population changes within individual areas in relation to socio-economic conditions, namely the proportion of total population dependent on agriculture and forestry in 1910, and the relative increase or decline in the population figure of 1880 as a result of migration during the period 1880 to 1910).

	Population growth (in %), 1869-1910	Population in agriculture and forestry (in %)	Migration balance, 1880-1910
Lower Austria (incl. Vienna)	77.4	18.0	+ 22.1
Donau-Tisza plain (incl. Budapest)	76.0	46.1	+ 14.1
Bukovina	55.9	71.1	− 8.7
Maritime region (incl. Trieste)	48.8	46.0	+ 4.8
Silesia	47.5	29.2	− 4.3
Galicia	47.4	73.1	−14.3
Croatia, Slavonia	43.7	78.8	− 6.0
Dalmatia	41.3	82.6	−12.2
Salzburg	40.2	40.1	+ 12.0
Left Tisza bank	37.8	70.1	− 5.1
Bohemia (incl. Prague)	31.7	32.3	− 8.8
Moravia	30.0	41.3	−10.4
Right Danube bank	27.9	65.2	−15.8
Styria	26.9	53.2	− 1.0
Left Danube bank (incl. Pressburg)	26.1	61.7	−13.8
Siebenbürgen	24.4	71.7	− 4.5
Tyrol and Vorarlberg	23.3	51.2	+ 0.2
Tisza-Mures plain	22.2	69.1	− 6.6
Right Tisza bank	18.8	61.3	−20.7
Carinthia	17.3	51.1	− 6.9
Upper Austria	15.8	46.9	− 5.4
Carniola	12.8	62.0	−18.1

In the period between 1869 and 1910 nine of these areas had an outstandingly high rate of population growth. In the lead were the districts of Lower Austria and the Danube-Tisza plain, the former being considerably influenced by the growth of Vienna, the latter by the development of the city of Budapest. Both areas, as a result of rapid urban growth, benefited substantially from migration gains. This was also true of the maritime region, although to a lesser extent, where the harbour town of Trieste exercised a similar role in attracting migrants, and in the case of Salzburg. The third place in the general classification was taken by Bukovina, which was still a highly agricultural area in 1910, but where high fertility was strong enough to cause not only a significant increase in population, but also to

maintain the number of inhabitants in the region at a permanently
high level. Of the areas with a higher than average growth rate, the
same characteristics are also shared by Galicia, Croatia-Slavonia and
Dalmatia. Thus in the northeast and southeast the monarchy was
surrounded by a band of territories which were characterised by an
extensive agrarian population and also by marked rates of population
growth. This presents an unusual picture in comparison with the
present-day situation in Central Europe, which is characterised by
stretches of border areas with shrinking population and so-called
'dead borders'.

In the years between 1869 and 1910, however, thirteen areas had
a growth rate consistently below the average. These districts were
predominantly agricultural areas of Hungary and the Austrian Carniola,
whose natural rate of growth was offset by continuous deficits as a
result of migration. This large and persistent exodus is also the reason
why Bohemia too has the place it does in the overall classification,
despite its important industrial base which had developed earlier. It is
noticeable that five of the seven Austrian Alpine areas are to be found
at the end of the table. Despite the various industries which had already
been established, particularly in Upper Austria and Upper Styria, 'their
time' had not as yet come, and the Alpine regions as a whole were
losing more people than they were gaining through immigration.

An examination of the decennial population surveys produces the
following picture (Appendix Table 1.3): in the first decade (1869 to
1880) the average annual growth rate of the population in Austria-
Hungary only amounted to 0.49 per cent, but what is even more
striking was the very low rate of increase in the Kingdom of Hungary
(0.13 per cent). In the official commentary on the census results in
1881 it was stated that 'This very small increase is by no means to be
considered as normal and can be most adequately explained by the
numerous natural disasters which have repeatedly befallen our country
in the past decade, and by the lamentable economic conditions
presently endured by a large part of our mother country.'[13] In
particular certain parts of the country had been devastated by a
cholera epidemic in 1872 and 1873, which led to a very small rate
of increase or to a net decline in population on the left and right bank
of the Tisza, in Siebenbürgen and on the Tisza-Mures plain. In contrast
the growth rate in the population of the Austrian Crown Lands was
far steadier at an annual average rate of 0.75 per cent. Apart from
Lower Austria, including Vienna, the highest growth rates were
recorded in Silesia, Galicia and Bukovina.

During the second decade, between 1880 and 1890 the growth rate in the Austrian Crown Lands remained essentially the same as it had been in the previous decade, whereas the annual average growth rate in Hungary, of 1.05 per cent, marked a significant improvement over the previous performance. Indeed the Hungarian growth rate lay well above the average for the Empire as a whole, and this phenomenon was particularly noticeable in many areas of the country which had experienced a catastrophe as far as population development was concerned in the previous decade. As the official commentary reported, it was 'the time of a renewal of population, but also the beginning of emigration'.[14] Apart from this trend, the power of the urban centres to attract immigrant population increased. Population thronged to the growing coal, iron and steel industries and to other industrial centres such as Borsod on the right bank of the Tisza, and Hunyad in Siebenbürgen.

It was in the third decade, between 1890 and 1900, however, that the highest annual average growth rates were recorded, reaching 0.94 per cent for the monarchy as a whole, with the rate for Hungary just marginally above this figure, and the rate in the Austrian Crown Lands fractionally below. The net increase in Hungary, moreover, was more evenly spread out than it had been in the previous decades and in the Austrian half of the Empire only Upper Austria, Carinthia, the Tyrol and Carniola fell noticeably behind the general pace of development.

In the last decade of the population survey, between 1900 and 1910, a certain tailing off in the rate of growth was evident in Austria-Hungary. The figure for the average annual growth rate for the Empire as a whole stood at 0.86 per cent, with the rate for the Austrian half of the monarchy being above this figure, and that of the Hungarian half below it. This general trend was clearly evident in the case of the two central areas (Lower Austria, including Vienna, and the Danube-Tisza plain, including Budapest), where the rate of annual increase in population fell back to 1.31 per cent and 1.39 per cent respectively. In order to understand more clearly the significance of these figures, it will be important to examine on the one hand the natural changes in total population, and on the other hand the general process of migration.

In the first instance, however, attention must once again be focused on Bosnia-Hercegovina. According to the results of the population surveys, this particular territory which had been under Austro-Hungarian administration from 1878 onwards, had a high average annual growth in population of 2.41 per cent (1879-85),

1.61 per cent (1885-95) and 1.30 per cent (1895-1910). Indeed only
on exceptional occasions were these growth rates exceeded or even
matched in either of the two major halves of the monarchy as a whole.
It cannot be denied, however, that at the time of the first survey the
particular area was barely organised on a comprehensive basis, and
that this led to the under-registration of population. In the course of
the later surveys this fault had been eliminated, with the result that
the rate of growth, at least for the first period, was probably
overestimated. From the second census period onwards, the registered
rate of increase would seem to correspond to the actual situation in the
territory. The principal reason for the significant growth of population
in this relatively sparsely populated area, which even in 1885 still had
only 27 inhabitants per sq.km., can be found in the process of
colonisation by settlers from Austria-Hungary, after its initial
annexation. In 1910, for example, the effective civilian population
in this district contained 46,859 individuals with Austrian citizenship,
61,151 with Hungarian citizenship and a further 6,581 inhabitants
who had migrated from other areas into Bosnia-Hercegovina. In relation
.to their actual individual nationality these foreigners were grouped into
58,113 Serbo-Croats, 20,585 Germans, 6,201 Magyars, 6,906 Czechs
and Slovaks, with the remainder being drawn from other minority
groups within the dual monarchy.

The Multinational State

Towards the end of its existence, the Austrian-Hungarian monarchy,
including Bosnia and Hercegovina, comprised the following nationalities,
which constituted in turn a total indigenous population of
approximately 50.9 million inhabitants.

	Total (in millions)	%	Distributed in the following main areas (in millions)	
Germans	12.0	24	6.2	Alpine lands
			3.5	Sudeten lands
			2.0	Hungary
Magyars	10.1	20	6.9	Trans-Danube and Alföld
			1.7	Northern Hungary
			1.5	Other parts of Hungary
Czechs and Slovaks	8.5	17	6.4	Sudeten lands
			1.7	Northern Hungary (Slovakia)
			0.2	Lower Austria (Vienna)

	Total (in millions)	%	Distributed in the following main areas (in millions)	
Serbs and Croats	5.4	11	2.3	Croatia, Slavonia, Tisza-Mures plain
			1.7	Bosnia, Hercegovina
			0.8	Karst lands
			0.6	Southern Hungary
Poles	5.0	10	4.8	Galicia
			0.2	Silesia
Ruthenians	4.0	8	3.6	Galicia, Bukovina
			0.4	Northeast Hungary
Romanians	3.2	6	2.3	Siebenbürgen, Tisza-Mures plain
			0.6	Northeast Hungary
			0.3	Bukovina
Slovenes	1.3	3		Alpine and Karst regions
Italians, Ladins	0.8	2		Alpine and Karst regions
Others, unknown	0.6	0		

It is impossible, however, to arrive at a total for the whole Empire on the basis of the absolute figures incorporated in Appendix Table 1.4, as in each specific area, such as the Austrian Crown Lands, the kingdom of Hungary and Bosnia-Hercegovina, the figures used are based on differently defined concepts of total indigenous population. But the table does facilitate some assessment of the relative dominance of individual nationalities in the different parts of the Empire. The Germans were clearly predominant in the Alpine regions; the Hungarians in the Trans-Danube and Alföld region; the Czechs and Slovaks, albeit with a markedly significant German component, in the Sudeten lands; and the Serbs and Croats in Croatia-Slavonia and Bosnia-Hercegovina. In the following regional districts there was an approximate balance between individual nationalities: Galicia (Poles and Ruthenians); Bukovina (Ruthenians and Romanians); Tisza-Mures plain (Romanians, Magyars, Germans); Siebenbürgen (Romanians, Magyars); and the Karst region (Serbs, Croats, Slovenes). If one examines the ethnic situation in even smaller territorial units, numerous other examples of an interweaving of various ethnic groups become obvious. These were not only intrinsically interesting, but in many cases were to become the focus of international attention at a later date. They would include the Sudetenland, prior to the final expulsion of the Sudeten Germans, and currently the South Tyrol. A theme which is still of great interest to contemporary students of this period is the differentiated process of development among the individual nationalities within the monarchy and the general process of assimilation, which included the tendency for linguistic minorities to suffer eventual absorption. It is now intended at this juncture to continue the study of the inner diversity within the population of Austria-Hungary by including a survey of the relative distribution of the various religious denominations. To some extent, of course, this distribution pattern closely corresponds with the role of specific nationalities, but this was not invariably the case.

It can be seen from Appendix Table 1.5, with its classification of the population according to religious denomination, that Austria-Hungary effectively brought together both the West and the East. The Roman Catholic creed was dominant in the western parts of the Empire, but it became increasingly less significant the further east the traveller went. It reached maximum proportions in the Alpine regions where 96.05 per cent of the population belonged to this faith, but only 95.04 per cent in the Sudeten lands, 94.24 per cent in the Karst regions, 71.37 per cent in Croatia-Slavonia (including Rijeka), 61.39 per cent in Northern Hungary, 55.14 per cent in the Trans-Danube and Alföld, 36.2 per cent in the Tisza-Mures plain, and finally only 12.65 per cent in Siebenbürgen. Two factors in particular accounted for this distribution pattern. In the first place the Ruthenians, Romanians and Serbs belonged in the main to the Christian churches of the East. The second largest religious denomination in the monarchy, Greek Catholic, was represented above all in the Carpathians, in Northeastern Hungary and in Siebenbürgen. Furthermore the main diffusion areas for the third largest creed, the Greek Orthodox faith, were Siebenbürgen, the Tisza-Mures plain and Croatia-Slavonia. Secondly, although the imperial family had succeeded in implementing the Counter-reformation in the Austrian Crown Lands, they failed to achieve this objective in the Hungarian territories. As a result there was a clear difference between the two halves of the Empire as far as the dissemination of Protestantism was concerned. Whereas Evangelists of the Augsburg faith only accounted for 1.32 per cent of all believers in Austria, their numbers in Hungary were on average 6.94 per cent, although this proportional representation could rise to as much as 12.04 per cent in Northern Hungary. Furthermore whereas Evangelists of the Helvetian faith ('Reformed') accounted for only 0.5 per cent of all believers in the Austrian half of the Empire, in Hungary they represented 12.8 per cent of the total, and were particularly strongly distributed in the Trans-Danube and Alföld areas (19.7 per cent), and in Siebenbürgen (14.6 per cent). There were also various members of the Jewish faith scattered in all parts of the Empire, although in 1890 they only constituted on average 4.5 per cent of the total population. However, they were strongly represented in the northeastern parts of the Empire, where they constituted 10 per cent of the population, in the northeastern *comitates* of Hungary (20 per cent), and 11.8 per cent in the Carpathian regions of Austria. In some towns, moreover, they were even more strongly concentrated, as a consequence of their widespread employment in urban vocations. Indeed in Budapest they formed 23.1 per cent of the total population.

In addition to the question of language and the prominence of different religious denominations, were the various levels of educational provision within the multinational state. It is perhaps symptomatic of contemporary attitudes, however, that none of the five population surveys from the period of the dual monarchy went beyond the basic criterion of whether individuals could read or write. And yet the educational issue had been debated by politicians for just as long as economic or legal matters, if not for longer. In 1766 a start had been made with the so-called 'Maria-Theresa School Reform', which had been followed by the 'General School Act' of 6 December 1774, which stipulated that schools should be established throughout the whole Empire. On 20 October 1781 came the imperial order that school attendance was to be made compulsory for all children between six and twelve years of age and district offices were instructed to use coercive methods to ensure full attendance. But the effectiveness of compulsory school attendance was impaired for some time by the continued practice of employing children in factories and the use made of peasant children in agricultural production. Further important developments were the act of 14 May 1869 which related to primary schools, and the acts of 1883 which led to the introduction at the secondary level of the 'civic school', improved teacher-training facilities and grammar schools. The most important aspect of these reforms, however, was the introduction of interdenominational state schools, the extension of compulsory education to eight years, the establishment of school counsels, at a regional, district and local level, as school supervisory agencies, and the expansion of grammar schools from six to eight forms, which meant that they now took over some of the tasks previously dealt with by the philosophical faculties of the universities.

It would be reasonable to suppose, therefore, that the basic skills of reading and writing would have been widely disseminated throughout the Empire by 1890, some 110 years after the initial introduction of compulsory education. Just how closely this did or did not correspond to reality in 1890 is revealed by the following classification of the Austrian Crown Lands and the various regions of Hungary based on the proportion of individuals above six years of age who could read and write (in %):

Lower Austria (incl. Vienna)	92.5	Danube-Tisza plain	64.1
Bohemia	91.8	Left bank of the Danube	60.1
Upper Austria	91.3	Maritime area	53.2
Vorarlberg	91.0	Carniola	52.0
Moravia	87.9	Tisza right bank	49.6
Salzburg	87.8	Tisza left bank	45.1
Tyrol	87.8	Siebenbürgen	32.9
Silesia	83.5	Croatia, Slavonia	32.3
Styria	74.2	Galicia	22.8
Danube right bank	69.1	Bukovina	19.3
Rijeka (town and area)	66.3	Dalmatia	16.2
Carinthia	65.6		

The average for the Austrian half of the Empire came to 65.5 per cent, and for the Hungarian half 50.6 per cent. It is striking, however, that regions within the Austrian half occupy both the first nine places in the table, as well as the last three. As far as elementary schooling was concerned there was an extremely large difference between regions at the hub of the Empire, such as Lower Austria (including Vienna), and Bukovina which had been acquired in 1775 and Dalmatia which had been initially acceded to Austria in 1797 and then again in 1815. This divergence in the rate of literacy was far more extensive than in the case of the various Hungarian territories.

The realisation that men had a readier access to education than women is not particularly modern. This fact was noted, for example, in the commentaries on the Austrian-Hungarian census of 1890, as well as on other occasions in the late nineteenth century. On average 68.5 per cent of the male population were literate in 1890, as opposed to only 62.6 per cent of the female population (at least of those aged six years and above). The difference was of course most pronounced in those regions with the least extensive provisions for elementary schooling. The relative proportions for men and women stood at 23.1 per cent and 9.3 per cent in Dalmatia; 23.1 per cent and 15.5 per cent in Bukovina; 27.4 per cent and 18.1 per cent in Galicia. The comparative figures for the two sexes in Lower Austria, however, were 94.0 per cent and 90.9 per cent; in Bohemia 94.0 per cent and 89.5 per cent and in Upper Austria 92.0 per cent and 90.6 per cent.

It was noted with some relief, however, that there was a progressive improvement from one survey to the next. The proportion of the population over six years of age which could read and write increased significantly between 1880 and 1900 (in %):

Year	Austria		Hungary		Total
	Male	Female	Male	Female	
1880	61.9	55.1	49.0	33.8	41.3
1890	68.5	62.6	57.0	43.9	50.6
1900	75.4	69.7	—	—	59.0

It was also correctly believed that there was an increasing equalisation in literacy levels between the two sexes, as a result of improved educational facilities for women. This was most apparent from an examination of comparative literacy rates according to individual age group, and based on the census returns of 1900.[15]

Age group	Proportion of those able to read and write		
	Male	Female	Percentage difference
6-11	60.1	56.7	3.4
12-14	77.1	71.9	5.2
15-19	75.6	69.5	6.1
20-29	74.9	64.2	10.7
30-39	67.8	51.5	16.3
40-49	61.7	41.9	19.8
50-59	56.2	33.6	22.6
60-69	47.2	25.7	21.8
70-79	42.9	22.7	20.2

Even in the last years of its existence the Austro-Hungarian monarchy was still able to demonstrate its effective skill and expertise in the administration and development of Bosnia and Hercegovina, which was an area that had lagged behind the general trend. On the basis of the 1910 census, an appraisal was provided of the educational level of the local population.[16] At the time of the original occupation of this territory in 1878 there had only been fifty-four Roman Catholic and fifty-six Serbian Orthodox primary schools with a total of 5,913 pupils of both sexes, apart from the Moslem *mektebs*, which were religious schools in which the Turkish-Arabic alphabet was taught and the reading of the Koran practised. It had therefore been necessary to establish a system of state schools, despite the difficulties posed by the general absence of teaching staff. However, by 1910-11 there were already 487 primary schools, of which 331 were general schools, 146 denominational and 10 were private. Together they had a total of 42,578 pupils of both sexes. In addition courses for illiterate adults had also been established. Furthermore, numerous nationals had been taught to read and write during their active military service. Accordingly once the network of schools had been sufficiently expanded, it was deemed to be appropriate to make school attendance 'relatively compulsory' on a legal basis. At the time of the 1910 census the following proportion of the population (in %) in Bosnia-Hercegovina were able to read and write:

Age group	Male	Female	Total
7-20	18.0	7.1	12.6
21-30	20.6	7.4	14.0
30+	13.9	5.4	10.2
Total	16.8	6.5	12.0

It is highly probable that the relative backwardness of large parts of the Austro-Hungarian monarchy in the field of elementary education was closely connected with their economic situation. Even in 1910 in the Austrian half of the Empire, 48.4 per cent of the total population were still involved in the primary sector, including forestry, horticulture and the fishing industry, either as direct employees, or as dependants. In Hungary the proportion was 64.5 per cent, and in Bosnia-Hercegovina 85.6 per cent. Even for that period, the relative role of the primary sector was still very substantial. On the basis of the sectoral distribution of the work force (employees, excluding dependants), the following proportional distribution pattern is obtained for the various European states (in %):[17]

Country	Primary production	Mining, industry and trade	Others
Hungary	68.6	17.5	13.9
Italy	59.4	31.0	8.7
Russia	58.3	25.0	16.7
Austria	58.2	29.6	12.2
Sweden	49.8	28.4	21.8

Country	Primary production	Mining, industry and trade	Others
Denmark	48.0	36.7	15.3
Ireland	44.6	37.6	17.8
France	41.8	45.0	13.2
Norway	41.0	41.7	17.3
German Empire	37.5	48.0	14.5
Switzerland	30.9	57.9	11.2
Netherlands	30.7	50.9	18.4
Belgium	21.1	53.3	25.6
Scotland	12.0	72.8	15.2
England	8.0	71.3	20.7

In the United States the comparative proportions were 35.9, 40.4 and 23.7 per cent respectively. Even at the turn of the last century the Austro-Hungarian monarchy was still essentially an agrarian state. That things might have been better as far as the national economy was concerned will be argued effectively below (see p.48 *et seq.*), which will also take into consideration from the demographer's point of view the problem of emigration. Clearly this tremendously large economic area, with its traditional system of agricultural production and its insufficiently developed secondary sector, at least in comparison with other European states, was unable to assimilate the increasingly large surplus of births. An extensive publication has recently appeared on the historical problems of economic development in Austria-Hungary and has served to highlight the peculiar situation in which the Empire found itself, and the dichotomy which inevitably arose between its aspirations and what could be effectively achieved; between national expediency and the laws of economics.[18]

There were of course considerable differences in economic structure within the monarchy itself. As can be seen from Appendix Table 1.6, the areas with the highest agricultural quota, excluding both Bosnia-Hercegovina (85.6 per cent) and Dalmatia (82.6 per cent), were to be found in the Kingdom of Hungary, in the Carpathian regions of Austria and in Carniola, where the proportion of wage earners employed in the primary sector fluctuated between 61.3 per cent (the right bank of the Tisza) and 78.8 per cent (Croatia, Slavonia). In Hungary only the Danube-Tisza plain, including Budapest, had a lower agricultural quota as far as the structure of employment was concerned (46.1 per cent), which corresponded approximately to the figure of 46.0 per cent for the Austrian maritime region, including Trieste. In the Alpine and Sudeten regions agriculture was less important, with the employment quota being well below the average for the Empire as a whole. Although the overall average for this particular region stood at 56.4 per cent, in the case of certain areas the proportion employed in agriculture was significantly less, including Bohemia (32.3 per cent), Vorarlberg (31.6 per cent), Silesia (29.2 per cent) and Lower Austria including Vienna (18.0 per cent). The highest quotas for employment in trade and industry were to be found in Silesia (46.3 per cent), Vorarlberg (44.1 per cent), Lower Austria (40.4 per cent), Moravia (35.0 per cent), Upper Austria (26.7 per cent) and the Danube-Tisza plain, including Budapest (25.1 per cent). Table 1.6 also serves to pinpoint the general decline in the proportional significance of the agricultural population in the Austrian half of the Empire, which fell from 52.4 per cent to 48.4 per cent between 1900 and 1910. In the Hungarian half the corresponding fall was from 68.4 per cent to 64.5 per cent, which was also accompanied by a concomitant rise in the level of sectoral employment in trade and industry. Indeed this trend was part of a process which occurred in most, if not all, areas of the monarchy.

An equally significant aspect to emerge from this analysis is the proportion of dependent employees in both the primary and secondary sectors of the economy. The respective figures for the two halves of the Empire were 70.1 per cent and 82.6 per cent in Austria, and 64.6 per cent and 68.4 per cent in Hungary. Indeed it was a matter of some concern to contemporaries that the proportion of self-employed or independent workers in relation to the labour force as a whole was tending to fall in the closing decades of the nineteenth century. This was also accompanied by an equivalent increase in the proportion of dependent employees, including civil servants and workers in the service industries. Doubts were expressed as to whether such a development was unavoidably engendered by economic necessity that promoted the centralisation of production in larger concerns, or whether it was occasioned by an actual decline in the economy. It was also feared that the decline in the number of independent workers would mean that the population would be 'progressively turned into a proletariat'.[19] Between 1890 and 1900 alone, for example, the proportion of dependent employees in relation to the total number of wage earners in Hungary had been reduced from 35.2 per cent to 30.9 per cent and this trend had been particularly marked in the primary sector where the ratio had fallen from 35.1 per cent to 30.7 per cent, but it had also been evident in industry and trade, where the respective figures were 45.5 per cent and 37.2 per cent. There had been a corresponding rise in the proportion of dependent employees in both sectors. Within the two halves of the Empire, however, there were clear regional differences in the proportion of wage earners, which can be attributed to the existence of special circumstances and combinations of circumstances. On the basis of the 1890 census results, H. Rauchberg has pointed out the following significant differences. There was a comparatively high proportion of wage earners in the primary sector of the Alpine regions, including Carinthia, Salzburg, Styria and Upper Austria, where the figures in 1910 fluctuated between 81.3 per cent and 72.3 per cent. On the other hand, an equally high proportion was recorded in the Sudeten regions, including Bohemia (71.7 per cent), Silesia (71.1 per cent) and Moravia (67.9 per cent), although the factors which had given rise to this situation were clearly different in the two general regions.[20] In the Alpine regions, for example, the system of agricultural holdings based on the self-contained but fairly substantial peasant tenement was prevalent, which in turn gave rise to a uniform pattern of settlement. In the Sudeten regions, on the other hand, the tendency was towards large-scale landed properties, although these failed to impose a uniform type of settlement on the area in question. They still left enough scope for the emergence of numerous small-scale farmers. Although their earlier dependent position still lingered on in the form of various mutual relationships between them and their former landlords, even after the implementation of peasant emancipation, their effective independence could no longer be doubted. Lower Austria (70.0 per cent) and neighbouring Moravia (67.9 per cent) also belonged to this type of region.

Galicia and Bukovina, with a 68.6 per cent and 69.7 per cent proportion respectively of wage earners in the total labour force employed in agriculture and forestry, constituted a clearly different type of region. They were essentially areas of small agricultural concerns and dwarf holdings, as far as general land endowment was concerned. For that reason the proportion of independent producers tended to increase along a west-east axis, and the proportion of wage earners correspondingly fell. Significantly the region with the lowest proportion of wage earners in the primary sector was located in the western part of the Empire. Vorarlberg registered a proportion of only 59.5 per cent, which, in direct contrast to the two Crown Lands in the extreme eastern part of the Empire cited above, was almost entirely the result of the prevalence of an intensive system of agricultural production. A further group of territories, including the Tyrol, Carniola and the maritime region, where the proportion of dependent

wage earners in the primary sector corresponded roughly with the
average for the Austrian half of the Empire as a whole, had in common
with one another a widely divergent pattern of production, with
intensive cultivation in the valleys and an extensive system of
agriculture in the mountainous regions.

In Hungary the proportion of wage earners in the primary sector
was significantly lower by 1910 than in the Austrian half of the Empire.
The proportions were particularly low in Croatia and Slavonia (62.8
per cent) and in Siebenbürgen (60.3 per cent). The agricultural crisis
of the late nineteenth century, which severely affected many parts of
Hungary, however, tended to raise the proportion of wage earners in
the primary sector and it was felt that the collapse of many small farms
and the accumulation of land in the hands of large property owners
was both economically and nationally a disadvantageous trend.[21]

The proportion of wage earners in industry and trade, including
mining, can be taken as a criterion for the extent of industrialisation.
The following regions were noted for their above average proportion
of the work force in this category, relative to the average of 82.6 per
cent for the Austrian half of the Empire as a whole: Silesia (89.1 per
cent), Moravia (85.5 per cent), Bohemia (85.1 per cent), Lower Austria
including Vienna (84.8 per cent) and Styria, including the mining and
industrial region of Upper Styria (83.6 per cent). This was equally the
case in the Hungarian territories, where the development of mining and
industrial production meant that the following regions had an average
proportion higher than the general figure of 68.4 per cent: the Danube-
Tisza plain, including Budapest (75.2 per cent), the left bank of the
Danube (71.9 per cent) and the right bank of the Tisza (69.8 per cent).

Fertility, Mortality and Migration

In order to be able to interpret correctly the development of the two
main components of natural population change in Austria-Hungary,
namely the movement in births and deaths, it is necessary in the first
instance to examine the longest series of annual figures for the period
1819 to 1913, which, however, is only available for the Austrian part
of the Empire (Figure 1.2).[22] Two periods, very different from each
other, are immediately distinguishable. The earlier period, lasting until
1875, is characterised by extensive short-term fluctuations, particularly
in relation to the death rate, which were clearly the result of wars and
epidemics. Between the years in which such catastrophes occurred the
birth rate stood at 40 (per 1,000) and the death rate at 30 (per 1,000).
From 1875 onwards the curves of the birth and death rates for the

Austrian half of the Empire follow the classic pattern of the demographic transition, as the population structure shifted from its original agrarian base to an industrial one. Short-term fluctuations as a result of isolated occurrences have also disappeared and the curves have become smoother, as their scissor shape has become increasingly defined through the continuing relative stability of the birth rate and the corresponding gradual decline in mortality. By the end of the century, however, this phase had come to an end, with the excess of births having reached its peak at over 12 per 1,000. There now followed a second period when the scissors began to close again, largely as a result of a relative decline in the birth rate which exceeded the comparative fall in mortality. In the last few years before the outbreak of the First World War the surplus of births over deaths in the Austrian half of the Empire had fallen to only 9 to 10 (per 1,000), as the birth rate had declined from 37 (per 1,000) at the turn of the century to 30 (per 1,000), whereas the death rate had fallen from 25 to 20 (per 1,000). These figures, in turn, illustrate in a very positive way the effectiveness of the measures undertaken by the Austrian government in the second half of the nineteenth century in the fields of social policy and public hygiene.

It is only from 1861 onwards, however, that published time series are available for the Hungarian part of the Empire. As a result they only cover a short section of that first phase when the development in mortality rates and to a lesser extent in fertility were still governed by national vicissitudes such as war and epidemics. The cholera epidemic of 1872-3, for example, produced a dramatic increase in mortality from 30 to over 60 (per 1,000), which was clearly more marked than in the Austrian half. But this was then followed by a far more stable process of development, with the death rate falling from just below 30 (1875) to 23 (per 1,000) in 1913, and the birth rate declining from over 45 to under 35 per 1,000. Once again these trends led to a surplus of births over deaths by a substantial margin of 12 (per 1,000). The intervening phase of the demographic transition did not operate in the Hungarian part of the Empire, as the pattern of population development in the latter part of the nineteenth century was determined by a premature decline in the birth rate, which has been the subject of a recent and interesting study by Demeny, although this has failed to provide an effective explanation for this phenomenon.[23]

Figure 1.2: The Natural Movement of Population in Austria-Hungary
1819/61-1913

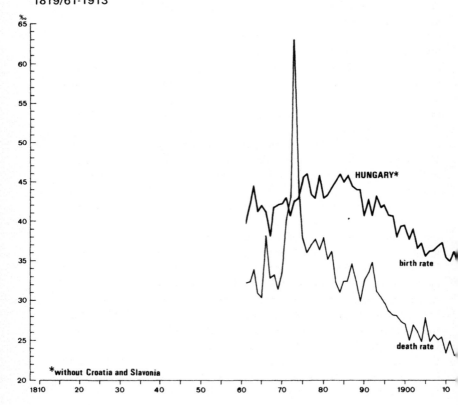

Figure 1.2 *(contd.)*

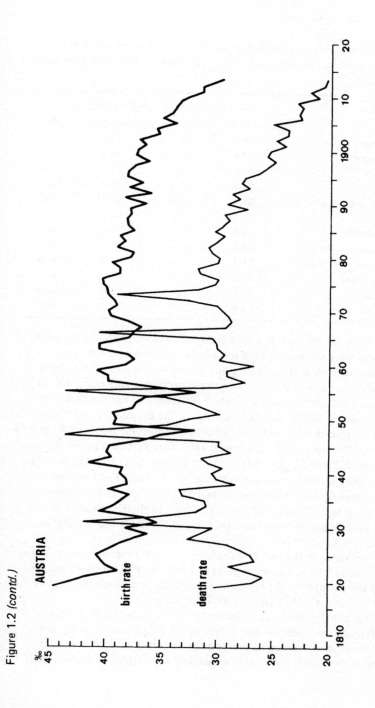

A comparative examination of the various European states reveals that the birth rate in both Hungary and Austria was among the highest recorded.[24]

Country	Birth rate (per 1,000 inhabitants)			
	c.1876-85	c.1886-95	c.1896-1905	1908-13
Romania	44.4	45.7	40.5	43.1
Hungary	44.4	42.5	38.3	36.0
Serbia	42.7	43.4	39.7	38.2
Austria	38.4	37.6	36.4	31.9
German Empire	38.0	36.5	35.2	29.5
Italy	37.3	36.6	33.2	32.4
Netherlands	35.9	33.6	32.2	29.1
England and Wales	34.2	30.9	28.6	24.9
Belgium	31.7	29.5	28.8	23.4
Switzerland	30.0	27.8	28.2	24.7
Sweden	29.8	28.1	26.4	24.4
France	24.9	22.8	21.8	19.5

The regional differences in the birth rate lead one to suspect that these figures were influenced by a specific factor, such as the prevalence of a particular nationality, a religious denomination, the relative level of educational attainment, or the actual structure of the economy. But the mechanism which gave rise to these differences is neither clear nor monocausal. Within the Austrian half of the Empire the two Carpathian regions of Bukovina and Galicia had the highest birth rate of 43 and 44 per 1,000 respectively. The lowest rates were recorded in the Alpine regions (27 and 30 per 1,000), with the exception of Lower Austria. The latter territory together with the Sudeten and Karst regions had mid-range figures of between 32 and 38 per 1,000. The average for the Austrian half of the Empire stood at 36.7. In the Hungarian half, on the other hand, the areas to either side of the Tisza had the highest figures (44 and 47 per 1,000) and the Transdanube in the west and Siebenbürgen in the east had the lowest figures (approximately 38 per thousand). The remaining regions had figures of between 41 and 43 and the average for the Hungarian territories as a whole stood at 41.6 per 1,000 in 1890-91 (Appendix Table 1.7).

It is equally important, however, to examine any noteworthy differences between the two halves of the Empire as far as the age distribution of the population and the sex ratio was concerned, as both these factors could have influenced the pattern of demographic development as it has been described. However this was not the case. In both Austria and Hungary the sex ratio was on average equally balanced, although this was particularly the case in the Hungarian territories. Indeed this, in turn, prompted many contemporary commentators to examine more closely the minor factors which may have influenced the overall balance between the sexes, such as the influence of the number of soldiers on active military service on the sex ratio of a garrison town; the shift in the ratio within a defined area due to the impact of immigration or rural exodus, etc. For every 1,000 females the following number of males was recorded:

Year	Austria	Hungary
1880	955	982
1890	958	985
1900	967	991
1910	965	981

The following distribution pattern of total population (per cent) can also be made on the basis of the three main age groups, embracing childhood (0-15 years), the active working age group (15 to 60 years) and the elderly (60 years and above):

Year	Austria			Hungary[a]		
	0-15	15-60	60+	0-15	15-60	60+
1880	34.0	58.4	7.6	35.2	58.4	6.4
1890	34.2	58.8	7.0	36.7	56.5	6.8
1900	34.4	58.4	7.2	35.6	56.8	7.6
1910	34.8	56.9	8.3	35.6	56.2	8.2

a. The 1880 figures refer only to civilian population, although all other figures relate to total population.

The following table also shows the general trend in the number of women of child-bearing age, the number of live births and the general level of fertility for the two halves of the Empire. The decline in fertility which started in Austria around the turn of the century, was evident in the Hungarian half of the Empire at least a decade earlier:

Year	Women aged between 15 and 45 years		Live births		General fertility rate	
	Austria	Hungary	Austria	Hungary	Austria	Hungary
1880	5,123,884	3,711,081	831,159	674,621	162.2	181.8
1890	5,443,985	3,876,627	895,004	721,759	164.4	186.2
1900	5,918,262	4,275,251	964,720	742,219	163.0	173.6
1910	6,383,902	4,581,147	911,123	737,833	142.7	161.1

The death rate in the Hungarian half of the Empire was decidedly greater than in the Austrian Crown Lands. After the normalisation of mortality following the last cholera epidemic in Austria-Hungary in 1872-3, the death rate in the Austrian half of the Empire fell from 30 to 20 per 1,000, and the equivalent fall in the Hungarian half was from 37 to 23 per thousand. The most frequent causes of death were infectious diseases and in particular tuberculosis and 'inborn debility'. During the same period there was a decline in the frequency of diseases characteristic of old age, such as organic heart disease, cerebral apoplexy and malignant neoplasm. In one particular year, 1880, 30.8 per cent of all deceased in Austria were under 1 year of age, 50.3 per cent were under 5 years and 60.0 per cent under 15. In the Hungarian part of the Empire the corresponding proportional mortality for these age groups was 32.6 per cent, 52.5 per cent and 60.8 per cent respectively in the year 1891. Infant mortality to a large extent determined the overall death rate. However, in the Austrian half of the Empire the infant mortality rate fell from 250 to below 200 per 1,000 between 1881 and the turn of the century (Appendix Table 1.7) and a similar process can be found in the Hungarian territories where infant mortality had fallen to approximately the same level.

However, the best criterion for assessing the effectiveness of state measures in the sphere of social policy and sanitary legislation can be found in the increase in life expectancy, which can be determined on the basis of a calculation of mortality tables. A general mortality table was constructed for the Austrian half of the Empire from the available age structure figures, according to individual years, of both the male and female population recorded at each census.[25]   Appendix Table 1.8 lists life expectancy figures at birth and at every successive ten-year period on the basis of the population surveys taken in 1869, 1900 and 1910. The increase in life expectancy during this forty-year period was as follows (in years):

	Male	Female
for newly born	+10.26	+ 9.74
for 10 year olds	+ 5.97	+ 5.57
for 20 year olds	+ 5.01	+ 4.88
for 30 year olds	+ 3.75	+ 4.34
for 40 year olds	+ 2.75	+ 3.48
for 50 year olds	+ 1.76	+ 2.54
for 60 year olds	+ 1.08	+ 1.63
for 70 year olds	+ 0.58	+ 0.94
for 80 year olds	+ 0.30	+ 0.48
for 90 year olds	+ 0.16	+ 0.05

What is particularly striking is that the greater life expectancy of
women around 1870 was not maintained throughout all the different
age groups. After the age of 60 (or to be precise after 58), men in those
days had a greater life expectancy than women of the same age. But as
early as the 1900 census it is clear that the modern pattern was
beginning to emerge, with women having a uniformly higher life
expectancy in all age groups.

As far as the Hungarian half of the Empire was concerned, a general
mortality table was not calculated until the census of 1900, but this
did then cover the different regions of Hungary,[26] although its main
aim was to determine not life expectancy, but the 'probable life span'.
This was defined as the median age at death of the population at risk,
that is to say the age by which any age group cohort would have
shrunk to half its original complement. The following table presents
the results of this calculation, together with figures for the Austrian
half of the Empire derived by the same method:

Age	Austria, 1901-05		Hungary, 1900-01	
	men	women	men	women
0	45.7	48.3	40.3	39.4
5	61.8	63.1	61.2	60.4
10	62.6	64.0	62.7	62.0
20	63.6	65.2	63.9	63.5
30	65.2	66.8	65.5	65.4
40	66.9	68.4	67.1	67.2
50	69.1	70.1	69.0	68.9
60	72.3	72.6	72.4	72.1
70	76.9	77.0	76.7	76.5

The most striking difference between the two halves of the Empire was that the probable life span for women was always shorter than that for men of a similar age in the Hungarian territories. This was probably occasioned by the special conditions operating in Croatia and Slavonia. If these areas are excluded from the calculation, the life span for women in the remaining regions was longer, as it was in Austria as a whole.

Mention must also be made of a fact which may seem surprising to us, although contemporary demographers devoted a lot of attention and careful commentary to it. Austria-Hungary had a growing negative emigration balance. It can be seen (Appendix Table 1.9) that the state as a whole evinced a migration deficit of −1.0 per cent, −1.3 per cent and −2.9 per cent respectively in the periods 1881-90, 1891-1900 and 1901-10, measured in each case as a percentage of the base figure. In absolute terms the deficit amounted to a population loss during the three periods of 379,796, 565,187 and 1,329,970 individuals respectively. As there was some return migration into Austria-Hungary, the total number of emigrants must have been even larger, but absolute figures were only partly registered in continuous emigration statistics by the harbour authorities in the ports of embarkation, and particularly in Hamburg and Bremen.

Table 1.9, however, also provides an indication of the considerable inner migration within the Austrian-Hungarian monarchy. Migration to centres of attraction within the monarchy, which was unleashed by overpopulation in several agricultural areas, took place on a comparatively large scale. The migratory gains of Lower Austria in the periods between 1880, 1890, 1900 and 1910 amounted to 7.3 per cent, 7.0 per cent and 5.1 per cent, or in absolute terms a total of 515,100 individuals, and this can be explained by the attraction of Vienna and the surrounding region. Similarly the attraction of Budapest explains the migratory gains of 4.0 per cent, 5.5 per cent and 2.6 per cent of the Danube-Tisza plain in the same periods, producing a total net gain of 331,400 individuals. It would be beyond the scope of this survey, however, to examine the diverse centres of attraction, the areas of population exodus and the direction of the streams of inner migration within Austria-Hungary, although the process is substantially reflected in the development of the fourteen largest towns of the monarchy:

Town	1869 Civil population	1910		% change (civil population)
		Civil population	Total population	
Vienna	607,514	2,004,939	2,031,498	230.0
Budapest	254,474	863,735	880,371	239.4
Prague	157,713	218,573	223,741	38.6
Lemberg (Lvov)	87,109	195,796	206,113	124.8
Graz	81,119	146,507	151,781	80.6
Brno	73,771	122,144	125,737	65.5
Trieste	70,274	226,458	229,510	222.3
Szeged	70,179	115,306	118,328	64.3
Szabadka	56,323	93,232	94,610	65.5
Krakow	49,835	142,518	151,886	186.0
Pressburg (Bratislava)	46,540	73,459	78,223	57.8
Debrecen	46,111	90,153	92,729	95.5
Kecskemét	41,195	65,716	66,834	59.5
Chernovtsy	33,884	84,214	87,128	148.5

In general, however, the exchange of people between the two halves of the Empire was relatively slight. Although formally classified as 'emigration', when the actual population was counted it was clear that it only related to 'temporary domicile' in other parts of the Empire. The time of the 'colonisation of the southeast', which had prompted extensive migration to Hungary in the eighteenth century, was long since past.

However, before the collapse of the unified state the First World War occurred, with an extensive loss of life suffered by all nationalities within the monarchy. This event was to have a substantial demographic effect. One and a half million were killed in the war, 0.5 million as a result of increased mortality; a further 3.8 million loss in the number of births meant that total population loss amounted to 5.8 million.[27] The number of those killed constituted 2.9 per cent of the pre-war population and total losses ran at 11 per cent of this figure. The last survey carried out by the authorities responsible for official population statistics thus dealt with this final tragic event. On average 23.9 per thousand lost their lives (as a proportion of the total indigenous population on 31 December 1910), although the figure in the Austrian half amounted to 23.3 per thousand, in Hungary to 25 per thousand and in Bosnia-Hercegovina to 19.1 per thousand.[28]

A Short Survey of the Succession States

Before the close of 1918 the Succession States of the monarchy had
claimed their right of existence through proclamations made by
provisional national assemblies: the Republic of Czechoslovakia on
28 October; the German-Austrian Republic on 12 November; the
Republic of Hungary, which later became the Kingdom of Hungary
between 1920 and 1946, on 16 November and the Kingdom of the
Serbs, Croats and Slovenes on 1 December 1918. These states were
recognised internationally by the treaties of Versailles, Saint-Germain
and Trianon. The remaining parts of the monarchy fell to several states:
Galicia partly to Poland and partly to Russia, together with the larger
part of Bukovina. After World War II the Soviet Union also took over
the Carpathian Ukraine; Siebenbürgen fell to Romania and the South
Tyrol was allotted to Italy (Figure 1.3). However, in the following
table only those three Succession States which originated entirely from
the former monarchy are dealt with.

	Austria	Czechoslovakia[a]	Hungary
Present-day surface area (sq.km.)	83,849	127,869	93,030
Population (1920/21/23)	6,534,742	13,003,446	7,986,875
Population (1970/71)	7,456,403	14,344,986	10,322,099
Difference (per cent)	+14.1	+10.3	+29.2
Population density (1971)	89	115	111

a. Present-day territorial state.

The Succession States not only had to struggle with substantial
economic problems, but they also inherited from the former monarchy
a problem of nationality. In the case of Czechoslovakia, with 3.3 million
Sudeten Germans and 0.6 million Hungarians among others, this grew
into an international crisis. Only through voluntary flight, expulsion
and resettlement as a result of World War II was the problem to some
extent resolved.

With regard to natural population change, however, all three states
soon followed the general pattern in Central Europe. The birth rate
fell more dramatically than the mortality rate, and Hungary was quick
to catch up with the general trend. After short-term fluctuations
resulting from war the trend of declining fertility and a stable, or of
late a slightly rising mortality continued:

		Austria	Czechoslovakia	Hungary
Birth rate	(per 1,000)			
	1920-24	22.6	22.6	30.2
	1935-37	13.3	16.6	20.5
	1955-59	17.2	18.5	17.8
	1971	14.6	16.5	14.3
Death rate	(per 1,000)			
	1920-24	16.7	16.5	20.9
	1930-37	13.4	13.1	14.5
	1955-59	12.5	9.7	10.3
	1971	13.1	11.5	11.9
General fertility figure (women between 15 and 50 years of age, 1972)		61.5	69.4	56.9
Infant mortality (1973)		23.8	21.2	33.8
Life expectancy (1970, in years)				
	newly born males	67.4	66.2	66.9
	newly born females	74.7	72.9	72.6
	aged 60 males	15.7	14.6	15.6
	aged 60 females	19.8	18.3	18.6

In terms of overall age structure the proportion of children and elderly in Austria is significantly different from the two neighbouring states:

Age group	Proportional distribution (%)		
	Austria	Czechoslovakia	Hungary
0-15	24.0	22.8	20.0
15-60	61.3	65.7	67.8
60+	14.7	11.6	12.2

Industrialisation developed rapidly in all three states and the proportion of urban population grew. In Hungary this process was governed by the agglomeration of Budapest and its surrounding district, whereas in Austria the initial preponderance of Vienna has been reduced by developments in other federal regions. Of the three states Hungary has the largest primary sector, and Austria has a strikingly high proportion of individuals employed in service industries, although this can be attributed not only to the size of the administration but also to tourism.

Figure 1.3: The Successor States of the Austro-Hungarian Monarchy after 1945

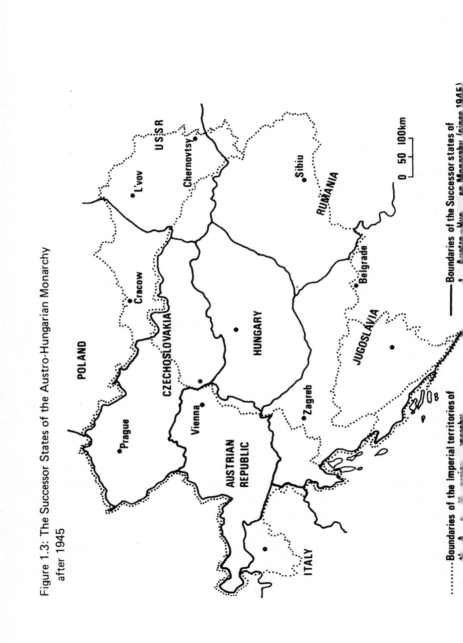

POLAND

USSR

•L'vov

•Cracow

•Chernovtsy

CZECHOSLOVAKIA

•Prague

HUNGARY

RUMANIA

•Sibiu

Vienna•

AUSTRIAN
REPUBLIC

•Zagreb

JUGOSLAVIA

•Belgrade

ITALY

0 50 100km

—— Boundaries of the Successor states of

.... Boundaries of the Imperial territories of

Employment distribution (1974)

Employment sector	Proportional distribution		
	Austria	Czechoslovakia	Hungary
Agriculture and forestry	13.0	15.7	23.0
Mining, industry and trade	40.9	47.6	44.0
Tertiary sector	46.1	36.7	33.0

Of the capital cities of the three states, Budapest with 2 million inhabitants is clearly the largest. The population of Vienna has fallen from 2.2 to 1.6 million (1916-71), and this trend is still continuing. Prague has grown to 1.1 million inhabitants. In addition Hungary has a further five large towns (Debrecen, Györ [Raab], Miskolc, Pecs [Fünfkirchen] and Szeged), with a combined population of 816,000. Austria has four large towns (Graz, Linz, Salzburg and Innsbruck), with a total population of 716,000 and Czechoslovakia five large towns (Brno, Pressburg [Bratislava], Ostrava, Kosice and Plzen), with a total of 1,285,000 inhabitants. Future projections of population growth to the year 2,000 envisage a further rise both in Czechoslovakia and Hungary to a total of 17.0 and 10.5 millions respectively, although the population of Austria is expected to remain at the same level, or even to decline slightly.

Notes

1. Erich Zöllner, *Geschichte Oesterreichs. Von den Anfängen bis zur Gegenwart*, Vienna, 1961, p.317.
2. Bukovina, with its capital Chernovtsy, is now largely part of the Soviet Republic of the Ukraine; the smaller part is incorporated into the Socialist People's Republic of Romania. Ibid., p.317.
3. Paul Demeny, 'Early Fertility Decline in Austria-Hungary: a Lesson in Demographic Transition', in D.V. Glass and R. Revelle (eds), *Population and Social Change*, London, 1972, p.155.
4. Christel Durdik, 'Bevölkerungs- und Sozialstatistik in Oesterreich im 18. und 19. Jahrhundert', in H. Helczmanovszki (ed.), *Beiträge zur Bevölkerungs- und Sozialgeschichte Oesterreichs. Nebst einem Ueberblick über die Entwicklung der Bevölkerungs- und Sozialstatistik*, Vienna, 1973, p.225 *et seq*. Gustav Borkor, *Geschichte und Organisation der amtlichen Statistik in Ungarn*, Budapest, 1896.
5. Volkszählung in den Ländern der ungarischen heil. Krone im Jahre 1900. Zehnter Teil. Zusammenfassung der Endergebnisse. Verfasst und herausgegeben vom königlichen ungarischen statistischen Zentralamt'. *Ungarische Statistische Mitteilungen*, N.S. Bd.27, Budapest, 1909.
6. Alföld refers to the vast plain in Hungary between the Danube and Romania.
7. Siebenbürgen is an historical area, comprising various towns in Romania (Cluj, Petrosani) and situated to the left of the southeast Carpathians.

62   Austria-Hungary

8. Kovacsics József, *Magyarország történeti demográfiája*, Budapest, 1963.
9. Heinrich Rauchberg, *Die Bevölkerung Oesterreichs auf Grund der Ergebnisse der Volkszählung vom 31 Dezember 1890*, Vienna, 1895.
10. 'Volkszählung in den Ländern der ungarischen heil. Krone im Jahre 1900', op.cit., p.1.
11. This figure excludes such areas of the Habsburg Empire as the provinces in the Netherlands, with approximately 2 million inhabitants; the 'Vorlande' in southwest Germany, with roughly 350,000, and Lombardy (Milan and Mantua) with a total of 1.3 million inhabitants. J. Vincenz Goehlert, 'Die Ergebnisse der in Oesterreich im vorigen Jahrhundert ausgeführten Volkszählungen im Vergleich mit jenen der neueren Zeit', in *Sitzungsberichte der kaiserlichen Akademie der Wissenschaften. Philosophisch-historische Classe*, XIV, Bd., I, Heft. Jhg, 1854, p.52 *et seq.* A. Ficker, *Bevölkerung der Oesterreichischen Monarchie in ihren wichtigsten Momenten statistisch dargestellt*, Gotha, 1860.
12. Kovacsics József, op.cit., p.175.
13. Ergebnisse der in den Ländern der ungarischen Krone am Anfange des Jahres 1881 vollgezogenen Volkszählung, I.Bd, Budapest, 1882, p.LIX.
14. 'Volkszählung in den Ländern der ungarischen heil. Krone im Jahre 1900', op.cit., p.40.
15. 'Volkszählung in den Ländern der ungarischen heil. Krone im Jahre 1900', op.cit., p.113.
16. Die Ergebnisse der Volkszählung in Bosnien und der Herzegovina vom 10.Oktober 1910. Zusammengestellt vom statistischen Department der Landesregierung. Sarajevo, 1912, p.XLII *et seq.*
17. 'Volkszählung in den Ländern der ungarischen heil. Krone im Jahre 1900', op.cit., p.126.
18. Oesterreichische Akademie der Wissenschaften, *Die Habsburger Monarchie, 1848-1918*, Bd.I, *Die wirtschaftliche Entwicklung*, edited by A. Brusatti, Vienna, 1973. In particular the contribution by N.T. Gross, 'Die Stellung der Habsburgermonarchie in der Weltwirtschaft', p.1 *et seq.*
19. 'Volkszählung in den Ländern der ungarischen heil. Krone im Jahre 1900', op.cit., p.139.
20. Heinrich Rauchberg, op.cit., p.364.
21. 'Volkszählung in den Ländern der ungarischen heil. Krone im Jahre 1900', op.cit., p.139.
22. K.K. Statistische Zentralkommission, *Statistische Rückblicke aus Oesterreich*, Vienna, 1913, p.6 *et seq.*
23. Paul Demeny, op.cit.
24. *Oesterreichisches Statistisches Handbuch 1916-1917*, Vienna, 1918, p.354. Slight differences or changes in the periods covered in the individual states do not impair the general comparability.
25. Oesterreichische Sterbetafeln, *Bearbeitet im Oesterreichischen Statistischen Zentralamt*, Vienna, 1967. Beiträge zur Osterreichischen Statistik, Heft.144.
26. 'Mortalitätstafel der Länder der ungarischen Krone. Bearbeitet im königlichen ungarischen Statistischen Zentralamt'. Ungarische Statistische Mitteilungen, N.F. Band II, Budapest, 1906.
27. C. Doring, 'Die Bevölkerungsbewegung im Weltkrieg (Deutschland, Oesterreich-Ungarn, England, Frankreich)', Archiv für soziale Hygiene und Demographie, Bd.13, Heft.4, Leipzig, 1920, p.366.
28. Wilhelm Winkler, *Die Totenverluste der Oesterreichischen-Ungarischen Monarchie nach Nationalitäten*, Vienna, 1919, edited by the Statistischer Dienst des Deutschösterreichischen Staatsamtes für Heerwesen.

APPENDIX

Table 1.1: Population, Area, Population Growth and Density in the Six Most Populated European States before the First World War (1910-11)

State	Population (in millions)	Area (in sq.km.)	Average yearly growth rate (in %) since the previous census	Population density (per sq.km.)
Russian Empire[a]	133.9	5,293,521		25.3
German Empire	64.9	540,858	1.42	125.0
Austria-Hungary	51.4	676,615	0.87	75.9
Great Britain and Ireland	45.2	315,683	0.87	143.3
France	39.2	536,464	0.06	73.1
Italy	34.7	286,610	0.64	120.9

a. European part.

Source: *Osterreichisches Statistisches Handbuch 1916-17*, Vienna, 1918, p.353.

Table 1.2: The Population of the Austrian Monarchy, 1786 to 1857[a]

Area	1786	1818	1828	Military	1838	Military	1851	1857	1786-1857 (in %)
Lower Austria	1,001,788	1,076,746	1,217,675	31,571	1,329,073	33,964	1,538,047	1,681,697	67.9
Upper Austria							706,316	707,450	
Salzburg	691,220	773,518	829,341	9,222	838,982	9,125	146,007	146,769	23.6
Steiermark	819,449	764,784	841,337	19,520	941,156	18,255	1,006,944	1,056,773	29.0
Carinthia	294,104	636,386	720,140	10,733	741,846	9,361	319,224	332,456	13.0
Carniola	412,409						463,956	451,941	9.6
Tyrol and Vorarlberg	681,631	735,114	786,437	4,713	819,988	12,489	858,203	851,106	24.8
Bohemia	2,745,018	3,275,900	3,785,972	77,909	4,017,571	62,013	4,385,894	4,705,525	71.4
Moravia	1,530,980	1,749,486	2,013,993	38,058	2,087,973	41,762	1,799,838	1,867,094	50.9
Silesia							438,586	443,912	
Galicia	3,277,087	3,760,319	4,439,811	61,276	4,538,254	76,819	4,555,477	4,597,470	54.2
Bukovina							380,826	456,920	
Görz, Gradisca, Triest	139,558	356,755	421,844	5,613	466,615	6,919	542,917	520,978	—
Dalmatia[b]	—	653,555	763,464	13,773	845,532	14,377	936,632	925,477	—
Hungary	7,044,462	9,824,977	10,892,491	65,787	11,790,100	55,467	7,864,262	8,125,785	49.5
Croatia, Slavonia							868,456	865,009	
Western Serbia							1,426,221	1,540,049	

Table 1.2 (contd.)

Area	1786	1818	1828	1828 Military	1838	1838 Military	1851	1857	1786-1857 (in %)
Military Zone	650,000	909,619	1,074,085	55,000	1,122,972	56,309	958,877	1,064,922	63.8
Siebenbürgen	1,416,035	1,625,508	1,860,401	12,337	2,023,700	8,601	2,073,737	2,172,748	53.4
The Austrian part of the Empire	11,521,244	13,425,808	15,398,210	266,775	16,200,375	278,165	17,534,950	18,224,500	58.2
The Hungarian part of the Empire	9,110,497	12,360,164	13,826,977	133,124	14,942,772	120,377	13,191,553	13,768,513	51.1
Total	20,631,741	25,785,972	29,225,187	399,899	31,143,147	398,542	30,726,503[c]	31,993,013[c]	55.1

a. 1786 – indigenous population, derived from J.V. Goehlert, 1854; 1818 – indigenous civil population; 1828 to 1857 – existing population (according to the official Tafeln zur Statistik der Österreichischen Monarchie, 1828, vol.11, 1838: New Series. vol.I, 1856; vol.III, Table 2, 1861). 1786 – excludes Vorlande, the Netherlands and Lombardy; 1818 to 1857 – excludes Lombardy and Venetia. The figures for the Hungarian part of the Empire between 1818 and 1857 are based on official estimates.

b. In 1786 Dalmatia was still part of the Republic of Venice.

c. In addition to the listed civil population in 1851 and 1857 there were respectively 560,000 and 564,989 military personnel. The figure for 1857 is derived from A. Ficker, 1860, p.15; the figure for 1851 is based on the estimate of A. Ficker of 648,000 active military personnel for the whole of the Empire and an assumption that the equivalent figure for Lombardy and Venetia was the same as in 1857 (c.88,000).

Table 1.3: The Population of the Austro-Hungarian Monarchy, 1869-1910[a]

Area	1869	1880	1890	1900	1910	Average yearly growth[b]			
						1869-80	1880-90	1890-1900	1900-10
Lower Austria	1,990,708	2,330,621	2,611,799	3,100,493	3,531,814	1.44	1.34	1.54	1.31
Upper Austria	736,557	759,620	785,831	810,246	853,006	0.28	0.34	0.31	0.52
Salzburg	153,159	163,570	173,510	192,763	214,737	0.60	0.59	1.06	1.09
Steiermark	1,137,990	1,213,597	1,282,708	1,356,494	1,444,157	0.56	0.59	1.06	0.63
Carinthia	337,694	384,730	361,008	367,324	396,200	0.29	0.35	0.17	0.76
Tyrol	885,789 }	805,176	812,696	852,712	946,613	0.27 }	0.09 }	0.48	1.05
Vorarlberg		107,373	116,073	129,237	145,408		0.78	1.08	1.19
Bohemia	5,140,544	5,560,819	5,843,094	6,318,697	6,796,548	0.72	0.50	0.79	0.69
Moravia	2,017,274	2,153,407	2,276,870	2,437,706	2,622,271	0.60	0.56	0.68	0.73
Silesia	513,352	565,475	605,649	680,422	756,949	0.88	0.69	1.17	1.07
Galicia	5,444,689	5,958,907	6,607,816	7,315,939	8,025,675	0.82	1.04	1.02	0.93
Bukovina	513,404	571,671	646,591	703,195	800,098	0.98	1.24	1.22	0.92
Carniola	466,334	481,243	498,958	508,150	525,995	0.29	0.36	0.18	0.35
Maritime region	600,525	647,934	695,384	756,546	893,797	0.69	0.71	0.85	1.68
Dalmatia	456,961	476,101	527,426	593,784	645,666	0.37	1.03	1.19	0.84
Right Donau bank	2,411,318	2,566,946	2,771,294	2,923,401	3,084,404	0.57	0.71	0.54	0.54
Donau-Tisza plain	2,141,338	2,343,384	2,778,514	3,284,233	3,769,658	0.82	1.63	1.69	1.39
Left Tisza bank	1,888,290	1,820,855	2,076,803	2,336,104	2,594,924	−0.33	1.29	1.18	1.06
Left Donau bank	1,725,458	1,752,049	1,889,099	2,049,611	2,175,924	0.14	0.70	0.82	0.60

Table 1.3 *(contd.)*

Area	1869	1880	1890	1900	1910	Average yearly growth[b]			
						1869-80	1880-90	1890-1900	1900-10
Right Tisza bank	1,489,283	1,440,028	1,529,259	1,674,241	1,769,681	−0.31	0.52	0.91	0.56
Siebenbürgen	2,152,805	2,084,048	2,267,935	2,476,998	2,678,367	−0.29	0.77	0.89	0.78
Tisza-Maros plain	1,752,753	1,721,312	1,918,623	2,054,712	2,141,769	−0.16	1.03	0.69	0.42
Rijeka and surrounding areas	17,884	20,981	30,337	38,955	49,806	1.46	3.46	2.53	2.49
Croatia and Slavonia	1,841,122	1,892,499	2,201,927	2,416,304	2,621,954	0.25	1.45	0.93	0.82
Austria	20,394,980	22,144,244	23,895,413	26,150,708	28,571,934	0.75	0.76	0.91	0.89
Hungary[c]	15,509,455	15,739,259	17,463,791	19,254,559	20,886,487	0.13	1.05	0.98	0.82
Total	35,904,435	37,883,503	41,359,204	45,405,267	49,458,421	0.49	0.88	0.94	0.86

	1879	1885	1895	1910	1879-85	1885-95	1895-1910
Bosnia and Hercegovina	1,158,164	1,336,091	1,591,036	1,931,802	2.41	1.61	1.30

a. Total population resident according to official sources with the following exceptions: for the Hungarian part of the Empire between 1869 and 1880, and for Bosnia and Hercegovina between 1879 and 1885 the figures only relate to total civilian population.
b. The calculated average yearly growth rate (in%) is based for the Hungarian parts of the monarchy between 1869-80 and 1880-90, as well as for Bosnia-Hercegovina for 1874-85 and 1885-95 on the total civilian population, whereas for the period, 1890-1900 and 1900-10 (1895-1910) the rates are based on total population.
c. The figures for the total population of Hungary for 1869 and 1880 are derived from József Kovacsics, *Magyarország történeti demográfiája*, Budapest, 1963, Appendix Table 6.

Table 1.4: The Population of the Austro-Hungarian Monarchy According to Language 1910[a] (in %)

Area	German	Hungarian	Czech	Polish	Ruthenian	Romanian	Serbo-Croatian	Slavonian	Italian	Others	Total
Alpine areas[b]	85.61	0.01	1.82	0.09	0.04	0.00	0.01	6.92	5.50	—	100.00
Sudetenland[c]	34.92	0.00	62.54	2.50	0.02	0.00	0.01	0.01	0.00	—	100.00
Galicia, Bukovina	2.95	0.12	0.11	53.66	40.04	3.12	0.00	0.00	0.00	—	100.00
The Karst Lands[d]	3.03	0.00	0.24	0.05	0.05	0.05	39.43	38.24	18.91	—	100.00
Austria	35.58	0.04	23.02	17.77	12.58	0.98	2.80	4.48	2.75	—	100.00
Trans-danube, Alföld[e]	10.55	72.89	2.00	5.09	2.18	6.64	3.64	0.79	0.02	1.20	100.00
North Hungary[f]	6.16	42.01	43.84	0.07	6.42	0.06	0.08	0.01	0.02	0.70	100.00
Siebenbürgen	8.74	34.28	0.14	0.06	0.07	54.96	0.04	0.01	0.05	1.65	100.00
Tisza-Maros plain	19.95	22.18	2.56	0.01	0.15	39.49	13.79	0.00	0.03	1.84	100.00
Croatia, Slavonia	5.10	4.21	2.04	0.09	0.31	0.04	85.96	0.68	1.06	0.51	100.00
Hungary	9.75	48.12	9.73	0.19	2.26	14.12	14.08	0.45	0.16	1.14	100.00
Bosnia-Hercegovina	1.21	0.34	0.40	0.58	0.39	0.03	96.02	0.16	0.13	0.74	100.00

a. Figures for Austria based on indigenous population present; for Hungary on total population and for Bosnia-Hercegovina on total civilian population present. For Austria the determining factor was the colloquial language: in Hungary and Bosnia-Hercegovina the mother tongue. There were no miscellaneous categories in Austria, as only the listed languages were officially allowed.
b. Upper and Lower Austria, Salzburg, Steiermark, Carinthia, Tyrol and Vorarlberg.
c. Bohemia, Moravia, Silesia.
d. Carniola, Görz and Gradisca, Triest, Istria and Dalmatia.
e. Trans-danube, Alföld, right bank of the Danube, Donau-Tisza plain and the left bank of the Tisza.
f. Left Donau bank, right Tisza bank.

Table 1.5: The Population of Austria-Hungary According to Religious Denomination, 1890[a]

Area	Roman Catholic	Greek Catholic	Evangelical AB	Evangelical HB	Greek Orthodox	Jewish	Muslim	Others	Total
Alpine region[b]	5,948,913	2,619	91,442	9,342	2,974	132,844	—	5,511	6,193,625
Bohemia, Moravia, Silesia	8,292,761	600	168,658	104,581	256	149,845	—	8,912	8,725,613
Galicia, Bukovina	3,069,819	2,810,259	54,157	5,466	452,202	854,930	—	7,574	7,254,407
Karst lands[c]	1,622,673	594	1,591	1,135	89,307	5,686	—	782	1,721,768
Trans-danube, Alföld[d]	4,179,126	610,160	506,294	1,489,019	359,934	425,272	—	8,663	7,578,468
North Hungary[e]	2,084,804	359,263	408,868	330,216	1,107	211,627	—	329	3,396,214
Siebenbürgen	284,808	636,178	208,758	328,064	694,902	39,148	—	59,358	2,251,216
Tisza-Maros plain	690,474	52,694	56,569	65,364	1,008,801	31,425	—	2,269	1,907,596
Croatia, Slavonia, Rijeka	1,581,558	12,387	23,551	12,463	567,588	17,570	—	607	2,215,904
Austria	18,934,166	2,814,072	315,828	120,524	544,739	1,143,305	—	22,779	23,895,413
Hungary	8,820,770	1,670,682	1,204,040	2,225,126	2,632,332	725,222	—	71,226	17,349,398
Total	27,754,936	4,484,754	1,519,868	2,345,650	3,177,071	1,868,527	—	94,005	41,244,811
Bosnia-Hercegovina (1885)	265,77	—	—	—	571,250	5,805	492,710	538	1,336,091

Table 1.5 (contd.)

Area	Roman Catholic	Greek Catholic	Evangelical AB	Evangelical HB	Greek Orthodox	Jewish	Muslim	Others	Total
				Proportional (in %)					
Alpine region[b]	96.05	0.04	1.48	0.15	0.05	2.14	–	0.10	100.00
Bohemia, Moravia, Silesia	95.04	0.01	1.93	1.20	0.00	1.72	–	0.10	100.00
Galicia, Bukovina	42.32	38.74	0.75	0.08	6.23	11.78	–	0.10	100.00
Karst lands[c]	94.24	0.03	0.09	0.07	5.19	0.33	–	0.05	100.00
Trans-danube, Alföld[d]	55.14	8.05	6.68	19.65	4.75	5.61	–	0.12	100.00
North Hungary[e]	61.39	10.58	12.04	9.72	0.03	6.23	–	0.01	100.00
Siebenbürgen	12.65	28.26	9.72	14.57	30.87	1.74	–	2.64	100.00
Tisza-Maros plain	36.20	2.76	2.96	3.43	52.88	1.65	–	0.14	100.00
Croatia, Slavonia, Rijeka	71.37	0.56	1.06	0.56	25.62	0.80	–	0.03	100.00
Austria	79.24	11.78	1.32	0.50	2.28	4.79	–	0.09	100.00
Hungary	50.84	9.63	6.94	12.83	15.17	4.18	...	0.41	100.00
Total	67.29	10.87	3.69	5.69	7.70	4.53	–	0.23	100.00
Bosnia-Hercegovina	19.89	–	–	–	42.76	0.43	36.88	0.04	100.00

a. Figures for Austria relate to total population present; for Hungary and Bosnia-Hercegovina to total civilian population. As the delineation according to religious denomination was not uniform in Austria, Hungary and Bosnia-Hercegovina. Muslims in Austria and Hungary as well as Greek Catholics and Evangelicals in Bosnia-Hercegovina are included in the 'Others' section.

b, c, d, e, f. cf. the footnotes in Table 4.

Table 1.6: The Sectoral Distribution of Employment of the Population and Proportion of Wage Earners in the Total Employed in Agriculture and Industry in Austria-Hungary (in %)[a]

| | Sectoral distribution of population | | | | | | | | Proportion of wage earners 1910 | |
| | Agriculture and forestry | | Industry and craft | | Trade and transport | | Public service and misc. | | Agriculture and forestry | Industry and craft |
	1900	1910	1900	1910	1900	1910	1900	1910		
Lower Austria	20.5	18.0	40.0	40.4	21.9	21.8	17.6	19.8	70.0	84.8
Upper Austria	49.4	46.9	26.2	26.7	11.3	11.2	13.1	15.2	72.3	78.0
Salzburg	45.1	40.1	21.7	23.4	15.8	16.2	17.4	20.3	78.3	78.5
Steiermark	58.4	53.2	20.5	21.9	8.4	9.8	12.7	15.1	73.0	83.6
Carinthia	58.4	51.1	19.9	21.7	8.6	11.0	13.1	16.2	81.3	79.4
Tyrol	59.8	54.3	17.1	18.9	9.8	11.7	13.3	15.1	69.3	75.2
Vorarlberg	34.3	31.6	43.9	44.1	11.2	11.6	10.6	12.7	59.5	81.0
Bohemia	35.7	32.3	40.2	41.1	12.4	13.2	11.7	13.4	71.7	85.1
Moravia	46.2	41.3	32.6	35.0	9.8	10.8	11.4	12.9	67.9	85.5
Silesia	35.1	29.2	44.5	46.3	9.1	11.2	11.3	13.3	71.1	89.1
Galicia	76.8	73.1	8.0	9.5	8.8	9.6	6.4	7.8	68.6	69.0
Bukovina	72.6	71.1	10.0	10.4	9.9	9.4	7.5	9.1	69.7	67.9
Carniola	69.8	62.0	15.1	17.5	5.6	7.5	9.5	13.0	70.6	71.3
Coastal areas	53.3	46.0	18.7	22.0	15.4	16.9	12.6	15.1	70.6	79.6
Dalmatia	83.7	82.6	4.6	4.8	4.8	4.8	6.9	7.8	79.3	63.7

Table 1.6 (contd.)

| | Sectoral distribution of population | | | | | | | | Proportion of wage earners 1910 | |
| | Agriculture and forestry | | Industry and craft | | Trade and transport | | Public service and misc. | | Agriculture and forestry | Industry and craft |
	1900	1910	1900	1910	1900	1910	1900	1910		
Right Donau bank	69.2	65.2	14.7	17.7	4.7	5.8	11.4	11.3	65.1	65.3
Donau-Tisza plain	51.0	46.1	21.2	25.1	9.5	11.4	18.3	17.4	67.0	75.2
Left Tisza bank	73.2	70.1	11.1	12.8	4.6	6.1	11.1	11.0	67.6	58.1
Left Donau bank	65.6	61.7	17.3	20.6	5.2	6.2	11.9	11.5	66.1	71.9
Right Tisza bank	65.0	61.3	16.8	19.2	5.3	6.8	12.9	12.7	64.3	69.8
Siebenbürgen	75.7	71.7	10.8	14.1	3.0	4.2	10.5	10.0	60.3	65.5
Tisza-Maros plain	71.8	69.1	12.7	14.4	4.2	5.4	11.3	11.1	65.3	63.1
Rijeka	4.8	3.2	34.2	38.9	28.4	30.5	32.6	27.4	62.1	84.8
Croatia, Slavonia	82.0	78.8	8.5	9.9	2.8	3.5	6.7	7.8	62.8	62.4
Austria	52.4	48.4	25.2	26.5	11.6	12.4	10.8	12.7	70.1	82.6
Hungary	68.4	64.5	14.4	17.1	5.2	6.5	12.0	11.9	64.6	68.4
Bosnia-Hercegovina	–	85.6	–	5.4	–	2.8	–	6.2	–	–

a. The calculations are based on total population present. Those employed in military service have been included in the column 'Public service and misc.'.

Table 1.7: The Natural Population Development of Austria-Hungary 1867-1913 (in % rates per 1,000 population)

Year	Austria				Hungary[a]			
	Birth rate	Death rate	Birth surplus	Infant mortality[b]	Birth rate	Death rate	Birth surplus	Infant mortality[b]
1867	36.9	29.5	7.4	—	38.0	32.8	5.2	—
1868	38.2	28.8	9.4	—	41.7	33.1	8.6	—
1869	39.7	29.2	10.5	—	41.9	31.3	10.6	—
1870	40.0	29.6	10.4	—	42.1	33.5	8.6	—
1871	39.3	30.2	9.1	—	42.8	40.1	2.7	—
1872	39.3	32.8	6.5	—	40.6	42.9	− 2.3	—
1873	39.9	39.1	0.8	—	42.4	62.9	−20.5	—
1874	40.0	32.0	8.0	—	42.8	43.3	− 0.5	—
1875	40.3	30.3	10.0	—	45.4	37.7	7.7	—
1876	40.4	30.0	10.4	—	45.9	36.0	9.9	—
1877	39.0	31.8	7.2	—	43.3	36.9	6.4	—
1878	38.8	31.8	7.0	—	42.8	37.7	5.1	—
1879	39.6	30.2	9.4	—	45.7	36.3	9.4	—
1880	38.0	30.0	8.0	—	42.8	37.8	5.0	—
1881	37.7	30.6	7.1	250.0	43.1	34.6	8.5	—
1882	39.2	30.9	8.3	255.9	44.1	35.5	8.6	—

Table 1.7 *(contd.)*

Year	Austria				Hungary[a]			
	Birth rate	Death rate	Birth surplus	Infant mortality[b]	Birth rate	Death rate	Birth surplus	Infant mortality[b]
1883	38.3	30.3	8.0	252.9	45.0	32.3	12.7	–
1884	38.9	29.6	9.3	247.1	45.9	31.2	14.7	–
1885	37.8	30.3	7.5	255.3	45.0	32.0	13.0	
1886	38.2	29.6	8.6	249.6	45.9	31.8	14.1	–
1887	38.5	29.1	9.4	244.1	44.4	33.9	10.5	–
1888	38.2	29.5	8.7	248.8	44.0	32.2	11.8	–
1889	38.3	27.6	10.7	236.3	44.0	30.0	14.0	–
1890	36.7	29.4	7.3	259.2	40.6	32.6	8.0	–
1891	38.5	28.2	10.3	242.8	42.6	33.3	9.3	255.1
1892	36.2	28.8	7.4	259.1	40.6	35.2	5.4	273.7
1893	38.2	27.3	10.9	231.8	42.8	31.3	11.5	239.0
1894	36.9	28.0	8.9	251.0	41.7	30.5	11.2	244.1
1895	38.2	27.7	10.5	240.9	41.8	29.7	12.1	240.3
1896	38.2	26.5	11.7	229.6	40.3	28.8	11.5	225.8
1897	37.7	25.8	11.9	228.3	40.3	28.5	11.8	221.6
1898	36.4	25.0	11.4	224.3	37.7	28.0	9.7	222.3
1899	37.5	25.7	11.8	218.6	39.3	27.2	12.1	206.1

Table 1.7 *(contd.)*

Year	Austria				Hungary[a]			
	Birth rate	Death rate	Birth surplus	Infant mortality[b]	Birth rate	Death rate	Birth surplus	Infant mortality[b]
1900	37.5	25.5	12.0	230.6	39.3	26.9	12.4	219.4
1901	36.7	24.1	12.6	209.0	37.8	25.4	12.4	205.5
1902	37.3	24.9	12.4	215.9	38.8	27.0	11.8	216.5
1903	35.4	23.9	11.5	214.7	36.7	26.1	10.6	212.3
1904	37.7	23.9	11.9	209.7	37.4	25.0	12.4	194.7
1905	33.9	25.2	8.7	231.0	36.1	28.0	8.1	229.9
1906	35.2	22.7	12.5	202.0	36.6	25.1	11.5	204.8
1907	34.1	22.8	11.3	208.6	36.6	25.6	11.0	208.5
1908	33.8	22.5	11.3	199.3	31.1	25.3	11.8	199.1
1909	33.5	23.0	10.5	208.6	37.7	25.6	12.1	211.7
1910	33.5	23.0	10.5	188.7	35.6	23.5	12.1	194.4
1911	31.5	22.0	9.5	207.5	35.0	25.1	9.9	206.8
1912	31.4	20.6	10.8	181.5	36.2	23.3	12.9	186.1
1913	29.7	20.3	9.4	189.8	34.5	23.5	11.0	201.3

a. 1867-80 figures for Hungary exclude Croatia-Slavonia.
b. Infant deaths in the first year of life per 1,000 live births.

Table 1.8: The Development in Life Expectancy in the Austrian
half of the Empire, 1865-75 to 1906-10

| | Male | | | Female | | |
Age	1865-75	1901-05	1906-10	1865-75	1901-05	1906-10
0	30.38	39.14	40.64	33.10	41.06	42.84
10	43.17	48.59	49.14	44.29	48.80	49.86
20	35.88	40.49	40.89	37.04	41.21	41.92
30	29.74	33.27	33.49	30.45	34.20	34.79
40	23.27	25.84	26.02	24.07	27.12	27.55
50	17.28	18.95	19.04	17.64	19.81	20.18
60	11.78	12.78	12.86	11.69	13.07	13.32
70	7.30	7.78	7.88	7.09	7.86	8.03
80	4.11	4.38	4.41	3.90	4.47	4.38
90	2.70	3.01	2.86	2.65	3.16	2.70

Source: *Österreichisches Statistisches Zentralamt.*

Table 1.9: The Balance of Births and Migration in Austria-Hungary (in % rates per 1,000 population)[a] 1881-90, 1891-1900 and 1901-10

	1881-90			1891-1900			1901-10		
	Total change	Birth surplus	Net migration balance	Total change	Birth surplus	Net migration balance	Total change	Birth surplus	Net migration balance
Upper Austria	14.2	6.9	7.3	16.5	9.5	7.0	13.9	8.8	5.1
Lower Austria	3.4	3.6	− 0.2	3.1	5.9	− 2.8	5.3	7.5	− 2.2
Salzburg	6.1	2.9	3.2	11.1	5.5	5.6	11.4	9.0	2.4
Steiermark	5.7	4.9	0.8	5.8	6.2	− 0.4	6.4	7.6	− 1.2
Carinthia	3.5	5.4	− 1.9	1.8	6.1	− 4.3	7.9	8.4	− 0.5
Tyrol	0.9	3.4	− 2.5	4.9	4.7	0.2	11.0	8.7	2.3
Vorarlberg	8.1	4.3	3.8	11.3	6.9	4.4	12.5	10.0	2.5
Bohemia	5.1	8.6	− 3.5	8.1	10.2	− 2.1	7.1	9.8	− 2.7
Moravia	5.7	8.2	− 2.5	7.1	10.4	− 3.3	7.6	11.4	− 3.8
Silesia	7.1	8.3	− 1.2	12.3	12.4	− 0.1	11.2	13.7	− 2.5
Galicia	10.9	11.9	− 1.0	10.7	15.3	− 4.6	9.7	16.4	− 6.7
Bukovina	13.1	13.2	− 0.1	12.9	15.0	− 2.1	9.6	14.4	− 4.8
Carniola	3.7	8.0	− 4.3	1.8	8.3	− 6.5	3.5	10.2	− 6.7
Coastal area	7.3	8.5	− 1.2	8.8	8.6	0.2	18.1	13.1	5.0
Dalmatia	10.8	13.7	− 2.9	12.6	15.0	− 2.4	8.7	14,1	− 5.4

Table 1.9 *(contd.)*

	1881-90			1891-1900			1901-10		
	Total change	Birth surplus	Net migration balance	Total change	Birth surplus	Net migration balance	Total change	Birth surplus	Net migration balance
Right Donau bank	7.3	11.3	− 4.0	5.5	10.2	− 4.7	5.5	11.4	− 5.9
Donau-Tisza plain	17.6	13.6	4.0	18.2	12.7	5.5	14.8	12.2	2.6
Left Tisza bank	13.7	13.8	− 0.1	12.5	13.5	− 1.0	11.1	14.0	− 2.9
Left Donau bank	7.3	10.0	− 2.7	8.5	11.7	− 3.2	6.2	12.7	− 6.5
Right Tisza bank	5.3	12.0	− 6.7	9.5	14.6	− 5.1	5.7	13.1	− 7.4
Siebenbürgen	8.0	10.6	− 2.6	9.2	9.2	0.0	8.1	9.7	− 1.6
Tisza-Maros plain	10.8	11.5	− 0.7	7.1	8.1	− 1.0	4.2	8.2	− 4.0
Rijeka	40.6	11.1	29.5	28.4	12.0	16.4	27.8	9.1	18.7
Croatia, Slavonia	15.5	14.5	1.0	9.7	10.4	− 0.7	8.5	13.4	− 4.9
Austria	7.9	8.8	− 0.9	9.4	11.1	− 1.7	9.3	11.9	− 2.6
Hungary	11.0	12.1	− 1.1	10.3	11.2	− 0.9	8.5	11.8	− 3.3
Total	9.2	10.2	− 1.0	9.8	11.1	− 1.3	8.9	11.8	− 2.9

a. The calculations are based on the total population present, with the following exception: for the Hungarian parts of the monarchy the proportional changes in the period 1881-90 have been calculated on the basis of the civilian population present. The figures for Hungary as a whole, however, relate to total population.

2 DENMARK

Otto Andersen

Introduction

Danish demographic data is so comprehensive and extends so far back in time, that it provides an excellent opportunity to trace the pattern of the demographic transition, as it operated in Denmark. Danish priests were required officially from about 1645 onwards to keep church records and these registers have been a natural starting-point for Danish demographic research. Unfortunately many of the older records have been lost in fires or due to mishandling, but those still remaining have constituted an effective basis for family reconstitution studies and other research. From about 1735 regular reports relating to births, marriages and deaths were also compiled by Danish officials. This chapter will draw substantially on these later statistics, which are generally regarded as reliable and effectively cover the whole of the kingdom of Denmark.

Of course vital statistics by themselves are not sufficient for a thorough demographic analysis. The size of the population and its distribution by sex and age are equally important. Information on these aspects is provided by several partial population counts, including those of 1645 and 1660, which were implemented primarily for taxation purposes. The reliability of these records, however, has been and still is a subject of debate in Denmark.[1] The first actual census was not held until 1769,[2] and was followed by further census enumerations in 1787, 1801 and 1834. From 1840 onwards a census has been held every fifth or tenth year. Furthermore the quality of the census material and of vital statistics in general has improved considerably through the years, but there still is a certain margin of error in the early data, although this does not invalidate their use for historical research and as a basis for a reliable assessment of demographic development in pre-industrial Denmark.

Even though Danish demographic data is very comprehensive, however, gaps do exist in the records. These are produced partly by the failure of the past generation to appreciate the possible uses of this data and partly by the difficulties connected with the collection and analysis of the data at that time. As a result the amount of demographic data structured according to socio-economic criteria is

79

relatively limited and most historical series follow the standard distribution according to sex, age and geographic area.

Trends in the Development of Demographic Components

In this section an attempt will be made to present the pattern of the demographic transition, as reflected in the general indices of population growth, mortality and fertility. As population pressure at various stages of the demographic transition often resulted in considerable external migration, which as a phenomenon was common to other industrialising countries, this will be subject to a separate discussion. This section will, therefore, concentrate on the presentation of basic data relevant to population development and the ancillary social and medical factors will be incorporated below (see p.89 *et seq.*).

Population Growth

If the annual excess of births is subtracted from the census figure of 1801, the probable population of Denmark in 1735 emerges as approximately 718,000.[3] Investigations concentrating on the period around 1670[4] suggest that the population at that time was approximately 600,000. These figures therefore indicate a rate of population growth ranging around 0.3 per cent p.a. in the period between 1670 and 1735. Indeed this rate of growth remained relatively unchanged until late in the eighteenth century, although in eight of the fifty-five years in the period 1735-90 the population growth rate was negative, due to excess mortality. Improved mortality conditions by the end of the eighteenth century, however, resulted in a higher rate of growth, which by about 1850 amounted to 1 per cent or even 1.5 per cent p.a. As the population of Denmark was effectively almost a closed population until the 1860s, as both immigration and emigration were very limited during this earlier period, the listed population growth rate and the natural rate of increase were therefore almost identical. However, from 1860 until the First World War Denmark had a net loss through emigration of approximately 250,000 individuals. As a result the difference between the growth rate of population and the natural rate of increase was thereby considerable during this period. While the natural rate of increase continued to range between 1 per cent and 1.5 per cent p.a., the growth rate of total population tended to decline somewhat. A decline in fertility, which started towards the end of the nineteenth century, has now effectively reduced the rate of population growth to under 1 per cent p.a., and only the larger cohorts of the 1940s have brought the rate of growth in any individual year to a point above this level. On a rough estimate the population of Denmark has increased from approximately 1 million (1811), to 2 million (1881), 3 million (1918), 4 million (1944) and finally to 5 million (1972). The natural rate of increase, as measured by the difference between the crude birth rate and the crude death rate, is illustrated in Figure 2.1.

Mortality

At the beginning of the nineteenth century the number of annual deaths ranged between 20,000 and 25,000, but increased towards the end of the century to approximately 40,000. This figure remained remarkably constant until the 1960s. Over time, however, appreciable variations have occurred in the level of mortality, as well as in the size and age-distribution of the Danish population. To account for these differences, other measures of mortality must be used. One of the measures most commonly used, but also the most unrefined, is the crude death rate (CDR), in which the annual number of deaths is related to mean population size. The CDR for Denmark, shown in Figure 2.1, is typical in its development of those countries that have already completed a large part of the demographic transition. CDR generally has declined from approximately 30 to approximately 10 per 1,000 population. Until the end of the eighteenth century mortality was clearly fairly constant and high, but was marked by large annual variations, caused by diseases and starvation, which will be discussed at greater length below (see p.89 *et seq.*). From the end of the eighteenth century, however, CDR has declined continuously and yearly variations have become consistently less prominent. This downward trend was only partially broken by a short-term increase in CDR which reached a peak in 1831 at 30.1 per 1,000. The immediate cause of this increase can be traced to a particular malaria epidemic in Denmark at that time,[5] which meant that 1831 was the only year since 1786 when the CDR was greater than the crude birth rate (CBR). Apart from this malaria epidemic, however, the general tendency was for the CDR to decline. Although the relative fall in CDR was generally small until 1900 (Figure 2.1), CDR had declined to approximately 20 per 1,000 by the turn of the century. The fall in CDR was much more pronounced after 1900 and yearly variations had almost disappeared, suggesting a far greater degree of control over both the food supply and disease.

The size of the CDR is dependent, among other factors, on the age structure of the population, which has changed considerably since 1900. To a large extent the increase in the CDR after 1960 is an expression of this particular factor, as an increase in the overall proportion of elderly individuals in the population of Denmark has resulted in an increase in the number of deaths, even though mortality in the individual age groups generally declined. Because of such a factor it is necessary to supplement CDR with other measures of mortality, including the rate of infant mortality and life expectancy at birth, both of which are illustrated in Table 2.1 for the period 1855 to 1950. Unfortunately Danish data does not allow any possible calculation of these two measures of mortality for the whole of the kingdom until 1835. Infant mortality, however, has been calculated in a single sample of Danish rural districts for the period 1780 to 1801 and found to have been approximately 18 per cent. To this must be added approximately 4.5 per cent, constituting the average share of still-births in total fertility.[6]

A fall in infant mortality can be traced until the period between 1835 and 1839. It is important to note, however, that there was no further improvement in this index between 1850 and 1900, in total contrast to the evidence provided from other countries, including Sweden. During this period the registered increase in life expectancy at birth was entirely due to a general fall in mortality in the remaining age groups. Mortality particularly in the younger age groups (Table 2.2) fell substantially, while the relative decline in the case of the older age groups was somewhat less pronounced. Table 2.3 illustrates the distribution of infant mortality according to the mother's marital status and indicates that around 1900 infant mortality for children born out of wedlock was approximately double that for legitimate offspring. Since 1900, however, the difference has been reduced to between 50 and 60 per cent, although there is still an appreciable difference between the two distinct groups. It is equally clear from the table that infant mortality as a whole has fallen quite markedly over time.

At the turn of the last century the number of registered still-births constituted approximately 2.5 per cent of total births. Although this proportion remained nearly constant until 1940, in the following years it has decreased both rapidly and steadily, so that today it only constitutes 0.5 per cent of the total.

Information is also provided (Tables 2.1-2.3) on mortality differences between males and females. Although female mortality is now uniformly lower than the male, during earlier periods female mortality was often comparatively higher in several of the age groups in the reproductive period (15-49 years of age). This is shown in Table 2.2. The reasons for this higher rate of female mortality are generally connected with complications arising from pregnancy during the earlier period. In addition a calculation of mortality rates according to marital status indicates that mortality is generally lowest amongst married persons and highest for divorced individuals.

Even though Denmark is a relatively small country, considerable regional differences in mortality existed. By and large there was a higher mortality rate in urban areas than in rural districts, with the highest mortality levels occurring in Copenhagen which in any case was much larger than any other urban centre in the country, having a total population in 1840 of approximately 121,000 individuals, or roughly 46 per cent of the total urban population of Denmark at that particular time. Regional differences in life expectancy at birth in the period 1840 to 1844 are shown in Table 2.4, which also indicates that there was little difference in female mortality between rural and urban areas (excluding Copenhagen), due largely to the relatively high rates of female mortality in rural regions. By and large, however, regional mortality differences have been greatly reduced since the mid-nineteenth century.

Unfortunately there is very little data which allows a breakdown of the population by economic or social status. However, an analysis of child mortality according to social group for Copenhagen around 1880 (Table 2.5) reveals pronounced differences in mortality, with the lowest income groups having the highest relative mortality rates. On the other hand, information relating to the cause of death has been publicised on a yearly basis since 1875,[7] although comparative analysis over extended time periods is made relatively difficult by changes in classification categories. Nevertheless it is still possible to delineate general trends in disease-specific mortality, particularly in the more modern period between 1921 and 1960 (Table 2.6). It can be clearly seen that the prevalence of certain diseases, including tuberculosis and other infectious diseases, has been greatly reduced, while other types of disease, such as malignant neoplasms, have acquired a relatively greater predominance. Furthermore the significant decline in infant mortality since 1931 has been accompanied by a radical shift in the general distribution of specific causes of death. In 1931 52.7 per cent of all deaths amongst infants under one year of age were caused by 'non-infectious diseases' (excluding pneumonia, 28.1 per cent by pneumonia and 19.2 per cent were caused by infectious diseases. By 1960 the same general categories of disease accounted for 89.0 per cent, 6.4 per cent and 4.6 per cent respectively of all registered deaths.[8] Between 1931 and 1960 it had become possible effectively to combat pneumonia and infectious diseases, but few improvements had been made in the treatment of infant-specific disabilities, such as malformation, prematurity, congenital debility and injury at birth. However, in the period after 1960 considerable improvements have been registered in this field and deaths in pregnancy and at childbirth, which had previously been appreciable, have now been reduced to a significantly lower level.

Fertility

At about the turn of the eighteenth century the annual number of live births was approximately 30,000, but this figure increased during the nineteenth century to roughly 70,000-75,000. During the course of the present century the number of live births has remained relatively constant. The general fall in fertility has tended to reduce the number of live births, but this has been counteracted by the effect of net population growth which has brought an increasing number of females into the reproductive age groups. The number of registered live births was particularly low during the 1930s (standing at 62,780 in 1933) and particularly high in the immediate post-war period, reaching a peak of 96,111 in 1946.

The general trends in CBR (Figure 2.1) indicate a relatively high level of fertility until about 1890, with an average figure of 30 to 35 per 1,000 inhabitants. In comparison with CDR, the short-term deviations in CBR are far less pronounced, but the two factors do tend to correlate to some extent. In periods marked by a rise in mortality, fertility tends to decline, as for example during the epidemics of the 1700s and around 1831. CBR was approximately 19 per 1,000 around 1950. The fall in fertility which set in towards the end of the nineteenth century was particularly marked and in many senses typical of those countries such as Denmark that had been through an industrial revolution (see p.89 *et seq.*). Furthermore, although fertility developments over the last 100 years will be analysed more closely in the following section, Figure 2.1 clearly shows the baby boom that followed the low fertility levels of the 1930s.

The age-specific fertility rates (Table 2.7) show that the decline in fertility has also impinged on the age structure of fertility in a typical and important way. Fertility around 1900 was characterised by a high rate in the age group 25-29 years, and a relatively high rate in the older age groups. In the course of the general decline in this index, fertility came to be concentrated in the younger age groups, particularly in the age group 20-24 years and to a lesser extent in the age group 15-19 years. By comparison the decline in fertility in the age groups over 30

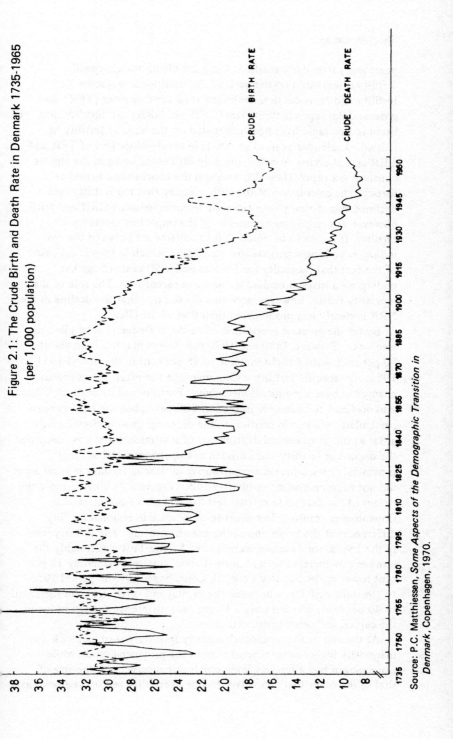

Figure 2.1: The Crude Birth and Death Rate in Denmark 1735-1965
(per 1,000 population)

CRUDE BIRTH RATE

CRUDE DEATH RATE

1735 1750 1765 1780 1795 1810 1825 1840 1855 1870 1885 1900 1915 1930 1945 1960

38 36 34 32 30 28 26 24 22 20 18 16 14 12 10 8

Source: P.C. Matthiessen, *Some Aspects of the Demographic Transition in Denmark*, Copenhagen, 1970.

years was particularly marked. Table 2.8 illustrates age-specific
fertility rates, listed on the basis of the traditional measures for
fertility and reproduction, including total fertility rates (TFR), and
gross and net reproduction rates (GRR and NRR). All fertility measures
listed in this table have been calculated on the basis of fertility in
individual calendar years. The trends in the development of TFR and
GRR are, of course, parallel, the only difference being in the almost
constant sex ratio. They also confirm the conclusions arrived at
through the calculation of the CBR, namely that the fertility rate
declined substantially over time. Differences between GRR and NRR,
however, are largely an expression of the impact of mortality on
fertility. It is also to be noted that the difference between the two
indices is no longer particularly significant, which in turn is indicative
of the fact that mortality for females under 50 years of age has
undergone a marked decline in the more recent past. The role of the
mortality factor, however, accounts for the fact that the decline in the
NRR is clearly less pronounced than that of the GRR.

By far the greatest proportion of births in Denmark take place in
wedlock.[9] Between 1880 and 1970 this proportion has been about
90 per cent, with a slight increase to 95 per cent in the period 1951 to
1955. Age-specific fertility within marriage therefore shows the same
changes as have been mentioned above. Fertility out of wedlock[10] has
also declined considerably in the last 100 years, but the fall has been
particularly marked in relation to the older age groups. Significantly
as far as the geographical distribution of marital fertility was concerned,
the decline in fertility was initiated in Copenhagen and in other
provincial cities, whereas a comparative decline in fertility in rural areas
did not become evident until after 1900 (Figure 2.2). Furthermore the
extent of the decline in marital fertility was also more marked in
Copenhagen, resulting in a short-term increase in regional fertility
differences at the beginning of the present century. The fertility level
in the 1880s, for example, as measured by the TFR was roughly the
same in provincial cities and in rural areas, but approximately 12 per
cent lower in the country's capital, Copenhagen. By the period 1956
to 1960 the difference between the capital and rural areas had increased
to 40 per cent, whereas only a 16 per cent difference existed between
the capital and other provincial cities.

At the end of the nineteenth century fertility out of wedlock was
marginally higher in rural areas than in the provincial cities, while
Copenhagen had a fertility level which was almost twice the size of
that in the other two areas. The decline in fertility out of wedlock has

Figure 2.2: Total Fertility in Wedlock,* Denmark 1880-1960

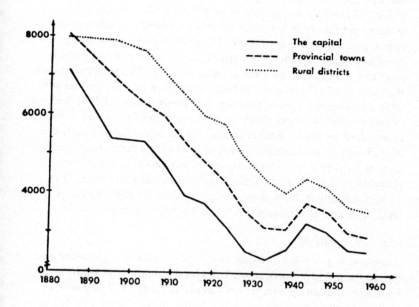

* Total fertility in wedlock expresses how many children 1,000 women will give
  birth to if they marry at the age of 15 and are living as married all through
  their reproductive period.

Source: *Fertilitetsforskelle i Danmark (Fertility Differences in Denmark),*
  Statistiske Undersøgelser, Copenhagen, 1965.

also been greatest in the capital and today there is little evidence of
any significant geographical variation in this factor. The differences
in the development of the TFR within wedlock in the three broad
geographic areas can be explained on the basis of an examination of
fertility according to socio-economic groups and by geographic region,
which is made possible by reference to the census returns of 1901 and
1940. The number of children per marriage, distributed according to

the socio-economic status of the head of the household, is illustrated in Table 2.9. At the turn of the last century fertility differences can be explained primarily as a result of comparatively lower fertility rates among specific social groups, including salaried office employees, civil servants employed in the capital and the self-employed. In the provincial cities, however, as well as in rural areas, the number of children per family in the different socio-economic groups was very nearly constant at 5-6 per family. The general decline in fertility, however, would seem to have aggravated differences in comparative rates of fertility between socio-economic groups. Differences between the three geographical areas, in turn, were often the result of fertility differences for the same socio-economic group within each of the three different areas. A worker in the capital, for example, showed a lower rate of fertility than a worker in a provincial city, who in turn had a lower fertility rate than an equivalent worker in a rural area. The high level of fertility in rural areas, however, was also due to the large proportion of farmers and agricultural workers in these areas, as in 1940, for example, both these two groups had the highest rate of fertility of any of the designated socio-economic groups.

External Migration

Comparatively less information exists in Denmark on emigration and immigration. Indeed official statistics on the numbers of both emigrants and immigrants are only available from 1929 onwards, as earlier published material was solely based on the simple calculation of net migration between individual census years. Furthermore an effective enumeration of migrants is made more difficult by the inevitable errors and omissions incorporated in each and every census and in the general registration of vital statistics. Emigration overseas, however, was officially recorded from 1869 onwards and this form of migration has been studied in substantial detail for the period between 1868 and 1914.[11] Before 1870 external migration both to and from Denmark was very limited. Only during the process of increased European migration overseas did emigration from Denmark become at all significant. Net migration for periods between individual census years up until 1930 is illustrated in Table 2.10. Apart from the period around the First World War, there has generally been a greater emigration from Denmark than immigration into the country. At least 285,000 individuals emigrated from Denmark to overseas countries in the period between 1869 and 1913, and approximately 90 per cent of these emigrants travelled to the United States, which throughout this whole period received the greatest share of overseas emigrants from Denmark at least until the onset of the depression of the 1930s, although other countries did tend to take an increasing share over time. In the period between 1914 and 1932 a total of 87,000 individuals emigrated from Denmark, 65.6 per cent of whom travelled to the United States and a further 23.8 per cent to Canada.[12] Increasingly restrictive immigration regulations after the Second World War, however, resulted in a change of direction for Danish emigrants with Australia becoming the major goal for overseas migrants. The extent of net migration has fluctuated frequently since 1930, corresponding to a large extent to economic conditions, war activities and changing immigration restrictions in the individual countries of the world.

Population and the Economy

An attempt will be made in this section to discuss the pattern of Danish economic development, particularly in relation to the process of the demographic transition.

The Period from 1700 to 1785

At the beginning of the eighteenth century Denmark was still essentially an underdeveloped country, characterised by a subsistence economy and a relatively low standard of living.[13] There was little indication of any significant progress in the near future. The rigid boundaries and distinctions that existed both between urban and rural areas and between individual crafts and occupations were important factors that had contributed to this general state of economic backwardness. Indeed in 1733, for example, residence restrictions were enforced upon the population of Denmark prohibiting many of the rural inhabitants between fourteen and thirty-six years of age from leaving the estates on which they had been born, on the grounds that an effective barrier was needed to prevent even internal migration during a period of relative economic depression. On the other hand, urban centres were given special privileges as economic units. Cities had an almost absolute monopoly on the right both to sell and to produce goods. Occupational employment in the cities, however, was severely regulated by strict rules, which effectively made it extremely difficult for an individual to establish his own place of business. All these regulations relating to employment were to seriously impede any rational use of the available labour force. By far the largest occupational group in eighteenth-century Denmark, however, were individuals employed in agriculture, forming approximately 60 per cent of the total population. The level of total output in the primary sector, however, seldom exceeded the amount necessary to cover unavoidable expenses and the indigenous needs of the agricultural workers. At the same time production in urban areas was extremely modest and even stagnating, as the level of demand from rural areas was not significant.

All of these conditions, taken together, help to explain the relative level of Danish mortality in the eighteenth century. It has already been shown that pronounced yearly variations in the level of mortality were extremely typical of this period, largely due to the influence of disease and starvation. These conditions, it would seem, were often aggravated by wars or by preparations for war within Europe.[14] A rise in mortality, for example, can be seen both before and during the Swedish wars, as well as at the time of military preparations for a war against Russia at the beginning of the 1740s, in the 1770s and at the end of the 1780s. This was equally the case during the war fought over the Austrian Succession (1740-48), during the Seven Years War (1756-63) and during troop concentrations in Denmark and Norway in 1762-3. Particular attention, however, has been focused on the fact that years of high mortality were frequently followed by years of low mortality rates, a phenomenon that tends to be a feature of short-term mortality changes in the eighteenth century. Indeed the view has been expressed in this context that 'death reaped also for the morrow'. The feeble and the exposed were often removed during these epidemics, whereas the strong and the less exposed tended to survive. The operation of this mechanism can be found in the significant fall in mortality rates in the years following major losses of population, including 1741, 1748, 1763 and 1786 respectively.

Fertility had to be high in a community with a high rate of mortality in order to insure the population against the possibility of extinction. In Denmark CBR was both high and relatively constant throughout the eighteenth century, even though it did not normally reach the level frequently found in the developing countries of the world today. This in turn can be explained by the fact that the average age at marriage was considerably higher in eighteenth-century Denmark than in today's developing countries, partly because of the many restrictions imposed on the act of marriage by the indigenous communities. It was common, for example, for marriage to be deferred until it could be shown that a man had sufficient means to support both a wife and children, either through regularised employment in the primary sector, or as a self-employed tradesman. In addition the fertility rate in Denmark during this period was kept marginally lower than in contemporary developing economies by the fact that proportion of women ever marrying was also significantly lower.

The wars during this period, however, were not completely detrimental to the economy, as shipping and foreign trade were frequently stimulated. By and large this positive side was very limited and if there were any ancillary benefits from involvement in wars, these largely accrued to urban residents in Copenhagen and not to the majority of the population.

The Period of Reform: 1785-1815

The period between 1785 and 1815 forms one of the great eras of reform in Danish history. Political changes in 1784 effectively brought to power a government which in turn proposed a complex of laws far in advance of their time. Many of the traditional restrictions on economic life were lifted and the preconditions for economic development were thereby provided. The reform proposals aimed at expanding the overall productivity of the labour force, by recommending the abolition, or at least the gradual reduction, of social and institutional barriers which had previously prevented the effective utilisation of the country's indigenous resources. It is important to note, however, that these efforts were primarily directed towards the modernisation of the system of production in the primary sector, at the cost of stimulating direct development in industry. This approach was significantly different to that adopted in many other European countries. During this period of reform, for example, serfdom was abolished and the labour force allowed to migrate at will. The traditional obligations of the agricultural worker to the seigneurial manor were relaxed and there was a concomitant increase in the number of self-employed in the primary sector. As a result of these changes agricultural workers themselves clearly became more interested in increasing total production. As a result of a net increase in the extent of cultivable land and an improvement in overall labour productivity, agricultural output increased considerably between 1770 and 1800. It has been estimated, for example, that grain production doubled during this brief period and there was a similar increase in the number of listed cattle and livestock, which, in turn, contributed to an improvement in the supply of manure for arable cultivation. Furthermore the increase in livestock was also accompanied by an improvement in net yields. In general the introduction of technological improvements was to a large extent facilitated by the specific nature of the reforms. Prior to this period fields had been cultivated in common with the result that an individual peasant could have his land spread over more than sixty separate pieces of land. The consolidation of land holdings, which was directly facilitated by the reform movement, also meant that land could be cultivated more rationally and with the use of a relatively higher level of technology. Furthermore a wider variety of plants, including potatoes and clover, could be successfully cultivated.[15]

There can be little doubt that the fall in mortality which occurred in the latter part of the eighteenth century was largely a result of these individual improvements in the primary sector.[16] Higher production led directly to a higher level of nutrition, and was also accompanied by an increasing awareness among the population as a whole of the importance of personal hygiene. The net result was an increased level of immunity against disease. A further important factor connected with these reforms, however, lay in the redistribution of farmsteads away from the traditional, densely populated village settlements. The locational dispersal of these farmsteads over the open countryside meant that housing standards as a whole were improved and the spread of epidemics to some extent impeded.

Significantly this particular period preceded the later advances in medical science, and it is therefore clear that the fall in mortality was brought about essentially by an improvement in the general standard of living, rather than as a result of medical progress. It must be noted, however, that the practice of smallpox vaccination was known in Denmark before 1800 and was made obligatory as early as 1810. Furthermore the first 'epidemic law' had been enacted in 1782 and in 1805 detailed rules and regulations had been introduced relating to the quarantine procedures for contagious diseases. The effect of these measures was to substantially limit the spread of epidemics and their net contribution to mortality can be seen in the gradual yearly reduction in the extent of variations in the CDR.

Danish agriculture has been characterised by the prominence of a large number of small farmsteads and their number grew particularly rapidly during this period of land reform. Between 1787 and 1801, 40,000 new farmsteads were established, although the increase in the number of men over 20 years of age during the same period only amounted to 25,000. As a result the opportunities for unmarried men in all age groups to acquire land of their own were substantially increased. The effects of this liberalisation of land tenure were far-reaching, but it found immediate expression in the rise in the crude marriage rate from 8 to approximately 10 per 1,000 inhabitants during this period, which in turn contributed to the rise in the number of live births registered in the period up until 1835.[17]

The international situation prior to 1807 was also favourable as far as Denmark was concerned. The country enjoyed the clear benefits of neutrality, including increased trade and shipping, while rising international price levels for agricultural products ensured a ready market for the increasing output from the primary sector. However, all of this changed in 1807, when Denmark was drawn into the international conflict on the side of Napoleon. The income from foreign trade disappeared and large sums had to be set aside for military preparations for war. In 1813 the Danish economic system collapsed completely, and between 1818 and 1828 the country experienced an extensive agricultural crisis as a result of the significant fall in the demand for primary sector produce following the termination of the war.

The Period from 1815 to 1890

During most of the nineteenth century Danish economic development was characterised by a relatively limited rate of growth. Gross national product (GNP) seems to have increased by only about 2 per cent p.a., while the increase in GNP per capita was about 0.9 per cent p.a. The period is also marked by regularly recurring economic fluctuations, which increasingly tended to conform to general international cycles. Furthermore towards the middle of the century trade connections with England were so intense, that an almost parallel development in the price structure of the two countries took place. The agricultural export quota was approximately 30 per cent around 1845, and had effectively doubled from the early 1820s. Between 1860 and 1880 significant infrastructural developments took place and the railway network in particular was expanded enormously. This development, in turn, also helped to raise the export quota to approximately 60 per cent. During the early part of the nineteenth century the most important single export product had been grain, but after the major fall in prices initiated during the mid-1870s, Danish agriculture effected an important structural reorganisation, with increasing emphasis being laid on livestock and animal production. As a proportion of total agricultural exports, products from the livestock sector increased significantly from 20 per cent in the 1850s to approximately 85 per cent at the beginning of the 1890s.

Despite the fact that the overall rate of economic growth was limited during this period, important changes did nevertheless take place in the country's occupational structure (Table 2.11). The share of GNP constituted by agriculture fell during the course of this period from approximately 60 per cent to about 38 per cent, while a significant increase was registered in the contribution made by trade, due largely to the increasing division of labour between English industry on the one hand and Danish agricultural producers on the other. As a result of increasing foreign trade activities the importance of trade itself as a component of GNP had risen markedly by about 1890, when it accounted for approximately 16 per cent of the total. A contributory factor behind this change had been the liberalisation of urban occupations, which had helped to ease the general establishment of trading facilities. In comparison, however, the development of handicraft and industrial production was very much slower. Between 1860 and 1890 industry's share of GNP only increased from approximately 4 per cent to 6.57 per cent. The reason for this, as mentioned earlier, is to be found in the explicit intention of contemporaries to increase production from the primary sector in the first instance, as the initial priority for economic growth.

In the period prior to 1890 fertility had been high and relatively constant, which reflected the continued prominence of agriculture in the Danish economy. Mortality, on the other hand, had declined somewhat (p.81-4), largely as a result of the higher living standards, which had been brought about by the reform legislation, and partly due to certain advances in medicine during this period. This general decline in mortality was only interrupted by a serious epidemic of malaria, known to contemporaries as 'cold fever', which reached its peak in 1831.[18] Nevertheless this disease was particularly rampant in Denmark during the early nineteenth century, especially in the southern parts of the country, in Lolland-Falster and southern Sealand, which because of their low-lying areas were particularly exposed to the disease. The epidemic of 1831 can indeed be traced back to 1825, when a severe storm broke the southern dikes and caused extensive flooding in the surrounding inland areas. This event, together with a series of warm summers and damp winters, helped to spread the disease. There is evidence to suggest that over 40 per cent of the population on Lolland-Falster contracted this fever in 1831, with the result that the CDR rose to 49.8 per 1,000 population, in contrast to the normal mortality rate of approximately 20 per 1,000. By and large a relatively small proportion of Denmark's population bore the brunt of this particular epidemic and its impact on a localised basis was clearly quite severe. Malaria itself was finally eliminated from Denmark around the

end of the nineteenth century and its final eradication was largely due
to the improvement of dikes and extended drainage of land. The
cholera epidemic of 1853 in Copenhagen was probably equally
important within the general context of Danish demographic history,
because of both its short- and long-range effects. In 1853 the number
of cholera cases was estimated at between 10,000 and 11,000 and the
number of deaths at between 6,000 and 7,000.[19] The high mortality
created by this epidemic, however, was the main reason for the final
introduction of an effective sewerage system in Copenhagen and for
the general improvement and purification of drinking water.

The Breakthrough of Industrialisation: 1890-1914

Even though it is difficult to give a precise date for the breakthrough
of industrialisation, there is evidence to suggest that distinct changes
did occur during the period from the mid-1890s to the First World War.
Danish industry had traditionally been strongly orientated towards the
home market and to this extent benefited substantially from the fall
in the price level for agricultural produce during the period of the
'great depression' between 1876 and 1894. Low food prices, combined
with rising real wages and an increased demand for industrial products
as a result of the further mechanisation of the primary sector, created
a far wider market for industrial products. Industry's proportion of
GNP (Table 2.11) increased substantially, to approximately 11 per cent
immediately prior to the outbreak of the First World War. As might
have been expected the share of GNP constituted by handicraft
production underwent a comparative fall during the same period.
Commerce, however, continued to expand and as a function of the
increased division of labour within the Danish economy there was a
significant increase in occupational employment outside agriculture,
in shipping and other forms of transportation and within professional
groups and public administration. Figure 2.3 illustrates the rate of
growth of GNP during this period in 1929 prices and on a logarithmic
scale. This confirms the extent of the real increase in GNP during this
period and emphasises the almost explosive development both in
commerce and industry. Indeed by the end of this period industry
had attained rough parity with the more traditional handicraft sector.

As might have been expected in this context, the demographic
components, mortality, fertility and migration, also underwent decisive
changes during this period. Industrialisation in all probability
contributed to those factors which were helping to reduce general levels
of mortality and had a particular impact on the role of medicine, by

Figure 2.3: GNP in Fixed Prices (1929 price level), Denmark, 1880-1923

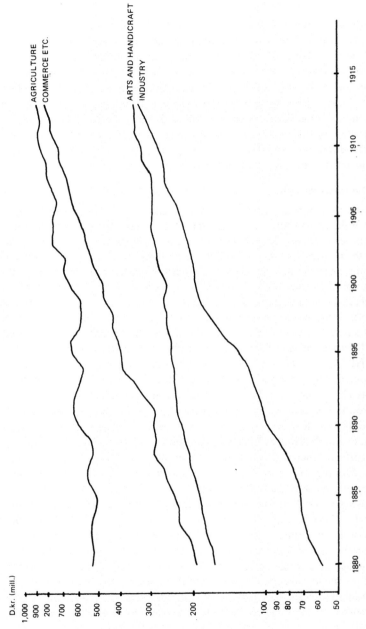

D.kr. (mill.)

AGRICULTURE
COMMERCE ETC.

ARTS AND HANDICRAFT
INDUSTRY

Source: Svend Aage Hansen, Økenouisk rekst, Danmark (Economic Growth in Denmark), Copenhagen, 1972.

facilitating the mass production of inexpensive medicines as advances were made in medical science. Increasing industrial production was also accompanied by higher levels of output of both food and clothing and an extension in the housing stock, which in turn led to a reduction in costs in these important areas of consumption. One of the immediate results was a fall in infant mortality and an accelerated increase in life expectancy. It is equally important to note that fertility also began to decline during this period, which effectively confirms the general theory of the demographic transition.

By the 1890s the process of change within the Danish economy was substantially advanced and almost certainly had created both economic and social pressures on individual families to reduce the number of children born. The initial decline in fertility (see p.84-8 and Figure 2.2), was significantly to be found in the urban areas, where the rate of decline was also most pronounced. Indeed it was in the cities that the increasing economic pressures must have been most severe, a situation aggravated by the fact that urban family structure as a result of the separation of home from work differed substantially from that still to be found in rural areas. Children in the cities were not to the same extent an integral part of the labour force and as early as 1873[20] a law had been enacted prohibiting businesses in Denmark from employing children under ten years of age. In 1901 this age limit was further increased to 12 years. Moreover a limited form of old age pensions had been introduced in 1891, which to some extent removed responsibility for the care of the old and elderly from the occupationally active age groups to the state.

However, the decline in fertility started in a period when contraceptive techniques were relatively incomplete and inadequate and dependence was placed mainly on coitus interruptus. Yet in spite of this, the pressures on individual families must have been so substantial during this period that a reduction in average family size was nevertheless achieved. Gradually, however, the decline in fertility became a general phenomenon within Danish society and also became apparent in agricultural areas.

External migration, on the other hand, had already become important in Denmark prior to 1870 (see p.88-9) largely as a function of the increase in total population as a result of the significant decline in mortality. At the same time, however, the level of migration was clearly more moderate than that which was to be found in Norway and Sweden. Overseas migration from Denmark itself only constituted about 15 per cent of total emigration from Scandinavia as a whole. In

relation to the registered excess of births, emigration from Norway and
Sweden was double that from Denmark, where emigration in the period
1850 to 1914 only contributed to a reduction of approximately 16
per cent in the natural rate of increase (Table 2.12). In relation to the
listed excess of births, the net losses through migration tended to
reach a peak between 1880 and 1889 when they amounted to 26 per
cent. The fact that emigration from Denmark was generally lower than
that from Norway and Sweden can be attributed to a large extent to
the achievements of the Danish economy and the general social and
economic conditions which were thereby created. Developments
within the primary sector, including the reclamation of land and the
introduction of intensive agricultural techniques, served to increase the
relative level of demand for labour. Equally the growth of a service
sector designed to meet the needs of agricultural expansion had a
similarly positive effect on relative labour demand.

The Inter-War Years: 1920-1939[21]

By and large conditions during the First World War and in the years
immediately following were favourable for Danish industry. Prior to
1920 this sector was able to expand its share of GNP to 15 per cent
(Table 2.11). In 1920, however, the international economic crisis
generated by the termination of war time activity finally reached
Denmark. Retail prices which had more than doubled or even trebled
since the beginning of the war, were now halved during the following
two years. The industrial sector had to struggle with enormous problems
of readjustment, as several firms which had been founded during the
protective isolation of the war period were now found to be relatively
uncompetitive. Other firms which were inherently sound suffered from
inflated costs, as they had purchased their raw materials at a period
when prices were still rising. The situation was aggravated by the
relative stickiness of wages, which did not fall as fast as prices.
Nevertheless despite the fact that the downswing in prices for
agricultural products was particularly pronounced during this period,
agriculture retained its position as the leading sector in the economy
throughout the 1920s. The extensive fall in prices for feedstuffs
benefited directly the livestock sector, which was not as severely
affected by the recession as grain production. Furthermore the Danish
government facilitated the establishment of approximately 10,000
new farmsteads during this period. By the beginning of the 1930s,
therefore, agriculture still contributed approximately 25 per cent of
GNP and employed roughly 33 per cent of the active population. In

addition the primary sector accounted for almost 80 per cent of total Danish exports. The following period from 1925 to 1931 was characterised by relatively good economic conditions and adjustment problems were minimal. These conditions continued to exist until 1931 when Denmark was drawn into the great international recession. Rapid developments, however, were taking place in other sectors of employment during this period and particularly in building and construction which underwent a disproportional increase in activity in order to compensate for relative under-production during the war period. Activity in this sector was also stimulated by the need to meet the new demands created by the extensive use of motorised transport.

Even though growth in the industrial sector was fairly limited, important changes in the actual structure of Danish society still took place during this period and these in turn had a substantial impact on the demographic components. Both fertility and mortality continued to decline. Indeed the fall in fertility was so marked during the recession of the 1930s, that the NRR fell to a point below the level of reproduction, which in turn provoked heated discussions among contemporaries on 'the approach of extinction' in Scandinavia as a whole. The actual decline in fertility, however, was far from being so pronounced. Although this period does show a reduced difference between CBR and CDR, there was little indication of a negative rate of natural increase. In 1935, for example, the rate of natural growth stood at 6.6 per 1,000 inhabitants, as against a rate of 10.2 in 1925. The fears of a declining population, however, vanished completely during the 'baby boom' of the 1940s and it could be argued that if fertility in the 1930s had been strongly influenced by adverse economic conditions, the population utilised the later improvements in the general economic situation to 'make up the difference'

Wages and Working Conditions before the First World War

Wage trends in Denmark are difficult to assess because of the absence of any early nationwide compilation of statistics on this subject. However, it is possible to describe certain developments from about 1840 onwards on the basis of individual surveys and wage statistics for individual occupations.[22] The general impression is that both money and real wages have increased significantly over time, even though there have been periods of relative decline due to changing economic conditions. From 1840 to 1870 money wages for an urban worker increased by approximately 120 per cent, while real wages seem to have risen by roughly 55 per cent. The trend in real wages has often been rather irregular during this period. A marked decline took place at the beginning of the 1850s, and the period from 1857 to the late 1860s was one of stagnation. From 1870 to 1890, however, there was a parallel development in both money and real wages, with a net increase of approximately 45 per cent. In the following period, from 1890 to 1900 money wages continued to rise at a time when prices were falling, so that the increase in real wages was as great as 30 per cent. From 1900 until the outbreak of the First World War, however, increases were very limited indeed.

The period as a whole, however, was characterised by extensive differences in relative wage levels. A trained craftsman earned a great deal more than an untrained worker and women earned an absolutely minimal wage. Agricultural workers were often paid in kind and although this often makes an effective comparison with other occupational groups relatively difficult, it would seem that their general living standards were roughly the same as those of urban workers. The process of fixing the wage level, however, did change radically between 1850 and 1914.[23] Negotiations between the individual worker and his employer were gradually replaced by collective agreements between employer and labour organisations. Although these organisations had been regarded at an earlier stage with a certain degree of apprehension, after the turn of the century they came to be viewed as an integral part of Danish society. In 1899 a general agreement was made between the labour organisations and the employers' associations, which regulated the right to strike and the practice of lock-outs. As a result by 1910 roughly 50 per cent of Danish workers were members of a labour organisation, a proportion which seems very high in the context of contemporary conditions in other parts of Western Europe. Similar improvements were made in respect to working hours. If a male industrial worker around 1870 had regularly had a working day of approximately eleven hours, the slow process of change in the following period had produced a situation in 1914 when the number of hours worked per day had generally fallen to approximately 9.3.

In the middle of the nineteenth century sanitary conditions in the factories and handicraft shops had largely been unsatisfactory and this had contributed to the poor health of factory workers.[24] Only in the 1880s were any significant improvements undertaken in this context and even then they were largely the result of individual initiative. Public legislation during this period was still largely concerned with the attempted limitation of child labour and it was only later that laws were enacted to protect workers who performed particularly hazardous jobs.

The fact that living standards by and large had been continuously rising during the nineteenth century is reflected in the pattern of family expenditure of income during this period.[25] About 1840, for example, approximately 53 per cent of total family income was normally used in the purchase of food. The gradual improvement in the standard of living, however, led to a noticeable shift in income expenditure away from food and towards other commodities. By the turn of the century the proportion of income used for basic food purchases had declined to roughly 41 per cent. At the same time, however, the average diet became more varied, as meat became a central staple in the diet at least in urban areas. It must be noted, however, that substantial dietary differences continued to exist between the different socio-economic groups within Danish society.

Wages and Working Conditions in the Inter-War Years

The fluctuating economic conditions of the inter-war years led to an uneven pattern of development as far as real wages were concerned, which contrasted markedly with the established trend in the pre-war period.[26] During the last years of the war and in 1919 the Danish labour organisations did manage to negotiate definite wage increases, with the result that the real hourly wage for a worker in this period was roughly 40 per cent above the 1914 level. Calculated on a yearly basis and with an allowance for fluctuations in the level of unemployment, real wages on the whole appear to have been 20 per cent higher than they had been in 1914. Between 1927 and 1931, however, the previous short-term variations in real wages were replaced by a general increase of approximately 20 per cent. However, the crisis of the 1930s brought Danish unemployment to a peak of 32 per cent in 1932 which in turn generated a more reserved attitude to increases in money wages among the labour organisations. From 1931 to 1939 real wages actually fell by approximately 15 per cent, although in other respects and specifically in the sphere of social welfare, the country's population gained a great many benefits during these years. Living standards apparently continued to improve throughout the 1920s, so that by 1931 the share of family income utilised for food purchases had fallen to 33 per cent.

The Occupational Distribution

The changes in the structure of the Danish economy will be described in more detail in the following section, although initial attention will be paid to a brief analysis of the trends in population distribution by occupation. Because of the frequent changes in classification categories between each census, it is particularly difficult to present a thorough numerical analysis of long-term trends in this area. The main emphasis in this section will therefore be centred on the distribution of the population between agricultural and urban occupations. This distribution over time is illustrated in Table 2.13, which also includes additional information on those population groups not included as part of the active labour force. Congruent with the declining proportion of agriculture in GNP, the share of the population involved in this sector also fell from 67 per cent in 1801 to 21 per cent in 1950. Although the primary sector was able to increase its absolute share of population until 1880, from this date until 1940 the number of individuals actively employed in agriculture remained relatively stable at around one million persons. A closer analysis of this trend indicates that there must have been a substantial and sizeable migration of labour from the agricultural sector into other industries. Up until 1901 the agricultural population increased by 61 per cent, whereas the population in other occupations grew by 377 per cent. Similarly between 1901 and 1950 the agricultural population actually fell by 11 per cent, at a time when the population in other sectors increased by 113 per cent. Individuals born in agricultural areas, as a result of the net excess in the number of registered births, could only find limited employment opportunities in the primary sector. As a result there was a massive process of migration from the rural regions. It has been calculated[27] that between 1801 and 1901 alone, there must have been an out-migration of more than 360,000 individuals from the agricultural areas. Furthermore 143,000 of these individuals left agriculture between 1881 and 1890. The net loss from this sector between 1901 and 1950, in comparison, was probably over 850,000.

Inevitably the actual size of the labour force is smaller than the final figures listed in Table 2.13. In about 1840 the active labour force in agriculture amounted to approximately 53 per cent of the total population supported directly by that sector. In the following period this proportion has not declined significantly, as far as agriculture is concerned. In other sectors, however, the dependency ratio had noticeably increased by 1950, when the proportion of those actively employed to total population had fallen to 47 per cent, despite the fact that in the more recent period the productive age groups within Danish society have tended to constitute an increasing proportion of total population. This fall is often seen as reflecting the impact of the increasing number of years devoted to education within the population as a whole. Of course the actual labour force is not necessarily equivalent to the level of the labour supply. Changing economic conditions in Denmark have inevitably had their effect on the rate of unemployment, which reached record proportions during the 1930s.

The Process of Urbanisation

Changes in the structure of the economy and in occupation distribution have also been accompanied by increasing urbanisation (Table 2.14). Denmark is characterised by the presence of one major metropolis, but the general trend has also been in the direction of a spread in urbanisation. In 1801 Copenhagen had approximately 101,000 inhabitants, while the next largest city, Odense on Funen, had only roughly 5,800 inhabitants. In 1950, however, Copenhagen incorporated roughly 975,000 individuals, while the second most important city, Aarhus in Jutland, had a total population of 116,000. Over time the process of urban development has been marked by the formation of suburban areas around the larger cities, which have attracted settlement both from the urban centres and from rural communities. This pattern of migration has become particularly prominent after 1950, with the result that the actual population of Copenhagen has undergone a net numerical decline. The urban population of Denmark as a whole, however, has increased from 21 per cent of total population in 1801 to 67 per cent in 1950 (Table 2.14). In general during the earlier period the high levels of mortality in the urban areas and particularly in Copenhagen itself resulted in a net population deficit, which by and large was counterbalanced by a net excess of new migrants. Copenhagen acted generally as a focal point for migration, because of the economic and employment opportunities which the city provided.

Age Distribution

During the process of the demographic transition the age distribution of the population has changed considerably. The population pyramids for Denmark clearly illustrate these changes and at the same time confirm the fact that the relative age structure of the population has only been marginally altered by the secular fall in mortality, whereas the impact of declining fertility has been considerable (Figure 2.4). The fall in mortality was a phenomenon common to all age groups, only perhaps being marginally more significant in relation to the younger age groups in the population. As a result the changes in age

Figure 2.4: The Age Distribution at the Ausns in 1840, 1890 and 1950, Denmark.

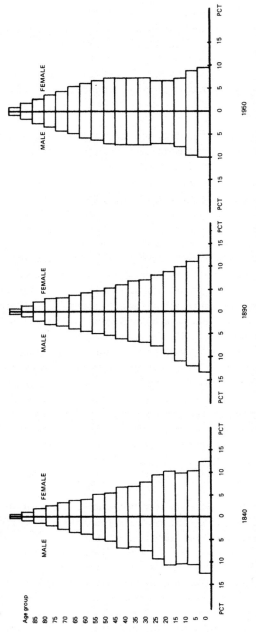

structure were relatively minimal, as all age groups benefited numerically from the mortality decline. The fall in fertility, however changed the total shape of the pyramid and reduced in particular the relative importance of the younger age groups. The net result was the complete disappearance of the traditional pyramid shape, which was increasingly transformed into a barrel. Between 1840 and 1890 only mortality declined significantly in Denmark, with the result that the population pyramid for these two bench-mark years is essentially similar. After 1890, however, with an increasing decline in fertility, the population pyramids, as for the years 1890 and 1950, begin to diverge considerably from each other.

Age structure is usually expressed in terms of the dependency ratio, where groups of young people (0-14 years of age) and of the elderly (65 years of age and above) are compared with the number of individuals in the occupationally active age groups (15-64 years of age). The dependency ratio in Denmark (Table 2.15) reveals that a decline in the proportion of younger individuals since 1890 has been counterbalanced by an increasing proportion of elderly, although the occupationally active age group has also increased somewhat in size. Indeed all these changes are synonymous with the 'ageing of the population', a process which has continued after 1950. Whereas the young previously constituted the largest dependent group, this role has now been usurped by the elderly. Economically this change in the demographic components necessitates a drastic alteration in the major investment goals in both the social and educational sectors. Indeed the positive growth in the overall size of the occupationally active group has been partly nullified by the impact of the ageing process on labour supply, as the ageing process itself has had a long range effect on the general willingness of labour to migrate within the labour market.

The Sex Ratio

The proportion of male and female live births in Denmark, as in other countries, has shown a marked stability over time. Between 1901 and 1950, for example, the number of male births per 1,000 live births has fluctuated between 512 and 515. As a result of higher male mortality, however, the initial excess of males in each generation declines over time and is finally replaced by an excess of females. In 1901 this transition occurred when the generation was between 20 and 25 years of age and in 1950 at a slightly later date (25 to 30 years of age). This postponement of the shift can be attributed to the general fall in mortality, as low mortality increases the number of years after birth before the initial excess of males is transformed into an excess of females. Pronounced geographical differences, however, exist in the sex ratio. The rural areas are characterised by an excess of males in almost all age groups, whereas an excess of females occurs earlier in urban areas. These differences effectively mirror the divergent economic opportunities existing in the two broad areas, which are also revealed in the pattern of internal migration.

Marital Status

The distribution of population by marital status has shown definite changes in Denmark during the twentieth century. The most decisive change has been in the proportional increase of married persons and a decline in the number of unmarried individuals, although the proportion of divorcees has also been on the increase (Table 2.16). Higher levels of male mortality have also produced a greater proportion of widows than widowers. These changes, in turn, have been the result of several fundamental shifts in the population's marriage patterns, as the number of marriages has risen significantly over time. Around 1900 approximately 18,000 new families were formed each year, whereas by 1950 this figure had increased to approximately 40,000. This has been partly a result of the general growth in population size, but was also a function of a very pronounced increase in age specific marriage rates, particularly in the younger age groups. The average age at marriage has also declined from 1900 onwards. Average age at first marriage in the period 1921-5 stood at 27.7 for males and 25.1 for females, whereas by 1951-5 the corresponding rates were 26.8 and 23.7 respectively. The age differences between the two sexes indicate that women generally marry at an earlier age than men and as a general rule are younger than the men they marry.

A connection exists, however, between the age at marriage and fertility (see p.89-91). The relatively high age at marriage in Denmark exercised a restrictive control on the level of fertility and it would be natural to expect an increase in fertility as a function of both higher marriage rates and a declining age at marriage. The opposite, however, was the case. This in turn must be attributed to the presence of more powerful factors which have tended to counteract the illustrated changes in the marriage component.

The Household and the Family

In the sociological context the family is traditionally defined as a social group bound together by lineage and/or marriage, or by relationships resembling marriage. The family has a mutual economy and normally includes adults of both sexes and children, if any. Danish statistics have often included the concept of the 'private household', defined on the basis of 'place of residence'. But because a household can also include non-related individuals, including domestic servants or agricultural workers, the sociological definition and the statistical concept of the 'household' do not always overlap. Nevertheless household size can be used as an approximate criterion for tracing the development of family size. Average household size in Denmark has declined over time from approximately 5.00 (1840), to 4.75 (1880) and 4.33 (1901) and this has mainly been the result of continuous urbanisation and the onset of the decline in fertility from about 1890 onwards. Census material after 1901, however, has contained a far greater wealth of detail relating to household distribution (Table 2.17) and reveals a further decline in average household size from 4.33 (1901) to 3.14 (1950). Furthermore it is apparent that family size was greatest in rural districts and lowest in Copenhagen, with provincial cities holding an intermediate position.

Education

Statistics regarding the level of educational attainment of the Danish population are unfortunately very deficient. Although educational requirements were introduced for both sexes as early as 1814, it is difficult to establish any precise or positive correlation between improved educational facilities and demographic trends, such as the decline in fertility. Indeed it could be argued that formal education in any case was only a partial expression of assimilated knowledge and skills which would be even more difficult to relate to long-term demographic trends.

Summary

Since the eighteenth century Denmark has passed through most of the process defined as the demographic transition. Both mortality and fertility were high in the eighteenth century, while the population growth rate was very limited. By the end of the transition period, after the Second World War, the rate of growth was equally low, but both fertility and mortality in the intervening period had declined substantially. The fall in mortality was apparent as early as c.1775 and clearly predated major discoveries in the medical sphere. It was primarily the result of effective reforms in the primary sector. On the other hand the fall in fertility did not become significant until after 1890. It reflected substantive structural changes within the community which in turn generated both economic and social pressures in favour of a smaller family size. Furthermore this reduction in average family size was realised before the time when techniques of contraception had become effective. Emigration, however, has also played a fundamental role in the long-term development of Danish population. Approximately 285,000 Danes emigrated overseas during the period of greatest population growth between 1869 and 1913 and roughly 90 per cent of these emigrants settled in the USA. In the two centuries under review Danish society has also changed from a nation with a very low standard of living to one of the most affluent in the present world. Development in this context has also been characterised by changes in occupational structure, with the secondary and tertiary sectors contributing an increasing share of GNP. The most important single factor to emerge from this analysis, however, is that no single component in this process of change can be examined in total isolation. The case of Denmark in this context only serves to emphasise the close and inter-related nature of both demographic, economic and social development from the late eighteenth century to the present day.

Notes

1. A.V.K. Frederiksen (1976); Hans Chr. Johansen (1975); Aksel Lassen (1965 and 1966).
2. A brief history of Danish census taking and registration of vital statistics is found in: P.C. Matthiessen (1970), Appendix 1, pp.193-200 and in O. Andersen (1977), pp.137-45.
3. O. Andersen (1973).
4. A.V.K. Frederiksen (1976), Chapter 4, p.52.
5. O. Andersen (1976).
6. Hans Chr. Johansen (1975), p.119.
7. *Dødsårsagerne i Danmark* (Causes of Death in the Kingdom of Denmark). Sundhedsstyrelsen. Yearly publication.
8. Infant Mortality in Denmark. Statistical Inquiries. Danmarks Statistik. Copenhagen, 1965.
9. *Fertilitetsforskelle i Danmark* (Fertility Differences in Denmark). Statistiske Undersøgelser. Copenhagen, 1965.
10. *Fertiliteten udenfor aegteskab* (Fertility out of Wedlock). Statistiske Undersøgelser No.21, Copenhagen, 1965.
11. K. Hvidt (1971).
12. O. Andersen (1977).
13. Svend Aage Hansen (1972), Part I and II. The economic and social history as presented in this chapter is based mainly on these books.
14. Aksel Lassen (1964), p.294.
15. Sven Aage Hansen (1972), Part I, Chapter III.
16. Otto Andersen (1973).
17. Svend Aage Hansen (1972), Part I, p.67 and p.81.
18. Otto Andersen (1976).

19. *Befolkningsforholdene i det 19. århundrede* (The Population of Denmark in the nineteenth century), Copenhagen, 1905, p.155.
20. Svend Aage Hansen (1972), Part I, p.259.
21. Ibid. (1972), Part II, Chapter XIII, pp.22-90.
22. Ibid. (1972), Part I, pp.254-73.
23. Ibid. (1972), Part I, pp.247-54.
24. Ibid. (1972), Part I, p.259.
25. Ibid. (1972), Part I, pp.260-67.
26. Ibid. (1972), Part II, pp.20-90.
27. Holger Gad (1966).

Bibliography

Otto Andersen, *Dødelighedsforholdene i Danmark 1735-1839* (Mortality Conditions in Denmark 1735-1839), Nationaløkonomisk Tidsskrift 2/1973, Copenhagen. (Danish version).
Otto Andersen, *A Malaria Epidemic in Denmark*, Research Report No.30, Institute of Statistics, University of Copenhagen, 1976.
Otto Andersen, *The Population of Denmark*, A population monograph in CICRED series, Copenhagen, 1977.
Anders V. Kaare Frederiksen, *Familierekonstitution* (Family Reconstitution. A model study of population trends in Sejø parish 1663-1813), Copenhagen, 1976 (English summary).
Holger Gad, *Befolknings- og arbejdsforhold i Dansk Landbrug* (The Population and the Working Conditions in Danish Agriculture), Aarhus, Denmark, 1966 (English summary).
Svend Aage Hansen, *Early Industrialisation in Denmark*, Copenhagen, 1970.
Svend Aage Hansen, *Økonomisk vaekst i Danmark, Bind I og II* (Economic Growth in Denmark), Copenhagen, 1972 (Danish version).
Kristian Hvidt, *Flugten til Amerika* (Flight to America), Aarhus, Denmark, 1971 (English summary).
Hans Chr. Johansen, *Befolkningsudvikling og familie-struktur i det 18. århundrede* (Population Development and Family Structure in the Eighteenth Century), Odense, Denmark, 1975 (Danish version).
Aksel Lassen, *Fald og fremgang. Traek af befolkningsudviklingen i Danmark 1645-1960* (Decline and Increase. Aspects of the population development in Denmark 1645-1960), Aarhus, Denmark, 1965 (Danish version).
Aksel Lassen, 'The population of Denmark 1660-1960', *The Scandinavian Economic History Review*, vol.XIV, no.2, Copenhagen, 1966.
P.C. Matthiessen, *Some Aspects of the Demographic Transition in Denmark*, Copenhagen, 1970.

Official Statistics

Danish Censuses and Vital Statistics:

Befolkningsforholdene i det 19. århundrede (The Population of Denmark in the Nineteenth Century), Statistisk Tabelvaerk VA5, Copenhagen, 1905.
Befolkningsudvikling og Sundhedsforhold 1901-1960 (Population Development and Health Conditions 1901-1960), Statistiske Undersøgelser No.19, Copenhagen, 1966.

110   *Denmark*

Folketal, Areal og Klima 1901-1960 (Population, Area and Climate 1901-1960), Statistiske Undersøgelser No.10, Copenhagen, 1964.

Fertilitetsforskelle i Danmark (Fertility Differences in Denmark), Statistiske Undersøgelser, Copenhagen, 1965.

Fertiliteten udenfor aegteskab (Fertility out of Wedlock), Statistiske Undersøgelser No.21, Copenhagen, 1968.

Infant Mortality in Denmark 1931-1960, Statistical Inquiries, Copenhagen, 1965.

Levevilkår i Danmark (Living Conditions in Denmark), Danmarks Statistik og Socialforskningsinstituttet, Copenhagen, 1976.

Dødsårsagerne i Danmark (Causes of Death in the Kingdom of Denmark), Sundhedsstyrelsen, Copenhagen, Yearly.

APPENDIX

Table 2.1: Infant Mortality Rate per 1,000 Live-born Children and
Life Expectancy at Birth (in years): Denmark, 1835-1950

| Period | Male | | Female | |
	Infant mortality rate	Life expectancy at birth	Infant mortality rate	Life expectancy at birth
1835-1839	158	41.3	134	43.7
1840-1849	155	42.9	132	45.0
1850-1859	145	43.1	124	45.4
1860-1869	145	43.7	124	45.6
1870-1879	148	45.5	128	47.2
1880-1889	149	46.8	125	48.9
1890-1900	149	48.6	122	51.4
1901-1905	131	52.9	104	56.2
1906-1910	121	54.9	98	57.9
1911-1915	111	56.2	89	℩.2
1916-1920	103	55.8	81	58.1
1921-1925	94	60.3	72	61.9
1926-1930	91	60.9	71	62.6
1931-1935	82	62.0	63	63.8
1936-1940	71	63.5	54	65.8
1941-1945	55	65.6	42	67.7
1946-1950	45	67.8	35	70.1

Source: Calculated on the basis of Danish life tables.

Table 2.2: Age-Specific Death Rates (per 1,000): Denmark, 1840-1950

Age group	Male					Female				
	1840-49	1890-1900	1921-25	1931-35	1946-50	1840-49	1890-1900	1921-25	1931-35	1946-50
1- 4	25.1	16.2	5.5	4.2	2.0	24.4	15.4	4.8	3.4	1.7
5- 9	8.1	5.6	1.6	1.3	0.7	8.6	6.0	1.6	1.1	0.5
10-14	5.0	3.6	1.4	1.1	0.6	6.0	4.6	1.4	0.9	0.4
15-19	5.4	4.5	2.3	1.9	1.1	5.8	4.7	2.3	1.7	0.7
20-24	8.6	6.0	3.2	2.6	1.6	6.8	4.9	3.2	2.3	1.1
25-29	7.4	5.5	3.2	2.7	1.7	7.6	5.6	3.2	2.9	1.4
30-34	8.6	6.1	3.2	2.8	1.9	9.9	6.5	3.2	3.2	1.7
35-39	10.1	7.7	3.8	3.4	2.3	10.8	7.5	3.8	4.0	2.3
40-44	12.8	9.3	4.9	4.5	3.4	11.9	8.2	4.9	4.9	3.0
45-49	17.1	11.6	6.8	6.5	5.3	13.1	9.1	6.8	6.6	4.6
50-54	21.8	15.7	10.0	9.9	8.0	16.4	11.8	10.0	9.3	6.5
55-59	30.2	22.0	14.7	14.8	12.2	23.6	16.4	14.7	13.7	9.9
60-64	41.6	30.7	23.3	23.0	19.5	34.4	24.2	23.6	21.1	16.5
65-69	55.6	44.7	36.5	37.0	30.9	48.5	36.7	36.5	34.2	27.5
70-74	91.6	74.5	57.5	59.8	50.8	81.8	65.0	57.5	57.7	47.3
75-79	122.8	115.0	96.3	98.6	84.0	108.1	98.9	96.3	96.0	78.9
80-84	186.7	169.4	159.2	155.3	140.5	175.9	151.6	159.2	153.2	132.1

Source: Calculated on the basis of Danish life tables.

Appendix

Table 2.3: Infant Mortality Rate[a] per 1,000 Live-born Children for Births in and out of Wedlock: Denmark, 1901-1949

Period	In wedlock		Out of wedlock	
	Boys	Girls	Boys	Girls
1901-09	116	91	227	175
1910-19	97	77	176	141
1920-29	88	68	136	106
1930-39	75	57	103	83
1940-49	48	37	77	60
1950-59	29	21	44	35

a. Average of the individual years.

Source: *Befolkningsudvikling og Sundhedsforhold (Population Development and Health Conditions)*, Copenhagen, 1966, pp.94-5.

Table 2.4: Life Expectancy at Birth (in years): Denmark, 1840-1844

	Male	Female
Copenhagen	33.2	37.1
Urban areas excl. Copenhagen	41.8	46.5
Rural areas	45.9	47.1
All Denmark	44.1	46.0

Source: Calculated by the author on the basis of Danish official statistics.

Table 2.5: Child Mortality for Legitimate Children, by Social Group in Copenhagen, Census of 1880

Social group	q(1)	q(2)	q(3)	q(5)
1. Officials, professionals, and manufacturers	.140	.178	.197	.231
2. Master artisans and shopkeepers	.180	.229	.242	.306
3. Teachers and clerks	.169	.215	.249	.258
4. Minor clerks and servants	.187	.238	.247	.273
5. Working class	.203	.259	.273	.309
Total	.192	.245	.256	.293

Note: q(a): Probability of death between birth and exact age a.

Source: P.C. Matthiessen, 'Application of the Brass-Sullivan Method to Historical Data', *Population Index*, October-December 1972.

Table 2.6: Causes of Death in Denmark, per 100,000 Population, 1921-1960

	1921-30	1931-40	1941-45	1946-50	1951-55	1956-60
1. Tuberculosis	84	50	34	24	9	4
2. Infectious diseases (excl. tuberculosis)	71	44	38	20	12	7
3. Malignant neoplasms	139	151	162	163	185	204
4. Apoplexy and senility	200	182	173	125	159	149
5. Diseases of the heart	118	167	180	245	263	298
6. Diseases of the respiratory system	185	146	89	84	43	41
7. Diseases of the digestive system	—[a]	51	52	47	38	37
8. Diseases of the genito-urinary system	—[a]	47	45	36	32	36
9. Congenital malformations	11	11	12	10	10	10
10. Diseases of perinatal period	41	39	42	35	27	23
11. Suicide	15	19	21	25	23	21
12. Homicide	1	1	1	1	1	1
13. Accidents	28	32	47	42	43	45
14. All other causes of death	222	132	110	75	48	49
Total	1,115	1,072	1,006	932	893	925

a. Figures for diseases of the digestive and the genito-urinary system are included in: All other causes of death.

Source: *Dødsårsager i Kongeriget Danmark (Causes of Death in the Kingdom of Denmark)*, Sundhedsstyrelsen, 1973.

Appendix

Table 2.7: Age Specific Fertility Rates in Five-Year Age Groups
(per 1,000 Females): Denmark, 1901-1961

Year	15-19	20-24	25-29	Age 30-34	35-39	40-44	45-49
1901	19.2	147.4	221.4	204.9	152.2	75.0	7.7
1911	24.2	140.1	196.8	168.1	128.7	56.0	5.9
1921	24.6	130.3	172.9	143.0	103.1	43.7	4.5
1931	22.9	101.5	125.3	97.6	65.5	25.5	2.2
1941	25.8	120.7	133.6	93.5	54.5	18.7	1.5
1951	38.4	153.8	147.3	93.0	50.1	16.8	1.1
1961	45.6	170.5	156.2	87.2	38.5	10.7	0.7

Source: *Befolkningsudvikling og sundhedsforhold (Population Development and Health Conditions)*, Copenhagen, 1966, p.87.

Table 2.8: Reproduction Rates (per 1,000 Females): Denmark, 1901-1961

Year	Total fertility rates TFR	Gross reproduction rates GRR	Net reproduction rates NRR
1901	4,139	2,028	1,580
1911	3,599	1,760	1,439
1921	3,111	1,515	1,295
1931	2,203	1,068	944
1941	2,242	1,087	1,002
1951	2,502	1,208	1,162
1961	2,547	1,240	1,203

Source: *Befolkningsudvikling og Sundhedsforhold (Population Development and Health Conditions)*, Copenhagen, 1966, p.67.

Table 2.9: Number of Children per Family, by Socio-economic Status, and Residence of the Head of the Household: Denmark, 1901 and 1940

	Number of children per family	
	1901[a]	1940[b]
I. Copenhagen		
A. Self-employed	4.8	1.3
B. Salaried employees and civil servants	4.7	1.3
C. Trained and untrained workers	5.7	1.4
II. Provincial cities		
A. Self-employed	5.5	1.7
B. Salaried employees and civil servants	5.6	1.6
C. Trained and untrained workers	5.9	1.9
III. Rural areas		
A. Self-employed		
1. In agriculture	5.5	2.5
2. Outside agriculture	5.9	2.0
B. Salaried employees and civil servants	—	1.9
C. Trained and untrained workers	5.7	—
1. In agriculture	—	2.7
2. Outside agriculture	—	2.4

a. Marriages, which at the time of the census 1 February 1901 had existed 25 years or more.
b. Marriages, which at the time of the census 5 November 1940 had existed for from 12 to 15 years.

Source: *Fertilitetsforskelle i Danmark (Fertility Differences in Denmark)*, Statistiske Undersøgelser, Copenhagen, 1965.

Table 2.10: Net Migration between Censuses: Denmark, 1870-1930

Period	Net migration[a]
1/2 1870 − 1/2 1880	−39,902
1/2 1880 − 1/2 1890	−73,016
1/2 1890 − 1/2 1901	−40,664
1/2 1901 − 1/2 1910	−65,085
1/2 1911 − 1/2 1916	−18,194
1/2 1916 − 1/2 1921	+23,700
1/2 1921 − 1/2 1930	−39,978

a. −indicates net emigration, + indicates net immigration

Source: *Befolkningsudvikling og Sundhedsforhold (Population Development and Health Conditions)*, Copenhagen, 1966, pp.168-9.

Table 2.11: The Relative Distribution of the Gross National Product (GNP): Denmark, 1820-1940, Current Prices

Year	Agriculture, etc.	Industry	Arts and crafts	Commerce, etc.	Rest	Total %	Total Mill. D.kr.
1820	54.7	14.9		5.9	24.5	100.0	188
1830	55.7	16.0		6.7	21.6	100.0	194
1840	53.0	16.9		7.6	22.5	100.0	236
1850	44.8	17.1		8.6	29.5	100.0	315
1860	48.1	4.3	14.7	9.0	23.9	100.0	464
1870	50.0	4.2	12.1	10.5	23.2	100.0	669
1880	44.9	5.2	10.8	13.7	25.4	100.0	840
1890	37.8	6.5	12.2	15.7	27.8	100.0	965
1895	34.7	7.8	11.5	17.5	28.5	100.0	1,039
1900	30.2	9.9	9.9	18.5	31.5	100.0	1,322
1905	31.5	9.6	9.2	19.9	29.8	100.0	1,588
1910	30.3	9.9	8.6	20.9	30.3	100.0	1,922
1915	30.5	10.6	6.8	21.2	30.9	100.0	2,887
1920	23.6	15.2	8.2	25.8	27.2	100.0	7,396
1925	24.5	11.3	7.4	24.6	32.2	100.0	6,153
1930	21.1	11.6	8.7	23.2	35.4	100.0	5,705
1935	18.0	14.7	9.5	21.3	36.5	100.0	6,380
1939	18.6	15.5	9.4	21.6	34.9	100.0	8,127

Source: Svend Aage Hansen, *Økonomisk Vaekst i Danmark (Economic Growth in Denmark)*, Copenhagen, 1972.

Table 2.12: Net Emigration in per cent of the Excess of Births,
Denmark, Norway and Sweden: 1850-1914

Period	Denmark	Norway	Sweden
1850-1859	− 3	11	8
1860-1869	5	28	25
1870-1879	18	26	23
1880-1889	26	71	64
1890-1899	14	18	37
1900-1909	16	50	33
1910-1914	32	39	21
Total	16	37	32

Source: Svend Aage Hansen, *Økonomisk Vaekst i Danmark (Economic Growth in Denmark)*, Copenhagen, 1972.

Table 2.13: Distribution of the Population by Occupation:
1801-1950, Census Data, Denmark

Year	Agriculture		Other occupations		Total population	
	Number 1,000	Pct.	Number 1,000	Pct.	Number 1,000	Pct.
1801	628	67	301	33	929	100
1834	704	58	527	42	1,231	100
1840	720	56	569	44	1,289	100
1845	744	55	613	45	1,357	100
1855	816	54	691	46	1,507	100
1860	853	53	755	47	1,608	100
1870	934	52	851	48	1,785	100
1880	1,006	51	963	49	1,969	100
1890	997	46	1,175	54	2,172	100
1901	1,015[a]	41	1,435	59	2,450	100
1901	1,001[b]	39	1,579	61	2,580	100
1911	1,051	36	1,852	64	2,903	100
1921	1,043	32	2,225	68	3,268	100
1930	1,027	29	2,524	71	3,551	100
1940	964	25	2,880	75	3,844	100
1950	887	21	3,362	79	4,249	100

a. From 1801 to 1901, the agricultural population includes also forestry, garden farming, and fishing.
b. From 1901 to 1950, 'agriculture' includes only farming. The numbers for 1901 and 1911 include estimates for the population employed in the various occupations in the territory which in 1920 was accorded to Denmark (southern Jutland).

Source: Holger Gad, *Befolknings- og Arbejdsforhold i Dansk Landbrug (The Population and the Working Conditions in Danish Agriculture)*, vol.I, Aarhus, 1956, pp.14, 33.

Table 2.14: Urban and Rural Population (in 1,000s) Denmark:
1769-1965

Year	Copenhagen	Suburbs of Copenhagen	Other urban areas	Rural areas	The whole country	The urban population in per cent of the total population
1801	101	—	93	735	929	21
1860	163	—	214	1,231	1,608	23
1870	198	—	245	1,341	1,784	25
1880	261	—	291	1,417	1,969	28
1890	360	—	362	1,450	2,172	33
1901	455	—	482	1,513	2,450	38
1911	559	—	550	1,647	2,756	40
1921	701	10	1,065[a]	1,494	3,270	54
1930	771	25	1,279	1,476	3,551	58
1940	890	118	1,432	1,404	3,844	63
1950	975	194	1,715	1,397	4,281	67

a. From 1921 a redefinition of the urban areas includes townships with at least
250 inhabitants.

Source: *Folketal, Areal og Klima 1901-60 (Population, Area and Climate,
1901-60)*, Statistiske Undersøgelser Nr.10, Copenhagen, 1964.

Appendix 121

Table 2.15: The Age Distribution and the Dependency Ratio in
Denmark, as given in the Censuses since 1840

Census year	Age groups, distribution by per cent			Dependency ratio[a]		
	0-14 years of age	15-64 years of age	65 years of age or more	0-14 and 65+	0-14	65+
1840	32.82	61.73	5.45	62.0	53.2	8.8
1845	32.76	61.76	5.48	61.9	53.0	8.9
1855	33.28	61.49	5.23	62.6	54.1	8.5
1860	33.69	61.11	5.20	63.6	55.1	8.5
1870	33.38	60.81	5.81	64.5	54.9	9.6
1880	33.79	60.13	6.08	66.3	56.2	10.1
1890	34.81	58.22	6.97	71.8	59.8	12.0
1901	33.94	59.40	6.66	68.4	57.1	11.2
1911	33.63	59.73	6.64	67.4	56.3	11.1
1921	31.18	61.98	6.84	61.3	50.3	11.0
1930	27.47	65.23	7.30	53.3	42.1	11.2
1940	23.97	68.21	7.82	46.6	35.1	11.5
1950	26.36	64.60	9.04	54.8	40.8	14.0
1960	25.09	64.27	10.64	55.6	39.0	16.6
1970	23.29	64.44	12.27	55.2	36.1	19.0

a. Number of persons in the given 'dependent' age group, in per cent of the
persons 15-64 years of age.

Source: Statistisk Tabelvaerk, VA5, *Befolkningsforholdene i Danmark i det 19.
Århundrede (The Population of Denmark in the 19th Century)*, Copenhagen,
1905. Statistiske Undersøgelser nr.19, *Befolkningsudvikling og
Sundhedsforhold, 1901-60 (Population Development and Health Conditions,
1901-60)*, Copenhagen, 1966.

Table 2.16: Marital Status (per cent), Denmark: 1901-1950

| | Male | | | Female | | |
	1901	1930	1950	1901	1930	1950
Unmarried	60.7	55.6	48.4	58.0	53.2	44.4
Married or separated	35.5	40.5	47.1	33.8	39.0	46.5
Widowed	3.7	3.5	3.3	8.0	7.0	7.2
Divorced	0.1	0.4	1.1	0.2	0.8	1.9
Total	100.0	100.0	100.0	100.0	100.0	100.0

Source: Danish Census data from 1901, 1930 and 1950.

Table 2.17: Private Households, Distributed by Size (per cent),
 Denmark: 1901-1950

	1901	1911	1930	1940	1950
Size of household					
1 person	9	10	11	13	14
2 persons	17	18	22	26	27
3 persons	18	18	22	24	23
4 persons	16	16	17	17	18
5 persons	13	13	12	10	10
6 or more	27	25	16	10	8
Total	100	100	100	100	100
Average number of persons per household	4.3	4.1	3.7	3.2	3.1

Source: *Levevilkår i Danmark (Living Conditions in Denmark)*, Copenhagen,
 1976.

3 FRANCE

Etienne van de Walle

The notion of a Malthusian equilibrium continues to dominate our vision of the historical past prior to the nineteenth century. According to the standard interpretation the lands of Western Europe were full until the population broke out of the stagnation of institutions and technology, thanks to the agricultural revolution that released it from its dependence on autarkic subsistence, and to the industrial revolution that provided an outlet for surplus farm labour. The carrying capacity of the land determined the number of the people. And if perchance numbers were increasing faster than the material base of society, then positive checks (in Malthus's terms) would quickly cut back the excessive growth. Thus, the level of mortality was endogenous, i.e. induced by the very pressure of population on limited resources.[1]

It is true that the size of villages in France, expressed in numbers of hearths, often exhibits a remarkable stability over the available statistical record.[2] E. Le Roy Ladurie, in a lecture devoted to 'immobile history', has noted that the population of France may have been approximately the same size in 1720 as in 1320: between 17 million and 20 million within the borders of 1720. Even though a trough was reached between these dates, as a result of plagues and wars (according to Le Roy Ladurie, the population plunged under the ten million mark in about 1440), he holds that the equilibrium figure was reached at either end of the period, and that it was a function of the constancy of agricultural technology.[3] If so, one of the most urgent tasks of the historian is to account for the long-term population growth in the eighteenth century.

It had generally been agreed that the population was growing during the decades preceding the Revolution. But it is now possible to take a fresh look at the history of the French population since 1740. One of the major ventures attempted in historical demography is now coming to fruition. The sample study of French parishes, initiated almost two decades ago by Louis Henry and his colleagues at the National Institute for Demographic Studies (INED), is now yielding results for the whole country.[4] There were 24.5 million inhabitants in 1750, 29.1 million in 1800, and 36.35 million in 1850 in the borders of 1861 (i.e. including Nice and the Savoys). With less certainty, Henry and Blayo estimate

123

the population at 21.5 million in 1700. These estimates are based on a reconstruction of the population from enumerated totals in the fourteenth century, and from the births and deaths registered in the sample of parishes. It turns out that there was a great deal of under-registration of deaths. The amount, but not the age distribution of the omitted deaths could be assessed; as a result the 1700 and 1750 estimates of population given above, are presented as *minimum* values. The authors conclude that 'France was more populated in the middle of the eighteenth century, and population growth between 1750 and 1800 was less than was thought until now'.[5] Nevertheless, population was increasing, and at an accelerating rate: 3 million additional people between 1700 and 1750, for an overall growth of 14 per cent in 50 years; then, 4.6 million between 1750 and 1800 (19 per cent growth) and 6.2 million between 1800 and 1850 (25 per cent). Later, we shall elaborate on the nineteenth-century statistics. Two issues remain to be discussed concerning the early part of our story: the component of population increase; and its implication for the Malthusian model.

The INED probe into the past has not yet reached the period prior to 1740; but between 1740 and the Revolution at least, there is little indication of a trend either in the birth or in the death rate. During these years, the crude birth rate was close to 40 (births per thousand persons), and the crude death rate close to 36 (deaths per thousand persons). Expectation of life at birth was between 27 and 28 years, and infant mortality remained close to 280 (infant deaths per thousand births).[6] If there was an acceleration of population growth during the century, the cause would seem to have been a very slight mortality decline. Not that the usual wretched living conditions improved: rather, catastrophic mortality receded somewhat between the first and second half of the century. But life expectancy, and health conditions in general, remained abysmally low in pre-revolutionary France.

Was high mortality the result of overpopulation, as the Malthusian model would have it? Does the population increase of the eighteenth century therefore presuppose a rise in the productivity of agriculture and a diversification of the economy? The available evidence indicates that there was no agricultural revolution, no economic takeoff in eighteenth-century France.[7] The *monde plein* (full world) postulate presupposes an extraordinarily fine tuning of the Malthusian equilibrium between population and resources, that has no basis in fact. The quality of resources, and the technology that exploits them, itself depends on the number of people. The experience of sustained population growth since the beginning of this century or earlier, in most of the less developed countries, suggests that a decline of the death rate without a substantial rise of individual consumption does not necessarily and automatically lead to a relapse into high mortality. Population size may determine total output rather than be determined by it. We suspect that the great scourges of the past — war, pestilence, even famine — were exogenous factors, historical accidents that could often have been avoided at the cost of minor political or administrative decisions. Lack of information and the irresponsiveness of institutions, rather than a mechanism tying the number of births rigorously to the number of deaths, explain high mortality. Growth is the fate of populations that do not limit their births — even when it is followed by the periodic collapse of numbers in the wake of catastrophic mortality. But in France, by the end of the eighteenth century, the catastrophes had become rarer.

The situation that has been described is not exclusively French. Other countries in Western Europe appear to have been subjected to sustained population growth, and their economy had to adapt to the growing numbers. The adjustments during the nineteenth century became part of what has been called the Industrial Revolution. Various regions of Europe reached original solutions to the general problem of accommodating the growing numbers within the available space. Before we review the solutions adopted in France, it is fitting to present the demographic backcloth, since it became highly distinctive in France from about the time of the French revolution. We shall review the evolution of mortality and fertility in succession.

Mortality

Available series of female expectation of life at birth are presented in Table 3.1. War losses and migration make the computation of the series for males less easy, but the course of mortality illustrated by these figures for female life expectancy, is generally characteristic for both sexes. For example, the following comparisons can be made:

	Male $\overset{o}{e}_o$	Female $\overset{o}{e}_o$
INED Series[8]		
1740-1749	23.8	25.7
1780-1789	27.5	28.1
1820-1829	38.3	39.3
INSEE-INED Series[9]		
1861-1865	39.1	40.6
1898-1903	48.5	52.4
1946-1949	61.9	67.5

A remarkable inflection in the series of mortality occurs at the time of the Revolution. Blayo notes that infant mortality decreases by one third between 1789 and 1829, to reach 180 per thousand at the latter date and he comments as follows: 'It is remarkable that this decline of infant mortality antedates the introduction, and *a fortiori* the generalisation in the rural environment, of preventive medicine, particularly vaccination against smallpox.'[10] The exact role of inoculation and vaccination remains to be established. It is certain, however, that the continuing mortality decline was not the result of any one factor. Moreover, infant mortality may have responded to specific influences and is not a particularly good index of overall mortality at that time, in France at least. Table 3.2 gives unadjusted values of infant mortality, computed from official statistics, at various points in time. These figures reveal little if any decline before the last quarter of the century. The mortality of infants and young children was affected by persistent customs having little to do with general economic progress. Predominant among those were the abandonment of children — what has been termed by some a disguised form of infanticide — and the custom of wet-nursing. The impact of such customs is imperfectly documented, although they were attracting the scandalised attention of contemporaries. For a period of nine years between 1824 and 1832, there were 30,300 foundlings recorded, or 3.5 per cent of all births in France.[11] To judge from the Parisian experience, which is well documented for a period at the end of the nineteenth century, the mortality of foundlings was appallingly high; 35 per cent of the infants abandoned in 1874-8 had died before they were one year old. The wet-nurse industry, moreover, by moving tens of thousands of new-born babies over large distances and by subjecting them to substandard care, was contributing to high mortality in the neighbourhood of large metropolises. This extraordinary custom too is well documented for Paris after 1880. It was then involving more than one fourth of the births occurring in the capital.[12] Wet-nurses were hired by members of the provincial bourgeoisie as well, but estimates of the numbers involved are hard to come by. The 1872 census published the results of a question identifying nurslings living outside of their parents' home; 51,000 or 1.5 per cent of all children under the age of five, were reported for the whole country. The highest concentrations (2 per cent or more) were encountered in thirteen *départements* around Paris, five *départements* around Lyons, and two around Marseilles. The proportion of nurslings was significantly correlated (r = 0.63) with infant mortality at the time. The latter was thus highest in some of the most prosperous areas in the neighbourhood of large cities.

It is possible to compute estimations of life expectancy at birth that exclude the effect of disrupting factors affecting childhood mortality. Such estimates for the nineteenth century at the level of the *départements* show a positive relationship to the level of rural incomes, and a negative relationship to the proportion of the urban population. Urban mortality is high, and seems long to remain unaffected by the factors that are causing rural mortality to decline. The sanitary problems of high density living in fast-growing metropolises such as Paris, Lyons and Marseilles, were insuperable without a sound theory about the transmission of disease. Public works strove to improve the urban environment, but as long as the mechanism of waterborne diseases — including cholera, the nineteenth-century plague — was not understood, mortality showed little decline. While Hausmann's efforts were directed towards enlarging streets and improving the housing, Vaisse in Lyons succeeded in providing abundant water and sewerage. In Marseilles, finally, the water ducts from the Durance were badly polluted before reaching the city, and there were no sewers to speak of — a condition that permitted the last big cholera epidemic in the country (1884). The contrasts in water supply and sewage go far to explain the different course of mortality in the three cities: whereas they all had life expectancies at birth close to thirty-three years until mid-century, the Rhône *département* reached forty years by 1876-80, Seine by 1891-5, and Bouches-du-Rhône only in 1896-1900.[13]

Unfortunately, in contrast with England, little information is available on causes of death before 1880. The scraps of information that exist suggest that respiratory tuberculosis was increasing in Paris until the early 1880s. The reasons for its subsequent decline remain conjectural. The importance of water- and food-borne diseases in urban mortality, particularly among children, is noteworthy. By 1880, when distributions of deaths by cause become regularly available for the capital, typhoid fever and diarrhoeas remained a more important factor than in London. Tuberculosis and typhoid fever were to remain unusually high in France by Western European standards well into the twentieth century. It is the behaviour of French fertility, however, that confers a unique character to the demography of that country.

Fertility

The momentous new fact for the first time in history at the level of a country, is that the birth rate of France has started its secular decline.

The INED study provides a series of adjusted crude birth rates showing a clear break at the time of the Revolution. From 38.8 births per thousand people in 1785-9, the birth rate had decreased to 32.9 in 1800-04, and to 31.0 in 1825-9.[14] It is clear, moreover, that the early part of the decline was not due to a temporary disturbance of nuptiality resulting from the great loss of lives during the wars of the Revolution and the Empire. It is estimated that 1.3 million young men died in the conflict, mostly from the diseases that accompanied large armies in the field.[15] Nuptiality reacted to the large disturbances in the marriage market, but only to a remarkably minor extent. We shall come back to a discussion of changes in age at marriage and in the proportions ever married, but it is undoubtedly marital fertility that deserves the limelight here.

By the beginning of the nineteenth century, a radically new behaviour had erupted in married life itself: family limitation by voluntary control of fertility was responsible for the drop of the birth rate. The appearance of contraception, moreover, was not restricted to privileged social classes or to small regions of France. It is possible to identify the influence of deliberate fertility control on marital fertility curves. The technique of family reconstitution has produced such curves from parish records, and it is clear that fertility began to be controlled, at the end of the eighteenth century, in widely dispersed regions of France. Contraception appeared even in areas that would maintain high fertility levels during the nineteenth century, such as Brittany, Alsace or the Nord *département*.[16] Why such a radical departure from past behaviour appears at about the same time over such a large section of the French territory — and not in other countries — remains one of the mysteries of demographic history. Is it an accident that the political upheavals of the Revolution coincided with a profound revision of the attitudes towards reproduction? Did the forces of Reason invade an area that had been hitherto ruled by arbitrariness and tradition, at the same time as other restraints on the principle of self-administration were crumbling? Did massive conscription serve as a medium for the diffusion of birth control? After all, is sex not a favourite subject of conversation among men drafted into the army?

There is no lack of hypotheses on the causes of the decline of fertility. We shall restrict ourselves here to a factual description of the course of overall fertility and its components, marital fertility, illegitimate fertility, and the proportion married. We shall briefly review some of the ecological associations between fertility and nuptiality on the one hand, and various socio-economic or demographic factors on the other hand, that could have played a role in determining their levels and trends. We shall use standardised indices of fertility: I_f, overall fertility; I_g, marital fertility; I_h, illegitimate fertility; and I_m, the proportion married. These indices are systematically used in a project on the decline of fertility in Europe, and they have been fully described elsewhere.[17] It is sufficient to say here that I_f, I_g and I_h express respectively the fertility of all women, of married women, and of single women, on a scale where the fertility of married Hutterite women would be 'one'. (The choice of the Hutterities, a North American religious sect proscribing the use of contraception, is prompted by the fact that their fertility schedule is the highest on record.) Thus, I_h, the index of illegitimate fertility (for example) would be equal to 'one' if all non-married women had the fertility of married Hutterites, a standard which implies regular sexual intercourse and no fertility control. Needless to say, non-married women are not subjected to these conditions, and I_h is therefore usually quite low, less than 0.05 for France. But the marital fertility of a population can be more fairly compared to that of the standard population. Most European countries exhibited I_gs of 0.70 (70 per cent of the Hutterites) or more during most of the nineteenth century. Finally, I_f, overall fertility, is determined by the combined effect of the proportion married, I_m, and of marital and illegitimate fertility. Neglecting the latter, $I_f \simeq I_g \times I_m$. These indices are given for the whole of France in Table 3.3, for the period 1831 to 1931.

We cannot compute the fertility indices prior to 1831, for lack of age distributions of the population by marital status. By 1831, marital fertility for France was already well below the level that usually prevails in countries where family limitation is not widely practised. In fact, France stands out among all countries of Europe at mid-century. Her I_g of 0.478 (or 47.8 per cent of Hutterite marital fertility) compares with 0.831 for the Netherlands, 0.784 for Belgium, 0.677 in Denmark and 0.673 in Sweden at the time. French marital fertility, moreover, was declining almost continuously, in contrast to the trend in other countries. An empirical generalisation regarding the demographic transition is that the earlier its beginning, the slower the pace of fertility decline. Thus, it took Taiwan only twenty years to reach the degree of birth control achieved by Sweden in about one hundred years.[18] It is therefore not surprising that France, the forerunner, was involved continuously in the decline of I_g between 1831 and 1931. (Actually the decline started earlier than shown by our figure, from an

I_g level probably superior to 0.7.) Of course, the slow pace of the
transition for France as a whole resulted in part from the phasing of
the fertility decline among very diverse *départements*. By 1831, three
départements in Normandy and three in the Garonne Valley had I_gs
of less than 0.4, their marital fertility being almost stabilised by
then at this low level. Conversely, in 1901, there were still pockets
of high fertility in Brittany and the Massif Central.

There was a peculiar temporary relapse into higher fertility in many
départements at mid-century, a feature that is also apparent in the
series for France given in Table 3.3. I_g declined in practically every
département of France between 1831 and 1856, and between 1876
and 1901; but it increased in 43 *départements* (out of 82) between
1856 and 1876.[19] There was a baby boom in France during the Second
Empire. The reasons for this interruption of the secular trend are
unknown. It is possible that the diffusion of contraception that had
widely started by 1830, stopped and even lost ground in some regions
during this era of prosperity. Many more local studies of fertility, at
the micro-level of families and couples, will be required for the
nineteenth century. There are rich statistical sources for the period,
such as the vital registration, the census lists, and the nominal
information available in cadastres, taxation rolls and notary records.
The period has been shunned by historical demographers, perhaps because so
much information becomes available then at the aggregate level of the
larger administrative units.

A general view of the relationship between the course of fertility
and socio-economic or cultural variables must therefore still rest on
the unsatisfactory evidence available for the *départements*. Ecological
correlations between variables indicate that the stage of advancement
reached in the fertility decline was clearly related to (a) the level of
expectation of life at birth in the *départements*; (b) the level of rural
income. Strangely enough, in view of the role generally attributed to
urbanisation and industrialisation in theories of the demographic
transition, the people in cities were not the first to adopt family
limitation. It is true that Paris had attained low marital fertility by
the time of its first published census: I_g was 0.392 in 1817. But many
of the other large cities, in particular the fast growing industrial centres,
were maintaining exceptionally high levels of fertility. The mining
regions and the centres of textile manufacture, including such poles
of the Industrial Revolution in France as the Nord *département*, Alsace
or Loire, were lagging in this respect behind the agricultural areas of

Normandy or Aquitaine. It is true that industry and the cities were providing work for the growing population, whereas the number of rural dwellers was shrinking. Nevertheless, the early decline of fertility in rural France is an original feature of the French transition.

The urban proletariat had higher illegitimate fertility. Table 3.3 suggests that there was little change in the illegitimacy rate in France as a whole, but the impression is misleading. In general, illegitimacy decreased in the large cities in the southern half of the country, while it increased in the northern half. The regions of high illegitimacy were generally also those where the most children were legitimated by subsequent marriage − an indication that consensual unions were a socially acceptable way of starting married life, at least for some social classes and in some regions. The decline of marital fertility in France, at any rate, does not seem to have been accompanied by a parallel decline of illegitimate fertility.

Table 3.3 also records the evolution of I_m, the standardised proportion of women married. In general, a rise of I_m accompanies the decline of marital fertility, and appears determined by it. It seems that the traditional checks to marriage, which prevailed under the old demographic régime, were relaxed when marital fertility became controlled. The relationship between marital fertility (I_g) and the proportion married (I_m) in the *départements*, results consistently in a zero order correlation coefficient close to −0.8 during the period between 1831 and 1901. Those *départements* with an early decline of fertility also showed a drop in the age at marriage, whereas the areas where marital fertility maintained high levels were also those where the age at marriage went up. Contrasting a *département* in the Garonne Valley with one in Brittany is instructive in this respect. Lot-et-Garonne. with I_gs of 0.351 and 0.231 respectively in 1831 and 1901, saw its female mean age at first marriage drop from 23.3 to 21.5 years during the period. Meanwhile, Finistère where I_g had only dropped, belatedly, from 0.815 to 0.718 from 1831 to 1901, witnessed a rise in the age at first marriage from 23.9 to 26.0 years.

Age at marriage is but one aspect of nuptiality. Another important variable is the proportion of the population that eventually gets married. One cannot help being struck by the long-term stability of the proportion of women married over two centuries of observation. Not only is this proportion remarkably constant over time for the whole of France, a feature that was noted by Chasteland and Pressat; the available information indicates that regional differences in the proportions ever-married that were established in the middle of the eighteenth century, were to persist into the twentieth.[20] In recent decades, many rural regions of France have evolved high proportions of male celibacy, because young women have increasingly deserted the countryside for a more comfortable life in the cities.[21] Surveys reveal that parents themselves deem the occupation of farmer suitable for their sons, since they wish to see the farm perpetuated, but that they reject the condition of peasant's wife for their daughters.[22] Universal and early marriage has become the norm in modern life, but the flight from the land has created a category of single men who were left behind by the urbanisation of society.

Population Growth

The trends in mortality and fertility reviewed in earlier sections of this chapter were from an early date combining to yield very low rates of natural increase, even by the European standards of the time. Rural societies in Europe were using diverse methods to cope with increasing populations within the finite land resources available. These methods included the resort to cottage industry, migrations either seasonal or permanent, and the intensification of agriculture. Although all these methods were used to varying degrees in France during the nineteenth century, the distinctive character of French demography is that population growth was very low overall and that it was even negative in many regions. When low reproduction combined with the flight from the land to urban and non-agricultural occupations, the result was a striking picture of declining population on the land which was quite unique for the time. Out-migration was not as intense as in other countries, and it can truly be said that 'denatality was the moving force of rural depopulation'.[23]

A majority of the *départements* reached their largest historical population size at some time during the nineteenth century, and then declined in absolute numbers. This maximum size was achieved before 1841 for 10 *départements*; and for an additional 34 *départements* before 1861. By the middle of the century, half of the national territory was losing population. Figure 3.1 illustrates the process.

The *départements* that declined early were either those where fertility had first been reduced (Normandy and the Garonne Valley) or mountainous areas (Alps, Jura, Massif Central) with substandard subsistence agriculture and sustained out-migration streams. Conversely, areas of persistent high fertility, such as Brittany, or of in-migration − the urban and industrialising regions − underwent population growth.

The extent of decline of the rural population in fifty years, between

Figure 3.1: Date when Maximum Population was Reached

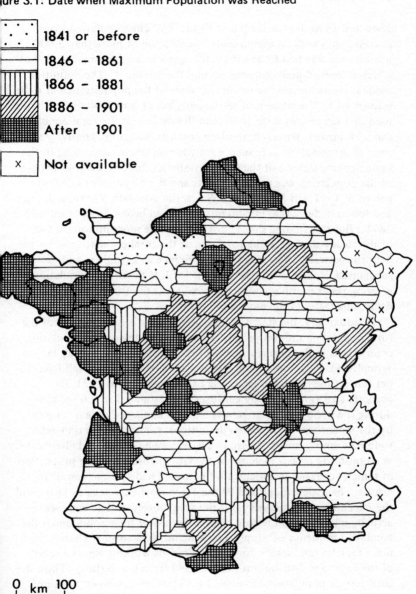

- 1841 or before
- 1846 – 1861
- 1866 – 1881
- 1886 – 1901
- After 1901

x Not available

0   km 100

miles 100

1846 and 1896, is represented in Figure 3.2. The population living
in communes with an agglomerated population of more than 2,000
inhabitants, was said to be urban; the agglomerated population is that
which is 'immediately grouped around the steeple'.[24] The definition
tends to overestimate the urban character of the population, and to be
influenced by the pattern of settlement; but at least it was consistently
used by each census since 1846, and the decline of the rural population
can be followed. Writers have often commented on the relatively slow
pace of urbanisation in France, even when measured according to the
undemanding criteria of the official statistics. Indeed, only 41 per cent
of the population was urban in 1901, and the 50 per cent mark was
passed in 1931. (In England and Wales, the population in rural districts
and towns under 2,000 inhabitants had fallen below 50 per cent before
1871.) But this finding should not obscure the more important fact
of the steady decline in the total size of the rural population − by 15
per cent between 1846 and 1896 for France as a whole − and the
substantial decline of numbers on the land. If the urban population is
growing faster in other countries, nowhere is the rural population
decreasing faster in the nineteenth century.

Paradoxically, the statistics indicate that the general decline of the
rural population did not prevent an increase of the active population
enumerated in the primary sector of the economy (i.e. mostly in
agriculture). Even though the relative share of that sector fell from 53
per cent of the labour force in 1851 to 41 per cent in 1921, its
absolute size as recorded by censuses, rose from 8.3 to 9.0 million
during the period.[25] These results must be explained at least in part
by the inconsistency of census definitions, particularly as they relate
to female employment. A farmer's wife may be considered alternatively
as a housewife or as a member of the labour force, and the proportion
of females engaged in agriculture fluctuated widely from census to
census. The male agricultural labour force reached a peak in 1876, and
then declined continuously. It is possible, however, that there was
actually an increase in female employment over the period, under the
combined influence of supply and demand mechanisms. There were
more females (and males, for that matter) of working age as a result
of the older age distribution that resulted from low fertility. Thus, the
total female population increased by 33 per cent between 1801 and
1901, but the female population between the ages of 15 and 65 grew
by 45 per cent.[26] Moreover, there may well have been a rise in labour
participation rates (the number of working persons per 1,000 persons
of working age), above all among females. This resulted from the overall

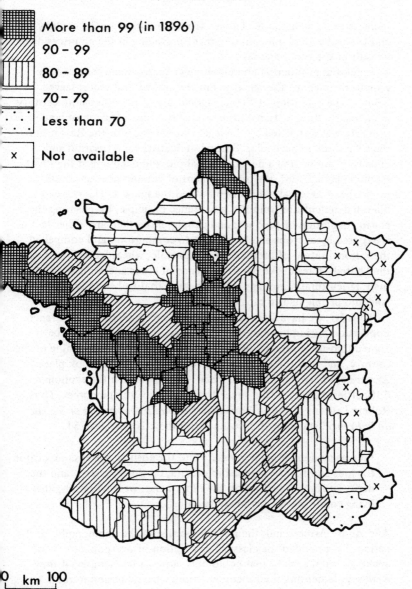

Figure 3.2: Growth of Rural Population, 1846-96

More than 99 (in 1896)
90 – 99
80 – 89
70 – 79
Less than 70

x   Not available

0   km 100

miles 100

increase in the demand for labour, from the middle of the century on, and the reabsorbed underemployment prevailing in the countryside as a result of the economic take-off.

Industrial production and employment were undergoing steady growth throughout the century, but the agricultural sector lagged behind. The evolution of French agriculture in the nineteenth century is shaped by three external influences. First, the diffusion of landed property was permitted by the legal consequences of the Revolution, the Civil Code in particular. Second, industrial centralisation and expansion stimulated a demand for labour and encouraged the flight from the land. Third, the improvement of communications, both internal and external, radically modified the market. The railroad liberated agriculture from the subsistence principle, by ensuring the cheap circulation of products and people; more than any other factor, it exposed local crops and handicraft to competition and compelled the rationalisation of production. Meanwhile, wheat from Russia and the United States broke the dependence of cities and industries on their agricultural hinterland. The old rules that had been tying together land and people had to break down.

Thus far, we have stressed the slow rate of increase of the French population during the nineteenth century. It has nevertheless been argued that the countryside was overpopulated at the beginning of the century, and that the moderate amount of growth that took place — 25 per cent between 1800 and 1850 — compounded the economic difficulties that led to the general stagnation of rural incomes. Thus, Robert Laurent in the authoritative *Histoire Économique et Sociale de la France*, states the following about the crisis of 1846-51:

> Increasing demographic pressure and the ensuing bitter competition for jobs and for the ownership of land, on the one hand, and the decay of rural industries on the other hand, were worsening the living conditions of the lowly people.[27]

And André Armengaud, the major specialist in the demography of the period, has provided the classical description of overpopulation by evoking a rural society that could only support its members if they were supplementing their incomes through participation in rural industries and temporary migration.[28]

The diagnosis of overpopulation, however, must be qualified. There is little evidence that population growth *per se* was hitting some predetermined ceiling of resources, and that living conditions were

worsening during the period as a result. The symbiosis of agriculture
and rural industries represented a traditional and highly rational form
of economic organisation, but it was being superseded in the course of
the nineteenth century. During what has been called the proto-
industrialisation period, the textile industry was decentralised, and
hundreds of other crafts were also practised in cottages and small
factories. The location of industry depended more on the existence of
cheap labour than on the availability of power sources and raw
materials. The advent of new sources of energy, new technologies,
and the importation of raw materials such as cotton, ultimately gave
a competitive advantage to manufacturers. The equation of industrial
production was transformed, and the viability of agriculture was
affected in the process. Although population growth may have made
it more painful, it cannot be blamed for the dislocations of the
Industrial Revolution.

Seasonal migration had also long been an established way of
complementing agricultural resources, above all in the more isolated
mountain regions:

In 1852, the agricultural survey enumerated more than 878,000
seasonal workers employed in the harvest; around 1846, some
20,000 temporary migrants were leaving the Puy-du-Dôme to
carry out non-agricultural activities; and Raoul Blanchard has
estimated that towards the middle of the nineteenth century,
60,000 winter and 30,000 summer seasonal workers were migrating
from the French Alps — without counting those staying away for
more than one season.[29]

The new factor seems to have been the establishment of no-return
migration streams, not only from these regions, but also from all the
agricultural areas. Here too, it appears simplistic to view the process as
a simple reaction to population pressure, although the sustained natural
increase of the population was feeding the migration stream in some
regions, while it was drying up in others for lack of people. From the
middle of the century on, while migration picks up momentum, the
respondents in agricultural surveys are complaining about the lack of
workers and the cost of the labour force. Agricultural salaries and prices
began to rise, and the mid-century appears as a divide separating a period
of stagnation from one of prosperity.[30]

Armengaud has interpreted the flight from the land after 1851 as a
primary consequence of the improvement in agricultural productivity.

According to him, the new technology allowed more product for less
work, and thus liberated workers who found employment in the
urban-industrial sector.[31] The interpretation may be valid in some parts
of France; in Lower Normandy, tillage was converted to pasture and the
dairy economy was less labour-intensive.[32] But it fails to account for
the general rise of agricultural salaries, and for the feeling of
contemporaries that there was a serious shortage of workers on the land.
The agricultural revolution that was taking place then was not
necessarily characterised by less intensive, labour-saving techniques.
The substitution of fodder crops for fallow in the new régimes of
rotation, the shift to plants such as potatoes and sugar beet that had
to be planted in rows into well prepared soil and required careful
weeding — these and other innovations required more rather than less
labour.[33] In other terms, the currents of migration rose at the very time
when agriculture needed more arms. They were the results of economic
forces that were over-riding the demand for labour in rural areas:
industrial salaries were higher than what agriculture could offer.
Migration went, as usual, from low to higher income regions.[34] The
result was that the productivity of labour had to rise in agriculture. The
tightening labour market that resulted from the demand from both the
agricultural and the industrial sector, led to attempts at mechanisation,
or at least to the resort to new tools such as the scythe or the iron
plough, that were more sparing of human labour. In brief, the gains in
productivity were a consequence, rather than a cause, of rural-urban
migration. It has been observed that the decay of cottage industry, far
from making more labour available for agriculture, contributed to the
shortage:

> The need in agriculture was for labor at the harvest peak, not
> year-round; the inroads of modern industries deprived rural
> populations of opportunities to maintain themselves the rest of
> the year, and so threatened the supply of harvest labor. French
> landowners thus found themselves short of labor paradoxically
> just because rural people had lost other work.[35]

The economic forces that were transforming industry and agriculture
were also at work in other European countries. But they were operating
within a different labour market — and with other legal and institutional
constraints. The type of rural society that emerged in France was
unique. It was made out of small peasant proprietors. They were the
ones who stayed behind, while the labour market was progressively

purged of servants and day labourers. The family farm, exploiting its own labour, was a compromise that could preserve a labour-intensive agriculture and pay their workers below the going rates — i.e. what they could have obtained in salaries in the industrial sector — without losing them. This may be why the country that had the lowest population increase on the land in Europe, also kept the highest proportion of its labour force in agriculture.

Slow growth, and the unsatisfied demand for labour, have accounted for another unique characteristic of France among the countries of Europe: the importance of immigration, and the relative insignificance of emigration among Frenchmen. Foreigners have accounted for a substantial proportion of the country's overall growth. It has been estimated that net migration approached 2 million between 1801 and 1911 (with a strong concentration at the end of the period), and exceeded one million between 1921 and 1931. By the later date, foreigners represented 7 per cent of the total population.[36] Italian and Belgian contingents were the largest. The foreign stock became largely assimilated — one million acquired French nationality between 1872 and 1911. The migrants went overwhelmingly into the urban and industrial sectors; but large streams of seasonal labourers were crossing the borders from Flanders in the North for the beet harvest, and from Italy to work in the vineyards.

Conclusion

By the 1930s the fertility of France had ceased to be remarkable by European standards. It rose after the war, and has been declining since 1964 — an experience not unlike that of its neighbours. The demographic originality of France lies in its past. Whereas populations in most European countries were multiplied two or three times between 1800 and 1940, France grew by less than 50 per cent. Jacqueline Beaujeu-Garnier has summarised the distinctive features of the French population in 1968 as follows:

> . . .densities much lower than most of its neighbors, an age distribution remarkable both by the abundance of young and old people, a strongly positive migratory balance and that almost continuously for more than a century and a half, a dominance of life in the countryside and of rural occupations, which is suddenly in the process of disappearing. . .[37]

The economic, political and cultural consequences of France's slow growth have been endlessly debated. No clear relationship can be established between the living standards of various Western nations and their rate of growth. What would have happened to the international prestige, the military power, the colonial expansion of France under different demographic conditions, has been the subject of much speculative literature. This essay must abstain from value judgements. The French were forerunners in adopting low fertility. At the time when their population was lagging behind that of their powerful neighbours, this led to much concern. But the individual, if not collective wisdom of fertility control was eventually recognised by all people of Europe.

Notes

1. For a modern statement of this thesis, see E.A. Wrigley, *Population and History*, World University Library, 1969.

2. See the detailed evidence in Jacques Dupâquier *et al.*, *Paroisses et communes de France, Dictionnaire d'histoire administrative et démographique — Région parisienne*, Editions du CNRS, Paris, 1974, and other volumes in the same series.

3. Emmanuel Le Roy Ladurie, 'L'histoire immobile', *Annales ESC* (29)3, May-June 1974, p.679 ff.

4. Louis Henry and Yves Blayo, 'La population de la France de 1740 a 1860', *Population* (Special Issue: *Démographie Historique*), November 1975, pp.71-122. See also other articles in the same issue.

5. Henry and Blayo, ibid., pp.110-11.

6. Ibid., p.108 ff; also, Yves Blayo, 'La mortalité en France de 1740 a 1829', in *Population*, op.cit., pp.123-42.

7. M. Morineau, *Les faux-semblants d'un démarrage économique: agriculture et démographie en France au XVIIIe siecle*, Cahiers des Annales, no.30, A. Colin, Paris, 1971.

8. Blayo, loc.cit., p.141.

9. Alain Mounier, 'La mortalité', *Population* (Special Issue: *La population de la France*), June 1974, p.107.

10. Ibid., p.130.

11. *Documents statistiques sur la France publiés par le Ministre du Commerce*, Paris, Imprimerie Royale, 1835, p.25 ff.

12. Foundlings and nurslings from Paris are discussed in Etienne van de Walle and Samuel H. Preston, 'Mortalité de l'enfance au XIXe siècle à Paris et dans le département de la Seine', *Population* (29)1, January-February 1974, pp.103-6.

13. Samuel H. Preston and Etienne van de Walle, 'Urban French Mortality in the Nineteenth Century', *Population Studies*, 1978.

14. Henry and Blayo, op.cit., p.109.

15. Ibid., p.107.

16. For Brittany, see Louis Henry and Jacques Houdaille, 'Fécondité des marriages dans le quart nord-ouest de la France de 1670 a 1829', *Population* (28), p.873-922. For Alsace, see Jacques Houdaille, 'La population de Boulay (Moselle) avant 1850', *Population* (22), pp.1055-84. For the Nord, see Raymond Deniel and Louis Henry, 'La population d'un village du nord de la France, Sainghin-en-Melantois, de 1665 à 1851', *Population* (20), pp.563-602.

17. Ansley J. Coale, 'The Decline of Fertility in Europe from the French Revolution to World War II', in S.J. Behrman, Leslie Corsa and Ronald Freedman (eds), *Fertility and Family Planning: A World View*, Ann Arbor, 1969, pp.3-24.

18. John Knodel, 'Family Limitation and the Fertility Transition: Evidence from the Age Patterns of Fertility in Europe and Asia', *Population Studies* (31)2, July 1977, pp.219-49.

19. Louis Henry, 'Evolution de la fécondité en France au XIXe siècle', Notes et documents, *Population* (30), pp.905-14.

20. Jean-Claude Chastelland and Roland Pressat, 'La nuptialité des générations françaises depuis un siècle', *Population* (17), 1962, pp.215-40. For the earlier period: Etienne van de Walle, 'La nuptialité des Françaises avant 1851, d'après l'état civil des décédrés', *Population* (Special Issue: La mesure des phénomènes démographiques. Hommage à Louis Henry), March 1977.

21. For a case study in one part of France, Bearn, see: Pierre Bourdieu, 'Célibat et condition paysanne', *Etudes rurales*, 5-6, 1962, pp.32-135.

22. Henri Mendras, *The Vanishing Peasant*, MIT Press, Cambridge, Mass., 1970, pp.173-5.

23. Paul Hohenberg, 'Migrations et fluctuations démographiques dans la France rurale, 1836-1901', *Annales ESC* (29)2, March-April 1974, p.494.

24. France, *Résultats statistiques du dénombrement de 1891*, Paris, Imprimerie Nationale, 1894, p.61.

25. André Armengaud, 'Industrialisation et démographie dans la France du XIXe siècle', in *L'industrialisation en Europe au XIXe siècle*, Colloques Internationaux du CNRS, Paris, 1972, p.188.

26. Calculated from estimates in E. van de Walle, *The Female Population of France*, pp.125-6.

27. In Fernand Braudel and Ernest Labrousse (eds), *Histoire économique et sociale de la France*, Book III, vol.2, Presses Universitaires de France, Paris, 1976, p.758.

28. See for example Chapter II, 'La rôle de la démographie', in Garonne and Labrousse, op.cit., Book III, vol.1, p.222 ff.

29. André Armengaud, *La population française au XIXe siècle*, 'Que Sais-je?' Presses Universitaires de France, Paris, 1971, p.27.

30. Braudel and Labrousse, vol.2, op.cit., p.746.

31. Ibid., vol.1, p.225.

32. Gabriel Desert, 'Le dépeuplement des campagnes bas-normandes pendant la première moitié du XIXe siècle', in Hommage à Marcel Reinhard, *Sur la population française au XVIIIe et au XIXe siècles*, Société de démographie historique, Paris, 1973, pp.193-214.

33. E.J.T. Collins, 'Labour Supply and Demand in European Agriculture 1800-1880', in E.L. Jones and S.L. Woolf (eds), *Agrarian Change and Economic Development*, Methuen, London, 1969.

34. L.M. Goreux, 'Les migrations agricoles en France depuis un siècle et leur relation avec certains facteurs économiques', *Etudes et Conjoncture*, xi, 1956, pp.327-74.

35. Paul Hohenberg, 'Change in Rural France in the Period of Industrialization, 1830-1914', *The Journal of Economic History*, vol.XXXII, 1, March 1972, p.229.

36. Jaqueline Beaujeu-Garnier, *La population française*, Armand Colin, Paris, p.77.

37. Ibid., p.5.

APPENDIX

Table 3.1: Female Expectation of Life at Birth, France

(1) INED series		(2) van de Walle		(3) Official statistics	
Dates	$\overset{o}{e}_o$	Dates	$\overset{o}{e}_o$	Dates	$\overset{o}{e}_o$
1740-1749	25.7				
1750-1759	28.7				
1760-1769	29.0				
1770-1779	29.6				
1780-1789	28.1				
1790-1799	32.1				
1800-1809	34.9	1801-1810	36.4		
1810-1819	37.5	1811-1820	38.3		
1820-1829	39.3	1821-1830	38.6		
		1831-1840	38.8		
		1841-1850	40.9		
		1851-1860	40.4	1861-1865	40.6
		1861-1870	41.8	1877-1881	43.6
		1871-1880	43.0		
		1881-1890	45.1	1899-1903	48.7
		1891-1900	46.0	1908-1913	52.4
				1920-1923	55.9
				1928-1933	59.0
				1933-1938	61.6
				1946-1949	67.4
				1952-1956	71.2
1960-				1960-1964	74.4
				1966-1970	75.4

Note: $\overset{o}{e}_o$ = life expectancy

Sources: (1) Yves Blayo, 'La mortalité en France de 1740 a 1829', in
Démographie Historique, special issue of *Population*, November 1975, p.141;
(2) Etienne van de Walle, 'La mortalité des départements français ruraux au
XIXe siècle', in Hommage à Marcel Reinhard, *Sur la population française au
XVIIIe et an XIXe siècles*, Société de démographie historique, Paris, 1973,
p.584; (3) Alain Monnier, 'La mortalité', in *La population de la France*,
special issue of *Population*, June 1974, p.107.

Table 3.2: Infant Mortality Rate, France

1802-1811*	188
1864-1868	178
1869-1873	187
1874-1878	164
1879-1883	167
1884-1888	169
1909-1913	120
1929-1933	80

Sources: *Arithmetical mean of 5 years (year X and XI, 1806, 1810 and 1811)
given in Dominique Minet, 'Statistiques de mortalité infantile sous le
Consulat et l'Empire', in Hommage à Marcel Reinhard, *Sur la population
française au XVIIIe et au XIXe siècles*, Société de démographie historique,
Paris, 1973, p.217. Other rates computed from data in *Statistique de la
France, passim.*

Table 3.3: Fertility and Nuptiality Indices, France, 1831 to 1931

	Overall fertility I_f	Marital fertility I_g	Illegitimate fertility I_h	Proportion married I_m
1831	.297	.537	.044	.514
1841	.286	.515	.043	.516
1851	.271	.478	.041	.526
1861	.275	.478	.045	.531
1871	.282	.494	.044	.529
1881	.267	.460	.043	.538
1891	.242	.410	.045	.540
1901	.228	.383	.044	.543
1911	.204	.315	.043	.591
1921	.189	.321	.039	.534
1931	.182	.273	.037	.613

Sources: Etienne van de Walle, *The Female Population of France in the
Nineteenth Century*, Princeton University Press, 1974, p.127. For 1911,
1921 and 1931: computed from official statistics.

4 GERMANY

Robert Lee

Despite the significant contribution of German academics such as
Süssmilch, Jastrow, Neumann and O.K. Roller to the early development
of demography, only in recent years have attempts been made to
reassess the role of the demographic variable in the process of German
economic growth.[1] This rehabilitation of historical demography is long
overdue, given the comprehensive nature of extant archival material,
much of which still awaits analysis.[2] The present contribution will be
concerned primarily with the actual mechanism of population growth
and its social and economic repercussions and will be based on official
statistical series and local monograph studies. Emphasis will be placed
on the causative mechanism behind the initial growth in population,
the late nineteenth-century phenomena of migration and fertility
decline and will be concluded with a postscript on twentieth-century
developments.

Certainly there can be no doubt concerning the overall magnitude
of population growth. Within the territorial borders of 1913, but
excluding Alsace-Lorraine, German population grew from 24,833,396
in 1816 to 60,641,278 by 1913 and 69,314,000 in 1939.[3] However,
the pattern of growth was highly diversified. Between 1816 and 1864
the annual growth rate fluctuated between 2.30 per cent in Pomerania
and 0.37 per cent in Hohenzollern. The first half of the nineteenth
century evinced a high rate of population increase in the eastern
agricultural districts of Prussia, including East and West Prussia,
Pomerania and Brandenburg, slightly lower but significant growth rates
in the nascent industrial centres of Saxony, the Rhineland and
Westphalia, and markedly low rates in the southern states of Bavaria,
Baden and Württemberg (Table 4.1). Although regional differences
were equally prominent in the later nineteenth century, there had
been an important shift in emphasis, with the industrialising regions
becoming the centres of population growth and the eastern territories
losing their earlier predominance. This shift was reinforced by
increasing urbanisation in those areas associated with secondary and
tertiary sector development. The twentieth century was also marked
by equally important trends; the rapid decline in fertility, structural
changes in the age composition of the population, and radical short-

term fluctuations occasioned by the two World Wars.

Regional differences, however, were already apparent in the initial period of growth in the second half of the eighteenth century. Although total population in the German territories is assumed to have risen by 33.3 per cent,[4] the annual growth rate fluctuated between 0.71 per cent in Württemberg (1750-94), 0.69 per cent in Braunschweig (1760-1803) to 0.31 per cent in Saxony (1755-92).[5] These rates were to some extent influenced by expansionist government policies embodying the ideas of Pufendorf and Lau,[6] but they continued to be evident during the opening decades of the nineteenth century. Indeed many territories registered peak growth rates during this period, which were not exceeded until the turn of the nineteenth century. In Bavaria the annual growth rate declined from a peak of 1 per cent (1817-20) to 0.11 per cent (1849-52) and a similar trend was evident in Prussia after the peak figures of 1817/19-1820/22.[7] The causal factors behind these trends, however, are more difficult to delineate. Broadly speaking a distinction can be made between essentially Malthusian explanations which emphasise the inter-related dependence of population growth on underlying economic expansion, and alternative interpretations which stress the exogenous function of the demographic variable.

The endogenous explanation originated in the writings of German neo-Malthusians, such as Weinheld, who posited a positive correlation between population growth and nascent industrialisation.[8] In the majority of states, however, the causative mechanism was agricultural reform, embodied in the Prussian legislation of 1807 and 1811, which in turn was symptomatic of structural changes in the primary sector of a number of individual German states.[9] Increased agricultural output facilitated a fall in both the average age at marriage and infant mortality, which generated a significant increase in the population growth rate.[10] Indeed in Baden and Württemberg the precise chronology of agricultural reform apparently determined the actual timing of population growth.[11] Even where it is admitted that agricultural reform was initially a function of an increased population density on the basis of the Boserup model, as in Lippe and Westphalia, further population growth is viewed in a Malthusian context, irrespective of whether the determining mechanism operated through a reduced death rate or higher fertility.[12]

Certainly economic growth could theoretically have influenced the trend of demographic development in Germany. An increase in the demand for labour, whether as a result of nascent industrialisation or agricultural development, may have affected fertility through facilitating changes in the land-holding system, or by providing additional employment opportunities. If as a result the average marriage age fell, successive periods would produce a greater generation frequency and further increases in total population without ancillary changes in marital fertility. The proportion of unmarried adults, which was frequently very high in pre-industrial economies, would also be reduced.[13]

If the component elements of fertility are examined, however, little support emerges for such an explanation of population growth. Under certain conditions, such as the absence of contraception and a traditionally accepted custom of breast-feeding, the major determinant of fertility would be the woman's age at marriage.[14] There is no concrete evidence of any significant shift in this index, however, during the crucial period of early population growth. The marriage age remained relatively stable, or in certain instances, as in Lower Saxony, Massenhausen and Mittelberg, actually rose (Table 4.2). No significant fall occurred in the majority of states until the final decade of the nineteenth century, when average age at first marriage was still fairly high: 27.6 years in Oldenburg (1855-64); 27.9 in Prussia (1867-9); 26.2 in Saxony (1876-8).[15]

Indeed the failure of industrial growth to activate this mechanism is reinforced by an analysis of marriage age according to occupational classification. The average age of women at first marriage in Prussia in the 1880s in agricultural provinces, such as Bromberg and Posen, was frequently lower than in urban centres.[16] Urban industrial employment for women, which should have provided optimal conditions for the operation of this mechanism, did not have the expected effect, as industrial workers throughout the nineteenth century had a high marriage age.[17] Furthermore the pattern of agricultural development may have had a negative influence, by encouraging a proportional increase in small-holdings. Certainly in agricultural settlements in Hanover and Bavaria and in the village of Göhlen, small-holders tended to marry at a later age than peasants on larger tenements.[18] As a result the negative aspects of a high marriage age, which had already been highlighted by Süssmilch, would not have been removed.

An endogenous rise in population could also have been initiated by an increase in the proportion of adults eventually marrying (I_m)*, which could have been a prime determinant of the crude reproduction rate (CRR).[19] In agricultural regions this would have been facilitated

---

* See Appendix 1, p.177.

by the increased settlement possibilities, initiated according to the Ipsen hypothesis by the land reforms of the early nineteenth century. Although early census data seldom provides a breakdown of population according to marital status, the available evidence fails to indicate any radical alteration in this index until the mid-nineteenth century. In Volkhardinghausen and Kreuth there was a slight deterioration in marriage opportunities between 1760-99 and 1800-19. Only a slight change was evident in Prussia and in Bavaria a rise in celibacy is posited for the early nineteenth century, particularly for tenants of larger agricultural holdings.[20] Indeed the general rate of population growth during this period, as far as this affected specific age groups within the population, may have adversely affected the possibility of marriage, and the situation would not have been improved by the reimposition of restrictive marriage legislation in a number of states in the early decades of the century.[21]

Further confirmation of the failure of economic growth, whether in the primary or secondary sector, to generate a rise in population can be found through an examination of nuptiality and the birth rate. Long-term fluctuations in the marriage rate were not evident between 1750 and 1850 (Table 4.3). If anything there was a downward trend in marriage frequency. Nicolai recorded a fall in the marriage rate in Wittenberg from 8.77 (per 1,000) between 1741 and 1750, to 5.84 (1771-1800) and this negative impression is confirmed in the case of Tiefenbach, Winterthur, Zittow and Oldenburg.[22] Indeed this evidence is derived from a sufficiently diverse selection of localities as to indicate that the downward trend was a common phenomenon in many different parts of Germany in the late eighteenth century. Early nineteenth-century data fails to reveal any change in this trend. Süssmilch had established an average marriage rate of 10.2 and 9.2 respectively for urban and rural districts in the mid-eighteenth century, and only in Friedersdorf (Silesia) of all the regional localities examined, were these rates consistently exceeded in the period prior to 1850. Although the marriage rate was artificially inflated immediately following the Napoleonic Wars, the index remained stable, or even tended to decline somewhat in the 1830s. This pattern was also punctuated by an occasional collapse of the marriage rate to exceptionally low levels, as in Massenhausen (Bavaria) where the rate fell from 9.68 in 1752 to a mere 4.45 in 1820.[23]

As in the case of the I_m index it has been argued that stringent regulations governing marriage and settlement contributed to this phenomenon, particularly in those states where Malthusian ideas were increasingly accepted. But it is unlikely that legislative enactments would have kept marriage rates at a low level in the majority of German states in the early nineteenth century when significant increases in total output and economic productivity were being recorded. In the specific case of Bavaria, where highly restrictive controls over marriage were imposed in the 1820s, there was no positive correlation between changes in official legislation and long-term movements in nuptiality. The lowest marriage rates registered for the whole of the nineteenth century preceded the restrictive legislation of 1825.[24] Furthermore Gugumus' analysis of the pattern of marriage in Saxony in the post-1820 period has revealed that the narrow correlation posited by contemporary authors between agricultural output and the marriage rate did not necessarily exist.[25] Significant growth in the primary sector would not have given rise to a comparative improvement in nuptiality, as the marriage rate was not sensitive in the short term to fluctuations in the price level of such agricultural commodities as potatoes. Although the underlying factors which produced a comparatively low rate of marriage, both in the late eighteenth and early nineteenth century, were clearly complex in nature, the endogenous mechanism was certainly not operative.

As far as the birth rate was concerned a similar element of stability is evident between 1750 and 1850 (Table 4.4). Indeed in certain cases, such as the city of Winterthur and Lübeck, there was a distinct fall in the number of registered births. In Berloch and Meidelstetten (Württemberg) this trend was accentuated in the early nineteenth century. A number of points need to be made in this context. First, in some areas, such as Friedersdorf, Böhringen and the Black Forest, birth rates were already fairly high at the beginning of this period, before any substantial economic growth was readily visible. Secondly, the initial regional differences in birth rates evident in the mid-eighteenth century, were retained throughout this period, despite significant changes in the economic structure of specific areas and settlements. Thirdly, the consistently high birth rates in the Black Forest were achieved in an area almost entirely isolated from the general process of economic change and were determined not by economic factors, but by the relative level of infant mortality. If the endogenous mechanism had in fact been the major determinant of birth rate trends, then short-term changes in the economic structure of individual regions should have produced a corresponding response in natality. This was clearly not the case in Germany during the crucial period of initial population growth.

Indeed, if detailed evidence of birth rate fluctuations in Bavaria is examined, it is clear that there was no improvement in the early nineteenth century. Birth rates in the 1820s and 1830s were particularly low although this cannot be accounted for by such standard factors as a rising proportion of childless marriages, or shifts in the age structure of the population.[26] However, it does provide evidence of family limitation, despite a recent claim that this practice did not become widespread until the end of the nineteenth century.[27] Age-specific marital fertility in the latter decades of the eighteenth century was noticeably lower than the equivalent rates for the period 1800-49. All the traditional criteria, including birth frequency and mean birth intervals, particularly between the penultimate and last birth in completed marriages, reinforce the impression of some form of family limitation. Indeed tentative evidence of a similar practice can be found in other areas of Germany prior to the secular decline in fertility.[28] It is important to note, however, that this evidence of a deliberate non-utilisation of the physical child-bearing capacity of married women stems from a period when economic growth particularly in the primary sector should have encouraged a relaxation of earlier restraints and produced a significant rise in the crude birth rate (CBR).

An explanation of the significant rise in German population in the late eighteenth and early nineteenth centuries must therefore be sought in the operation of the other major demographic variable, namely mortality. Indeed the significance of the fall in mortality, as the prime causal factor behind the overall growth in population in Western Europe during this period, has been generally recognised and such a view is substantially supported by German data (Table 4.5). In the Kurmark and Neumark of Prussia, for example, the death rate declined from 29.4 per 1,000 (1748-93) to 26.3 (1816-49). In Hanover a rate of 29.4 in the late eighteenth century had given way to one of 26.3 by the 1830s. Further evidence of a significant fall in mortality can be found in such diverse localities as Zittow, Treisberg and Finsternthal (Taunus), the city of Winsen and the Elbe island of Finkenwärder.[29] Indeed even in urban areas, where mortality was traditionally higher than surrounding rural districts, a similar trend was visible. In Königsberg, for example, the death rate fell from 35.2 (1700-79) to only 30.4 (1800-03).[30] Although there were isolated exceptions to this general trend, the overall impression remains that a decline in mortality was the most significant factor in determining population growth rates in Germany in the period prior to 1850.

However, if the decline in mortality can be successfully isolated as the causal factor behind population growth, the question still remains as to the specific mechanism which can account for the almost uniform fall in the death rate in areas which on the basis of their economic structure and geographical location were clearly very dissimilar and disparate. A number of different hypotheses have inevitably been advanced, and in order to clarify the precise nature and effect of this important development attention must be focused on each specific hypothesis in turn.

Traditionally gains in life expectancy from the late eighteenth century onwards were attributed to advancements in medical science and improved medical facilities. However, this view has now been subjected to a great deal of trenchant criticism. The major breakthroughs in medical science invariably post-dated the initial mortality decline, and in many cases infrastructural improvements in medical provision may have actually aggravated the death rate.[31] On the other hand there was a marked expansion in medical facilities throughout Germany in the late eighteenth and early nineteenth centuries. The first midwifery school had been founded in Prussia in 1725, and was clearly needed if the comments of contemporaries on both pre- and post-natal care are to be taken seriously. This was followed by eleven similar foundations in other states by 1792.[32] Developments in the field of physiology also facilitated improvements in the quality of instruction.[33] There was an increase in medical personnel in other spheres. The number of doctors in Prussia, for example, rose by 53.2 per cent between 1827 and 1842, and the number of medical assistants in Bavaria increased from 57,884 (1844-5) to 62,847 (1850-51).[34] Indeed this trend was evident in almost every individual state, with the result that by the mid-nineteenth century the overall number of patients per doctor seldom exceeded 4,000 (Table 4.6). There was also a corresponding increase in the provision of hospitals, with new institutions being founded at Frankfurt a.M. (1770), Braunschweig (1780), Göttingen (1780), Kiel (1789) and Halle (1806).[35] The pace of development in the early nineteenth century was even more dramatic, with the number of hospitals in Prussia, for example, rising from 155 in 1822 to 409 (1846) and 684 (1855). The catchment area of each hospital fell accordingly from 75,252 to 24,840 inhabitants.

It is of course difficult to evaluate the precise impact of these institutional changes. Certainly individual hospitals were not hesitant in advancing claims of high recovery rates (Table 4.7) and in Bavaria in 1851-2 only 4.64 per cent of all patients are known to have died during their period of hospitalisation. Recovery chances by the mid-nineteenth century varied from 48.1 per cent for heart diseases to 96.9 per cent for diseases affecting the skin and cellular tissue.[36] Naturally these figures must be viewed with some caution, particularly as terminal cases were frequently discharged prematurely from hospitals, but the records do seem to indicate that conditions were not necessarily as catastrophic as critics of institutional medical reform have made out. Indeed the net effect of improved medicalisation could have been enhanced by a concentration of available resources on the treatment of the economically active age groups within society, including agricultural labourers, factory workers and craftsmen. In Munich in 1853-4 over 40 per cent of the patients treated in the General Hospital were in the age group 21-30 and a similar emphasis in medical treatment appears to have existed in rural areas.[37] To this extent institutional changes in the provision of medicine during this initial period of population growth may have played a minor role in facilitating the decline in mortality, even if the original hypothesis can no longer be fully maintained.

It has also been argued in the context of medical improvements that the central factor affecting mortality was the introduction of smallpox inoculation.[38] Certainly smallpox mortality in the late eighteenth century could often be substantial, constituting approximately 16 per cent of all deaths in Bavaria in 1802, and accounting for an annual loss of 180,000 in Germany as a whole.[39] Equally significant was the positive reaction of individual states to the introduction of compulsory inoculation, with Bavaria (1806), Hesse (1807), Baden (1815) and Württemberg (1817) in the forefront. But once again this hypothesis is open to criticism and in most areas of Germany there is little evidence to support the claims made for smallpox inoculation. Mortality from this disease was particularly prominent in the eighteenth century among younger age groups, with the highest age-specific death rate in Königsberg in the age group 1-2 years, followed by infants under six months of age.[40] Unfortunately infant mortality, as a component of the overall death rate, remained relatively high during this period and it can only be surmised that infants who would have succumbed to smallpox in the late eighteenth century now died in the post-inoculation period from other diseases. Furthermore it has been estimated that in order for inoculation to have had a major effect on mortality, it would have had to constitute up to 25 per cent of all fatalities. Although there were regular outbreaks in many parts of Germany in the late eighteenth century, smallpox tended to follow a three- to five-year cycle, so that even if inoculation had been optimally effective, the complete eradication of the disease would still not have had a sufficiently dramatic impact on mortality to account for the recorded fall in the death rate in various German provinces. However, the effectiveness of inoculation was in any case jeopardised by administrative weaknesses and inadequate financial provision and fresh legislation was needed in the 1860s in a number of states to tighten up the existing system.

It has also been argued that the fall in mortality was facilitated by the adoption of effective quarantine measures, which prevented any further outbreak of epidemic plague after 1750 and also meant that traditional subsistence crises were no longer accompanied by inflated mortality.[41] In Germany the centralised nature of state power provided an effective basis for the implementation of such measures and many states, such as Saxony, Prussia and Bavaria, did attempt to isolate outbreaks of epidemic disease. The last outbreak of plague in Saxony was reported in 1680-84, and the 1710-11 outbreak was only severe in certain eastern provinces of Prussia.[42] One of the central duties of the 'health police' (*Gesundheitspolizei*) was to report the occurrence of local epidemics and to take necessary steps to restrict population movement in order to minimise the latent danger of contagious infection. Clearly such co-ordinated activities could have helped to reduce the geographical virulence of specific diseases, but the impact of quarantine measures was probably mitigated by the continuing inefficiency of the local bureaucracy. There is little evidence that such measures effectively limited the spread of typhus during the crisis years of 1770-72, nor the initial cholera outbreak in the early 1830s.[43] In the case of the Reichstadt Kempten the eventual disappearance of major epidemics in the late eighteenth century, irrespective of the precise cause, did not initiate a new balance between births and deaths.[44] But perhaps the crucial fact which this hypothesis fails to explain, is the long-term divergence in regional mortality trends. If quarantine measures were implemented by most German states, why was there still a significant difference in regional mortality by the mid-nineteenth century?

Finally, attention must be focused on the hypothesis, formulated by Mckeown, which emphasises the importance of a general increase in food supplies, as a result of the increasingly intensive system of agricultural cultivation.[45] Agricultural improvement laid the basis for long-term population growth by facilitating a reduction in the number of deaths from a broad group of infectious diseases which were sensitive to nutrition levels and living standards as a whole. Theoretically this hypothesis should also be applicable to Germany during the early period of population growth, as agricultural output improved significantly. On the one hand there was a marked expansion in the cultivable area, which in the case of the northeastern provinces of Prussia (East Prussia, Pomerania and Posen) witnessed an increase from 3.2 to 7.4 million hectares. On the other hand there was a widespread intensification of cultivation using the methods usually associated with the 'agricultural revolution'. The net impact on the total output level of the German primary sector was considerable (Table 4.8), producing an increase of 135 per cent between 1816 and 1865 for all agricultural commodities, or an annual growth of 1.3 per cent between 1800 and 1883.[46] Although there were regional differences, almost every area of Germany participated in this process of agricultural expansion. In the period 1800-1850/51, for example, grain production rose by an estimated 62 per cent in Württemberg, 70.3 per cent in Prussia, 108 per cent in Saxony and 210 per cent in Bavaria.[47] This should have influenced significantly age-specific mortality rates and allowed the postulated mechanism of population growth to have operated.

The application of this hypothesis to German data, however, raises a number of problems. Within Germany there were a number of regions where an improvement in primary sector production was not accompanied by a fall in mortality. Despite an increased output of both grain and livestock during the first half of the nineteenth century, the death rate in Bavaria remained above the national average. A crude death rate (per 1,000) of 43.5 in the Landgericht Freising in 1833 had only fallen marginally to 43.4 by 1840. On a more localised level life expectancy for adults continued to decline during the early nineteenth century until the marital cohort of the 1840s, with the lowest life expectancy being registered in the decade 1830-39 at 35.0 years.[48] A similar situation existed in the eastern provinces of Prussia, where grain production increased dramatically, partly as a result of the 1807 and 1811 reforms, and partly due to buoyant foreign demand for German grain.[49] Mortality, however, showed no sign of declining (Table 4.9) and life expectancy at birth, even after the initial phase of agricultural expansion, was still considerably lower than in many other German districts. The absence of a correlation between increased agricultural output and falling mortality is also evident in Württemberg. Despite an increase of 62 per cent in output (1804-1852/5) the death rate actually rose from 28.96 (per 1,000) in the late 1820s to 31.9 in the 1850s. It could of course be argued that the main beneficiary of higher agricultural output in the eastern provinces was not the indigenous peasantry, but the growing urban population in industrialising countries such as England, but neither Bavaria nor Württemberg participated actively in the international export trade and relative price movements in all these three areas indicate that some of the benefits of increased production did in fact percolate down to the local population, without initiating a significant fall in mortality.

A number of factors reduced the possible impact of increased agricultural production on the relative mortality level. An intensification of cultivation inevitably required a higher input of both labour and capital. Indeed by the mid-nineteenth century many agricultural producers were suffering from increased indebtedness. The value of agricultural mortgages in Prussia rose from 224 million Marks in 1820 to 346 million by 1852, and in Württemberg the number of registered bankruptcies in the primary sector increased from 1,062 in 1840 to 8,813 by 1854.[50] On the other hand the increased labour requirements of agriculture were partly resolved by a more effective exploitation of existing resources, particularly on large-scale estates following the process of peasant emancipation. The small-scale producer, however, was frequently forced to increase his own level of labour input and that of his immediate family in order to keep pace with the labour-intensive trend of agricultural reform.

Given the need to increase both capital investment and labour input, the benefits of any improvement in agricultural output would have been far more differentiated than the original hypothesis has allowed. A number of factors would have determined the actual operation of this mechanism of population growth. First the benefits of intensified production would have been dependent on the pattern of land-holding. In such areas as Lower Saxony where there was a broad section of substantial peasant holdings with an effective control over the basic factors of production, the indigenous population would almost certainly have benefited from increased agricultural output and an expansion in the nutrition base. In direct contrast small-scale producers in parts of South Germany would have been placed under considerable strain through participation in the general process of agricultural reform. Second the net return on increased investment would have been jeopardised by contemporary price movements for agricultural commodities. Price indices in the early nineteenth century, partly as a result of increased total output, remained relatively stable. In Bavaria, for example, the index for wheat had only risen from a base of 100 (1750-59) to 106 in the 1830s, and throughout many areas of Germany the 1820s and early 1830s were characterised by the classical symptoms of overproduction.[51] As a result important sections of rural society, such as small-scale producers, may not have benefited in the long term from the process of agricultural reform, which may well have contributed to a deterioration in their relative economic position. Significantly the broad group of infectious diseases which were supposedly sensitive to the nutrition level did not undergo any decline in virulence in Bavaria during this critical period, although further research is necessary to establish whether this was a more general phenomenon.[52]

Indeed the limitations of this hypothesis clearly emerge from an examination of infant mortality, which remained a major component of total mortality until the late nineteenth century.[53] The available data does not reveal any significant improvement in this index during the early nineteenth century, but rather a deterioration in Prussia (1816/20-1851/60), Saxony (1831/40-1871/80) and Bavaria (1831/40-1861/70) (Tables 4.10, 4.11). Indeed many of the regions which registered an improvement in agricultural production visibly failed to benefit from a fall in infant mortality. This was the case in Upper and Lower Bavaria and Swabia, together with the eastern provinces of East and West Prussia and Posen, which consistently suffered from higher infant mortality rates than the western territories of Westphalia and Rhineland (Table 4.12). Indeed areas in northern Germany where the rise in primary sector output was well below the level achieved in the eastern provinces also had a lower infant mortality. In Oldenburg, for example, a rate of 12.3 (per 100 live births) was recorded between 1855 and 1864 and the comparative rate in Schleswig-Holstein was 13.5 (1855-9).[54]

Although the rate of infant mortality was influenced by a number of complex factors, including the proficiency of the midwifery service and the ethnic mix of the indigenous population, the major factor was the method of infant feeding.[55] Certainly parental income levels did not play a significant role, either in Prussia or certain Bavarian estates.[56] Indeed in Göhlen and Lohmen (Mecklenburg) small-holders and craftsmen frequently had a lower infant mortality rate between 1750 and 1875 than families of larger tenements. The reasons for the failure to breast-feed children are difficult to establish,[57] but there can be little doubt that this factor was responsible for the variegated infant mortality pattern throughout Germany. The substitutes for natural milk were frequently lethal, ranging from a mixture of biscuits and sugar to poppy seed.[58] However, there was no correlation between the practice of breast-feeding and regional levels of agricultural output. Indeed the average duration of breast-feeding tended to decline along a north-south axis,[59] and as a result a fundamental determinant of total mortality would have maintained an independent role unaffected by the pace of agricultural reform, or even improvements in relative living standards. Furthermore the rise in illegitimacy in many parts of Germany in the early nineteenth century would not have improved the situation, as illegitimate infant mortality was invariably higher than that of legitimate offspring.[60]

By the mid-nineteenth century, however, death rates had fallen quite significantly, and they were to remain stable or even to decline further in the course of the following decades. The main beneficiaries of this trend were individuals in the younger age groups 1-2, 2-3, 10-19 and 20-29 (Table 4.13), where the highest gains in life expectancy were recorded. The net result of this mechanism was a significant increase in the proportion of total population in the economically active age group 20-39. In Prussia, for example, this age group underwent an increase of 46:68 per cent between 1816 and 1840, and one of 58.90 per cent between 1816 and 1858, and evidence from other states confirms the fact that the crucial expansion in this age group was primarily a phenomenon of the first half of the nineteenth century.[61] Still-births and perinatal mortality, on the other hand, show no significant changes during this period. Pregnancy wastage in Baden in the late eighteenth century had fluctuated around 5 per cent of all births and in Durlach the corresponding rate had been 3.28 per cent. By the end of the nineteenth century, however, the proportion of still-births had not noticeably altered, varying from 3.4 per cent in Saxony, 3.3 per cent in Prussia, 3.2 per cent in Württemberg, 3.1 per cent in Bavaria to 2.7 per cent in Baden. Indeed as far as Prussia was concerned there had been a slight deterioration in this index in the early nineteenth century, until a maximum rate of 4.12 per cent had been reached between 1861 and 1870.[62]

Despite the general downward trend in mortality, however, distinct regional variations continued to exist. Infant mortality continued to be disproportionally high in both Bavaria and Württemberg, and within Prussia the death rate for this important age group between 1876 and 1895 still fluctuated between 27.7 (per 100 live births) in Liegnitz and 10.5 in Aurich. By and large infant mortality was still above average in the eastern provinces and below average in the industrialising areas of Westphalia, the Rhineland and Hanover (Table 4.12). Indeed the high variance in the infant mortality rate became even more accentuated towards the very end of the nineteenth century and was still to some extent visible in the overall death rate for the age group 0-15

(Table 4.14). Regional differences, however, were not so clearly marked in relation to the central age group 15-45, and the overall similarity in adult death rates is equally visible in extant life tables. However, given the overall importance of infant mortality, the crude death rate still varied considerably by the end of this period. Death rates were relatively high in Bavaria, Silesia, East and West Prussia, at least in comparison with the below average rates recorded in Schleswig-Holstein, Hanover, Oldenburg and Hesse-Nassau. Equally the death rate in many urban centres was often lower than in surrounding rural districts, but as a result of the favourable age structure of migrants, rather than better living conditions.

It is important to note, however, that given a comparative stability in the birth rate, the overall level of mortality from the early nineteenth century onwards would have been sufficient to generate an annual surplus of births, except for a small number of years characterised by isolated epidemics or severely adverse economic conditions. Indeed given the deferred adoption of widespread family limitation until the late nineteenth century, the cumulative tendency of the death rate to fall would have magnified the overall rate of population growth during this period. Social welfare legislation towards the end of the century, including the wider availability of *Krankenkassen* (health insurance agencies) in the 1850s and 1860s could have further contributed to the overall decline in mortality, and thereby reinforced the general process of population growth.

Information on the cause of death by disease is only available on a national basis for the latter decades of the nineteenth century, although sufficient data does exist for earlier periods for reasonable conclusions to be drawn on the nature of long-term trends. Apart from illnesses linked with infancy, the greatest cause of death throughout most of the nineteenth century was tuberculosis. Even as late as 1892 this disease accounted for 259.1 deaths per 100,000 inhabitants (Table 4.15). This disease is traditionally linked to the adverse effects of increasing industrialisation, but even in such a primarily agricultural region as Bavaria tuberculosis mortality continued to rise during the nineteenth century, finally reaching a peak of 327 deaths (per 100,000 inhabitants) in 1881-90. Furthermore it was equally prominent in both urban and rural areas.[63] The final decline in the incidence of tuberculosis towards the very end of the century was attributed to a significant rise in real wages and to the foundation of a large number of sanatoria.[64] However, the very fact that tuberculosis mortality in the early 1890s was hardly dissimilar in incidence from what it had been in Breslau in 1687-91 highlights a further crucial weakness in the Mckeown hypothesis which seeks to find an explanation for the general fall in mortality in increased agricultural output. As in the case of infant mortality, the virulence of tuberculosis remained comparatively unaffected by the substantial increase in total primary sector output.

Nevertheless although controversy still shrouds any discussion of the secular decline in the death rate in Germany, the solution clearly cannot be sought in a simple monocausal explanation. None of the major hypotheses is sufficiently supported by available data, and it may well be that other factors such as climatic changes and a shift in the balance between the virulence of specific diseases and the relative immunity of the human host were more important in accounting for the secular decline in mortality. On the other hand there can be no doubt that the fall in mortality was the prime factor which influenced the overall rate of population growth. Indeed the evidence provided by Köllmann of an excess supply of labour in the opening decades of the nineteenth century only serves to emphasise the exogenous nature of population growth, and its strict independence of either increased agricultural output, or nascent industrialisation.[65]

However, given that the decline in the crude death rate (CDR) was an exogenous variable, both the chronology and nature of this trend would have had a significant impact on the process of German economic growth. In the first case it increased the supply of labour, particularly of those individuals in the active age groups. By the 1890s 57.3 per cent of the total population were aged between fifteen and sixty years, and in certain regions, such as Saxony, the proportion was marginally higher.[66] As a result during a crucial period of economic development labour costs remained comparatively low. By the 1840s between 50 and 60 per cent of the German population may well have been living on the bare limits of subsistence. In Bavaria in the 1820s over 26 per cent of the population are estimated to have earned less than 200 Gulden annually, at a time when the average maintenance costs for a single child were well over 40 Gulden.[67] This in turn affected the viability of labour-intensive innovation, particularly in the primary sector. Secondly, in those areas where the natural productivity of the soil was limited, the independent growth of population encouraged the development of domestic craft industries as an alternative or subsidiary source of income supply and this diversification process itself played an important role in the gradual emergence of centralised industrial production.[68] Finally the highest rates of population growth were frequently recorded in the first few decades of the nineteenth century.

For the German Empire as a whole growth rates had peaked at 1.43 per cent p.a. between 1816 and 1820 and this figure was not to be surpassed until the first five-year period in the twentieth century. This initial burst, however, would have had a lasting effect on the economy, by influencing such variables as average savings, the relative productivity of investment, as well as the size of the labour force. Equally the high rates of population growth in the late nineteenth and early twentieth centuries may well have provided a further impulse for technical innovation, via the mechanism of increased demand and it has in fact been claimed that 'nearly half of the German capital goods industry has so far been entirely dependent upon the increase in population'.[69] Furthermore exogenous population growth may well have generated waves of population-sensitive and other types of capital formation, the differential productivity of which would in turn have influenced the rate of expansion of aggregate supply and thus of economic growth in general.[70]

But if population growth in the nineteenth century had a direct bearing on economic development, its social ramifications at least in the short term were not as significant. It has recently been argued that one of the immediate results of the interaction of population growth, which inevitably led to individual states attempting to control marriage and settlement, and economic change during the early nineteenth century, was a marked rise in illegitimacy.[71] Certainly many areas of Germany showed a significant rise in illegitimacy (Table 4.16), but it is important to note that this was often most apparent in such areas as Bavaria where both the rate of population growth and the 'modernisation' of the economy was less substantial than in other parts of the country. Indeed the social phenomenon of rising illegitimacy rates was only marginally influenced by population growth, and more a response to a relaxation of legal constraints and an improvement in real wage levels for domestic and agricultural servants. Nor did this change amount to a sexual revolution in German society.[72] Equally the traditional pattern of the sex ratio does not appear to have been altered as a result of population growth. Although there was a slight increase in the proportion of women in German society between 1852 and 1861, the earlier balance was largely retained. Indeed despite the secular movement in the CDR, this did not affect the differential mortality between the two sexes. In Bavaria between 1817-18 and 1838-9 life expectancy for men and women had stood at 31.27 and 34.16 years respectively, and by the 1880s and 1890s a similar pattern was evident. Overall mortality for men may have fallen to 26.9 (per

1,000) in 1876-85, but the equivalent rate for women was still significantly lower at 23.7.[73] Indeed this element of stability in trends which could have affected the social composition of Germany was equally evident in relation to average family size, at least until the onset of the secular decline in fertility in the late nineteenth century. There is no evidence of extended family structures either in the late eighteenth or early nineteenth centuries. In Schleusingen average family size in the period 1700-1846 stood at 4.7 and in Bavaria in 1810-11 the figure fluctuated between 3.5 and 5.5 according to administrative area.[74] If gains in child and adult mortality positively influenced family size, this was counterbalanced by the tendency of infant mortality to increase over the same period. Furthermore despite extensive population growth there is clear evidence that social attitudes were slow to change. The catchment area for marriage partners did not significantly alter during the early decades of the nineteenth century and attitudes to professional medication remained cautious and reserved.[75] The social framework of Germany was therefore not seriously affected by the initial growth in population.

However, by the mid-nineteenth century population growth had in fact produced a major socio-economic phenomenon. The scale of German overseas migration cannot be doubted (Table 4.17). Migration in the eighteenth century had still been largely determined by ideological factors, but with the easing of restrictions on migration in the Act of Confederation (1815)[76] the pattern of migration underwent a significant change. Although pull factors, such as the Californian gold discoveries of the 1840s, were often important, migration was increasingly determined by the push mechanism generated by a deteriorating economic position.[77] Of crucial significance in this context was the population growth rate which in the early decades of the nineteenth century frequently exceeded the growth of GNP, as well as the pattern of inheritance in the southwestern areas of Germany, where continuous subdivision had already led to overpopulation by the beginning of this period. The interaction of these two factors can be seen in the emigration statistics. Peak emigration figures were recorded in 1816-17, 1847 and 1853, and on each occasion corresponded either with an acute harvest failure or potato blight. A high proportion of all emigrants during this early period came from the southwest, reaching 98.9 per cent in 1830-34 and remaining fairly significant in the 1850s at 24.9 per cent.[78] By the mid-1860s, however, a shift in the migration pattern can be detected. The period of rapid development in the primary sector of the northeastern provinces, such as Brandenburg,

Posen and East Prussia, with its attendant demand for labour, was now over and the underlying structural weaknesses in agriculture were severely exposed during the 1870s when increased overseas competition produced a dramatic fall in the internal price level for agricultural commodities. As a result agricultural labourers were increasingly forced to emigrate (Table 4.18). At the same time the relatively large number of emigrants from the western areas of Germany can be explained by the fact that industrial expansion was not yet sufficiently advanced to provide adequate employment opportunities for the growing population. However, from the 1870s onwards GNP grew at a faster rate than population and the incentive to emigrate for economic reasons was gradually reduced.

The unprecedented scale of emigration during the nineteenth century generated a great deal of controversy, with Burgdörfer estimating the net loss to Germany at 200,000 million Marks.[79] Certainly the high proportion of males among total emigrants affected the sex ratio and the prominence of the younger age groups (20-29, 30-39) would have impinged on the overall age structure of the remaining population. By and large, however, although the impact of cyclical emigration on the home market and domestic investment is still relatively unclear, in the context of relative overpopulation prior to the period of industrial take-off in the 1860s and 1870s, overseas migration effectively minimised the social costs which would have been activated by rising unemployment, pauperism and class antagonism. In areas where there was a disproportional loss of active men, emigration would have stimulated the trend towards the full-time employment of women in the labour force and even during the period from 1871 to 1910 external migration only reduced the natural rate of population growth by 10 per cent.

The pattern of overseas migration, however, was only part of the increasing locational mobility of the German population. Although internal migration had taken place in the past, largely in connection with state-supported colonisation schemes,[80] it became particularly noticeable in the latter decades of the nineteenth century. In 1907, from a total population of 60.4 million, 29 million (or 48.0 per cent) had been involved in some form of internal migration, whether short-distance or inter-state. To a large extent this significant growth in internal migration was a function of underlying economic changes and rapid industrialisation, which led to significant shifts in the sectoral distribution of employment. In 1882, 42.5 per cent of the total population were still dependent on agriculture and only 35 per cent on mining and industry, and a further 22 per cent on trade, transport and service industries. By 1907 the proportional distribution had altered significantly to 28.6 per cent, 42.8 per cent and 28.6 per cent respectively. Indeed extensive industrialisation in Germany between the foundation of the Empire (1870-71) and 1913-14 was to a large extent facilitated by the high regional mobility of the population, which meant that the growing labour requirements of heavy industry could be met at a low opportunity cost. As early as the 1871 census the pattern of extensive migration to the major cities, particularly to the Ruhr complex, was already apparent. For example, 23.78 per cent of the population of the mining town of Bochum were recent immigrants and in Hamburg, Germany's principal port, 38.3 per cent of the population came from other German states.[81] Although local short-distance migration was very common, the most significant single facet of this phenomenon was the extensive migration from the eastern provinces to the expanding industries of the Ruhr in the 1880s and 1890s, which was to some extent linked with infrastructural improvements in the transport system.[82] In the period 1860-1914 approximately 15-16 million individuals migrated within Germany across state boundaries.

The factors that influenced the migration pattern were often connected with the system of land-holding. In those areas of the eastern provinces where small peasant tenements predominated and compensatory industrial employment was not available the highest migration rates were recorded. Internal migration was particularly extensive as well in the Schiefergebirge, the Hunsrück, the western Eifel, Westerwald and the Kreis Wipperfürth, where similar factors were operative.[83] However, it was also symptomatic of the general mobility of the population as a whole during this period that inter-urban migration was also significant. In the case of Halle in 1899, for example, 65.8 per cent of total immigrants had come from other urban areas and not directly from agriculture, and the average length of domicile for all migrants in Berlin (1871-1910) only amounted to two years.[84]

From a demographic point of view extensive migration had substantial repercussions. The fact that the younger active age groups were prominent in internal migration increased the disparity in the age structure between expanding and declining areas. In 1900, for example, males between sixteen and thirty years of age constituted 26.3 per cent of the population of Rhineland-Westphalia, but only 21.7 per cent in the northeastern provinces of Prussia, where emigration had been considerable. Equally the higher relative mobility of men affected the sex ratio. In the northeastern provinces of Prussia there were 107 women per 100 men, whereas the corresponding figures in West Germany and in the Empire as a whole stood at 97 and 103 respectively. In certain areas, such as the Walsertal, where male emigration had been fairly continuous during the late nineteenth century, the inevitable result was a local surplus of women.[85] On the other hand the increasing disproportional representation of the younger age groups in the urban areas also meant that mortality tended to decline at a faster rate in cities than in the surrounding rural areas. In Prussia in 1890-91 the death rate (per 1,000) for migrants in the age group 15-20 stood at 3.5, but at 4.3 for the indigenous population of the same age, which would also seem to indicate that migrants as a whole were healthier than the existing urban population. In the economic sphere large-scale internal migration was vital to the growth process, in that it transferred an important factor of production to those areas with a high capacity for expansion, although from the point of view of domestic demand the effect of cyclical waves of immigration into expanding urban centres has yet to be effectively examined. As a result the urban population of Germany grew dramatically in the three or four decades prior to 1913 (Table 4.19), although in the early years of the twentieth century new migrants were increasingly directed into the independent suburbs of such cities as Berlin, Essen, Cologne, Hanover and Dresden. If only 23.7 per cent of the total population in 1871 had lived in urban areas of over 5,000 inhabitants, by 1910 this had risen to 48.8 per cent. The number of large cities (with over 100,000 inhabitants) had risen from four to forty-eight. The locational distribution of Germany's population had therefore been fundamentally altered within a very short space of time.

From a sociological point of view the direct effect of rapid urbanisation is more difficult to chart. It has been argued, for example, that migrants from the eastern provinces tended to retain their traditional value systems, including a strong religiosity and behavioural norms consolidated in folk tales and children's games. However the rapid pace of migration, accompanied by social mobility and a pattern of short-term domicile, may well have prevented the emergence of social or cultural diversity in urban centres affected by extensive immigration.[86] On the other hand there is evidence that a larger proportion of migrants achieved higher social positions, as civil servants and independent producers, than the indigenous population, which may have aggravated any initial barriers between the two groups.

Of crucial importance in the process of demographic transition was the secular decline in fertility towards the end of the nineteenth century. Although fertility in 1900 was still quite high, with two provinces within 10 per cent of the Hutterite schedule, between 1871 and the early 1930s overall fertility (I_f)* fell by 60 per cent, marital fertility by 65 per cent and illegitimate fertility by 54 per cent. I_f per 1,000 women between the ages of 15 and 45 years fell from 159 (= 100) in 1876-85 to 128.0 (80.5) in 1910-11 and to 90 (56.6) by 1922. Furthermore this remarkable change cannot be attributed to any alteration in nuptiality, as the proportion of women in the fertile age group actually married increased during this period. A wide variety of factors has been offered as possible explanations of this phenomenon, including physical degeneration, rationalisation of sexual activities, an increase in venereal disease and the impact of urbanisation.[87] It is clearly difficult to separate the individual influences acting on fertility and particularly on marital fertility during a period of substantial economic change, but it would appear from Knodel's analysis that the earliest instance of a 10 per cent decline in fertility is to be found in 1879, with the last area of Germany undergoing the same process in 1914.[88] If the traditional socio-economic variables affecting fertility are examined, however, the complex nature of this phenomenon becomes relatively clearer. In the first instance increasing urbanisation does not appear to have played a fundamental causative role. Although fertility decline often started in urban areas, it was closely followed by a parallel trend in surrounding rural districts and the urban-rural differential which continued to exist in the 1930s was at a substantially lower level of fertility. Secondly, although differences did exist in the level of marital fertility according to profession before the onset of the secular decline, it is unlikely that shifts in the occupational structure could account for this trend, as all economic groups underwent the same basic process. Indeed factory workers, on the basis of Prussian data for 1895-1906, were relatively slow to adopt the new fertility pattern (Table 4.20), and only the more 'privileged' elements within the urban proletariat were in the forefront of the decline in fertility.[89] Thirdly, although there were significant differences in the rate at which marital fertility declined according to religious denomination, with the CBR of Catholics remaining significantly higher than that of both Protestants and particularly Jewish families, all three denominations were affected by the secular decline. In Bavaria which remained staunchly Catholic throughout this

* See Appendix 1, p.177.

period the index of marital fertility (I_g)* fell from 0.84 (1871) to 0.60 (1910).[90] It was recognised even by contemporaries, however, that an improvement in infant mortality, by affecting domestic arrangements and through the operation of lactation and postpartum amenorrhea, may have had a negative impact on fertility.[91] Significantly during the period of fertility decline infant mortality also fell by 70 per cent, which contrasts sharply with the resilience of this rate in the central decades of the nineteenth century. Although there would appear to be close links between the two phenomena, with areas of high infant mortality such as Bavaria and other parts of South Germany witnessing an earlier and more rapid decline in fertility, further research needs to be undertaken to determine whether the relationship was causal or not. Certainly the gradual decline in illegitimacy may have reinforced this trend, as infant mortality was invariably higher for children born out of wedlock and in Braunschweig, for example, the fall in illegitimate conceptions preceded the decline in fertility.[92] It is equally plausible that improved educational provisions may have affected this secular decline, by producing a change in tastes and altering the apparent trade-off between children and consumer goods which were now becoming more readily available. Furthermore a control of fertility would have required a more rational appraisal of optimal utility which education may well have provided. A positive correlation, however, is once again difficult to ascertain, as fertility was to decline initially in such areas as Bavaria, where educational provisions were still inadequate in the mid-nineteenth century, rather than in parts of Prussia, where literacy levels had improved at a comparatively earlier date.[93] Finally rapid industrial expansion may have contributed to the secular fall in fertility, particularly when it is borne in mind that GNP rose by approximately 500 per cent between 1851 and 1913. Fertility levels were directly influenced by such indices as relative savings and the proportional role of the secondary sector, although other aspects of 'modernisation', such as the level of female employment, do not appear to have played a causal role. However despite the complexity of this phenomenon, two aspects clearly stand out. On the one hand the secular decline in fertility was symptomatic of a wider awareness of contraceptive techniques, which involved a more general acceptance of traditional methods on a more than localised scale, or the application of new methods of contraception. On the other hand the reduction in I_f was accomplished in a remarkably short time span.

---

*See Appendix 1, p.177.

As far as twentieth-century developments were concerned, the post
1918-19 period witnessed the continued operation of trends which had
been largely apparent in the pre-war period. The immediate short-term
losses occasioned by the war, however, were considerable, including 2.4
million military casualties, an increased level of civilian deaths (0.3
million) largely as a result of the influenza epidemic of 1918-19, as well
as a lower population growth rate due to deferred conceptions. Although
the war years 1915-18 witnessed a net fall in population, the expansion
and reallocation of war industries reinforced the pattern of internal
migration, with certain areas such as the Ruhr and the Neckarkreis
(Württemberg) benefiting substantially from this factor. However, the
Treaty of Versailles brought about a loss of 6,476,000 inhabitants in
territories now ceded from the Empire, and the revival of emigration in
the immediate post-war years also helped to minimise the pace of
internal population growth. Both the birth and death rates continued to
decline. In the latter case this can be attributed to further improvements
in medical and social welfare services and a rise in real income levels.
Life expectancy at birth which had stood at only 35.6 and 38.5 years
respectively for men and women in 1871-80 rose to 67.4 and 73.5 years
by 1967-9. The decline in natality, on the other hand, was aggravated in
the late 1920s and 1930s by the international economic crisis, which was
felt particularly severely in Germany (Table 4.21). However, the Nazi
seizure of power in 1933, together with the cyclical upswing in the
economy which was already underway in 1932, brought this trend to
an end. Indeed the National Socialist regime was able to raise the birth
rate through the mechanism of marriage loans (*Ehestandsdarlehen*),
increased child and maternity allowances, and a restructuring of the
taxation system in 1936 in favour of large families. The birth rate rose
from 14.7 (per 1,000) in 1933, to 18.0 (1934) and 18.9 (1935) and in
individual localities the increase was even more significant, with the
equivalent rate for the Landkreis Wittersberg (Bezirksamt Halle), for
example, rising from 14.6 (1933) to 21.7 (1935). The upward trend was
reinforced by a further fall in the average age at first marriage and by
ideological pressures exercised by such Nazi organisations as *Mutter und
Kind.* At the same time it is arguable that a large part of this revival in
natality could be attributed to the economic recovery of Germany
which was part of a general cyclical pattern and clearly underway before
1933. Indeed far from restoring the primacy of family life as far as
women were concerned and reviving the purity of the Germanic race,
the large-scale rearmament programme initiated by the National
Socialists had the reverse effect as far as demographic aspects were

concerned. The increasing demand for labour by the late 1930s had been met not only with a rise in the number of women in full-time employment, but also by a new wave of foreign immigration into the Empire. In 1937-8, for example, 120,000 Italians and 77,000 Poles emigrated into Germany.

Indeed there were underlying trends in the inter-war years which continued to operate almost exogenously. With the continued fall in the birth rate the age structure of the population underwent further changes, with a proportional increase in the active age groups (15-65). There was a significant increase in the utilisation of female labour. Although the pace of assimilation into the work force was governed by the underlying economic structure of each specific region, with the prominence of textile production in Saxony, for example, facilitating the early employment of women,[94] this process had been speeded up during this period by rationalisation within the German secondary sector, where increasing mechanisation created a growing demand for female semi-skilled and unskilled labour. Irrespective of the Nazi attempts to remove women from the work force, the economic pressures of the 1930s and the growth of a war economy only served to reinforce the long-term trend. Economic necessity had triumphed over political ideology.

The precise inter-relationship between population development, economic growth and social change is clearly difficult to define and its multifarious aspects cannot be entirely covered in a brief contribution. Nevertheless the importance of population growth should not be underestimated. Most demographic indices in Germany preceded economic trends and this was particularly evident in relation to mortality.[95] By the mid-nineteenth century Germany was increasingly integrated into the developing capitalist economic structure and it has even been stated that the resulting cyclical pattern of development which was to influence substantially the process of industrial growth was 'urged on by an extraordinary and heavy increase in population'.[96] By the early twentieth century Germany had effectively passed through the three stages of the 'vital revolution' and its pattern of demographic development was now to be characterised by both low fertility and mortality levels. Equally important, however, was the gradual erosion of regional differentials. Extensive fluctuations in the basic indices of fertility, infant mortality and illegitimacy, which had been a pronounced facet of the early decades of the nineteenth century, tended to disappear over time. If differentials continued to exist, as figures on net fertility rates for 1920 would seem to indicate,[97]

Figure 4.1: Administrative Areas of Germany, 1900

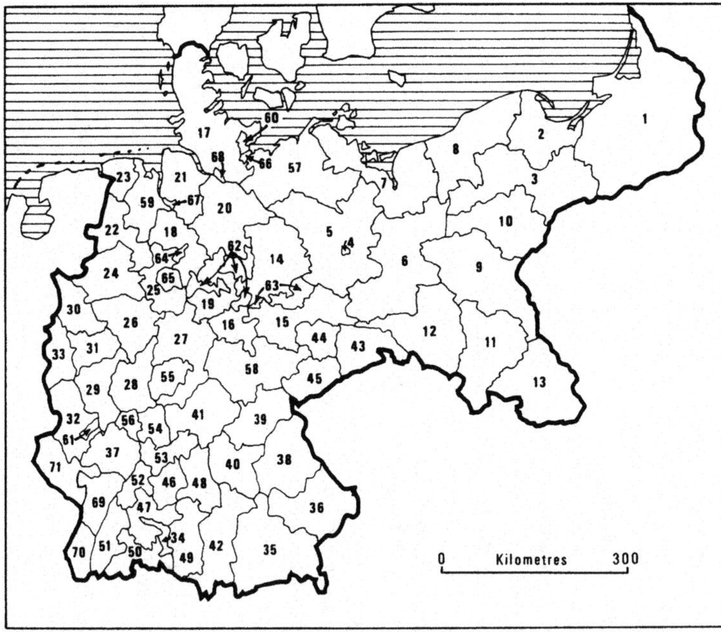

1 Ostpreussen
2 Danzig
3 Marienwerder
4 Berlin
5 Potsdam
6 Frankfurt an der Oder
7 Stettin-Stralsund
8 Köslin
9 Posen
10 Bromberg
11 Breslau
12 Liegnitz
13 Oppeln
14 Magdeburg
15 Merseburg
16 Erfurt
17 Schleswig
18 Hannover
19 Hildesheim
20 Lüneburg
21 Stade
22 Osnabrück
23 Aurich
24 Münster

25 Minden
26 Arnsberg
27 Kassel
28 Wiesbaden
29 Koblenz
30 Düsseldorf
31 Köln
32 Trier
33 Aachen
34 Sigmaringen
35 Oberbayern
36 Niederbayern
37 Pfalz
38 Oberpfalz
39 Oberfranken
40 Mittelfranken
41 Unterfranken
42 Schwaben
43 Dresden
44 Leipzig
45 Zwickau
46 Neckarkreis
47 Schwarzwaldkreis
48 Jagstkreis

49 Donaukreis
50 Konstanz
51 Freiburg
52 Karlsruhe
53 Mannheim
54 Starkenburg
55 Oberhessen
56 Rheinhessen
57 Mecklenburg
58 Thüringen
59 H. Oldenburg
60 F. Lübeck
61 Birkenfeld
62 Braunschweig
63 Anhalt
64 Schaumburg-Lippe
65 Lippe
66 Lübeck
67 Bremen
68 Hamburg
69 Unterelsass
70 Oberelsass
71 Lothringen

0   Kilometres   300

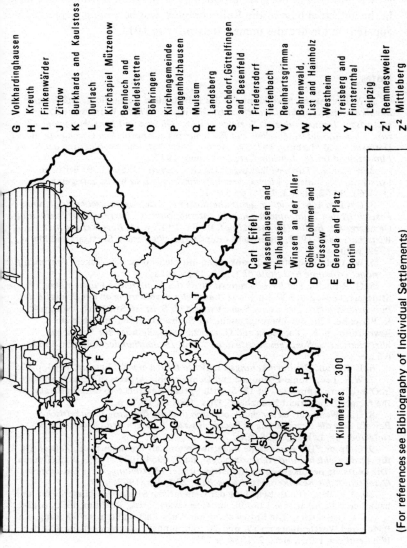

A	Carl (Eifel)
B	Massenhausen and Thalhausen
C	Winsen an der Aller
D	Göhlen Lohmen and Grüssow
E	Geroda and Platz
F	Boitin

G	Volkhardinghausen
H	Kreuth
I	Finkenwärder
J	Zittow
K	Burkhards and Kaulstoss
L	Durlach
M	Kirchspiel Mützenow
N	Bernloch and Meidelstetten
O	Böhringen
P	Kirchengemeinde Langenholzhausen
Q	Mulsum
R	Landsberg
S	Hochdorf, Göttelfingen and Besenfeld
T	Friedersdorf
U	Tiefenbach
V	Reinhartsgrimma
W	Bahrenwald, List and Hainholz
X	Westheim
Y	Treisberg and Finsternthal
Z	Leipzig
Z¹	Remmesweiler
Z²	Mittleberg

(For references see Bibliography of Individual Settlements)

they were no longer dependent on isolated regional factors, but were determined by variables which had a uniform applicability thoughout the whole of the country. It is perhaps even more ironic that the erosion of regional differentials took place at a time when the economic dichotomy which had been created by the process of imbalanced growth, initially in the grain-producing northeastern provinces and then in the industrial base of the Ruhr complex, was becoming increasingly apparent in the decades immediately prior to 1914.[98]

Notes

1. W. Köllmann, 'Bevölkerung in der industriellen Revolution', *Studien zur Bevölkerungsgeschichte Deutschlands*, Göttingen, 1974; A.E. Imhof (ed.), *Historische Demographie als Sozialgeschichte. Giessen und Umgebung vom. 17. zum 19. Jahrhundert. Quellen und Forschungen zur hessischen Geschichte*, Bd.31, Darmstadt and Marburg, 1975; W. Herbig, *Wirtschaft und Bevölkerung der Stadt Lüdenscheid im 19. Jahrhundert*, Dortmund, 1977.

2. W.R. Lee, 'Zur Bevölkerungsgeschichte Bayerns 1750-1850: Britische Forschungsergebnisse', *Vierteljahrschrift für Sozial- und Wirtschaftsgeschichte (VSWG)*, Bd.62, Heft 3, 1975, pp.310-11.

3. *Das Deutsche Reich in gesundheitlicher und demographischer Beziehung. Festschrift den Teilnehmern am XIV. Internationalen Köngress für Hygiene und Demographie, Berlin 1907 gewidmet*, Berlin, 1907, p.11. *Bevölkerung und Wirtschaft 1871-1972*, Statistisches Bundesamt Wiesbaden. Stuttgart and Mainz, 1972, p.90.

4. W. Abel, 'Wachstumschwankungen mitteleuropäischer Völker', *Jahrbuch für Nationalökonomie und Statistik (JNS)*, 1935, p.187.

5. G. Rümelin, *Die Bevölkerungsstatistik des Königreichs Württemberg*, Stuttgart, 1884, p.5; E.W. Buchholz, *Ländliche Bevölkerung an der Schwelle des Industriezeitalters. Der Raum Braunschweig als Beispiel*, Stuttgart, 1966, p.4; K. Blaschke, 'Zur Bevölkerungsgeschichte Sachsens vor der industriellen Revolution', in E. Giersiepen and D. Lösche (eds), *Beiträge zur Deutschen Wirtschafts- und Sozialgeschichte des 18. und 19. Jahrhunderts*, Berlin, 1962, p.51.

6. E. Keyser, *Die Bevölkerungsgeschichte Deutschlands*, Leipzig, 1943, p.395.

7. W.R. Lee, 'Some Economic and Demographic Aspects of Peasant Society in Oberbayern from 1752 to 1855, with Special Reference to Certain Estates in the former Landgericht Kranzberg', Diss., Oxford, 1972, p.22.

8. C.A. Weinheld, *Ueber die Population und die Industrie oder kritischer Beweis, dass die Bevölkerung in hochkultivirten Ländern den Gewerbefleiss stets übereile*, Leipzig, 1828, p.vi.

9. G. Ipsen, 'Die preussische Bauernbefreiung als Landesausbau', *Zeitschrift für Agrargeschichte und Agrarsoziologie*, Bd.2, 1954, p.29 et seq.; W. Köllmann, 'Die deutsche Bevölkerung im Industriezeitalter', *Mitteilungen der Deutschen Gesellschaft für Bevölkerungswissenschaft*, 27 Folge, 1962, p.57.

10. A.v. Nell, 'Die Entwicklung der Generativen Strukturen bürgerlicher und bäuerlicher Familien von 1750 bis zur Gegenwart', Diss., Bochum, 1973, p.134.

11. J. Griesmeier, 'Die Entwicklung der Wirtschaft und der Bevölkerung von Baden und Württemberg im 19. und 20. Jahrhundert', *Jahrbücher für Baden-Württemberg*, I Jhg., Heft. 2, 1954, p.125.

12. E. Boserup, *The Conditions of Agricultural Growth*, London, 1965, *passim*; H. Ueköffer, 'Die Bevölkerungsbewegung in Westfalen und Lippe, 1818-1933', Diss., Münster, 1941, p.20.

13. J. Hajnal, 'European Marriage Patterns in Historical Perspective', in D.V. Glass and D.E.C. Eversley (eds), *Population in History*, London, 1965, pp.101-43.

14. E.A. Wrigley, 'Family Limitation in Pre-industrial England', *Economic History Review (EHR)*, vol.XIX, 1966, p.86.

15. F. Prinzing, 'Die Wandlungen der Heiratshäufigkeit und des mittleren Heiratsalters', *Allgemeines Statistisches Archiv (ASA)*, 1897, pp.662-5.

16. A. Frhr. v. Fircks, 'Rückblick auf die Bewegung der Bevölkerung im preussischen Staate', *Preussische Statistik*, XLVIII, A, Berlin, 1879, p.132.

17. H. Brandt, 'Ueber Veränderungen des Heiratsalters sowie seine Beziehungen zur Kinderzahl', *Archiv für Rassen- und Gesellschaftsbiologie*, vol.31, 1937, p.414.

18. P. Fried, 'Historisch-statistische Beiträge zur Geschichte des Kleinbauerntums (Söldnertums) im westlichen Oberbayern', Mitteilungen der Geographischen Gesellschaft in München, Bd.51, 1966, p.19; W.R. Lee, op.cit. (1972), pp.194-6; H. Müller, *Bauerntum am Rande der Grossstadt. Bevölkerungsbiologie der Dörfer Hainholz, Bahrenwald und List (Hannover)*, Leipzig, 1940, p.14; I. Kothe, *Das Mecklenburgische Landvolk in seiner bevölkerungsbiologischen Entwicklung, dargestellt am Beispiel der Dörfer Göhlen, Lohmen und Grüssow*, Leipzig, 1941, p.58.

19. A.M. Guest, 'The Relationship of the Crude Birth Rate and its Components to Social and Economic Development', *Demography*, vol.11, no.3, 1974, p.463.

20. J. Houdaille, 'Quelques Résultats sur la démographie de 3 Villages d'Allemagne de 1750 à 1879', *Population*, 1970, p.651; A. Frhr. v. Fircks, op.cit., p.142; J.M. Phayer, *Sexual Liberation and Religion in 19th-century Europe*, London, 1977, pp.62-3.

21. J. Knodel, 'Law, Marriage and Illegitimacy in 19th-century Germany', *Population Studies (PS)*, 1967, p.279 et seq.

22. F. Nicolai, *Beschreibung einer Reise durch Deutschland und die Schweiz im Jahre 1781*, Stettin, 1787, p.25; R. Dertsch and H. Homann, 'Bevölkerungsgeschichte und Bevölkerungsbiologie von Tiefenbach bei Oberstorf', *Zeitschrift des Historischen Vereins für Schwaben und Neuburg*, Bd.52, 1936, p.204; E. Albrecht, 'Die Bevölkerungsbewegung einer Mecklenburgischen Landgemeinde (Zittow bei Schwerin) vom 17. bis zum 20. Jahrhundert', *Archiv für Bevölkerungswissenschaft und Bevölkerungspolitik (ABB)*, 1940, pp.101-02; J. Wernicke, *Das Verhältnis zwischen Geborenen und Gestorbenen in historischer Entwicklung*, Jena, 1896, p.54.

23. W.R. Lee, op.cit. (1972), p.60.

24. Ibid., p.62.

25. J. Gugumus, 'Konjunktur und Eheschliessung im Deutschen Reich seit 1820', Diss., Köln, 1940, p.33.

26. W.R. Lee, op.cit. (1972), pp.46-8.

27. J. Knodel, 'Two- and-a-half Centuries of Demographic History in a Bavarian Village', *PS*, 1970, pp.353-76.

28. W.R. Lee, op.cit. (1975), pp.327-8; J. Krausse, 'Unterschiedliche Fortpflanzung im 17. und 18. Jahrhundert', *ABB*, 1940, p.28 et seq.; I. Kothe, op.cit., p.61.

29. K. Biedermann, *Deutschlands politische, materielle und soziale Zustände im 18. Jahrhundert*, Leipzig, 1880, p.340. For other localities see map bibliography.

30. K. Kisskalt, 'Die Sterblichkeit im. 18 Jahrhundert', *Zeitschrift für Hygiene*

172   *Germany*

und Infektionskrankheiten (ZHI), 1921, p.111.
    31. T. Mckeown and R.G. Record, 'Reasons for the decline of mortality in England and Wales during the 19th century', *PS*, vol.16, 1962, pp.94-122.
    32. Th. Maser, *Dissertatio inauguratio de erroribus obstetricorum*, Argentorati, 1726; J.D.E. Brunner, *Entdeckung der Irrtümer und Bosheiten der Hebammen*, Solingen, 1740; H. Baas, *Die geschichtliche Entwicklung des ärztlichen Standes und der medizinischen Wissenschaften*, Berlin, 1896, p.333.
    33. A. Hirsch, *Geschichte der medizinischen Wissenschaften in Deutschland*, Munich and Leipzig, 1893, p.676.
    34. K. Finkenrath, 'Die Medizinalreform. Die Geschichte der ersten deutschen ärztlichen Standesbewegung von 1800-1850', *Studien zur Geschichte der Medizin*, Heft 17, Leipzig, 1929, pp.4, 9; *Aerztliches Intelligenzblatt*, 11 Jhg., Munich, 1855, p.291.
    35. G. Fischer, *Chirurgie vor 100 Jahren*, Leipzig, 1876, p.110.
    36. *Aerztliches Intelligenzblatt*, 3 Jhg., Munich, 1856, p.415.
    37. Ibid., p.414.
    38. P. Razzell, 'Population change in 18th century England. A Reinterpretation' *EHR*, 2nd Series, vol.XVIII, no.2, 1965, pp.312-32.
    39. Anon, *Was that Baierns Regierung bisher für die Kuhpocken*, Munich, 1802, p.3; J.C.W. Juncker, *Archiv der Aerzte und Seelsorger wider die Pockennoth* Bd.III, Leipzig, 1797, p.83.
    40. K. Kisskalt and C. Stoppenbrink, 'Die Alterssterblichkeit an Pocken vor Einführung der Impfung', *ZHI*, Bd.19, no.3, 1920, p.485.
    41. J.D. Post, 'Famine, Mortality and Epidemic Disease in the Process of Modernisation', *EHR*, vol.XXIX, 1976, pp.14-37.
    42. K. Blaschke, op.cit., p.121.
    43. J.N.A. Leuthner, *Betrachtungen der Gallen- und Faulfieber*, Nürnberg, 1776; M. v. Pettenkofer, *Untersuchungen und Beobachtungen über die Verbreitungen der Cholera*, Munich, 1855, *passim*.
    44. W. Ehrhart, 'Die Sterblichkeit in der Reichstadt Kempten (Allgäu) in den Jahren 1606-1624 und 1686-1870', *Archiv für Hygiene und Bevölkerungspolitik*, 1936, p.118 *et seq*.
    45. T. Mckeown, R.G. Brown and R.G. Record, 'An Interpretation of the Modern Rise of Population in Europe', *PS*, vol.26, 1972, pp.345-82; T. Mckeown, *The Modern Rise of Population*, London, 1976, p.142 *et seq*.
    46. W. Köllmann, 'Grundzüge der Bevölkerungsgeschichte Deutschlands im 19. und 20. Jahrhundert', *Studium Generale*, Jhg.12, 1959, p.384; W.G. Hoffmann 'The Take-off in Germany', in W.W. Rostow (ed.), *The Economics of Take-off into Sustained Growth*, London, 1963, p.103.
    47. G. Helling, 'Berechnung einer Index der Agrarproduktion in Deutschland im 19. Jahrhundert', *Jahrbuch für Wirtschaftsgeschichte*, 1965, no.IV, p.128.
    48. W.R. Lee, op.cit. (1972), p.22.
    49. H.W. Graf v. Finckenstein, *Die Entwicklung der Landwirtschaft in Preussen und Deutschland, und in den Neun Alten Preussischen Provinzen von 1800-1930*, Bern, 1959, Bd.III, Tables 1-4.
    50. W.G. Hoffmann, *Das Wachstum der Deutschen Wirtschaft seit der Mitte des 19. Jahrhunderts*, Berlin, Heidelberg and New York, 1965, p.742; E.C. Dinckel, 'Ueber die bäuerliche Credit-Verhältnisse in Württemberg', *Zeitschrift für die gesamte Staatswissenschaft*, vol.XII, 1856, pp.557, 573.
    51. G.H. Haumann, *Ueber die zur Zeit in Deutschland herrschende Noth des Landwirtschaftlichen Standes*, Ilmenau, 1826; J. Kuczynski, 'Studien zur Geschichte der zyklischen Ueberproduktionskrisen in Deutschland, 1826-1866', in *Die Geschichte der Lage der Arbeiter unter dem Kapitalismus*, I.11, 1961, p.28.
    52. W.R. Lee, 'Primary Sector Output and Mortality Changes in early 19th

century Bavaria', *The Journal of European Economic History*, vol.6, no.1, Spring 1977, pp.133-62.

53. A.E. Imhof, 'Sterblichkeitsstrukturen im 18. Jahrhundert auf Grund von massen-statistischen Analysen', *Zeitschrift für Bevölkerungswissenschaft*, 1976, Heft 3, p.107; *Das Deutsche Reich*, op.cit., pp.31-42.

54. C. Becker, *Statistische Nachrichten uber das Grossherzogtum Oldenburg*, Heft XI, Oldenburg, 1870, p.131.

55. A. Frhr. v. Fircks, op.cit., pp.98-9; P. Biedert, *Die Kinderernährung im Säuglingsalter*, Stuttgart, 1900, p.156; A. Groth and M. Hahn, 'Die Säuglingsverhältnisse in Bayern', *Zeitschrift des Bayerischen Statistischen Landesamts*, Munich, 1910, *passim.*

56. Von Behr Pinnow and F. Winkler, *Statistische Beiträge für die Beurteilung der Säuglingssterblichkeit in Preussen*, Charlottenburg, N.d., p.117.

57. G. Lange, 'Die Ernährungsweise der im Grossherzogtum Baden geborenen Kinder während des ersten Lebensjahres', *Sozial-historische Mitteilungen für Baden*, 1917, p.134 *et seq.* According to the 1910 survey the following factors accounted for the failure to breast-feed children: faulty development of the nipples, deficient milk secretion, weakness of the child, lack of goodwill on the part of the mother, indifference, family opposition and the economic necessity of returning as quickly as possible to work.

58. W.R. Lee, op.cit. (1972), pp.124-6; H. Bernheim, 'Die Intensitäts-Schwankungen der Sterblichkeit in Bayern und Sachsen und dessen Factoren', *Zeitschrift fur Hygiene*, 1888, p.577.

59. C. Röse, 'Die Wichtigkeit der Mutterbrust für die körperliche und geistige Entwicklung der Menschen', *Monatsschrift für Zahnheilkunde*, vol.XXIII, 1905; C.A. Würzburg, *Die Säuglingssterblichkeit im Deutschen Reiche während der Jahre 1875-7. Arbeiten aus dem kaiserlichen Gesundheitsamt*, Berlin, 1888, 4 Bd., p.55. Infant mortality in Prussia was particularly high in such areas as the Bezirksamt Liegnitz and Sigmaringen, where breast-feeding was comparatively rare.

60. G. Mayr, 'Die Sterblichkeit der Kinder während der ersten Lebensjahre in Süddeutschland, insbesonders in Bayern', *Zeitschrift des kgl. Bayerischen Statistischen Bureaus*, 2 Jhg., 1870, p.210 *et seq.* In Bavaria, although the increase in infant mortality during the period 1835/6-1868/9 was practically the same for both legitimate and illegitimate children, the former rose from 37.3 to 39.6 (per 100 live births), whereas the latter rose from 38.9 to 42.0.

61. G. Meyer, 'Die mittlere Lebensdauer', *Jahrbücher für Nationalökonomie und Statistik*, Jena, 1867, 5 Jhg., p.31.

62. A. Gottstein, 'Zur Statistik der Totgeburten seit 200 Jahren', *Zeitschrift fur Sociale Medizin*, Bd.1, 1906, pp.6-14; F. Prinzing, 'Die Ursachen der Totgeburten', *ASA*, Bd.7, 1907, p.22; O.K. Roller, *Die Einwohnerschaft der Stadt Durlach im 18. Jahrhundert*, Karlsruhe, 1907, p.46.

63. F. Prinzing, *Handbuch der medizinischen Statistik*, Jena, 1930-1, p.509; C. Ballod, *Die Mittlere Lebensdauer in Stadt und Land*, Leipzig, 1899, p.46.

64. 'Die Lungentuberkulose und ihre Bekämpfung in Bayern', *Zeitschrift des kgl. Bayerischen Statistischen Landesamts*, Munich, 1910, p.230. In Bavaria eleven sanatoria were established between 1898 and 1907.

65. W. Köllmann, 'Bevölkerung und Arbeitskräftepotential in Deutschland, 1815-65. Ein Beitrag zur Analyse der Problematik des Pauperismus', *Jahrbuch des Landes Nordrhein-Westfalen*, 1968, pp.209-54.

66. R. Wuttke, *Stand und Wachstum: Sächsische Volkskunde*, Dresden, 1900 p.89.

67. H.R. Giebel, 'Strukturanalyse der Gesellschaft des Königreichs Bayern im Vormärz, 1818-48', Diss., Munich, 1971, p.287; W. Conze, 'Vom "Pöbel" zum "Proletariat"', *VSWG*, 1954, *passim*; E. Anegg, 'Zur Gewerbestruktur und

174   Germany

Gewerbepolitik Bayerns, während der Regierung Montgelas', Diss., Munich, 1965, p.65 et seq.; Münchner Intelligenzblatt, Munich, 1799, p.348.

68. F.F. Mendels, 'Proto-industrialisation: the First Phase of the Industrialisation Process', Journal of Economic History (JEH), 1972, pp.241-61.

69. A. Lorsch, ' Population cycles as a cause of business cycles', Quarterly Journal of Economics, LI, 1937, p.659.

70. A.C. Kelley, 'Demographic Cycles and Economic Growth: The Long Swing Reconsidered', JEH, 1969, p.636.

71. E. Shorter, 'Illegitimacy, sexual revolution and social change in modern Europe', Journal of Interdisciplinary History (JIH), vol.2, no.2, 1971, pp.237-72.

72. W.R. Lee, 'Bastardy and the Socio-economic Structure of South Germany', JIH, vol.7, no.3, 1977, pp.403-25.

73. F. Prinzing, op.cit. (1930-1), p.32.

74. E. Keyser, op.cit., p.407; W.R. Lee, op.cit. (1972), pp.389-90.

75. H. Zwerenz, Westheim bei Kitzingen am Main. Schriften aus dem rassenpolitischen Amt der NSDAP, Würzburg, 1937, p.15; Generalbericht über die Sanitätsverwaltung im Königreich Bayern, Munich, 1904, p.91.

76. P. Marschalck, Deutsche Ueberseewanderung im 19. Jahrhundert, Stuttgart, 1973, p.33. In the eighteenth century the following states had prohibited emigration: Prussia (1721), Baden (1749), Mecklenburg (1760-66), Bavaria (1764), Saxony (1723, 1764), and Hessen (1787). Only Württemberg had allowed freedom of movement from 1514 onwards.

77. M. Walker, Germany and the Emigration, 1816-65, Cambridge Mass., 1964, pp.8-9.

78. W. Köllmann and P. Marschalck, 'German Emigration to the United States', Perspectives in American History, vol.7, 1974, p.520.

79. F. Burgdörfer, 'Die Wanderungen über die deutschen Reichsgrenzen im letzten Jahrhundert', ASA, vol.20, 1930, p.161 et seq.

80. W.O. Henderson, Studies in the Economic Policy of Frederick the Great, London, 1963, pp.128-30.

81. Statistisches und Wahlamt der Stadt Bochum, Das Bevölkerungs-mässige Wachstum und Werden der Industrie-Gesellschaft Bochum, 1719-1936, Bochum, 1937, passim; K. Brämer, 'Heimatsinn und Wandertrieb der Bevölkerung des preussischen Staats', Zeitschrift des kgl. Preussischen Statistischen Bureaus, Bd.XII, 1873, p.342.

82. H. Haufe, 'Die nordostdeutsche Bevölkerungsbewegung, 1817-1933. Entstädterung und Verstädterung', ABB, vol.5, 1935, p.325.

83. H. Golding, 'Die Wanderbewegung in Ostpreussen seit der Jahrhundertwende mit besonderer Berücksichtigung der Abwanderung vom Lande', Zeitschrift des Preussischen Statistischen Landesamts, 69 Jhg., 1930, p.216; M. Sering, Die Verteilung des Grundbesitzes und die Abwanderung vom Lande, Berlin, 1910, p.4.

84. A. Steinhart, Untersuchung zur Gebürtigkeit der deutschen Grossstadtbevölkerung, Berlin, 1912, p.71.

85. A. Bek, 'Die Bevölkerungsbewegung im ländlichen Raum in der letzten 250 Jahren dargestellt am Beispiel der Gemeinde Mittelberg (kleines Walsertal)', Diss., Hohenheim, 1958, p.73.

86. W. Brepohl, Industrievolk im Wandel von der agraren zur industriellen Daseinsform dargestellt am Ruhrgebiet, Tübingen, 1957, p.240; W. Köllmann, 'Die deutsche Bevölkerung im Industriezeitalter', Mitteilungen der Deutschen Gesellschaft für Bevölkerungswissenschaft, 27 Folge, 1962, reprinted in ibid. Bevölkerung in der industriellen Revolution, Göttingen, 1974, p.39.

87. R. Seeberg, Der Geburtenrückgang in Deutschland, Leipzig, 1913, pp.13-15; J. Borntraeger, Der Geburtenrückgang in Deutschland. Seine Bewertung

und Bekämpfung, Würzburg, 1913, p.33; M. Hecht, 'Die Geburtenrhythmus Badens in den letzten 100 Jahre', *ABB*, 1935, p.350. According to one source gonorrhea accounted for an annual loss of 20,000 births (F. Löhne, *Volksvermehrung und Bevölkerungspolitik vom nationalökonomisch-medizinischen Standpunkt*, Wiesbaden, 1927, p.12).

88. J. Knodel, *The Decline of Fertility in Germany, 1871-1939*, Princeton, 1974, Chapter II.

89. K. Astel and E. Weber, 'Die Unterschiedliche Fortpflanzung und Untersuchungen über die Fortpflanzung von 14,000 Handwerkmeistern und selbständigen Handwerkern Mittelthüringens', *Politische Biologie*, Heft 8, Munich, 1939, p.4.

90. J. Knodel and E. v. de Walle, 'Breast-feeding, fertility and infant mortality: an analysis of some early German data', *PS*, 1967, p.111.

91. F. Burgdörfer, 'Geburtenhäufigkeit und Säuglingssterblichkeit mit besonderer Berücksichtigung bayerischer Verhältnisse', *ASA*, vol.7, 1907, pp.63-154.

92. 'Die Bewegung der Bevölkerung in den 20 Jahren 1853-1872', *Beiträge zur Statistik des Herzogtums Braunschweig. Heft 1*, p.IX.

93. W.R. Lee, *Population Growth, Economic Development and Social Change in Bavaria, 1750-1850*, New York, 1977, pp.337-55.

94. J. Reulecke, 'Veränderungen des Arbeitskräftepotentials im Deutschen Reich 1900-1933', in *Industrielles System und politische Entwicklung in der Weimarer Republik*, Bochum, 1973, p.91.

95. M.B. Hexter, *Social Consequences of Business Cycles*, Boston, 1925, p.175.

96. W. Röpke, *Crises and Cycles*, London, 1936, p.41.

97. Dr Simon, 'Die Entwicklung der Geburtenziffer in Preussen seit 1875, insbesonders seit 1901', *Zeitschrift des kgl. Preussischen Statistisches Bureaus*, Bd.61, Berlin, 1922, p.189. Fertility rates (live births per 1,000 women between 15 and 45 years) fluctuated between 58.75 (Stadtkreis Berlin) and 135.59 (Regicrungsbezirk Oppeln), with the national average standing at 101.39.

98. F.B. Tipton, *Regional Variations in the Economic Development of Germany during the 19th century*, Middletown, Connecticut, 1976, *passim*.

Bibliography of Individual Settlements (see Figure 4.2)

A. A. Simonis, 'Sippen- und bevölkerungskundliche Untersuchungen eines Eifeldorfes', *Archiv für Bevölkerungswissenschaft und Bevölkerungspolitik (ABB)*, 1936, Heft 1, p.37 *et seq.*

B. W.R. Lee, 'Some Economic and Demographic Aspects of Peasant Society in Oberbayern from 1752 to 1855, with Special Reference to Certain Estates in the former Landgerich Kranzberg', Diss., Oxford, 1972.

C. L. Wülker, 'Zur Bevölkerungskunde von Winsen (Aller)', *ABB*, vol.XV, 1941, p.261 *et seq.*

D. I. Kothe, *Das Mecklenburgische Landvolk in seiner bevölkerungsbiologischen Entwicklung, dargestellt am Beispiel der Dörfer Göhlen, Lohmen und Grüssow*, Leipzig, 1941.

E. J. Amrhein, *Die Bevölkerungspolitische Lage der beiden Rhondörfer Geroda und Platz*, Würzburg, 1937.

F.)J. Houdaille, 'Quelques Résultats sur la démographie de 3 Villages d'Allemagne
G.)de 1750 à 1879', *Population*, 1970, pp.649-54.
H.)

I. W. Scheidt, 'Niedersächsische Bauern II. Bevölkerungsbiologie der Elbinsel Finkenwärder vom Dreissigjährigen Krieg bis zur Gegenwart', *Deutsche Rassenkunde*, Bd.10, Jena, 1932.

J. E. Albrecht, 'Die Bevölkerungsbewegung einer mecklenburgischen Landgemeinde (Zittow bei Schwerin) vom 17. bis zum 20. Jahrhundert', *ABB*, vol.XIV, 1940.

K. B. Richter, *Burkhards und Kaulstoss. Zwei Oberhessische Dörfer*, Jena, 1936, *Deutsche Rassenkunde*, Bd. 14.

L. O.K. Roller, *Die Einwohnerschaft der Stadt Durlach im 18. Jahrhundert*, Karlsruhe, 1907.

M. R. Schuppius, 'Statistisches aus einem alten Kirchenbuch', *Archiv für Sippenforschung und alle verwandten Gebiete*, 10 Jhg., Heft 2, 1933, p.33 *et seq.*

N. ( ). Wagner, 'Bevölkerungsstatistisches aus der Gemeinden Bernloch und Meidelstatten, OA. Münsingen', *Württembergisches Jahrbuch für Statistik und Landeskunde*, Stuttgart, 1916, pp.30, 64.

O. G. Heckh, 'Bevölkerungsgeschichte und Bevölkerungsbewegung des Kirchspiels Böhringen auf der Uracher Alb vom 16. Jahrhundert bis zur Gegenwart', *Archiv fur Rassen- und Gesellschaftsbiologie*, Bd.33, 1939, pp.126-69.

P. P. Benkelberg, 'Die Bevölkerungsentwicklung einer lippischen Kirchengemeinde seit 1760', *ABB*, 1940.

Q. W. Klenck, *Das Dorfbuch von Mulsum, Kreis Wesermünde*, Niedersachsen, 1959.

R. F. and T. Schmölz, 'Die Sterblichkeit in Landsberg am Lech von 1585-1875', *Archiv für Hygiene und Bakteriologie*, Bd.136, Heft 5, 1952, pp.504-40.

S. I. Müller, 'Bevölkerungsgeschichtliche Untersuchungen in drei Gemeinden des württembergischen Schwarzwaldes', *ABB*, 1939, p.108 *et seq.*

T. H. Göllner, *Volks- und Rassenkunde der Bevölkerung von Friedersdorf (Kreis Lauban/Schlesien)*, Jena, 1932.

U. R. Dertsch and H. Homann, 'Bevölkerungsgeschichte und Bevölkerungsbiologie von Tiefenbach bei Oberstorf', *Zeitschrift des Historischen Vereins für Schwaben und Neuburg*, Bd.52, 1936, p.170 *et seq.*

V. J. Krausse, 'Unterschiedliche Fortpflanzung im 17. und 18. Jahrhundert', *ABB*, 1940, p.24 *et seq.*

W. H. Wülker, *Bauerntum am Rande der Grossstadt. Bevölkerungsbiologie der Dörfer Hainholz, Bahrenwald und List (Hannover)*, Leipzig, 1940.

X. H. Zwerenz, 'Westheim, ein sterbendes Bauerndorf', *Schriften aus dem Rassenpolitischen Amt der NSDAP bei der Gauleitung Mainfranken*, Bd.11, 1937.

Y. W. Döll, 'Treisberg und Finsternthal, zwei Taunusdörfer', *ABB*, vol.XI, 1941, pp.374-83.

Z. G.F. Knapp, 'Die Kindersterblichkeit in Leipzig 1751-1870', *Mitteilungen des Leipziger Statistischen Bureaus*, Heft 8, 1874.

Z[1]. J. Houdaille, 'La Population de Remmesweiler en Sarre aux XVIIIe et XIXe siècle', *Population*, 1970, pp.1185-9.

Z[2]. A. Bek, 'Die Bevölkerungsbewegung im ländlichen Raum in der letzten 250 Jahren dargestellt am Beispiel der Gemeinde Mittelberg (Kleines Walsertal)', Diss., Hohenheim, 1958.

APPENDIX 1

I_m a measure of the proportion married

I_f a measure of overall fertility

I_g a measure of legitimate fertility

$$I_g \quad \frac{BL}{\Sigma F_i m_i}$$

$$I_m \quad \frac{\Sigma F_i m_i}{\Sigma F_i w_i}$$

$$I_f \quad \frac{B}{\Sigma F_i w_i}$$

where — BL represents the number of legitimate births during the period of 5 years centred on the date of estimation

m_i and w_i represent respectively the married women and the total number of women in the age group at the date of estimation

F_i represents the marital fertility of a high fertility standard population, namely the Hutterites, in the 5 year age group i

B represents the total number of births of the five-year period

These are standard indices described by A.J. Coale, 'The Decline of Fertility in Europe from the French Revolution to World War II', in S. J. Behrman, L. Corsa and R. Freedman (eds.), *Family Planning: A World View*, Ann Arbor, 1969, pp.3-24.

APPENDIX 2

Table 4.1: General Rates of Population Growth (p.a.): 1816-64, 1864-1910

Province/state	1816-64			1864-1910		
	Absolute increase (1000)	%	% p.a.	Absolute increase (1000)	%	% p.a.
East Prussia	875	98.75	2.05	303	17.20	0.37
West Prussia	682	119.43	2.48	451	35.99	0.78
Stadt Berlin	435	219.69	4.57	1,438	227.17	4.93
Brandenburg	898	82.68	1.72	2,109	106.30	2.31
Pomerania	755	110.54	2.30	279	19.40	0.42
Posen	704	85.85	1.78	576	37.79	0.82
Silesia	1,609	84.59	1.76	1,715	48.84	1.06
Saxony	848	70.84	1.47	1,044	51.05	1.10
Schleswig-Holstein	302	43.32	0.90	622	62.26	1.35
Hanover	316	19.62	0.40	1,016	52.75	1.14
Westphalia	601	56.37	1.17	2,458	147.45	3.20
Hesse-Nassau	430	44.88	0.93	833	60.01	1.30
Rhineland	1,462	76.54	1.59	3,749	111.09	2.41
Hohenzollern	10	18.18	0.37	6	9.23	0.20
Total (Prussia)	9,873	72.01	1.50	16,583	70.32	1.52
Bavaria	1,168	32.38	0.67	2,112	44.23	0.96
Saxony	1,143	95.72	1.99	2,470	105.69	2.29
Württemberg	337	23.88	0.49	689	39.41	0.85
Baden	436	43.33	0.90	711	49.65	1.07
Mecklenburg-Schwerin	245	79.54	1.65	87	16.32	0.35
Gross-Sachsen	87	45.07	0.93	137	48.92	1.06
Mecklenburg-Strelitz	27	37.50	0.78	7	7.07	0.15
Oldenburg	80	34.18	0.71	169	53.82	1.17
Braunschweig	67	29.64	0.61	201	68.60	1.49
Sachsen-Meiningen	57	47.10	0.98	101	56.74	1.23
Sachsen-Altenberg	46	47.91	0.99	74	52.11	1.13
Sachsen-Coburg-Gotha	53	47.32	0.98	92	55.75	1.21
Anhalt	73	60.83	1.26	138	71.50	1.55
Schwarzburg-Sonderhausen	21	46.66	0.97	24	36.36	0.79
Schwarzburg-Rudolstadt	20	37.03	0.77	27	36.48	0.79
Waldeck	7	13.46	0.28	3	5.08	0.11
Lippe	30	37.03	0.77	40	36.03	0.78
Elsass-Lothringen	366	30.04	0.62	290	18.30	0.39
Hesse	255	45.37	0.94	465	56.91	1.23
Total (excl. the three Hansa towns)	14,559	58.62	1.22	25,534	64.82	1.40

Source: Compiled from official sources.

Table 4.2: Average Age at First Marriage for Women (in Years)

Locality	Period		
	1750-1799	1800-1849	1850-1875
Kitzingen a.M.	25.3		
Tiefenbach	30.0	28.9	
Massenhausen	26.9	27.1	
Thalhausen	31.1	29.3	
Reinhartsgrimma	25.4 (1755)	23.3 (1799)	
Saxony, Mecklenburg, South Hannover	24.6 (1780-90)	24.5 (1840/49)	
Bavaria (excl. Palatinate)		29.9 (1815/60)	26.2 (1862/68)
Palatinate		26.4 (1815/60)	26.2 (1862/68)
Winsen a.d. Aller	26.6	26.3	28.0
Gde. Mittelberg	25.1	28.5	
Göhlen			
Bauernfrauen	22.1 (1775/	23.9 (1825/30)	
Häuserfrauen	1800)	28.1 (1800/25)	28.8
Handwerkerfrauen		21.5	25.1
Böhringen	24.8	24.8 (1800/09)	
Gde. Carl (Eifel)	23.1	26.2 (1801/50)	
Geroda and Platz			26.6 (1850/59)
Boitin	25.6 (1780/ 1809)	26.4 (1810/59)	
Volkhardinghausen	26.0 (1780/ 1809)	24.6 (1810/59)	
Kreuth	31.5 (1780/ 1809)	30.6 (1810/59)	
Hochdorf, Besenfeld, Göttelfingen	23.96	24.74	
Finkenwärder	23.76	24.00 (1800/29)	
Württemberg families	22.7	24.1	25.6 (1850/99)

Sources: see bibliography of individual settlements, pp.175-6.

Table 4.3: Marriage Rates in German Territories (per 1,000)

Locality	1750/9	1760/9	1770/9	1780/9	1790/9	1800/9	1810/9	1820/9	1830/9	1840/9	1850/9
Friedersdorf	12.9	13.3	11.7	10.9	10.8	8.3	7.3	7.9	6.1	7.2	5.9
Mulsum	8.0	11.3	6.0	8.7	10.3	7.6	7.7	6.9	5.8	7.3	5.4
Böhringen	8.1	5.3	8.0	7.4	9.8						
Hainholz, List, Bahrenwald							9.5		9.1		9.6
Göhlen[a]						9.2	8.0	10.6	5.8	6.8	
Grüssow[a]						7.6	9.2	5.9	6.8	5.9	
Lohmen[a]							7.6	4.5	8.0	5.7	
Oldenburg		10.0	8.3	8.6	8.9[a]						
Prussia[a]							10.6[b]	8.9	9.1	8.6	8.4
Bavaria[a]								6.7[c]	6.5	6.6	6.4
Baden[a]							7.0[d]	6.6	7.9	7.2	6.0
Württemberg[a]									8.1	7.7	
Massenhausen[e]	9.6		8.6				6.4	4.4	6.4	7.7	
Thalhausen[f]	12.7		10.0			16.3	10.9		9.5	5.3	
Mecklenburg[a]							10.4	8.3	7.9	7.4	
Wittenberg[a]	7.8	7.9	5.8								
German Empire[a]										8.1	7.8

Note: a. 1801-10, etc.
     b. 1816-20.
     c. 1825-30.
     d. 1817-20.
     e. For the following years: 1752, 1771, 1813, 1820, 1832, 1840.
     f. For the following years: 1752, 1771, 1801, 1812, 1830, 1843.

Table 4.4: Crude Birth Rates in German Territories (per 1,000)

Locality	1750/9	1760/9	1770/9	1780/9	1790/9	1800/9	1810/9	1820/9	1830/9	1840/9	1850/9
Friedersdorf							40.0	41.5	43.4	40.2	37.6
Böhringen	52.4	47.2	43.8	50.7	50.9	55.5	47.7	47.8	44.2	52.6	
Durlach	24.8	25.5	25.8	26.8	29.7	30.5					
Burkhards and Kaulstoss		24.3	32.6						31.5	32.9	
Mulsum	38.3	41.3	30.0	26.3	32.0	31.3	33.7	38.8	29.7	29.2	29.5
Hochdorf, Besenfeld and Göttelfingen	43.5	40.9	35.3	38.7	41.5	40.3					
Massenhausen[b]	43.8		30.7				41.8	37.8	44.2	41.9	32.8
Thalhausen[b]	64.4		54.1				37.8	31.2	36.5	38.6	
Geroda and Platz									37.1	45.6	26.9[a]
Württemberg[a]							37.7[c]	38.7	42.0	42.5	37.3
Bavaria[a]								34.1[d]	35.0	35.2	34.4
Prussia[a]								41.7	39.6	39.7	40.5
Saxony[a]							44.3[e]		40.0	40.3	41.0
Baden[a]								42.2[f]		39.2	34.2
Fürstentum Waldeck		36.3[g]									
Oldenburg[a]		36.6	33.3	31.6	33.8	33.3	34.2	32.8		31.5[h]	
German Empire[a]										37.5	36.8

Note: a. 1801-10, etc.; b. Average decennial figures; c. 1816-20; d. 1826-30; e. 1816-20; f. 1826-30; g. 1760-90; h. 1846-60.

Table 4.5: Crude Death Rates in German Territories (per 1,000)

Locality	1750/9	1760/9	1770/9	1780/9	1790/9	1800/9	1810/9	1820/9	1830/9	1840/9	1850/9
Böhringen	35.6	36.4	32.7	36.1	49.7	40.5	45.0	31.9	34.8	36.0	
Durlach	35.9	28.8	32.0	30.8	31.9	40.1					
Hochdorf, Besenfeld and Göttelfingen[a]	27.6	29.2	26.9	21.2	25.3	26.1	25.1	17.5	28.4	26.6	
Burkhards and Kaulstoss		21.2		25.4					26.0	23.9	25.2
Mulsum	39.7	38.0	33.3	32.6	22.3	30.7	29.7	29.4	24.0	20.3	
Oldenburg		26.1	22.6	22.7[b]	29.7	30.5	26.9			30.5[c]	
Landsberg	31.	31.	31.	30.	32.	35.	35.	31.	31.	31.	
Friedersdorf							39.7	37.9	38.2	39.4	
Isarkreis[d]						38.4	31.1	28.9	27.6	32.5	
Freising[e]						42.6	37.2	35.8	43.5	43.4	
Württemberg[b]							33.3[f]	29.3	33.2	32.8	31.0
Baden[b]							28.8[f]	25.5	29.8	29.1	27.2
Prussia[b]							29.1[f]	28.3	30.5	28.2	28.1
Saxony[b]								28.4[g]	28.2	28.5	27.1
Bavaria[b]								27.4[h]	29.3	28.8	28.8
German Empire[b]										28.2	27.8

Note: a.Excluding still-births; b.1781-90, etc.; c.1840-60; d.For the years 1809,1818, 1827, 1834, 1848, e.For the years 1809, 1815, 1827, 1833, 1840; f.1816-20; g.1827-30; h.1826-30.

Table 4.6: The Doctor-Patient Ratio in Individual German Territories,
1849-53

State	Ratio	State	Ratio
Prussia	1:2,931	Braunschweig	1:2,583
Württemberg	1:3,948	Bavaria[a]	1:3,184
Baden	1:3,285	Upper Bavaria	1:3,251
Nassau	1:3,519	Swabia	1:3,449

a. 1854.

Source: Aertzliches Intelligenz-blatt. 11 Jhg., Munich, 1855, p.144, Bavaria
(1854); A. Fischer, *Geschichte des deutschen Gesundheitswesens*, Bd.2,
Berlin, 1933, p.369.

Table 4.7: The Registered Death Rate in Selected German Hospitals

Hospital	Year	Total no. of patients	No. of deaths	%
Fürth	1858/9	1,132	28	2.47
Bamberg	1790/1824	19,977	1,159	5.7
Rothenburg	1854/5	283	8	2.8
Munich	1853/4	9,028	749	8.2
Göttingen	1785/6	494	21	4.25

Table 4.8: The Development of Agricultural Production per Unit of Labour Input (LI) in Germany, 1800-1850 on the Basis of Grain Values (GV)

Period	Arable	Livestock	Total	Labour force (1,000)	Tons per LI	Index
			Production in 1,000 tons			
1800-10	14,500	7,555	22,055	9,525	2.32	100
1811-20	15,660	7,332	22,992	9,530	2.41	104
1821-25	19,140	8,100	27,240	10,100	2.70	116
1826-30	20,010	8,787	28,797	10,300	2.80	120
1831-35	22,910	11,205	34,115	10,600	3.22	139
1836-40	24,795	12,262	37,057	11,057	3.35	144
1841-45	26,825	13,719	40,544	11,662	3.48	150
1846-50	29,000	14,874	43,874	11,425	3.84	165

Source: G. Franz, 'Landwirtschaft, 1800-1850', in H. Aubin and W. Zorn (eds), *Handbuch der deutschen Wirtschafts- und Sozialgeschichte*, Bd.2, Stuttgart, 1976, p.313.

Table 4.9: Comparative Growth in Grain Production and Relative Mortality Rates in the Provinces of Posen and Silesia (1816-52)

Crude death rate (per 1,000 inhabitants)

	Posen	Silesia
1816-19	30.18	33.72
1820-24	27.88	30.23
1825-29	36.91	33.32
1830-34	38.99	33.84
1835-39	28.67	33.88
1840-44	30.48	29.90
1845-49	37.66	33.18

Grain production (1,000 tons at 1,000 kg.)

	Wheat		Rye		Barley		Oats	
	Posen	Silesia	Posen	Silesia	Posen	Silesia	Posen	Silesia
1816	6.8	62.4	70.2	396.0	23.5	145.6	58.2	380.8
1822	11.9	78.7	104.8	450.1	28.3	167.6	65.7	404.7
1831	19.6	103.1	156.7	531.3	35.4	200.5	77.0	440.5
1840	27.2	127.5	208.6	612.4	42.5	233.5	88.3	476.3
1846	26.3	105.3	153.0	386.1	25.6	171.7	76.2	279.5
1852	55.0	152.5	252.0	486.7	30.1	223.6	61.0	374.9
	48.2	90.1	181.8	90.7	6.6	78.0	2.8	− 5.9
%	708.82	144.3	258.9	22.9	28.1	53.5	4.8	− 1.5

Source: H.W. Graf Finckenstein, *Die Entwicklung der Landwirtschaft in Preussen und Deutschland und in den neuen alten Provinzen von 1800-1930*, Bern, 1959, Bd.III, Tabellen 1-4; F.W.C. Dieterici (ed.), *Mittheilungen des statistischen Bureau's in Berlin.9 Jhg.*, Berlin, 1856, pp.137-9, 153-5.

Table 4.10: Infant Mortality Rates in German Territories (per 100 live births)

Locality	1750/9	1760/9	1770/9	1780/9	1790/9	1800/9	1810/9	1820/9	1830/9	1840/9	1850/9
Hochdorf, Besenfeld and Göttelfingen	11.70	16.85	23.30	19.35	26.45	17.75	19.65	15.20	22.85	19.50	18.90
Burkhards and Kaulstoss	12.4	10.2	11.9	12.3	13.8	11.9	10.9	11.6	15.3	10.4	15.5
Böhringen	26.7	27.2	31.2	25.7	32.6	35.8	34.5	26.6	35.8	34.4	35.2 35.0 (1860/9)
Mittelberg	28.5	35.9	34.8	30.3	30.1	38.5	24.0	15.7	14.1	11.3	19.1
Massenhausen	36.7	41.94	36.19	25.87	32.45	37.71	39.43	36.58	38.98	41.80	
Thalhausen				40.00	36.36	45.45	37.14	62.50	60.00	54.34	
Mulsum	15.6	16.9	15.5	19.0	13.5	13.8	15.8	7.7	13.2	4.9	6.4
Friedersdorf[a]							13.9	13.6	14.8	14.9	13.6 13.2 (1860/9)
Leipzig[b]	34.8					32.41		23.0			21.2
Württemberg families[c]	18.6					23.3					22.4
Bernloch and Meidelstetten[c]	29.5					38.4					32.9
Göhlen[d]	21.0		19.5			19.0		21.7			16.6
Lohmen[d]	10.5		22.0			18.3		13.3			13.6
Remmesweiler[e]											
Catholic	14.0			14.6			11.5			14.7	
Protestant	8.3			15.7			15.1			10.3	
Boitin[f]						18.1	15.7				
Volkharding-hausen[f]						18.6	17.8				
Kreuth[f]						19.3	21.5				

Note: a. Per 1,000 inhabitants; b.For the period 1751-1800, 1801-20, 1821-50, 1851-70; c.For the period 1750-99, 1800-49, 1850-99;

Table 4.11: Infant Mortality in the Major German States (per 100 live births)

Period	German Empire	Prussia	Bavaria	Saxony	Württemberg	Baden
1811-20		16.9			32.1	
1821-30		17.4				23.2
1831-40		18.3	29.5	26.6		
1841-50		18.6	29.8	26.1	34.8	
1851-60		19.7	31.1	25.5		25.2
1861-70		21.1	32.7	26.7	36.0	27.6
1871-80	23.4	21.4	30.9	28.7	32.0	26.2
1881-90	22.5	20.8	28.4	28.2	26.9	23.0
1891-00	21.7	20.3	26.5	27.3	24.4	21.7
1901-05	19.9	19.0	24.0	24.6	21.7	20.2
1906-10	17.4	16.8	21.7	19.8	18.2	17.3

Source: F. Prinzing, *Handbuch der medizinischen Statistik*, Jena, 1930-31, p.375.

Table 4.12: Infant Mortality in Prussia, According to Province (1876/80-1891/95), per 1,000 live births

Province	1876/80	1881/85	1886/90	1891/95
East Prussia	309.0	303.7	329.6	341.1
West Prussia	358.7	347.9	391.7	393.5
Berlin (Stadt)	433.1	383.8	389.6	359.5
Brandenburg	357.9	347.0	370.0	386.9
Pomerania	324.3	303.8	330.4	352.5
Posen	361.6	349.0	375.8	381.0
Silesia	358.2	343.9	360.9	366.3
Saxony	326.0	325.2	341.4	353.7
Schleswig-Holstein	245.4	234.3	253.0	277.2
Hanover	223.7	217.4	230.2	243.1
Westphalia	244.9	237.1	260.0	277.4
Hesse-Nassau	245.1	221.8	217.9	224.5
Rhineland	280.0	279.1	299.0	316.5
Hohenzollern	408.1	362.8	329.6	304.0

Source: A. Frhr. v. Fircks, 'Die Sterblichkeitsverhältnisse der preussischen Bevölkerung', *Zeitschrift des kgl. Preussischen Statistischen Bureaus*, Jhg.37, Berlin, 1897, p.37.

Table 4.13: Life Tables for Men and Women: Various German Territories

Age	Bavaria 1817/8-23/4 m	Bavaria 1817/8-23/4 f	Saxony 1838/49	Oldenburg 1855/64 m	Oldenburg 1855/64 f	Prussia 1867/77 m	Prussia 1867/77 f	Mecklenburg 1867/81 m	Mecklenburg 1867/81 f	Oldenburg 1861/85 m	Oldenburg 1861/85 f	Prussia 1890/91 m	Prussia 1890/91 f	German Empire 1871/81 m	German Empire 1871/81 f
0	10,000	10,000	100,000	100,000	100,000	100,000	100,000	100,000	100,000	100,000	100,000	100,000	100,000	100,000	100,000
1	6,536	7,012													
2	5,985	6,638													
3	5,783	6,401													
4	5,621	6,197													
5	5,489	6,027	48,778	77,640	79,170	65,433	68,338	75,348	77,530	78,038	80,232	68,430	71,486	64,871	68,126
6	5,390	5,930													
7	5,308	5,850													
8	5,236	5,788													
9	5,175	5,735	46,035	73,830	75,250	62,296	65,086	72,175	74,285	74,527	76,649	66,119	68,954	62,089	65,237
10	5,129	5,689													
11	5,086	5,645													
12	5,046	5,603													
13	5,008	5,565													
14	4,974	5,530													
15	4,943	5,498	44,957	71,890	72,750	60,860	63,565	70,489	72,454	72,548	74,410	65,068	67,663	60,892	63,878
20	4,791	5,358	43,318	69,400	70,360	59,123	61,877	68,615	70,706	70,011	72,109	63,566	66,244	59,287	62,324
25	4,588	5,167	41,170	66,130	67,830	56,604	59,683	66,174	68,605	66,309	69,481	61,539	64,507	56,892	60,174
30	4,367	4,902	39,022	63,000	64,510	54,041	57,110	64,049	66,212	63,095	65,982	59,454	62,375	54,454	57,566
35	4,164	4,603	37,143	59,810	60,470	51,318	54,185	61,808	63,445	59,843	61,808	57,033	59,898	51,815	54,685
40	3,944	4,293	35,068	56,400	56,040	48,157	51,075	59,085	60,460	56,159	57,374	54,115	57,133	48,775	51,576
45	3,674	3,967	32,420	52,110	51,570	44,489	47,805	55,954	57,422	51,820	53,229	50,544	54,245	45,272	48,481
50	3,364	3,614	29,227	47,520	47,340	40,306	44,199	51,911	54,041	47,152	49,157	46,462	51,147	41,228	45,245
55	3,013	3,204	25,521	41,970	42,450	35,593	40,049	46,958	49,964	41,810	44,545	41,590	47,297	36,544	41,308
60	2,553	2,745	21,192	35,920	36,440	30,159	34,882	40,842	44,357	36,010	38,853	35,702	41,995	31,124	36,293
65	2,002	2,162	16,127	28,560	28,800	24,074	28,374	33,113	36,908	28,992	31,457	28,876	35,081	24,802	29,703
70	1,374	1,453	11,107	20,650	20,560	17,337	20,814	24,369	27,941	21,162	22,938	21,039	26,276	17,750	21,901
75	751	806	6,526	12,800	11,980	10,703	13,042	15,415	17,788	13,116	14,205	13,005	16,689	10,743	13,677
80	363	361	2,885	5,980	5,510	5,361	6,449	7,761	9,476	6,329	6,800	6,111	8,156	5,035	6,570
85	150	156	853	2,010	1,760	2,014	2,215	2,791	3,446	2,221	2,412	1,849	2,701	1,635	2,232
90	55	56	159	490	400	569	555	727	1,020	535	646	340	567	330	471
95	15	9	20	100	100	111	108	159	249	142	159	27	70	38	56
100				40	30	9	11			49	50	2	5	2	3

Table 4.14: Death Rates in Prussia (1876-95) According to Province and Administrative District for Specified Age Groups (per 1,000 Population)

Province	0-15 m	0-15 f	15-45 m	15-45 f	45-70 m	45-70 f	70-90 m	70-90 f
East Prussia	33.98	30.97	8.13	6.17	33.25	27.12	169.21	149.63
West Prussia	30.66	27.84	7.38	6.57	31.64	24.03	158.34	136.55
Berlin (Stadt)	32.79	29.56	8.99	6.43	37.32	23.67	196.83	159.91
Brandenburg	31.06	28.09	7.83	6.20	32.40	24.48	183.13	172.07
Pomerania	27.78	25.53	7.52	6.72	29.09	23.85	167.16	167.02
Posen	29.34	26.36	7.30	6.38	31.58	25.79	161.42	150.59
Silesia	34.08	30.69	9.26	7.88	36.91	30.37	210.87	189.60
Saxony	28.45	25.56	7.24	6.48	33.39	28.00	194.23	192.10
Schleswig-Holstein	22.39	20.48	7.91	7.09	27.85	24.82	165.78	159.29
Hanover	22.05	20.14	7.94	8.19	33.60	31.47	188.71	189.23
Westphalia	22.90	21.47	9.59	9.28	39.06	33.81	197.81	185.66
Hesse-Nassau	21.11	19.51	8.95	8.31	37.60	34.21	199.55	204.80
Rhineland	26.13	23.86	8.85	7.98	36.89	31.14	193.77	176.31
Hohenzollern	32.64	30.31	7.39	8.42	28.90	31.41	209.93	198.28
Regierungsbezirk								
Königsberg	33.37	30.74	8.35	6.04	33.34	27.09	172.03	153.22
Gumbinnen	34.89	31.30	7.79	6.36	33.14	27.16	164.99	144.64
Danzig	32.90	29.80	8.11	6.83	32.35	24.01	167.34	144.92
Marienwerder	29.22	26.55	6.86	6.38	31.13	24.07	152.17	131.56
Berlin (Stadt)	32.79	29.56	8.99	6.43	37.32	23.67	196.83	159.91
Potsdam	31.80	28.91	7.75	6.24	33.28	24.71	187.01	177.59
Frankfurt	30.12	27.01	7.99	6.17	31.38	24.22	179.44	167.39
Stettin	32.29	29.38	7.85	6.74	29.70	23.74	172.40	174.98
Köslin	22.36	20.93	6.57	6.40	28.21	24.12	159.97	160.67
Stralsund	27.05	24.86	8.82	7.46	28.44	23.54	167.80	157.28
Posen	28.81	25.62	7.41	6.33	31.56	25.82	170.92	152.63
Bromberg	30.25	27.62	7.13	6.46	31.61	25.76	147.65	146.76
Breslau	36.49	32.46	10.15	8.62	38.96	31.52	212.61	209.85
Liegnitz	34.63	31.24	8.33	7.78	36.51	29.36	227.38	210.04
Oppeln	31.93	29.10	8.98	7.17	34.86	29.87	195.19	175.68
Magdeburg	29.92	27.03	7.04	6.57	32.99	29.04	190.96	197.95
Merseburg	28.57	25.46	7.28	6.33	33.70	26.30	194.34	190.98
Erfurt	24.55	22.29	7.74	6.59	33.65	29.69	201.58	181.93
Schleswig	22.39	20.48	7.91	7.09	27.85	24.82	165.78	159.29
Hannover	24.17	22.25	8.42	8.00	36.95	33.73	198.51	206.32
Hildesheim	23.69	22.04	7.99	7.89	35.45	31.41	193.71	206.97
Lüneburg	22.75	20.24	7.17	6.80	33.91	32.37	197.05	196.42
Stade	21.07	19.16	8.50	9.55	32.95	34.28	194.36	194.92
Osnabrück	20.09	18.53	7.73	10.25	32.82	32.33	196.16	189.17
Aurich	16.49	14.70	7.61	7.37	23.79	20.34	145.01	141.89
Münster	23.10	21.60	9.07	10.19	35.17	33.95	192.80	190.55
Minden	20.17	19.23	8.93	9.54	38.23	37.05	195.20	194.56
Arnsberg	23.85	22.25	10.03	8.81	41.45	32.05	204.16	177.81
Kassel	20.20	18.93	8.63	8.34	37.73	34.77	199.57	212.68
Wiesbaden	22.09	20.13	9.24	8.30	37.51	33.40	199.34	196.89
Koblenz	24.31	21.97	8.34	8.24	36.41	36.03	216.19	209.66
Düsseldorf	25.04	23.30	9.59	7.72	38.54	29.49	191.21	171.94
Köln	30.86	28.18	9.24	8.10	38.18	31.22	195.60	166.28
Trier	24.91	22.40	7.72	8.79	35.51	33.07	201.86	200.40
Aachen	26.69	23.51	7.45	7.42	32.87	27.94	175.23	162.20
Sigmaringen	32.64	30.31	7.39	8.42	28.90	31.41	209.93	198.28
Average	28.24	25.71	8.39	7.34	34.45	28.58	186.38	174.53

Source: A. Frhr. v. Fircks, op.cit., p.67.

Table 4.15: Causes of Death in Germany (per 100,000 inhabitants),
 1892-1960

Disease	Date							
	1892	1900	1910	1920	1930	1938[a]	1950[b]	1960
Tuberculosis	259.1	224.6	163.5	154.2	78.8	62.3	40.6	16.5
Malignant neoplasms			79.0	87.2	117.6	146.7	174.0	201.0
Diseases of the circulatory system[d]			214.8	225.2	260.7	309.8	349.9	462.1
including diseases of the brain			60.2	57.6	62.4	100.2	128.3	177.3
Pneumonia	148.2	140.8	127.0	126.9	81.3	84.1	48.6	40.9
Digestive disorders			205.1	126.7	77.5	76.5	64.6	64.7
Female deaths of childbirth[c]	409.2	323.4	324.3	491.8	528.8	365.9	205.5	106.3
Decrepitude	232.6	221.3	163.0	163.9	101.9	98.9	74.6	53.8
Suicide	20.5	20.1	21.7	21.8	27.5	28.3	20.3	19.4
Accidents	37.8	41.1	36.0	47.3	39.5	48.5	43.7	55.9

Note: a.Territorial area as at 31 December 1937; b.The Federal Republic
 (excluding the Saarland and Berlin); c.The position at the end of the year;
 d.The Federal area excluding the Saarland.

Source: Bevölkerung und Wirtschaft, 1872-1972; Statistisches Bundesamt
 Wiesbaden, Wiesbaden, 1972, p.121.

Table 4.16: (A) Illegitimacy Rates per 100 Live Births: Various German and European States, 1845/50-1865/70

State	1845/50	1865/70
Bavaria	20.5	19.3
Saxony	14.8	15.1
Württemberg	11.8	15.7
Denmark	11.4	10.8
Austria	11.3	14.7
Scotland	9.8	9.6
Norway	8.3	9.2
Sweden	8.8	9.3
Belgium	8.1	7.2
France	7.4	7.6
Prussia	7.5	8.3
England	6.7	6.3
Netherlands	4.8	4.0
Spain	—	5.8
Italy	—	5.0

(B) Illegitimate Births in Bavaria (per 100 Live Births), 1835/60-1872

Period	Illegitimacy rate
1835/60	21.1
1860/68	22.2
1868/69	17.9
1869/70	16.4
1871	15.2
1872	14.4

Source: Die Bewegung der Bevölkerung des Königreichs Bayern im Jahre 1877, Zeitschrift des kgl. Bayerischen Statistischen Bureaus, Jhg. 11, Munich, 1879, p.259.

Table 4.17: German Overseas Emigration, 1816-1934

Period	Emigrants (1,000)	Immigrants to USA (1,000)	%	Annual average emigration rate[a]
1816-19	25.0			2.7
1820-24	9.8	1.9	19.4	1.0
1825-29	12.7	3.8	29.9	1.2
1830-34	51.1	39.3	76.9	2.2
1835-39	94.0	85.5	91.0	2.6
1840-44	110.6	100.5	90.9	2.4
1845-49	308.2	284.9	92.4	4.5
1850-54	728.3	654.3	89.8	9.0
1855-59	372.0	321.8	86.5	4.3
1860-64	225.9	204.1	90.4	2.5
1865-69	542.7	519.6	95.7	3.6
1870-74	484.6	450.5	93.0	2.3
1875-79	143.3	120.0	83.7	0.7
1880-84	864.3	797.9	92.3	3.8
1885-89	498.2	452.6	90.9	2.1
1890-94	462.2	428.8	92.8	1.8
1895-99	142.4	120.2	84.4	0.5
1900-04	140.8	128.6	91.3	0.5
1905-09	135.7	123.5	91.0	0.4
1910-14	104.3	84.1	80.6	0.3
1915-19	4.1	1.0	24.4	0.0
1920-24	242.3	150.4	62.1	0.8
1925-29	295.3	230.1	77.8	0.9
1930-34	88.1	62.1	70.6	0.3

Note: a. Based on the population of the areas affected by emigration.

Source: W. Köllmann and P. Marschalck, *German Emigration to the United States. Perspectives in American History*, vol.7, 1974, p.518; F. Burgdörfer, 'Die Wanderungen über die deutschen Reichsgrenzen im letzten Jahrhundert', *Allgemeines Statistisches Archiv*, vol.20, 1930, p.189 *et seq.*; W. Mönckmeier, *Die deutsche überseeische Auswanderung*, Jena, 1912, p.14.

Table 4.18: The Regional Distribution of German Emigrants
  (1871-1910) (in %)

Period	N.E.[a]	N.W.[b]	S.W.[c]	Central[d]	S.E.[e]	West[f]	Hanseatic towns[g]
1871-75	39.3	15.4	25.6	3.8	5.2	8.3	2.1
1876-80	35.4	15.2	25.3	4.2	7.2	9.8	3.1
1881-85	38.2	14.4	24.1	3.8	6.3	10.6	2.6
1886-90	37.7	12.0	28.9	3.2	5.1	10.1	3.0
1891-95	34.8	13.3	25.3	4.4	7.1	10.7	4.4
1896-00	28.6	14.8	26.1	4.8	6.9	10.8	8.0
1901-05	30.7	13.8	23.6	5.0	7.8	14.1	5.0
1906-10	27.5	13.3	23.4	5.2	8.7	15.7	6.2

Note: a.East and West Prussia, Pomerania, Posen, Brandenburg, Mecklenburg;
  b.Schleswig-Holstein, Oldenburg; c.Bavaria, Baden, Württemberg, Hesse,
  Alsace-Lorraine, Hohenzollern; d.Thuringia, Saxony (province), Brunswick-
  Anhalt; e.Silesia, Saxony (kingdom); f.Rhineland, Westphalia, Hesse-Nassau,
  Waldeck, Lippe; g.Hamburg, Bremen, Lübeck.

Source: W. Köllmann and P. Marschalck, op.cit., p.535.

Table 4.19: Distribution of Population (per 1,000) within the German
  Empire, According to Size of Gemeinde

Size of local authority	1871	1875	1880	1885	1890	1895	1900	1905
−2,000 (inhabitants)	639	610	586	563	575	501	456	426
2-5,000	124	126	127	124	103	118	122	118
5-20,000	112	120	126	129	115	135	135	137
20-100,000	77	82	89	89	93	107	122	129
100,000+	48	62	72	93	114	139	162	190

Source: M. Neefe, 'Bevölkerungsstand', *Statistisches Jahrbuch deutscher Städte.
  15 Jhg.*, Breslau, 1908, p.43.

Table 4.20: Marital Fertility According to Occupational Status in Prussia, 1895-1906

Professional occupation	No. of births per marriage
Agriculture	5.32
Industry (mining)	4.53
Factory work	4.37
Textiles	4.37
Metal industry	3.33
Public service	3.23
Health service	2.15

Source: L. Berger, 'Untersuchungen über den Zusammenhang zwischen Beruf und Fruchtbarkeit unter besonderer Berücksichtigung des Königreichs Preussen', *Zeitschrift des kgl. Preussischen Statistischen Landesamts*, 1912, p.233.

Table 4.21: Marriage, Birth and Death Rates in the German Empire and the Weimar Republic, 1871/5-1933 (per 1,000)

Period	Marriage rate	Birth rate	Death rate	Surplus of births over deaths
1871-75	9.4	39.0	28.3	10.7
1876-78	7.8	39.2	26.1	13.1
1879-89	7.8	36.8	25.1	11.7
1890-95	8.0	36.3	23.3	13.0
1896-00	8.4	36.0	21.2	14.7
1901-05	8.0	34.3	19.9	14.4
1906-10	7.9	31.6	17.5	14.1
1911	7.9	28.6	17.3	11.3
1912	7.9	28.3	15.6	12.7
1913	7.7	27.5	15.0	12.4
1914	6.8	26.8	19.0	7.8
1915	4.1	20.4	21.4	−1.0
1916	4.1	15.2	19.2	−4.0
1917	4.7	13.9	20.5	−6.6
1918	5.4	14.3	24.7	−10.5
1919	13.4	19.7	15.5	4.3
1920	14.5	25.8	15.1	10.7
1921	11.9	25.1	13.9	11.3
1922	11.1	23.0	14.4	8.6
1923	9.4	21.1	13.9	7.1
1924	7.1	20.5	12.3	8.2
1925	7.7	20.7	11.9	8.8
1926	7.7	19.5	11.7	7.9
1927	8.5	18.4	12.0	6.4
1928	9.2	18.6	11.6	7.0
1929	9.2	17.9	12.6	5.3
1930	8.8	17.5	11.1	6.5
1931	8.0	16.0	11.2	4.7
1932	7.9	15.1	10.8	4.3
1933	9.7	14.7	11.2	3.5

From official sources.

5 ITALY

Lorenzo del Panta

The Italian population, which amounted to 13.4 million people in 1700, rose to 15.5 million (1750) and 18.1 million (1800), with an average annual growth rate in the two fifty-year periods of 2.9 and 3.1 per 1,000 respectively. Within the European framework of eighteenth-century demographic development, however, this increase appears rather limited, given that the equivalent growth rates for Europe as a whole during the same two fifty-year periods stood at 4.1 and 6.2 per 1,000 respectively.[1] Nevertheless the pattern of Italian demographic development in the eighteenth century assumed a regularity significantly more pronounced than in previous periods. Improvements in sanitary conditions resulted in a progressive decline of infectious diseases and particularly in the disappearance of the plague. The relative stabilisation of mortality around more normal levels, although they remained quite high, probably contributed to a sustained level of population growth. Other factors, however, both political and economic, were important in this context. Following the treaties of Aquisgrana (18 October 1748) which signified the end of Spanish domination, Italy began to enjoy a long period of peace which, in turn, enabled the country to re-emerge within a European context after a long period of isolation.

The Italian economy of the eighteenth century, however, remained heterogeneous. In contrast to the first manifestations of capitalism in parts of the Po valley and in Tuscany, the mass of central and southern Italy retained its antiquated social structure and system of production. This factor, together with the disequilibrium that accompanied Italy's revival, was one of the reasons for the comparatively slower rate of population growth in Italy than in other areas of Europe.

During the Napoleonic period demographic data improve both in respect to quantity and reliability. Although internal political divisions until the second half of the nineteenth century preclude the enumeration of national data, surviving sources and later secondary work do provide a precise enough basis to trace population trends over the last two centuries (Table 5.1). Over time little change took place in annual growth rates, which fluctuated between 5.0 per 1,000 in the 90 years preceding unification (1771-1861) and 6.6 per 1,000 in

196

the following 100 years (1861-1961). During the Napoleonic period, however, the increase was rather modest due to the negative factors that burdened the country at that time; wars, military conscription and the general political and economic crisis. Mortality was particularly high, especially in the years 1816-17 on account of the national typhoid epidemic, and nuptiality failed to reach the high levels recorded during the last years of French domination when young people were able to evade military conscription. The pronounced increase in population during the decade 1821-31 was largely due to a strong revival in the number of marriages around 1820 which, in turn, created a significant increase in the number of births during the following years. Despite several serious mortality crises provoked by cholera epidemics (1835-7, 1855, 1866-7)[2] population growth was maintained at an average annual rate of 6 per 1,000 throughout the mid-nineteenth century. It should be noted, however, that at least until the very end of the century growth rates calculated on registered population figures significnatly underestimate the rate of natural growth. Emigration, which had been apparent immediately after unification (Table 5.2), increased further after 1880. The hardships generated by the agricultural crisis further compounded the pressure on resources created by the progressive rise in the natural growth rate of Italy's population. It is also clear from the table that although mortality declined during this entire period, a fall in the birth rate only becomes apparent after 1890. The natural growth rate, therefore, tended to increase continuously from 1880 to 1930, except for the decade marred by the First World War. The growth rate calculated on the basis of the registered population, however, followed a different pattern. Except for the two periods of war it remained stable at an annual rate of approximately 7 per 1,000. The difference between the two rates reflects the extensive exodus of large numbers of Italian workers from unification to the present day, which resulted from the limited absorption capacity of the internal labour market.

It is important to note, however, that the process of demographic transition which produced a fall in natality and mortality levels from those prevailing around the mid-nineteenth century to those of today did not occur at the same time and with the same modalities in all areas of the peninsula. Indeed these differences are not fully reflected in an analysis of population data on a territorial basis (Table 5.3), which reveals a substantial stability in growth between different regional areas,[3] although the central and southern regions appear to lag somewhat behind the North. Intense rates of migration, both external and internal (particularly from the South to the North) greatly

Figure 5.1: Regions and Geographical Areas of Italy

1 Piemonte
2 Val d'Aosta
3 Lombardia
4 Liguria

I Geographical Area: North West

  5 Trentino Alto-Adige
  6 Veneto
  7 Friuli
  8 Emilia-Romagna

II Geographical Area: North East

  9 Toscana
10 Umbria
11 Marche
12 Lazio

III Geographical Area: Centre

13 Abruzzi
14 Molise
15 Campania
16 Puglia
17 Basilicata
18 Calabria

IV Geographical Area: South

19 Sicilia
20 Sardegna

V Geographical Area: Islands

diminished the consequences resulting from differences in the demographic characteristics of the various regions.

As far as fertility is concerned pre-unification data for the various Italian states is insufficient for a complete analysis. On the basis of fragmentary evidence, however, it is possible to establish a sufficiently clear picture of natality and fertility trends during the first half of the nineteenth century.[4] Although an overall fertility decline did not develop decisively until towards the end of the century, there are indications for some regions and social groups that the decline in fact began several decades earlier. The numerous family reconstitution studies now available, although based on small parish communities, reflect rather modest fertility levels for the seventeenth and eighteenth centuries. In the context of contemporary nuptiality levels, this fertility resulted in an average completed family size of between five and six children.

In relation to the movement in the birth rate over time certain general trends can be established for the early nineteenth century. Indeed for two entire regions natality levels are available for several years of the eighteenth century. In Tuscany with a population of 975,000 the birth rate stood at 34.7 per 1,000 in the period 1779-83[5] and the equivalent figure for Lombardy with a population of approximately 1,200,000 stood at 40.5 for the period 1770-94.[6] A more general picture, however, emerges for the period of French domination (1807-13). During these years the Italian *départements*, which as part of the French Empire comprised approximately a quarter of the total Italian population, had an average birth rate of 36.3 per 1,000. During the same period the equivalent rate for the *département* of the Kingdom of Italy, which comprised a further one third of total population, stood at 39.2. The variation between *départements* appears rather limited, with a strong concentration of the birth rate between 35 and 40 per 1,000. This situation had not altered substantially by 1830, when the average stood at 38.4 per 1,000. Behind this apparent uniformity, however, significant differences existed, from the standpoint of both social stratification and regional location. The availability of records which permit a more detailed analysis significantly affects the apparent homogeneity of the birth rate. In Tuscany, with sufficiently complete and reliable statistics from the early nineteenth century, the average number of children per marriage fell steadily from 1820-24 to the end of the century from 5.6 to 4.2, although this change cannot be attributed either to mortality changes or to variations in the age at marriage. The fall therefore reflected a change in attitude in relation to optimal family size. A further example of differentiation in fertility levels from the early nineteenth century onwards can be found in the differences between urban and outlying rural districts. Data for Turin, Genoa, Bologna and Florence clearly show a level of legitimate fertility that was significantly lower in the cities than in the surrounding countryside (Table 5.4). Finally we should not overlook the example of two distinct social groups, namely the aristocracy and the Jewish community. Both groups show a demographic behaviour pattern that was significantly different from the rest of the population. Their fertility which before the nineteenth century was above average began to decline a century before that of the Italian population in general. By the end of the nineteenth century the birth rate of Jewish communities had reached levels which Italy as a whole would not attain until the mid-twentieth century.

From 1861 onwards Italian statistics become both richer and more regular and increasingly encompass the entire country.[7] As far as birth rates are concerned (Table 5.5), however, the same pre-unification levels continue to persist until about 1880. From that date onwards, both the birth rate and the standardised index of fertility (I_f) follow a similar trend.[8] A steady decline beginning around 1890 continues until 1920 after which the birth rate fell more rapidly until 1950 when the downward trend of the curve levels off. Within the space of a century therefore both indices had fallen by approximately 50 per cent. The index of marital fertility underwent a slow decline as early as 1862-6, fell sharply after 1921-6 and continued to decline slightly during the following decades. Illegitimacy also represents a modest component of general fertility. The increase in the decades following unification, however, did not reflect any real change, but simply reflected changes in marriage legislation in 1865. From the end of the last century a steady decline took place, with the index falling by approximately 80 per cent between 1880-82 and 1960-62. For the population as a whole, therefore, fertility began to decline significantly during the last two decades of the nineteenth century, although contraceptive practices were implemented by some sectors of the population during the first half of the century. At the same time, however, the decline took place from a rather moderate level, which was significantly lower than comparative levels in other countries of northwestern Europe.

Data is also available which permits an analysis of the principal characteristics of nuptiality (Tables 5.6, 5.7). The rate of nuptiality and the index I_m (the proportion ever married) fail to show a clear trend, due probably to the operation of stabilising factors such as the persistence of traditional social norms regulating the selection of spouses, the relative stability of the occupational structure at least until the Second World War and obligatory military service for all males under twenty-one years. However, the I_m index reaches its lowest point in 1921, reflecting the long-term effect of foreign emigration and the short-term impact of the losses incurred through the First World War. The age at first marriage, however, also fails to show any substantial change over time, except for a slight rise for both men and women, which in turn helps to explain the increasing proportion of celibate and unmarried women between the ages of twenty and twenty-four years. Finally the rise in the proportion of single women between fifty and fifty-four years during the last decades, as well as the contemporaneous diminution in male celibacy for the same age group, can be explained by emigration, which created a general scarcity of adult males, a situation further aggravated by high mortality rates for men during the Second World War.

The decline in fertility can be further clarified by a more detailed analysis according to geographical and socio-economic criteria. Table 5.8 shows the adjusted indices of marital fertility for each region of Italy during four distinct periods. The remarkable uniformity of the rates during the years 1862-6 contrasts significantly with the high variability of the three-year period 1950-52. The century following unification was characterised by a widening gulf between the fertility of the southern population and that of the rest of the country. Particularly during the post First World War period differences increased rapidly. A ranking of regions according to the period when the index of legitimate fertility first fell below 0.600 (Table 5.9) shows unequivocally the retarded decline in most of the southern regions.

There are, however, other fertility differentials which require attention, including those between urban and rural areas and those between different socio-economic groups.[9] Table 5.10 presents indices of marital fertility divided into the following categories: rural, semi-rural and urban.[10] Clear differences between urban and rural population existed by 1871, and the legitimate fertility of semi-urban areas was 10 per cent and that of urban areas 15 per cent below rural fertility levels. As far as regional variations were concerned, there were marked urban-rural differences in most of the central and northern districts, where marital fertility in the principal cities was already less than 200 per 1,000 by 1871, corresponding to an I_g index of less than 0.55 and clearly indicating the existence of a neo-Malthusian type of birth control. In the South and Islands, however, differences were minimal or even non-existent. Most of the large southern cities did not possess at that date any of the characteristics common to modern urban conglomerates, and there was no sharp distinction in the social structure of populations according to the size of community. In the period 1871-1931 legitimate fertility fell dramatically in all three categories throughout most of northern and central Italy, although the differentia between large and small communities did increase. In the South fertility began to decline slowly in large cities, but the difference between urban and rural areas remained limited. Data for 1951 is probably distorted by the increasing development of urban hospitals and clinics, producing a slightly overestimated urban fertility level, but it is still possible to establish a fall in legitimate fertility between 1931 and 1951 for every type of community in central and northern Italy, although there was now a reduction in urban-rural differentials. Fertility in the South also fell in all community categories, but the decline occurred with about the same speed in the cities as in the countryside and fertility difference remained modest. Neo-Malthusian behaviour patterns therefore developed in two specific directions: on the one hand from the urban to the rural population and on the other hand from the North to the South. Finally it is possible to calculate coefficients of variation for legitimate fertility indices (I_g)[11] on the basis of a division between the southern and the central-northern areas of the country.[12] In 1861 the relative dispersion of fertility rates between provinces was very low (about 6 per cent), suggesting a relative homogeneity in behaviour patterns in the pre-unification period (Table 5.11). During the following century, however, variability increases significantly, finally reaching 32.9 per cent in 1951. Moreover while the increase in variability is sluggish and limited in the South, the rise in the coefficients in the central-northern region occurs earlier (reaching a value of 17 per cent by 1911) and at a significantly faster rate. These differences arose largely from the fact that those areas marked by an early fertility decline witnessed a more extensive diffusion of the neo-Malthusian mentality which reflected profound social and economic changes. The more rapid acceptance of new behavioural norms by the cultured and wealthier classes and by the urban population in general occasioned an increase in urban-rural fertility differentials and differentials between provinces even within the same geographic region. In the South, on the other hand, where the population was economically and socially more homogeneous and less differentiated culturally, the acceptance of neo-Malthusian behaviour was relatively slow and did not therefore generate geographical differences in fertility.

Wealthier families at any point in the family cycle had a larger number of surviving children than poorer families in the early modern period. Although this difference can in part be attributed to lower levels of infant mortality in wealthier families, it also indicates fertility differences between social strata. During the nineteenth century, however, this situation changed. Effective family limitation by wealthier families quickly counterbalanced the benefits derived from lower infant mortality. From the end of the nineteenth century until the mid-1950s the less wealthy families bore more children whether measured by the actual number born or by those surviving to various ages.[13] Valuable information on fertility differences according to the husband's profession is furnished by the 1931 census (Table 5.12). The data show a clear inverse relationship between occupational status and fertility in the four geographical regions. Differences in the northern and central regions, however, are more noticeable than in the South and the Islands. In the North the difference in family size between large and small families is 2.6 children, whereas in the South it is only 1.5. In the post-1931 period the situation changed again with fertility differences diminishing as mortality differentials declined. The inverse relationship between fertility and socio-economic status was now substituted by a 'U' relationship.

An analysis of mortality in the pre-unification period is also hindered by the absence of adequate statistics. However, as in the case of fertility, existing local studies make it possible to trace general trends. Following the disappearance of the plague and a diminution of violent typhoid epidemics, eighteenth-century Italy was characterised by more stable mortality levels than in previous centuries.[14] The mortality rate in Lombardy between 1770-94 stood at 37.5 per 1,000,[15] and that of Tuscany between 1779-83 at 28.1 per 1,000.[16] On the basis of this evidence it can be concluded that 'normal' mortality levels did not change significantly until at least the third or fourth decade of the nineteenth century and that progress during this period was limited to a reduction in the frequency of exceptional crises. The period from 1800 to unification is characterised on the one hand by the disappearance of smallpox which had been a significant cause of infant and child mortality following the diffusion of vaccination and on the other hand by the appearance of several national crises: the epidemic of petechial typhoid fever in 1816-18 and the successive cholera epidemics of 1835-7, 1855 and 1866-7. These severe crises occasioned violent increases in mortality. In 1817, for example, in Lombardy, Tuscany and Puglia, mortality surpassed 50 per 1,000. It is possible, however, to perceive the beginnings of a change in 'normal' mortality rates before the mid-century, although it should be pointed out that available statistics are rather contradictory. Mortality rates presented according to region and excluding those periods of severe epidemics (Table 5.13) reveal the beginnings of a decline in mortality rates for Piedmont, Lombardy and the Veneto from 1840. The same cannot be said, however, for Liguria, Tuscany, Puglia and Calabria. Clearly mortality decline cannot be regarded as a general phenomenon until the decades following unification (Table 5.14). Between 1862-7 the national average rate was still 30.4 per 1,000, although in the period 1870 to 1950 mortality fell by about two thirds, from approximately 30 to 10 per 1,000.

The mortality rate, however, is influenced by a number of factors other than the actual level of mortality, including the age structure of the population, which changed rapidly during the last century largely as a consequence of the fertility decline. Mortality levels which ignore changes in the age structure can be ascertained from the evidence of life expectancy. Life expectancy figures for both sexes at ages 0, 10 and 50 (Table 5.15) based on census material reveal a doubling in life expectancy at birth which without doubt reflects progress in Italy, whether seen from the point of view of nutrition and improvements in general socio-economic conditions, or from that of better sanitary conditions resulting from medical and pharmaceutical discoveries. Although an improvement in life expectancy is recorded for all ages, it is particularly noticeable for life expectancy at birth. The percentage increases in life expectancy at ages 0, 10 and 50 between 1881-2 and 1960-2 were 91 per cent, 27 per cent and 25 per cent respectively for males and 102 per cent, 38 per cent and 42 per cent for females. As early as 1910-12, life expectancy for women was higher than for men and the gap between the sexes tended to increase over time.

The decline in infant mortality had a decisive impact on the general mortality decline. In the course of a century infant mortality fell by 87.7 per cent. It is clear, however (Table 5.16), that even in recent years the South has lagged behind the rest of the country. This sluggishness in the decline of infant mortality undoubtedly reflects the backward conditions of the southern population in terms of living standards and the limited diffusion of hygienic norms and sanitary facilities. For the more recent period, however, trends can be established for both natal and perinatal mortality (Table 5.17). Significantly these indices which reflect primarily endogenous factors such as the conditions of gestation and delivery as well as heredity rather than exogenous factors (the environment in which the baby lives) evince a rather different trend to that of infant mortality. In the case of natal mortality, observable for the entire century, an increase is noticeable until 1920-25. Even if this increase is in part fictitious, reflecting improvements in registration, it is none the less remarkable that official statistics do not show a return to the levels of 1871 until the end of the Second World War.

As far as the causes of mortality were concerned, the most virulent and widespread epidemics in the nineteenth century, after the disappearance of smallpox and the typhoid epidemic of 1817, were cholera. Apart from these exceptional crises infectious diseases caused the greatest number of deaths during the entire nineteenth century. Even around 1890 serious infectious diseases were significantly more widespread than in other European countries. In 1887-91, for example, there were 880 deaths in Italy each year per million inhabitants due to typhoid fever, as opposed to only 196 in England and 250 in the Netherlands.[17] Equally deaths from malaria averaged annually 581 per million, as opposed to 6 in England and 40 in the Netherlands. Clearly infectious diseases still constituted the major cause of death at the end of the nineteenth century (Table 5.18). In the period 1889-92 from the general category of infectious and parasitic diseases, tuberculosis was responsible for the highest proportion of deaths (37.6 per cent), followed by typhoid fever (11.9 per cent), malaria (10.0 per cent), measles (9.2 per cent) and diphtheria (8.8 per cent).[18] Prior to 1929-33 the situation only changed gradually, with a slow diminution in the significance of infectious diseases and a gradual increase in those connected with the circulatory system. Ten years after the end of the Second World War, however, the situation had changed dramatically. New methods of therapy had significantly weakened the hold of infectious diseases, and the ensuing period was to be marked by an increasing prevalence of diseases of the circulatory system and of cancer as major causes of death.

An analysis of data on a geographic basis, however, often produces a significantly different picture. As far as mortality trends were concerned the South and the Islands are characterised by a distinct backwardness until just before the Second World War (Table 5.14). Only in the post-war period do these differences disappear, reflecting a slightly more favourable situation in these regions. Before the beginning of the decline in mortality, deaths from infectious diseases were considerably higher in the South and Islands.[19] In the period 1887-91, 83.1 per cent of all malaria deaths were recorded in these regions. Over time infectious diseases as a whole continued to remain more typical of the South. Indeed only in the case of infectious tuberculosis which was finally eliminated after World War II was a higher percentage of deaths recorded in the northern regions of the peninsula.

The process of demographic development in Italy was realised in a rather differentiated manner. The impression is of not one but of two distinctive demographic regimes: the Mediterranean type found in the South and the northwestern European type found in the North. The differences are particularly significant in relation to fertility and infant mortality, tied as they are to general socio-economic conditions. These differences were not simply causes but also consequences of the economic gap that separated the two parts of the country. The origins and development of this division over time must therefore be examined.

Although the origins of this disequilibrium are still debated among economic historians and effective analysis is hindered by the paucity of data before Italian unification,[20] the consensus view would place the beginnings of this problem as far back as the eleventh century, with the advent of the Norman monarchy, the late introduction of feudalism and the consequential decline of the southern cities at a time when communal civilisation in the North was beginning to flourish. These then are the distant origins of the crisis of the *Mezzogiorno*.[21] It is more important in the present context, however, to establish the extent and particularly the dynamic of this gap during the period from the end of the eighteenth century to 1861. Only by this means will it be possible to place in perspective the causative factors behind the further exacerbation of this division in the post-1861 period and to evaluate the relative contribution of government policies and more distant factors. The loss in velocity and weight of Italy's economic development compared to other countries of northwestern Europe emerges clearly in the period from the mid-eighteenth century to the early decades of the nineteenth century.[22] Only in some northwestern regions of Italy did an element of dynamism penetrate traditional conservatism. As a result the Italian economy did not lose ground completely to the more advanced European states and become entirely subjugated to them. On the contrary Italy was able to develop by emulation and benefited from international experience to the point of adopting a capitalistic structure as an efficacious mechanism for growth. But these rudimentary aspects of development in the pre-unification period could only emerge fully after a long and stormy process that continued for several decades after 1861 and this in turn contributed to the increasing level of regional division after unification.

In 1861 Italy's gross national income was about a third of that of France and Germany and one quarter of that of England.[23] Even if the peninsula had participated in the general process of European development, the distance dividing Italy from other nations remained enormous particularly in the spheres of primary sector development, manufacturing and commerce. On a national basis Italian development did not take place until the end of the nineteenth century.[24] Between 1863 and 1897 the annual average rate of increase in national income was almost zero; consumption, especially private consumption, only rose marginally and investment levels remained low. The proportion of GNP derived from industry did not increase at all in the forty years following unification (Table 5.19). Economic development was concentrated primarily in the period between the end of the nineteenth century and 1913-14 when national income rose by an annual average of 2.6 per cent and private consumption by 2.1 per cent. The weight of secondary and tertiary sector activity grew progressively in relation to gross product, although there were some improvements in agricultural productivity. After a pause caused by war, industrialisation continued until growth was arrested by the depression of 1929 and Italy's later involvement in the war with Ethiopia and World War II. Only during the twenty years following 1945 can one speak of a period of intense and progressive development, which transformed the Italian economy and led to the rise of the tertiary sector.

The process that brought Italy out of the vicious cycle of stagnation and transformed her into a modern industrial power was not uniform, but developed diverse rhythms both chronologically and spatially. In 1881, of the major socio-economic indicators, only that of illiteracy provided evidence of a gap between the two main zones (Centre-North and South). In the period between 1881 and 1951, however, the gap increased in relation to all the indicators used (Table 5.20).

It is clear, therefore, that during the period immediately preceding unification the *Mezzogiorno*, or as it was then the Kingdom of the Two Sicilies, was not in an entirely precarious position,[25] even if it did suffer from certain disadvantages; the retarded development of railway and highway networks, a greater poverty in minerals and fuels and its relative distance from economically more advanced nations. The principal causes of regional disequilibrium between the North and the South must be found in the position of agriculture, for the agrarian structure of the *Mezzogiorno* was largely antiquated.[26] The major responsibility for this must rest with the landed nobility, who succeeded in absorbing every innovative development and prevented the diffusion of modern systems of soil use and reform in general. Conditions in the North were fundamentally different, for during the first half of the nineteenth century it underwent a process of rapid development, particularly in the Po valley. Thus while the *Mezzogiorno* after 1861 remained anchored in conditions that were endemic in the more backward areas of the Mediterranean, the North had begun to develop as a European economy.

The major beneficiaries of unification were the northern and central regions, where government policy reinforced the nascent trend towards economic modernisation.[27] Public administration in the *Mezzogiorno*, by contrast, was entirely inadequate, particularly in relation to the primary sector. Plans for soil reclamation, the development of aqueducts, river transport improvements and forest protection hardly affected the South. Tariff unification adversely affected the possibility of southern industrial development and southern markets were flooded with products from the North and other European countries.[28] Half of Italy, namely the South, simply functioned as a consumers' market for several decades following unification,[29] and the situation was further aggravated by disproportionate taxation. As a result the extent of economic disequilibrium between these two broad regions became even more apparent in the post-1861 period.

The impact of economic factors on demographic development is, of course, difficult to determine, but it is clear that the North-South contrast was particularly important in relation to fertility. Without doubt the socio-economic backwardness of the southern population retarded the decline in fertility, but at the same time the maintenance of high fertility levels and large families had a negative impact on the possibility of economic development. Similarly high levels of infant mortality were a direct consequence of economic underdevelopment in the South, but they also contributed to a delayed fertility decline.

However, the component of demographic development most closely related to economic development and regional differences was without doubt migration, whether internal or external. During the last century (Table 5.21) more than 25 million Italians left the country, the vast majority seeking work abroad.[30] Just under half of these migrants emigrated across the oceans; roughly 6 million moving to the United States, 3 million to Argentina and the bulk of the remainder travelling to Brazil, Canada and Australia. Between 1862 and 1970 the net loss was approximately 9 million individuals. In the first two decades following unification emigration was not particularly extensive and affected primarily the northern regions because of their proximity to foreign states. Only from 1880-90 onwards did foreign migration become a mass phenomenon. Stimulated by various factors, including the severe economic crisis in the South, the growing demand for unskilled labour in North and South America and improved transport facilities, the number of emigrants grew rapidly until World War I. Emigration after the war declined significantly due to legislative measures in the United States (1921, 1924) designed to restrain immigration, fascist limitations on emigration particularly from 1930 onwards and finally the outbreak of a new world war. Post-1945 a new wave of trans-oceanic migration occurred which continued until the mid-1950s. In more recent years employment possibilities in neighbouring EEC countries have significantly altered the direction of the migration flow. By and large net migration has been greater in periods of high natural population increase (Table 5.2) and consequently has reduced the variability over time of the actual rate of population growth.

From 1861 to the present day the northern and central regions have had a natural rate of increase significantly lower than that of the southern areas. Their proportion of total population, however, has changed little, because of the growing emigration flow, both internally and internationally, which originated from the Southern regions, although regional rates of natural increase have moved further apart. Significantly the North and particularly the northeastern regions have dominated migration to European countries until 1945, whereas the South provided the majority of overseas migrants (Table 5.22). The relative role of the northern districts in European and overseas migration has tended to decline over time, except during 1921-42, when absolute migration rates were quite small. The exact opposite occurred in the *Mezzogiorno*, while the Centre retained a rather constant proportion.

These results are explicable in the context of Italian economic and social development. Prior to economic development in the latter years of the nineteenth century even the North recorded high rates of emigration, and a significant decline is only evident from the early twentieth century onwards. The growing economic gap between North and South is well reflected in the changing proportion of migrants originating from the South and the Islands. From 1876-1900 to 1958-62 the proportion of migrants from these regions emigrating to Europe rose from 6.9 to 64.1 per cent and the respective increase in overseas migration was from 50.8 to 75.1 per cent.

It has been maintained that foreign migration contributed in part to the delay in the decline of fertility and the retarded transformation of familial relations in the South.[31] On the other hand by removing the most healthy members of society, emigration probably contributed to a lowering in the fertility level of the remaining indigenous population. A more significant effect of this process, however, related not to the mechanism of biological selection, but to selection of a social and psychological nature. Emigration carried away from these regions those members most predisposed to change and most ready to adopt new ideas relating to reproduction and the family. It therefore reinforced the inherent conservatism of the indigenous population.

Increasing socio-economic disparity between various regions, together with divergent demographic trends, particularly in relation to fertility, also gradually generated an increasing migratory flow from the depressed areas of Italy to those regions characterised by economic development. Data on internal migration are only available from 1901 onwards, but it is probably safe to assume that internal mobility was not as significant in the nineteenth century.[32] In the sixty years following the census of 1901 (Table 5.23) only two regional areas consistently record positive rates of internal migration; the Northwest and Central Italy. But although all areas in the first regional group — the so-called 'Industrial Triangle' — have positive values, the positive record of the second group must be attributed exclusively to the strong force exerted by the capital. All other regional areas consistently present negative values. Apart from a migratory flow from the South to the Centre and North, there was also an intense flow from the northeast, which had only been marginally affected by industrialisation, to the industrial areas of the northwest. Particularly in the post-1945 period inter-regional migration has assumed alarming proportions, reflecting once again the relative underdevelopment of many large areas of the country.

The profound structural differences between the South and the Centre-North are equally apparent in any discussion of the modality and chronology of Italian urbanisation. In comparison with more developed European countries, Italian urbanisation has generally lagged behind and until the mid-nineteenth century was certainly less dramatic. At that time less than one fifth of all Italians were resident in communities with more than 20,000 inhabitants,[33] whereas the proportion in England was already over one third. Clearly the principal facts that have characterised the relationship between the city and the countryside have been: (1) the late development of a national state in comparison with almost every other European country; (2) the severe backwardness in industrialisation; and (3) the extreme economic, social and cultural imbalance between regions, particularly between the North and South.[34] As a result of traditional political divisions, a network of minor urban centres existed at the time of unification, which were particularly diffused in the Centre-North as the old capitals of traditional states. The process of urbanisation in communities of over 20,000 inhabitants (Table 5.24) during the last century has followed different patterns. The inter-war period, for example, was marked by a decline in urbanisation as a consequence of fascist legislation. The post-1945 period, on the other hand, witnessed a rapid increase in urbanisation concomitant with the general economic and industrial development of the country. Over time the most striking aspect of urbanisation has been the progressive increase in the importance of large urban communities. In 1808 there were only five centres with more than 100,000 inhabitants: Milan and Venice in the North; Rome in the Centre; and Naples and Palermo in the South.[35] By 1861 eleven cities had surpassed this level: six in the North; two in the Centre and three in the South and Islands. A century later there were thirty-two cities with at least 100,000 inhabitants of which sixteen were in the North, six in the Centre and ten in the South and Islands. But while in the North these centres are distributed along two axes (from Turin to Trieste and from Milan to Bologna) determining the framework of a territorial system articulated by numerous minor centres, in the South it is difficult to establish any continuity in the urban network.

There are, however, a number of further aspects of demographic development that require examination, particularly where population growth impinged on the Italian social structure. As far as sex ratios were concerned (Table 5.25) there is no evidence of disequilibrium except during the last decade. After intense male migration, however, females became predominant, particularly after 1913-14. Heavy losses of males during the First World War, however, counterbalanced the decline in emigration and there was no significant reduction in the relative surplus of women. The long-term resurgency of emigration, despite reduced accessibility and anti-emigration legislation, tended to reduce the sex ratio and this tendency continued, although on a smaller scale, after the Second World War. Interesting variations also took place in the relative proportions of men and women over fifteen years of age according to marital status (Table 5.26). Although celibate men are continuously more numerous than single women, the difference tends to diminish over time. In all other categories, however, women invariably outnumber men, with the proportional surplus rising from relatively small levels in relation to married couples, to significantly higher levels in relation to widows and widowers, which in turn reflected higher emigration rates among men and their higher age specific mortality.

As in other developed European countries the age structure of the Italian population has undergone rapid and profound changes during the last century.[36] Particularly as a result of the fertility decline, the population has aged progressively (Table 5.27) and the thinning out of the younger age groups has automatically increased the proportion of adults and aged. In 1861 those under fifteen years represented 34.2 per cent of the population, but only 25.2 per cent in 1961, while the proportion of elderly above sixty-five had more than doubled during the century, rising from 4.2 per cent to 9.7 per cent. The ratio of old to young, calculated as the relation between the number of individuals above sixty-five and those below fifteen years of age, clearly reflects the ageing of the population, moving from 12.2 to 38.3 in the course of a century. Regional differences are also evident in relation to changes in the age structure. The ageing of the population is significantly more accentuated in the Northwest, where fertility decline occurred earlier and more intensely, and less striking in the South, where fertility remained quite high until post 1945. The ratio moved from 14.4 in 1871 to 54.8 in 1961 in the Northwest, but only from 16.6 to 25.8 in the South during the same period.[37]

Variations in the active and non-active proportions of total population (Table 5.28) depend partly on the age composition of the population but primarily on the changing socio-economic conditions of the country.[38] The decline in the active proportion of the Italian population during the century following unification can be attributed largely to the sharp diminution in the proportion of active women. As far as men were concerned a decline in the proportion classified as active is a common phenomenon in all Western countries. In the case of women, however, their employment in the labour force often increased in the more developed countries.[39] An examination of the active population on the basis of sectoral economic activity (Table 5.29) reinforces the impression that industrialisation and economic development only began to assume importance in Italy at the beginning of the twentieth century. Between 1861 and 1911 the proportion of those employed in industry only rose from 18 per cent to 24 per cent, but had jumped to 40 per cent by 1961. It is not possible, however, to present in this context a detailed analysis of active population by geographical area and sectoral economic activity. It is clear from the evidence of general rates for specific geographical regions (Table 5.30) that differences were considerable. The national average was exceeded in the Northwest by 10.9 per cent in 1861 and by 11.0 per cent in 1961. In the Islands, on the other hand, the rate of activity was 19.3 per cent below the national average in 1861 and 18.4 per cent below a century later. The rates of activity for men declined in all age groups during the period observed (Table 5.31), with the exception of the age group 25-44 years, where the rate remained stable throughout the first fifty years of this century. In the case of women a decisive decline took place for all age groups. The reduction in the proportion active has been particularly strong for both sexes in the age groups under twenty-five and over sixty-five. This decline reflects, without doubt, the impact of economic progress. While the general rates of activity for all age groups and for both sexes fell by almost 13 per cent between 1901 and 1951, the average annual income per capita rose in real terms by 105 per cent during the same period.[40]

The decline in the rates of activity in the two specific age groups cited was directly influenced by shifts in sectoral employment.[41] In the primary sector children were employed in family concerns from an early age, and the elderly despite some diminution in their contribution, still retained some role in production. The shift of a large part of the population from the primary sector to other sectors of the economy clearly involved a significant reduction in the numbers of young and elderly classified as active. The introduction of social legislation, while promoting the increasingly earlier retirement of the elderly, also led to a progressive extension in compulsory education. As a result the extent of illiteracy among individuals of six years and above fell from 68.8 per cent in 1871 to 12.9 per cent in 1951.[42]

It is much more difficult, however, to explain the reduction even in absolute terms, of the number of economically active women. This trend was connected partly with the decline of certain industrial activities, such as textiles and the food industry, where the proportion of women employed had been traditionally significant at the beginning of the twentieth century.[43] Their overall participation in the work force, moreover, was weakened by a decline in emigration between the two World Wars, which coincided with industrial stagnation. Furthermore the anti-feminist orientation of the fascist regime constituted an additional obstacle of no mean importance to the emancipation of women in the field of labour.

Finally attention needs to be focused on the family. Despite the relative lack of systematic studies in this area, it is clear that the transition from an extended to a nuclear family cannot be regarded as a phenomenon specific to the process of industrialisation.[44] The nuclear family was typical even of pre-industrial, agrarian Italy. The major reduction in family size was a result not so much of a reduction in the number of relatives living together under the same roof, but of a fall in the number of children born. The reduction in the birth rate rather than a diminution of traditional cohabitation ties between relatives was the prime factor in accounting for the dramatic fall in average family size. Family structure, moreover, was connected over time with the prevailing nature of property relations. The possession or use of a small family plot, which was the typical holding of the majority of the rural population in regions characterised by the latifundia system, did not facilitate the emergence of several nuclear families on the same piece of land. The extended or enlarged family forms which existed in the case of the *mezzadria* were largely limited to single nuclear families supplemented either by another couple (that of a son) or by single individuals (widows, orphans, single men or women). More often than not it represented a household in transition and usually a household with an elderly couple living in the home of their son. But in every case the size and structure of the family depended on the form of productive activity and the concrete economic conditions available to the family, factors which in turn promoted a great deal of variation.

Even in 1930 family size was closely related to the extent of land under cultivation (Table 5.32). This correlation, indeed, is more apparent in the Centre-North than in the South and Islands where the large landowners could easily find cheap labour.[45] In pre-industrial times the extended family was primarily the model for noble families and the land-holding class in general, although they constituted only a minority of total population. Significantly a larger number of surviving children was traditionally found in wealthier families, and this evidence is corroborated by the few existing studies.[46] In Florence partial data from the Catasto of 1427 indicates that the relative difference in terms of children per household according to the age group of the mother varied from 17 per cent to 64 per cent between the wealthiest and poorest classes. Between the latter and the middle income groups the difference was less significant but still noticeable. At Bari in 1753 there was a constant increase in the number of children resident at home from 2.02 to 4.39 per family with the progressive increase in income between five broad income groups. Finally at Turin in 1802 while families of manual labourers had an average of 1.18 children resident at home, the figure for professional groups and those practising the liberal arts stood at 1.92. These differences can be partly accounted for by differences in mortality and perhaps in relative age at marriage, even if one cannot exclude a higher legitimate fertility among the wealthier groups. This relationship, however, changed radically during the period of the demographic transition.

Indeed the distinctiveness of the contemporary nuclear family cannot be examined merely in the context of average family size, but must be viewed in relation to the transformation of the family's economic function.[47] If the family in the pre-industrial period was primarily a unit of production, whether for subsistence or exchange, the modern family constitutes an economic entity in which the means for productive support gained elsewhere are distributed and utilised. As a result of this change in function, children today require substantial family support without being in a position to contribute in return. They constitute a major expenditure item and not a form of investment, and this is probably one of the factors behind the reduction in births that has accompanied the process of industrialisation in all developed countries. In relation to the history of the family, however, a comprehensive statistical analysis is only possible for the recent period. Between 1881 and 1911 the proportional increase in the number of families hardly differed from that of the population as a whole. After 1931, however, the number of families increased at a higher rate than population although it is only post-1945 that the disparity becomes accentuated and average family size declines significantly (Table 5.33). Besides purely demographic factors, however, the number of families obviously depends on economic and social factors.[48] Urbanisation, internal migration and the rise in income levels, which facilitate the formation of autonomous families at a comparatively younger age, and the growing sense of independence are certainly among the dominating factors that have contributed to a disproportional rise in the number of families in relation to population in the post-1945 period. As far as the average number of children per family is concerned, regional divisions remain significant.[49] While a decline is already apparent in the three regions of the Centre-North between 1911 and 1931, there is no evidence of any downward trend in the *Mezzogiorno* and the Islands until after the Second World War.

Clearly this divergence is connected with the sluggish decline in general fertility typical of the population in the South. But it must not be forgotten that during the fascist period the Italian population was subjugated to intense population propaganda and to a series of legislative measures aimed at stimulating marriage and fertility and at reinforcing the unity of the family, which in turn retarded the process of female emancipation.[50] Even if the direct and durable effect of these policies was modest, the twenty years of pro-natal propaganda undoubtedly contributed to a reinforcement of conservative elements in Italian society and impeded the diffusion of birth control. This process of reinforcement, however, was probably more pronounced in the less developed regions of the country and particularly in the *Mezzogiorno* where the emergence of a modern reproductive behaviour and a rational attitude towards the family have been delayed.

Notes

1. A. Bellettini, 'La popolazione italiana dall'inizio dell'era volgare si nostri giorni, Valutazioni e tendenze', in *Storia d'Italia—5—I documenti*, Einaudi, Torino, 1973, pp.515-25.

2. L. Del Panta and M. Livi Bacci, 'Chronologie, intensité et diffusion des crises de mortalité en Italie, 1600-1850', in 'La mesure des phénomènes démographiques Hommage à L. Henry', *Population*, Numéro Spécial, mars 1977, par.7.

3. In the enclosed map, boundaries of Italian regions and geographical areas are indicated.

4. M. Livi Bacci, *A History of Italian Fertility during the Last Two Centuries*, Princeton University Press, 1977, Chapter I.

5. L. Del Panta, *Una traccia di storia demografica della Toscana nei secoli XVI-XVIII*, Dipartimento Statistico, Firenze, 1974, p.51.

6. M. Romani, 'Il movimento demografico in Lombardia del 1750 al 1850', *Economia e Storia*, II, IV, 1955, p.415.

7. M. Livi Bacci, *A History of Italian Fertility*, Chapter II.

8. In Italy, birth statistics by age of mother and duration of marriage are available only since 1930: it is not possible, then, to calculate age-specific fertility rates for the previous period. This is the reason why we have used in the following tables (5-11), some fertility and nuptiality indices proposed by A.J. Coale: an index of general fertility (I_f); an index of marital fertility (I_g); an index of illegitimate fertility (I_h); and finally an index of the proportion married (I_m).

The relationship among the four measures is described by the following equation:

$$I_f = I_g \cdot I_m + I_h \cdot (1-I_m)$$

For the computation of these indices it is sufficient to have: (1) the age, sex and marital status distribution of the population; and (2) the annual number of live births by legitimacy.

These indices are practically standardised rates with the method of standard coefficients: the standard fertility schedule is the fertility of married Hutterite women (marriages of 1921-30); it is a very high fertility level, probably close to the maximum attainable in a large population.

This set of related indices has two main purposes: (1) to present the fertility of a given population as a percentage of the highest fertility on record; (2) to minimise the dependence of fertility measures on the age structure of a population.

9. M. Livi Bacci, *A History of Italian Fertility*, Chapter III.

10. A distinction of 'urban' from 'rural' population founded on *comuni*-size is certainly defective, but it is practically the only one which allows the use of homogeneous data for the whole century.

11. Provinces are intermediate administrative divisions between *comuni* and regions. In 1951 there were 92 Italian provinces.

12. M. Livi Bacci, *A History of Italian Fertility*, Chapter IV.

13. M. Livi Bacci, ibid., Chapter VI.

14. L. Del Panta and M. Livi Bacci, *Chronologie, intensité et diffusion des crises de mortalité*, para.6.

15. M. Romani, *Il movimento demografico in Lombardia*, p.428.

16. L. Del Panta, *Una traccia di storia demografica*, 51.

17. L. Bowelli, 'Pour l'histoire de la mortalité en Europe: la malarie en Italie', in *Actes du Colloque International de Démographie Historique*, Liège, 18-20 Avril 1963, p.426.

18. G. Canapera, A. Tizzano, C. Barbensi and S. Somogyi, 'Cause di morte', in *Sviluppo della popolazione italiana dal 1861 al 1961*, op.cit., p.470.

19. F. Bonelli, *Pour l'histoire de la mortalité en Europe*, p.427.

20. A. Caracciolo, 'La storia economica', in *Storia d'Italia—3—Dal primo settecento all'Unita*, Einaudi, Torino, 1973, p.685.

21. F. Compagna, 'Urbanizzazione Nord e Sud', in *Urbanizzazione e Modernizzazione* a cura di G. Germani, Il Mulino, Bologna, 1975, pp.394-5.

22. A. Caracciolo, *La storia economica*, op.cit., p.512.

23. V. Castronuovo, 'La storia economica', in *Storia d'Italia—4—Dall'Unità a oggi*, Einaudi, Torino, 1975, p.490.

24. A. Santini, *Nuzialità, natalità e cicli brevi dell'economia. L'esperienza italiana tra il 1863 e il 1965*, Dipartimento Statistico, Università di Firenzo, 1970, p.134.

25. O. Vitali, *Aspetti dello sviluppo economico italiano alla luce della ricostruzione della popolazione attiva*, Istituto di Demografia dell'Università di Roma, 1970, p.170.

26. V. Castronuovo, *La storia economica*, op.cit., p.49 *et seq.*

27. Ibid., pp.64-5.

28. O. Vitali, *Aspetti dello sviluppo economico*, p.171.

29. C. Vivanti, 'Lacerazioni e contrasti', in *Storia d'Italia—1—I caratteri originali*, Einaudi, Torino, 1972, p.936 *et seq.*

30. A. Santini, 'L'emigration', in *La population de l'Italie*, op.cit., p.50.

31. M. Livi Bacci, *A History of Italian Fertility*, Chapter VII.

32. A Golini, *Distribuzione della popolazione, migrazioni interne e urbanizzazione in Italia*, Istituto di Demografia dell'Università di Roma, 1974, pp.27-9.

33. C. Carozzi, 'Il processo di urbanizzazione', in *Urbanizzazione e Modernizzazione*, op.cit., pp.332-4.

34. Ibid., pp.325-7.

35. L. Gamdi, 'Da città ad area metropolitana', in *Storia d'Italia—5—I documenti*, Einaudi, Torino, 1973, p.372.

36. M. Natale, 'La composition de la population', in *La population de l'Italie*, p.59 *et seq.*

37. Ibid., p.61.

38. 'Active population' mentioned in Tables 25, 27 and 28 is surveyed by means of population censuses, and consists of people aged ten years and more who, (1) practise a profession, art or trade, on his own account, or in somebody else's service, or are looking for a job; (2) are temporarily unable to practise a profession, art or trade; (3) are looking for their first job. 'Active population in professional condition' (Table 5.29) refers only to people in categories (1) and (2).

218   *Italy*

39. M. Livi Bacci, *I fattori demografici dello sviluppo economico italiano*, p.79.
40. O. Vitali, *Aspetti dello sviluppo economic italiano*, p.204.
41. M. Livi Bacci, *I fattori demografici dello sviluppo*, p.79 *et seq.*
42. Ibid., p.106.
43. Ibid., p.81.
44. C. Saraceno, *La famiglia nella società contemporanea*, Loescher, Torino, 1975, p.13.
45. M. Livi Bacci, *A History of Italian Fertility*, Chapter VII.
46. Ibid., Chapter VI.
47. C. Saraceno, *La famiglia nella societa contempranea*, p.18.
48. M. Livi Bacci, *I fattori demografici dello sviluppo*, p.64.
49. M. Natale, 'La composition de la population', in *La population de l'Italia*, op.cit., p.67.
50. M. Livi Bacci, *A History of Italian Fertility*, Chapter VII.

Table 5.1: Growth and Density of the Italian Population (since 1861: De Facto Population), 1771-1961

Date	Population (in 000) within 1914 boundaries[a]	Intercensal annual increase (per 000)	Population (in 000) within contemporary boundaries[b]	Intercensal annual increase (per 000)	Population density (per sq. km.)
1771	16,033		17,000		56.4
1781	16,969	5.7			
1791	17,479	3.0			
1801	17,860	2.2			
1811	18,257	2.2			
1821	19,000	4.0	20,400	3.7	67.7
1831	21,088	10.5			
1841	22,355	5.9	23,300	6.7	77.3
1851	24,162	7.8			
1861	25,017	3.5	25,756	5.0	85.5
1871	26,081	4.2	27,578	6.6	91.5
1881	28,460	8.8	29,278	6.2	97.2
1901	32,475	6.6	33,370	7.0	110.8
1911	34,671	6.6	35,695	7.0	118.5
1921	37,143	6.9	37,404	4.8	124.2
1931	39,548	6.3	40,582	8.5	134.7
1936	41,186	8.1	42,303	8.5	140.4
1951	45,967	7.3	47,159	7.6	156.5
1961	48,677	5.7	49,904	5.8	165.7

Note: a. 1771-1851: V. Travaglini, *La popolazione italiana nel secolo anteriore all'Unificazione del Regno*, Padova, 1933, p.42; b. 1771-1841: C. Cipolla, Four Centuries of Italian Demographic Development', in *Population in History*, edited by D.V. Glass and D.E.C. Eversley, London, 1965, p.573.

Table 5.2: Demographic Development of the Italian Population, 1862-1961

Period	Birth rate (per 000)	Death rate (per 000)	Rate of natural increase (per 000)	Rate of net immigration (per 000)	Rate of increase (per 000)
1862-71	37.4	30.3	7.1	− 0.3	6.8
1872-81	36.9	29.6	7.3	− 1.3	6.0
1882-91	37.2	26.9	10.3	− 2.8	7.5
1892-1901	34.2	23.7	10.5	− 4.2	6.3
1902-11	32.2	21.3	10.9	− 4.1	6.8
1912-21	27.2	21.8	5.4	− 2.4	3.0
1922-31	27.5	16.3	11.3	− 2.3	9.0
1932-41	23.0	13.9	9.1	− 0.6	8.5
1942-51	20.1	12.8	7.3	− 1.4	5.9
1952-61	18.0	9.6	8.4	− 2.7	5.7

Source: M. Livi Bacci, *Italy*, from the Fifteenth Edition of Encyclopaedia Britannica, 1974, p.1096.

Table 5.3: Distribution of Italian Population by Geographical Area, 1771-1851 (1914 Boundaries)[a]

Date	Northwest	Northeast	Centre	South	Islands	Italy
1771	28.8	15.0	18.8	25.8	11.6	100.0
1811	26.7	15.0	19.8	26.5	12.0	100.0
1851	26.8	14.1	19.8	28.0	11.3	100.0

Distribution of Italian De Facto Population by Geographical Area, 1861-1951 (Contemporary Boundaries)[b]

Date	Northwest	Northeast	Centre	South	Islands	Italy
1861	26.4	20.0	16.8	25.3	11.6	100.0
1911	26.3	20.5	16.9	23.6	12.7	100.0
1951	24.7	19.8	18.2	25.1	12.2	100.0

Sources: a. V. Travaglini, op.cit., pp.38-40; b. S. Somogyi, 'Evoluzione della popolazione attraverso il tempo', in 'Sviluppo della popolazione italiana dal 1861 al 1961', *Annali di Statistica*, anno 94—Serie VIII, vol.17, Roma, 1965, p.21.

Table 5.4: Urban-Rural Differential Fertility, c.1840

	Turin 1837 Births per 1,000 marriages	Genoa	Bologna 1843 Live births per 1,000 women 15-50	Florence 1836-45 Legitimate live births per 1,000 married women
City	142.7	178.1	108.2	165.0
Rest of province	210.8	200.0	137.6	198.4
Ratio of rural to urban	147.7	112.3	127.2	120.2

Source: M. Livi Bacci, *A History of Italian Fertility during the Last Two Centuries*, Princeton University Press, 1977 (Tables 1.17, 1.19, 1.20), pp.37, 39.

Table 5.5: Birth Rate and other Demographic Indices (I_f, I_g and I_h): 1862-6 to 1960-62

Date	Birth rate	Overall fertility (I_f)	Marital fertility (I_g)	Illegitimate fertility (I_h)
1862-66	36.8	.399	.677	.044
1870-72	36.8	.389	.646	.050
1880-82	36.3	.384	.648	.063
1890-92	34.3	.376	.640	.055
1900-02	33.0	.369	.633	.048
1910-12	32.4	.346	.616	.037
1921-26	29.0	.304	.585	.029
1930-32	25.2	.255	.471	.027
1935-37	23.2	.236	.434	.022
1950-52	18.5	.192	.344	.014
1960-62	18.6	.200	.338	.011

Source: M. Livi Bacci, *A History of Italian Fertility*, Table 2.3, p.57.

Table 5.6: Nuptiality Indices: 1861 to 1961

Date	Crude nuptiality rate	Proportion married (I_m)	Percentage single by age			
			Males		Females	
			20-24	50-54	20-24	50-54
1861	7.8	.560	81.7	13.5	53.9	12.3
1881	7.7	.549	89.2	11.4	60.9	12.1
1901	7.2	.549	87.1	10.9	61.6	10.9
1921	8.8	.495	85.9	10.1	67.8	11.2
1936	7.6	.519	90.9	9.0	69.3	12.4
1951	7.2	.538	90.7	7.9	67.5	14.5
1961	7.8	.578	90.9	8.3	65.6	13.9

Source: M. Livi Bacci, *A History of Italian Fertility*, Table 2.21, p.100.

Table 5.7: Mean Age at Marriage, by Sex: 1896-1900 to 1956-1960

Date	Single males	Single females
1896-1900	27.5	23.9
1906-1910	27.1	23.6
1916-1920	28.9	23.4
1926-1930	27.4	23.9
1936-1940	28.3	24.9
1946-1950	28.9	25.1
1956-1960	28.6	24.9

Source: M. Livi Bacci, *A History of Italian Fertility*, Table 2.22, p.100.

Table 5.8: Adjusted Marital Fertility (I_g)[a], by Region: 1862-66 to 1950-52

Region		1862-66	1890-92	1921-26	1950-52
Northwest	Piedmont	.657	.631	.382	.228
	Liguria	.696	.601	.370	.226
	Lombardy	.669	.680	.526	.289
Northeast	Trentino-Alto Adige	—	—	.703	.430
	Veneto	—	.712	.712	.358
	Venezia Giulia	—	—	.518	.227
	Emilia	.653	.668	.538	.240
Centre	Tuscany	.737	.647	.477	.235
	Marche	.711	.725	.621	.299
	Umbria	.628	.661	.562	.256
	Lazio	—	.590	.517	.358
South	Abruzzi	.711	.701	.738	.361
	Campania	.689	.679	.797	.508
	Puglia	.744	.697	.743	.501
	Basilicata	.690	.682	.747	.474
	Calabria	.651	.649	.766	.515
Islands	Sicily	.705	.647	.624	.425
	Sardinia	.642	.648	.714	.589

a. Marital fertility indices are corrected for abnormal levels of illegitimacy after Unification, and for the effects of migration on sex composition of the population.

Source: M. Livi Bacci, *A History of Italian Fertility*, Table 2.13, pp.84-5.

Table 5.9: Regions Grouped by Date of Decline in Marital Fertility (I_g)

Date	Decline (I_g below .600)
1881-91	Lazio
1891-1901	Liguria
1901-11	Tuscany, Piedmont
1911-21	Emilia, Umbria, Lombardia
1921-31	Trentino, Marche, Sicily, Veneto
1931-36	Albruzzi
1936-51	Campania, Puglia, Basilicata, Calabria, Sardinia

Source: M. Livi Bacci, *A History of Italian Fertility*, Table 2.14, p.88.

Table 5.10: Marital Fertility Rate[a], Three Classes of *Comuni*: 1871 to 1951

Year	Less than 30,000	30,000 to 100,000	More than 100,000	Total
1871	247.7	223.5	210.2	243.8
1931	184.4	153.4	128.6	170.5
1951	125.1	122.9	100.0	119.6

a. Live legitimate births per 1,000 married women aged 15-49.
Source: M. Livi Bacci, *A History of Italian Fertility*, Table 3.9, p.122.

Table 5.11: Coefficient of Variation (Q/M) of Marital Fertility (I_g) by Provinces, North and Centre, South and Islands, all Italy, 1861-1951

Area	1861	1911	1951
North and Centre	6.7	16.7	27.2
South and Islands	5.3	8.3	16.0
Italy	6.2	14.0	32.9

Source: M. Livi Bacci, *A History of Italian Fertility*, Table 4.7, p.184

Table 5.12: Children Ever Born, by Occupation and Residence of
    Husband: 1931[a]

| Occupation | Geographical area | | | | |
	North	Centre	South	Islands	Italy
Agriculture					
self-employed	4.67	4.15	4.79	4.61	4.59
dependent workers	4.12	3.57	4.11	4.24	4.08
Commerce, industry, artisans					
self-employed	3.27	3.28	4.61	4.27	3.71
dependent workers	2.97	3.00	4.12	4.05	3.27
Clerical workers, etc.	2.06	2.22	3.39	3.08	2.42
Professionals, liberal arts	2.29	2.31	3.29	2.93	2.60
Not in labour force	4.46	4.15	5.30	5.07	4.66
All occupations	3.68	3.53	4.45	4.29	3.90

a. Data refer to mean number of children ever born to married women of all ages
   with husband present.

Source: M. Livi Bacci, *A History of Italian Fertility*, Table 6.10, p.237.

Table 5.13: Crude Mortality Rates for Selected Italian Regions, XIX Century[a]

Periods	Piemonte[b]	Liguria[c]	Lombardia[d]	Veneto[e]	Toscana[f]	Puglia[g]	Calabria[h]
1780-84			38.6		28.1[i]		
1810-14			39.0		30.6		
1820-29			33.0		27.8	31.8	28.3
1830-34	32.0	25.4					
1840-49			32.5	32.1[j]	26.7		
1860-64	27.8	27.4			30.3		
1870-73[k]	27.7	27.8	29.5	28.6	31.2	34.1	30.8

Note: a. Periods of major crises excluded; b. G. Muttini Conti, 'La popolazione del Piemonte nel secolo XIX', *Archivio Economico dell'Unificazione Italiana*, Serie II, vol.VI, Torino, 1962, p.147; c. G. Felloni, 'Popolazione e sviluppo economico della Liguria nel secolo XIX', *Archivio Economico dell' Unificazione Italiana*, Serie II, vol.IV, Torino, 1961, p.431; d. M. Romani, *Il movimento demografico in Lombardia*, p.428; e. C. Cipolla, *Four Centuries of Italian Demographic Development*, p.577; f. P. Bandettini, *La popolazione della Toscana dal 1810 al 1959*, Scuola di Statistica dell'Università, Firenze, 1961, p.12; g. F. Assante, *Città e campagne nella Puglia del secolo XIX. L'evoluzione demografica*, Librairie DROZ, Genève 1974, p.117; h. L. Izzo, *La popolazione calabrese nel secolo XIX*, Napoli, 1965, pp.196, 215; i. 1840-47; j. 1779-83; L. Del Panta, *Una traccia di storia demografica della Toscana*, p.51; k. A. Tizzano, 'Mortalità generale', in *Sviluppo della popolazione italiana dal 1861 al 1961*, p.461.

Table 5.14: Crude Mortality Rates by Geographical Areas, 1870-73 to 1960-63

Date	Areas					
	Northwest	Northeast	Centre	South	Islands	Italy
1870-73	28.6	29.4	30.4	33.0	29.5	29.8
1880-83	27.0	27.2	28.3	32.6	28.5	28.4
1899-1902	21.6	20.7	21.0	24.8	23.7	22.4
1909-13	19.0	18.9	18.7	22.0	21.3	20.0
1920-23	16.7	16.2	16.8	19.9	18.1	17.1
1929-33	14.2	13.3	13.3	17.2	15.9	14.8
1934-38	13.7	12.3	12.5	16.3	15.5	13.9
1950-53	11.1	9.5	9.3	9.9	9.8	10.0
1960-63	11.2	10.2	9.3	8.7	8.9	9.8

Source: A. Santini, 'La mortalité', in *La population de l'Italie*, CICRED Series, World Population Year, 1974, p.36.

Appendix   227

Table 5.15: Life Expectancy at 0, 10 and 50 Years, 1881-1962

Date	e_0		e_{10}		e_{50}	
	Males	Females	Males	Females	Males	Females
1881-82	35.2	35.7	48.2	47.6	19.5	19.6
1910-12	46.6	47.3	52.5	52.7	21.2	21.9
1930-32	53.8	56.0	55.5	57.2	22.5	23.9
1960-62	67.2	72.3	61.2	65.8	24.3	27.8

Source: A. Santini, 'La mortalité', in *La population de l'Italie*, p.40.

Table 5.16: Infant Mortality Rates, by Geographical Areas, 1870-1972 (per 1,000 births)

Date	Geographical areas					
	Northwest	Northeast	Centre	South	Islands	Italy
1870-72	220.3	250.1	225.4	226.2	218.8	228.6
1900-02	175.6	167.0	151.4	169.9	191.1	170.8
1930-32	109.5	92.2	85.2	125.5	125.1	109.0
1960-62	36.1	31.6	32.0	55.2	46.5	42.3
1970-72	24.9	21.8	22.5	36.3	32.8	28.2

Source: A. Santini, 'La mortalité', in *La population de l'Italie*, p.41.

228   *Appendix*

Table 5.17: Still-births per 1,000 Births (1871-1960) and Perinatal
Mortality (1931-1960) in Italy

Year	Still-born per 1,000 births[a]	Still-born and dead in the first week per 1,000 births[b]
1871-75	27.7	
1881-85	32.8	
1891-95	39.3	
1901-05	42.7	
1911-15	40.8	
1921-25	43.5	
1931-35	33.8	53.0
1941-45	28.7	49.6
1951-55	29.8	48.2
1956-60	26.0	43.7

a. Annali di Statistica, Anno 104, Serie VIII—vol.29, *Tendenze evolutive della mortalità infantile in Italia*, ISTAT, Roma, 1975, p.62; b. A. Tizzano, 'Mortalità generale', in *Sviluppo della popolazione italiana dal 1861 al 1961*, p.451.

Table 5.18: Distribution of Deaths by Cause, 1889-1957

Cause	1889-92	1909-13	1929-33	1954-57
Diseases attributable to micro-organisms	20.7	15.5	14.8	4.3
Cerebro-vascular diseases, ischaemic heart diseases, other cardiovascular diseases	10.1	16.7	22.1	42.8
Other diseases of breathing system	19.3	18.8	17.5	8.5
Other diseases of digestion system	15.3	15.6	13.3	6.0
Cancer	1.6	3.3	4.9	13.1
Other causes of death	33.0	30.1	27.4	25.3
All causes	100.0	100.0	100.0	100.0

Source: C. Canapera, A. Tizzano, G. Barbensi, S. Somogyi, 'Cause di morte', in *Sviluppo della popolazione italiana*, pp.470-537; L. Di Comite, *La mortalità in Italia*, Istituto di Demografia dell'Università di Roma, 1974, p.4.

Table 5.19: Distribution of Gross National Product by Sector of
Activity, 1861-1900

Sector of Activity	1861-70	1871-80	1881-90	1891-1900
Agriculture	57.5	56.6	50.9	50.4
Industry	19.8	19.0	20.7	19.3
Other activities	22.7	24.4	28.4	30.3
Total	100.0	100.0	100.0	100.0

Source: A. Bellettini, 'Accroissement de la population', in *La population de
l'Italie*, p.15.

Table 5.20: Mean Value of some Socio-Economic Variables, North
and Centre, South and Islands: 1881 and 1951

Variable	Date	Mean value	
		North and centre	South and islands
Marital fertility	1881	634.9	666.3
	1951	275.9	450.4
Infant mortality	1881	223.5	234.3
	1951	48.3	82.8
Ruralisation	1881	52.5	46.7
	1951	40.8	57.5
Industrialisation	1881	20.4	23.7
	1951	33.6	20.8
Male illiteracy	1881	39.8	68.3
	1951	2.1	14.8
Urbanisation	1881	20.7	15.6
	1951	31.7	26.3

Source: M. Livi Bacci, *A History of Italian Fertility*, Table 5.2, p.194.

Table 5.21: Emigration by Ten-Year Periods and by Destination, 1871-1970 (in 000)

Period	Europe	Total overseas		Total[a]
		US and Canada	Other	
1871-80	906	268	270	1,176
1881-90	929	245	950	1,879
1891-1900	1,288	514	1,547	2,835
1901-10	2,512	2,329	3,515	6,027
1911-20	1,696	1,567	2,132	3,821
1921-30	1,362	419	1,188	2,551
1931-40	414	115	288	703
1946-50	638	66	489	1,127
1951-60	1,767	193	1,170	2,937
1961-70	2,127	184	471	2,646

a. Figures do not add to total because of rounding.

Source: M. Livi Bacci, *Italy*, from the Fifteenth Edition of Encyclopaedia Britannica, 1974, p.1097.

Table 5.22: Distribution of Emigration by Geographical Area of Origin and by Destination, 1876-1962

Destination and geographical area of origin	Periods			
	1876-1900	1901-1920	1921-1942	1958-196:
European countries				
Northwest	29.1	30.6	40.5	7.7
Northeast	56.8	44.1	36.0	19.4
Centre	7.2	15.4	12.6	8.8
South	5.9	6.4	5.9	54.3
Islands	1.0	3.5	5.0	9.8
	100.0	100.0	100.0	100.0
Non-European countries				
Northwest	22.2	11.9	11.1	4.0
Northeast	19.6	5.7	13.0	9.3
Centre	7.4	11.3	10.0	11.6
South	42.9	49.6	46.7	57.5
Islands	7.9	21.5	19.2	17.6
	100.0	100.0	100.0	100.0

Source: G. Marrocchi, 'Movimento migratorio con l'estero', in *Sviluppo della popolazione italiana dal 1861 al 1961*, p.647.

Table 5.23: Balances of Internal Migration among Italian Geographical
Areas, according to Census Data, 1901-1961 (Values per 1,000
Inhabitants Born and Residing in Geographical Area)

Date	Geographical area				
	Northwest	Northeast	Centre	South	Islands
1901	+ 15.8	− 22.4	+ 15.4	−10.9	− 0.1
1911	+ 27.6	− 24.1	+ 6.5	−11.0	− 9.4
1921	+ 29.3	− 11.2	+ 12.3	−18.7	−16.6
1931	+ 64.4	− 40.3	+ 20.4	−29.2	−26.2
1951	+ 96.8	− 70.5	+ 49.6	−45.4	−40.3
1961	+178.0	−103.5	+ 69.4	−92.8	−73.0

Source: A. Golini, 'Distribution de la population, migrations interieures et
urbanisation', in *La population de l'Italie*, p.89.

Table 5.24: Percentage of Urban[a] to Total Population, 1861-1961

Date	% Urban population
1861	19.6
1871	21.5
1881	23.7
1901	28.1
1911	31.3
1921	32.2
1931	35.1
1936	35.5
1951	41.1
1961	47.7

a. Living in *comuni* with at least 20,000 inhabitants.

Source: C. Carozzi, 'Il processo di urbanizzazione', in *Urbanizzazione e
Modernizzazione*, p.330

232   *Appendix*

Table 5.25: Sex Ratio, De Facto Population within Contemporary
Boundaries, 1861-1961

Year	Males per 100 females
1861	100.4
1871	101.2
1881	100.4
1891	99.6
1901	98.5
1911	96.5
1921	97.2
1931	95.8
1941	95.6
1951	94.9
1961	94.0

Source: S. Somogyi, 'Evoluzione della popolazione attraverso il tempo', in
Sviluppo della popolazione italiana dal 1861 al 1961, p.23.

Table 5.26: Per Cent Difference between Female and Male Population
over 15 Years, by Marital Status, 1861-1951

Year	Unmarried women	Married women	Widows	Separated women
1861	−22.6	1.0	56.7	−
1911	− 9.1	5.1	56.7	16.0
1951	− 6.2	2.3	70.5	7.5

Source: S. Somogyi, 'Evoluzione della popolazione attraverso il tempo', in
Sviluppo della popolazione italiana dal 1861 al 1961, p.41.

Appendix

Table 5.27: Distribution of De Facto Population by Age Groups,
1861-1961

Year	Age groups			Old to young ratio[a]
	0-14	15-64	65 and more	
1861	34.2	61.6	4.2	12.2
1911	34.0	59.5	6.5	19.1
1961	25.2	65.1	9.7	38.3

a. $P_{65+}/P_{0-14} \cdot 100$

Source: M. Livi Bacci, *I fattori demografici dello sviluppo economico italiano*,
Istituto di Statistica Economica dell'Università di Roma, 1965, p.45.

Table 5.28: Per Cent Distribution of Active and Non-active Population,
by Sex, 1861-1961

Year	Males		Females		Total	
	Active	Non-active	Active	Non-active	Active	Non-active
1861	69.9	30.1	48.7	51.3	59.5	40.5
1911	67.2	32.8	28.8	71.2	48.2	51.8
1961	60.6	39.4	19.6	80.4	39.7	60.3

Source: C. D'Agata, 'Composizione della popolazione secondo l'attività
lavorativa', in *Sviluppo della popolazione italiana*, pp.219-20.

Table 5.29: Per Cent Distribution of Active Population in Professional
Condition by Field of Economic Activity, 1861-1961
(Contemporary Boundaries)

Year	Agriculture	Industry	Other activities	Total
1861	69.7	18.1	12.2	100.0
1911	58.4	23.7	17.9	100.0
1961	29.0	40.4	30.6	100.0

Source: C. D'Agata, 'Composizione della popolazione secondo l'attività
lavorativa', in *Sviluppo della popolazione italiana*, p.222.

234 234 *Appendix*

Table 5.30: Total Activity Rates (Active population per 1,000 inhabitants) by Geographical Area, 1861-1961

Geographical area	1861	1911	1961
Northwest	647	523	435
Northeast	572	474	421
Centre	585	494	395
South	616	473	376
Islands	480	408	324
Italy	595	482	397

Source: C. D'Agata, 'Composizione della popolazione secondo l'attività lavorative', in *Sviluppo della popolazione italiana*, p.223.

Table 5.31: Rates of Activity by Sex and Age Group, 1901 and 1951

Age group	Males		Females	
	1901	1951	1901	1951
10-14	638	231	409	121
15-24	894	755	556	352
25-44	952	958	381	291
45-64	933	891	354	209
65 and more	847	437	296	71

Source: M. Livi Bacci, *I fattori demografici dello sviluppo*, p.77.

Table 5.32: Mean Number of Persons per (Farm-owning) Family,
by Size of Farm, 1930

Size of farm (hectares)	Mean number of persons per family
less than 0.5	4.0
0.5— 1	4.0
1— 3	4.5
3— 5	5.3
5—10	6.4
10—20	8.3
20—50	8.5
All farms	5.1

Source: M. Livi Bacci, *A History of Italian Fertility*, Table 7.7.

Table 5.33: Population, Families and Mean Number of Persons per
Family in Italy, 1881-1961

Year	Index numbers 1881 = 100		Mean number of persons per family
	Population	Families	
1881	100.0	100.0	4.5
1901	114.1	112.5	4.5
1911	121.8	121.3	4.5
1931	144.7	151.9	4.2
1951	166.9	190.1	4.0
1961	177.8	220.1	3.6

Source: M. Livi Bacci, *I fattori demografici dello sviluppo*, p.64.

7 THE LOW COUNTRIES

Paul Deprez

Although both Belgium and the Netherlands were politically united until 1830 the data in this contribution has been presented separately, as consistent comparisons between the two countries are largely impossible. If this has resulted in a fragmented study we would like to request the reader's understanding. However, wherever possible we have emphasised similarities and attempted to synthesise the results.

Changes in Total Population

Because of frequent boundary changes, particularly in the case of Belgium, a solid and uniform base for the examination of population data does not exist. Prior to 1830 the Netherlands, Belgium and the Grand Duchy of Luxembourg were united under the Dutch crown. The revolt of Belgium in 1830, however, led to its formal secession from the Netherlands in 1839, although the following territories remained under Dutch administration: the northern half of the province of Limburg, and part of Flanders protecting the south bank of the Schelde estuary. The province of Luxembourg was also transformed into the Grand Duchy. This situation continued until World War I, when the Eupen-Malmedy area which had previously been part of the German Empire was ceded to Belgium in 1920, increasing its area by 1,026 sq.km. to 30,513 sq.km. The same problem, however, arises in the case of the Netherlands as a result of the territorial gains of 1839 and the reclamation of land from the sea, although in the latter case this did not generate a sudden increase in total population. For the purposes of this study the territorial boundaries established by the 1839 treaty have been taken as an analytical base, although population figures in the case of Belgium are listed for both the old and the expanded territory, with 1920 being taken as a transition year.

The trend in total population in Belgium as well as the growth index (1784 = 100), and population density per sq.km. are listed in Table 6.1. Significantly the highest rate of increase took place between 1866 and 1910, which will later emerge as a crucial period in Belgium's demographic history. However, there were significant differences between the various provinces, both in relation to net population

236

growth and relative density (Table 6.2). In terms of actual population growth both Flanders and Wallony grew at an almost identical rate up to 1830, although the rate was appreciably faster in the provinces of Brabant and Liège during the French period between 1796 and 1815. After 1830, however, the growth rate picked up in Wallony with both regions having identical rates of increase between 1866 and 1890. However, from the late nineteenth century onwards the continuous increase in population in Flanders was accompanied by a gradual stagnation in Wallony and the balance in terms of population distribution began to tilt in favour of Flanders. This in turn was to generate a number of problems which still plague Belgium today. The population in Brabant, however, grew at a faster rate than in any other region and this can be largely attributed to the considerable growth of the metropolitan area of Brussels.

As a rule the highest levels of population density, both in Belgium and the Netherlands, are found in the western provinces (Flanders, Antwerp, Brabant and Hainaut). Indeed a high density in East Flanders already existed in the eighteenth century where a figure of 150 inhabitants per sq.km. was not uncommon at the beginning of this period. The general trends between Flanders and Wallony are also evident in the consistently higher levels of population density in the former area, which followed the general pattern visible in the growth indices.

The population growth rate in the Netherlands between the late eighteenth century and 1947 was clearly higher than in Belgium (Table 6.1). However, two distinct periods emerge. Between 1795 and 1900 population growth was slower than in Belgium, but in the post-1900 period the rate of growth was considerably faster than in the Belgian territories. In terms of relative population density the sharp increase in Dutch population in the first half of the twentieth century has resulted in high density levels and by 1947 the Netherlands registered the highest population density of the two countries.

However, regional differences were equally significant in this case. The two least accessible provinces of Friesland and Zeeland in general returned the lowest rate of population growth (Table 6.3), whereas the highest rates occurred in the provinces of Utrecht, Noordholland and Zuidholland, Limburg and Drenthe. The figures for Limburg are explicable in terms of economic change (industrialisation and the growth of the mining industry), and the performance of Utrecht, Noord- and Zuidholland can be attributed to the impact of considerable urbanisation, but there would appear to be no satisfactory explanation

for the population growth of Drenthe. However, with the exception of
Drenthe, the rate of growth only began to diverge on a provincial basis
in the post-1849 period. Between 1849 and 1909 the lowest rates are
observed in the most northerly and southerly provinces (Friesland,
Zeeland, Noord-Brabant and Limburg), with most of the population
growth concentrated in Noord- and Zuidholland, Utrecht and Drenthe.
In the latter period (1909-47) the highest growth rates occurred in
Noord-Brabant, Limburg and Utrecht, and the lowest in Zeeland,
Friesland and Groningen. The marked increase in population growth
in the southeastern part of the country during this period can be
attributed to the development of the mining industry and secondary
sector expansion as a whole.

The only provinces with relatively high population densities in 1815
were Noord- and Zuidholland and Utrecht, which would seem to
indicate that this was primarily determined by the overall extent of
early urbanisation. However, this appears to have been a unique Dutch
phenomenon, as no correlation emerges between population density
and relative urbanisation in Belgium. The lowest densities in 1815 were
found in Drenthe, Overijssel and Zeeland, closely followed by the
remaining provinces. Furthermore Drenthe and Zeeland have maintained
low densities throughout this period, although this was equally true of
Friesland after 1909.

Age and Sex Structure

In the case of Belgium both sexes remained of equal strength until 1880,
although this was followed by an increasing predominance of women
until 1920 when the male/female ratio reached an all-time low of 0.969
(Table 6.4). Between 1920 and 1930 there is a slight increase in the
proportion of men (0.981), but from 1939 onwards there was a further
increase in the proportion of women which reduced the ratio to a new
low of 0.958 by 1961. The deterioration in the ratio within the periods
1910-20, and 1930-47, however, can be attributed to the impact of the
two World Wars.

Provincial differences are also apparent in this context (Table 6.5).
There was clearly a higher proportion of women in the four Flemish
provinces than in the Walloon provinces and although the difference is
only fractional, it is nevertheless consistent. Brabant, with Brussels as
its main urban centre, shows a continuous increase in female population,
with the sex ratio falling from 0.985 (1846) to 0.937 (1910) which can
be attributed to the growth of population in the capital, as a surplus of
women had been a common phenomenon of urban population from the

sixteenth century onwards.

As far as the age structure of the Belgian population was concerned, four distinct age groups have been isolated (0-14 years, 15-44, 45-64 and 65 years and above). In this we will first try to examine the male and female components of total population and then to clarify regional differences. With respect to the male population in the age group 0-14 years there is a significant decline between 1846 and 1856, which is equally apparent in their female counterparts (Table 6.6). Although the reasons for this trend are not very clear, the cholera epidemic of 1848 and the extensive emigration during this period may have been causal factors. Between 1856 and 1880 there was a proportional increase in the size of this age group, from 30.4 to 33.8 per cent for males and from 30.2 to 33.2 per cent for females. This was followed, however, by a continuous fall which meant that by 1947 their proportion of total population only stood at 21.2 per cent and 20 per cent respectively. At the other end of the spectrum the proportion of people aged sixty-five years or over increased by approximately 0.5 per cent for men (1846-80) and by the same rate for women (1846-90). After a relative decline prior to 1900, there is a continuous increase from 1910 onwards. Significantly prior to 1900 Belgium had the second highest proportion of people aged sixty-five years and over in Western Europe, being surpassed only by France, and although it has now been overtaken by the Scandinavian countries, it still ranks in the top group. The Netherlands, however, occupied a more central position in the nineteenth century, although it became after 1900 a country with one of the lowest percentages of old people.[1]

However, these percentage figures do not fully reflect the ageing process of the population as a whole. The ratio of the population of less than fifteen years of age over the population aged sixty-five years or more (Table 6.7) declined for both men and women between 1846 and 1866. Although there was a slight improvement in the position prior to 1900, this was followed by a continuous and sharp fall. The sharpest decline in the ratio occurred earlier for women (between 1920 and 1930) than for men (between 1930 and 1947), and in any case it is relatively clear that the ageing process for women was more pronounced and occurred at a comparatively earlier date than for men. However, the second series of ratios (population aged 65 years and over/ population aged between 15 and 64 years) reveals a remarkable stability with the effects of the ageing process only becoming apparent in 1947. It would seem, therefore, that the process of ageing in Belgium was mainly one of 'ageing at the base of the pyramid', with the effects of an 'ageing at the top' only apparent from 1920-30 onwards.

An interesting difference emerges, however, between the three main regions of Belgium (Flanders, Wallony and Brabant) as early as 1846. The proportion of young people aged fifteen years or less increased from 31.3 to 34.0 per cent in Flanders between 1846 and 1910, while it declined in Wallony from 33.5 to 27.4 per cent and in Brabant to a lesser extent. Equally from 1910 onwards although Flanders followed the general downward trend, the decline was less apparent than in other regions. For the population aged sixty-five years and over the proportions remained relatively unchanged in Wallony and Brabant between 1846 and 1890, while it actually increased in the case of Flanders (Table 6.8). Between 1890 and 1920 a decrease in the proportion of old people took place in Flanders, while an increase occurred in other regions. In the post-1920 period all three regions showed an increase, although this was highest in Brabant and lowest in Flanders. By the turn of the century, therefore, Flanders had not only the highest percentage of young, but also the highest proportion of aged, with a resultant loss of population in the active age groups. In Wallony, however, the basic change involved a narrowing of the base of the pyramid, indicated by a fall in the proportion of persons aged fifteen years or less. During the period 1846-1947 the young/old ratio (i.e. less than 15/65 and over) followed the fluctuations in the proportion of the younger age group, although the levels of the ratio were determined by the relative importance of the population aged sixty-five years and over. In other words the higher the percentage of the elderly, the lower the ratio and vice versa (Table 6.9). The ratio 65+/15-64 in the case of Brabant and Wallony does not alter significantly between 1846 and 1920, although the following years were marked by a significant decline. In Flanders, however, the situation was rather more complicated. Between 1846 and 1890 the ratio increased, only to decline between 1890 and 1920 and to increase again in the following years. Only in the years following World War II did Flanders finally acquire a more favourable ratio of active to retired population than either Wallony or Brabant.

In the Netherlands, on the other hand, there was a continuous increase in the male/female ratio between 1830 and 1947 (Table 6.10). In comparison with Belgium, therefore, it followed a totally divergent path: declining in Belgium and increasing in the Netherlands. On a regional basis only the provinces of Drenthe, Overijssel and Gelderland had a surplus of males in 1830 (Table 6.11). However, during the following period the situation changed drastically, with all the separate

provinces except Groningen, Utrecht, Noord- and Zuidholland
reporting a surplus of males in 1947. Of these four provinces Groningen
was probably a borderline case with a ratio of .99. The female surplus
in the other three provinces, however, was more pronounced (.96) and
is indication of extensive in-migration and a high incidence of urban
population growth. The trends in the proportion of males and females
(0-14 years) were largely identical (Table 6.12). If there was a fall in the
proportion between 1830 and 1859, this was counterbalanced by an increase
from 1859 to 1889. This was followed, however, by a continuous fall until
1947 when the post-war baby boom created an increase, which was
significantly not evident in the case of Belgium. The proportion of the
male population aged sixty-five years and over initially declined
between 1830 and 1859, only to be followed by a continuous increase.
The same trend is evident for females, although it is not as regular. The
ratios produced by a combination of the various age groups (Table 6.13)
indicate a considerable process of ageing over time, which resulted
largely from a reduction in the relative importance of the younger age
groups, with little or no ageing at the top of the population pyramid
and no increase in the burden of older people in relation to the active
adult population. However, the ratio 0-14/65+ indicates that the ageing
of the female population occurred at an earlier stage than for men,
although between 1830 and 1947 the general trend was identical for
both sexes. Further confirmation of the fact that the female population
was initially older and continued to remain so during the period under
consideration can be derived from the ratio 65+/15-64. However, in
direct contrast to Belgium there were no clear regional differences.

The percentage of young people (0-14 years) increased for both
sexes between 1849 and 1899, only to be followed by a later decline.
Moreover no province deviates from the general pattern. For the base
year (1849) the highest proportion of boys is to be found in the two
most northerly provinces of Groningen and Friesland, although no
significant pattern emerges for the rest of the country. The proportion
of girls in the youngest age group in 1849 was lowest in the three
provinces of Noord- and Zuidholland and Utrecht which had the
largest urban population, as well as in Noordbrabant. To some extent
this can be attributed to the large influx of women into the nascent
urban centres. By 1899, however, although there is a remarkable
element of similarity in relation to the male population with the
exception of Zuidholland (highest), Noordbrabant and Friesland
(lowest), no distinctive pattern emerges in the case of women. In 1947
the proportion for both sexes is relatively similar, with the highest

percentages in Drenthe, Limburg and Noordbrabant, characterised by
a high rate of population growth, and the lowest in Groningen, Zeeland,
Noord- and Zuidholland. However, the proportion of males was higher
than the percentages for women throughout the whole period.

The percentage of men and women aged sixty-five years and over
(Table 6.12) has increased continuously, except for a decline between
1899 and 1920 in Drenthe, Gelderland, Utrecht, Zuidholland,
Noordbrabant and Limburg. However, the increase in the percentage
was consistently higher for men than for women. The highest increases
for both sexes were registered in Groningen, Friesland, Noordholland
and Zeeland, although it should be noted that the percentages were
normally higher for women than for men. The highest 0-14/65+ ratios
in 1849 are found in Groningen, Friesland, Zeeland (all three for both
sexes), Noordholland (men only) and Drenthe (women only). By 1947
the ratios for both sexes were lowest in Groningen, Friesland and
Zeeland, which indicates that the ageing process was most advanced in
these provinces. The two northern provinces in this group were faced
with an ageing at the top, while Zeeland faced one at both the base
and the top of the pyramid. The lowest ratios in 1849 were registered
in Noordbrabant, Limburg, Utrecht (all three provinces for both sexes),
Overijssel and Gelderland (men only). By 1947 the highest ratios were
to be found in Noordbrabant and Limburg, which as provinces had
aged the least, as a result of the fact that they had the highest
proportion of people under fifteen years of age and a low proportion
of individuals aged sixty-five years and over. These regional differences
are confirmed by the ratio 65+/15-64, which indicates that the heaviest
burden of older people occurs in Groningen, Friesland and Zeeland,
with the lowest proportion of elderly in Noordbrabant and Limburg.

Internal and International Migration

In the case of Belgium data on migration, particularly for the pre-1890
period, is not especially abundant. For the years between 1815 and
1824, however, Smits observed a strong flow of rural migrants towards
Antwerp and the urban areas of East Flanders (specifically Ghent),
whereas the rural areas of East Flanders and Namur together with the
provinces of West Flanders, Liège, Limburg and Hainaut were the major
losers of population.[2] An indication of internal migration patterns is
provided by a breakdown of population according to their place of
birth (Table 6.14). Between 1846 and 1890 the proportion of
individuals involved in migration within their province of birth
increased uniformly throughout the country. This was not the case,

however, in relation to interprovincial migration, where the highest percentages in 1846 were encountered in Antwerp, Brabant and Namur and the lowest in West Flanders and Luxembourg. Indeed Brabant and Antwerp for administrative and economic reasons were the main growth centres of Belgium in the second quarter of the nineteenth century. However, the significance of interprovincial migration by 1866 had declined considerably, except in the case of Luxembourg, with the highest percentages recorded in Antwerp, Liège and Luxembourg. To a large extent this decline reflected the severity of the economic crisis of the 1840s and 1850s, when only provinces with a relatively strong industrial base were able to maintain their appeal as centres of in-migration. Between 1866 and 1890 the proportions increased again, although it is important to note that the 1866 pattern remained largely unchanged. For the period 1901-10, however, the provinces of Antwerp, Brabant, Hainaut and Liège recorded a positive net migration,[3] with the highest negative rates in Flanders, Limburg and Luxembourg. However, these provincial rates do not fully reveal the complexity of the overall migration pattern. Within the provinces of Antwerp, Brabant and Liège, for example, only those districts with a large urban base (Antwerp, Brussels and Liège) had a strong rate of in-migration, whereas other areas suffered a net loss in population. Similarly in Hainaut only those districts in the southern industrial belt had a positive balance. In the following years the major cities continued to act as poles of attraction, although by 1948-61 Liège had strengthened its position in comparison with both Brussels and Antwerp. However, by this date all the various districts (*arrondissements*) of Brabant gained from in-migration, whereas Hainaut, with the exception of Charleroi, no longer attracted migrants. West and East Flanders, and Luxembourg, however, remained the areas of highest out-migration.

Between 1930 and 1947 the pattern of interprovincial migration has remained relatively unchanged. Most migrants tended to move to a neighbouring province in the first instance, if it benefited from a favourable economic position.[4] Furthermore, with the exception of Brabant, most migrants tended to move to provinces within their own language area. Data from the years between 1891 and 1900 also confirms that most of the internal out-migration was generated in rural areas.[5] However, on the basis of recent research it would seem that migration was not responsible for differences in age structure in the individual provinces, but only served to accentuate trends that were already underway.[6]

The earliest data on emigration stems from the period 1830-44,[7] when both Flanders and Hainaut had the highest proportion of emigrants (33.7 per cent, 16.4 per cent and 17.9 per cent respectively for West Flanders, East Flanders and Hainaut). However, emigration was most prominent in specific *arrondissements*: Kortrijk (West Flanders), Ghent (East Flanders) and Tournai (Hainaut), and it seems likely that the decline of the rural textile industry was mainly responsible for this particular pattern. The proportion of emigrants from urban centres was significantly greater than from rural areas. Finally the peripheral areas of the country were most severely affected by emigration, as the principal destinations of migrants were France and the Netherlands which attracted migrants from the border provinces. However, two of the most 'closed' provinces (West Flanders and Luxembourg) generated most of the intercontinental migration. The process was also a two-way one, with both France and the Netherlands providing the bulk of immigrants, particularly in the border areas and the 1846 census reveals a distinct surplus of female immigrants from these two countries in contrast to a male surplus from other more distant areas of Europe.[8]

However, many of the characteristics of this pattern of migration reoccurred in later years, although satisfactory data for the period 1846-84 is lacking. There was almost no change in the destination of either Belgian emigrants or foreign immigrants, or indeed of the sex ratio of immigrants according to country of origin. However, between 1886 and 1900 the proportion of emigrants who settled in countries bordering on Belgium, including the British Isles, increased from 75 per cent (1886) to 87.6 per cent (1900).[9] Between 1830 and 1844 the proportion had stood at 86.3 per cent,[10] which would indicate an increasing importance of intercontinental migration in the period 1844 to 1886. In the last two decades of the nineteenth century overseas migration declined again, but increased significantly prior to World War I from 5.1 per cent (1896-1900) to 16.8 per cent (1901-13).[11] During the same period emigration to European countries declined, although this was most pronounced in relation to more distant migration. Emigration to neighbouring countries, however, also declined from 87.6 per cent (1896-1900) to 79.5 per cent (1901-13). The immediate post-war period witnessed a number of changes in the migration pattern which were to determine emigration up until 1947. Emigration declined rapidly to less than a third of its pre-1914 level.[1] Intercontinental migration was reduced to very small levels (5-6 per cent), although migration to the Belgian Congo (Zaïre) did increase, and within Europe France became an increasingly popular destination at the direct expense of Germany and the Netherlands.

During the nineteenth century France, the Netherlands and Germany, in that order, had provided the majority of immigrants. An increase in the importance of France between 1846 and 1900 was accompanied by a decline in the importance of the Netherlands, and although Germany became more significant prior to 1880, this was followed by a slight decline.[13] In the early twentieth century the importance of Germany fell even further (from 20.2 per cent in 1900 to 9 per cent between 1901 and 1913) and this was equally the case in relation to the Netherlands (25 per cent to 13 per cent). France, however, doubled its proportion of immigrants from 40.4 per cent to 76.6 per cent.[14] After the First World War Germany's significance declined even further and the number of French immigrants also fell. On the other hand there was an increase in Dutch and British immigration into Belgium, accompanied by an increasing proportion of Italians and Poles. By 1947 Italians were the largest body of immigrants (22.9 per cent), followed by the French (18 per cent) and the Dutch (17 per cent).[15]

In the Netherlands Noordbrabant and Zuidholland were the only provinces with considerable in-migration in the period 1815 to 1824.[16] However, interprovincial migration was much more important in the Netherlands and its significance increased during the period under examination (Table 6.15). Women were also more mobile than men, although this was more marked in relation to short-distance migration than interprovincial migration. On a regional basis the lowest level of interprovincial migration is to be found in the most northerly and southerly provinces (Groningen, Friesland, Zeeland, Noordbrabant and Limburg),[17] although this was partly compensated by a higher intra-provincial migration in the first four of these provinces. Although Limburg had percentage figures comparable with other provinces in the country, it had a much higher incidence of foreign-born people.[18] The interprovincial percentages for both sexes and for all provinces increased up till 1947 and there was also an increase in short-distance migration, except in Gelderland, Drenthe, Utrecht and Zuidholland where the percentages for both sexes declined. However, in Drenthe this was compensated by a strong increase in interprovincial migration. As far as net migration was concerned (Table 6.16) the provinces with the highest negative rates between 1840 and 1947 were Groningen, Friesland, Drenthe and Zeeland while Utrecht, Noord- and Zuidholland were the major centres of attraction.

Dutch international migration statistics, however, are relatively poor and only facilitate an examination of the general emigration flow and not the country of destination, as the only distinction made in official compilations was between Dutch colonies and non-specified foreign countries. Immigration statistics are even worse, as they include returning Dutch migrants. As a result reliance has had to be placed on census data rather than existing official statistics (Table 6.17). Almost all immigrants into the Netherlands came from either Belgium or Germany, although the proportion of Germans was naturally reduced during World War II. Immigration was also concentrated in the border provinces, with the German element particularly strong in Groningen, Drenthe, Overijssel, and Gelderland, and Belgians in Zeeland.

Nuptiality and Fertility

In this analysis crude rates have not been employed, because population size, particularly at the provincial level, was relatively small and crude rates would have been significantly influenced by differences in age structure as well as the sex ratio. However, in a number of instances crude birth rates were the only measurement available for an extended examination of regional differences, although they have been used very reluctantly.

In Belgium during the period 1829 to 1947 the proportion of men and women never married at age fifty has declined sharply, although this was more apparent for women than for men (Table 6.18). The fall in the proportion of single women was very marked (Table 6.19), being most apparent in the age group 30-39 and least noticeable in the age group 15-24. The increase in the proportion of single women between 1846 and 1856, which was evident in all age groups, can be attributed to the impact on nuptiality of the deteriorating economic situation of the 1840s and 1850s. In relation to this index for women on a provincial basis (Table 6.20) both East and West Flanders and Limburg had a proportion consistently above the national average, although by 1930 they had also been joined by Luxembourg. The percentage remained stable in Namur, increased in the southeastern provinces of the country and declined in Flanders, Antwerp and Hainaut.

The I_m index, or the proportion married among women of child-bearing age between fifteen and fifty years is the most sensitive indicator of nuptiality.[19] A high index is indicative of an early and intensive marriage pattern and a low index is frequently evidence of nuptiality restrictions. Moreover the index provides a useful link with changes in fertility. Over time all provinces have moved towards a more intense marriage pattern as a result of an increasing reduction in marriage restrictions (Table 6.21). However, a clear distinction can be drawn between the western and eastern part of the country. Whereas there was a sharp increase in the index in Antwerp, Brabant, Flanders and Hainaut, the change in the eastern and southeastern provinces was less pronounced. A distinction is equally evident between the relatively industrialised and agricultural provinces, or between the poor and rich areas. The more prosperous provinces of Antwerp, Brabant, Hainaut and Liège in 1930 had higher indices. However recent research has indicated that there was a sharp decline in the I_m index between 1806 and 1829 in all provinces.[20]

The fall in the average age at marriage, on the other hand, progressed by stages, although it was particularly rapid in the case of women (Table 6.22). On a regional basis the fall in the average age did not vary significantly between provinces in the period 1862-1930 (Table 6.23), although a marginally smaller decrease was observed in the three eastern provinces of Liège, Limburg and Luxembourg. The lowest average ages for 1862-6 are found in Hainaut, Liège, Namur and Luxembourg, in other words in the Walloon provinces. By 1896-1900, however, the group had lost Luxembourg, but been joined by Antwerp and Brabant. In 1926-30 the lowest figures were recorded in Hainaut and Namur.

The I_g index, however, is designed to indicate the extent to which marital fertility of a given population falls short of the highest obtainable fertility, based on the fertility of married Hutterite women. The higher the index value, the closer fertility will be to the expected maximum. It is fortunate, therefore, that this is one of the few consistent measurements available for Belgium over an extended period of time. For Belgium as a whole the I_g index increased between 1800 and 1829, only to decline between 1829 and 1846. During the period 1846-66 it increased again, but declined up until 1930 with a further sharp increase recorded after the end of World War II (Table 6.24). On a regional basis the absence of sufficient data for 1829 prevents an analysis of trends between 1800 and 1846. However, a comparison of the indices for 1800-12 and 1846 reveals a minimal rate of change between provinces, with the exception of Antwerp. The relative increase in the index between 1846 and 1866, however, reflects two contrary trends: a sharp rise in Flanders and a much smaller increase or even a decline in Wallony (Hainaut and Namur). Serious regional differences also emerged between 1866 and 1930. The largest decreases were observed in Brabant, Hainaut and Liège, with the result that these three provinces had the lowest I_g index by 1930. The decline in West Flanders and Limburg was comparatively less severe and by 1930 these two provinces had the highest index figure. Between 1930 and 1961 there was a similar dichotomy, with a very sharp increase being recorded in Hainaut, Liège, Namur and Brabant, and a significantly smaller rise in Flanders and Luxembourg. These results confirm the existence of a consistent difference between Flanders and Wallony. Within Wallony, however, the fact that Liège and Hainaut are highly industrialised and Luxembourg relatively less so has strongly influenced the overall level and evolution of fertility.[21]

In the Netherlands, however, the fall in the proportion of women never married has been considerably less than in Belgium, except for the age group 30-34 for both men and women (Table 6.25). Moreover in the majority of cases the significant decline only occurred between 1930 and 1947. For women the age groups 40-44 and 50-54 reveal little change and in the age group 20-24 the decline was only approximately 20 per cent, considerably less than in the case of Belgium. It is important to note, however, that the proportion never married in 1849 was already considerably lower in the Netherlands than in Belgium, although over the course of the following years this relationship was to change significantly. The fall in the proportion in the age group 20-24 was comparatively small in the Netherlands, with the result that by the turn of the century the incidence of single women in this age group was higher than in Belgium.[22] For the age group 50-54 hardly any fall was observed which resulted in a considerable narrowing of the original gap between the two countries.[23]

As far as the four major age groups were concerned, the age groups 40-44 and 50-54 underwent little change prior to 1930, although there was a slight increase in the proportion of women aged 50-54 between 1879 and 1920. For the age groups 20-24 and 30-34 an increase was registered between 1830 and 1849 which almost certainly reflected the political and economic difficulties following the break-up in 1830 of the union between Belgium and the Netherlands, which led to a general postponement of marriage. Thereafter the percentages decreased continuously, except for a slight increase in 1920-30 in the age group 20-24. As far as regional differences for women in the two age groups 20-24 and 50-54 were concerned (Table 6.26), there was a continuous decrease in the first age group in Drenthe, Overijssel, Gelderland, Utrecht, Zeeland, Noordbrabant and Limburg. With the exception of Drenthe, all these provinces had the highest percentage of never married women in 1947. However, by this date a clear regional pattern between high and low percentages had emerged, which had been lacking in the mid-nineteenth century. But irrespective of whether or not there was a continuous fall between 1849 and 1947, the actual rate of decrease was almost the same in all provinces. In the proportion of never married in the age group 50-54, however, little change occurred. By 1947 the highest proportion was recorded in the southern half of the country, which had largely been the case in 1849.

Data on the average age at marriage is unfortunately very scarce and although there was an overall fall, it was neither continuous nor extensive (Table 6.27). If there was a fall between 1851 and 1880, this was followed by a further rise until 1900, when a further decline set in. The overall fall was less than 10 per cent, although in Belgium the average age at marriage declined by approximately 16 per cent. If the average age at marriage had been higher in Belgium than in the Netherlands in 1852-6, the reverse was the case by the turn of the century.

The only available indicator of fertility for the whole period under examination is the general legitimate fertility rate. However, the situation is slightly complicated by the existence of three separate sets of data, with the first series published by Hofstee (number of births per 1.000 married women aged 15-45) consistently higher than the two later series compiled by Buissink.[24] Hofstee almost certainly failed to make a distinction between legitimate and illegitimate births, thus inflating the fertility rates, although this series does cover the largest time-span (1831-1950), whereas the two Buissink series only extend from 1850 to 1914.[25] In the final analysis the later Buissink series has been used as this directly relates the number of legitimate births to married women aged fifty years and under and therefore provides a more refined system of measurement. The Hofstee data has only been used to extend the period covered in the analysis (Table 6.28). The highest fertility rates in 1850-54 were found in Noord- and Zuidholland, Zeeland and Noordbrabant in the southwestern parts of the country. By 1880-84 differences were now reflected along a west-east axis, with the lowest fertility rates registered in the northern provinces of Noordholland, Friesland, Groningen, Drenthe and Overijssel. By 1900-04, however, the pattern had shifted again, with the lowest rates now being listed in Noordholland, Friesland, Groningen and Zeeland. The highest fertility occurred in Noordbrabant and Limburg. This general pattern was also present in 1910-14. For the Netherlands as a whole, fertility fell between 1850 and 1859, increased between 1860 and 1879 only to fall continuously from then onwards.

If the same periodisation is adopted at the provincial level, most provinces tend to follow the national pattern in the period 1850-59, with the exception of Limburg where there was a continuous increase in fertility until 1875-9 and Drenthe where no real changes were recorded until 1860-64. Between 1860 and 1879 there was a continuous increase in Groningen, Drenthe, Overijssel, Zuidholland, Noordbrabant and Limburg. In Gelderland, Utrecht and Noordholland the increase was interrupted during the years 1870-74. Friesland and Zeeland, however, were significant exceptions, with the decline in fertility starting in 1860-64 and 1870-74 respectively. The fall in fertility was relatively general after 1880-84 except in Drenthe where a sharp fall in the rate between 1875-9 and 1880-84 was followed by a recovery until 1900-04, and in Overijssel, Noordbrabant and Limburg, where a shorter period of initial decline was followed by a slight increase until the end of the century.

The overall increase in fertility rates between 1850-54 and 1875-9, however, was marked by regional differences. The highest increases are found in Noordbrabant and Limburg, and the smallest ones in the three western provinces of Noord- and Zuidholland and Zeeland. Part of this pattern was retained, when fertility rates began to fall, in the period 1880-84 to 1910-14. The highest rate of decrease was registered in the western provinces, including Utrecht, and the smallest in the eastern and southeastern provinces. The middle group was comprised of the two northern provinces of Groningen and Friesland.

The general similarity in the different sets of data, both for the period 1851-65 and 1900-14, although the Hofstee figures are consistently higher (Table 6.29), suggests that the analysis can be confidently extended both to earlier and later periods. For the years prior to 1850 there was a general increase in fertility, particularly between 1831 and 1840, with this trend continuing in Groningen, Drenthe and Zuidholland until 1845. However, this was followed by a short decline in fertility rates between 1845 and 1850, as a result of the crisis of 1846-8.[26] Although the rates increased after 1850 they still remained below the 1841-5 level. Two clear sub-periods emerge in the years following 1914. Between 1914 and 1940 fertility rates fell continuously, but this was followed by an increase after 1941. In the immediate post-1914 period the greatest fall occurred in Zuidholland and Zeeland, with the lowest decline registered in the eastern and southeastern provinces, except for Groningen. The recovery in fertility rates was most apparent in the highly urbanised provinces of Utrecht, Zuid- and Noordholland.

The discussion on the causal mechanism behind these significant changes has given rise to a number of different interpretations.

Buissink has argued, for example, that the agricultural depression of the late nineteenth century had a particularly adverse effect in Groningen, Friesland and Zeeland and caused an irreversible and dramatic fall in fertility.[27] However, his own data would seem to indicate that the fall in fertility was equally prominent in other provinces. Hofstee, on the other hand, has pointed out that the highest decline took place in the alluvial areas of the Netherlands, where the primary sector was naturally more predominant.[28] Furthermore the long-term trends attributed by Buissink to the crisis of the 1880s may have been the result of changing attitudes to fertility in the more urbanised provinces of the western Netherlands. However, Hofstee has also argued that there was a shift in the pattern of fertility decline from the northwest to the southwest,[29] which has been denied by Buissink,[30] and on the whole Hofstee may well have overstated his case in this respect.

The central debate on causality has involved proponents of religious factors as the main determinant of fertility decline (Van Heek, Buissink), and Hofstee who has argued for the primacy of non-religious and specifically economic factors. The former protagonists have argued that the Roman Catholic religion has tended from the early twentieth century onwards to retard the secular decline in fertility.[31] However, fertility differences between Catholics and non-Catholics in a given area were frequently smaller than the differences between Catholics in various individual provinces.[32] The arguments of Van Heek and Buissink, moreover, have been recently placed in some doubt by Van Poppel, as Catholic fertility rates were directly governed by the size of community. Large communities invariably had lower rates of fertility,[33] and the rate of fertility decline is also greater in larger communities. Although differences in fertility were clearly influenced by religious factors, non-religious variables were of prime importance in determining the mechanism of fertility decline. This has been further confirmed by Methorst who has highlighted the significance of income factors in urban and rural districts.[34] The same income group was likely to have more than four children per family in rural areas than in towns and a reverse relationship existed for families of less than four children. Furthermore large families were invariably found in comparatively poor districts, with small families effectively a privilege of the rich. By and large the lower the level of skill and income, the higher fertility rate tended to be.

Mortality

A swift glance at the trend in crude death rates in Belgium reveals that the major decline in mortality took place between 1875 and 1910

(Table 6.30). In 1815-24 the highest rates were recorded in East and West Flanders and Brabant (Table 6.31), although by 1880 all Flemish provinces, including Flanders, Antwerp and Limburg, as well as Brabant, had above average death rates. Between 1880 and 1959-61 this situation was reversed, with the highest rates now being found in Wallony (Hainaut, Liège, Luxembourg, Namur and Brabant). Indeed the trend towards an increase in mortality was already to be observed prior to 1880 in villages adjacent to the rivers Sambre and Meuse and in certain fringe areas of the Ardennes.[35] The relative fall in mortality in Flanders after 1880 was largely the result of lower rates in the coastal area of West Flanders and along the Brussels-Antwerp axis.[36] Significantly death rates between 1815 and 1841 were consistently lower in rural communities than in the urban centres.[37]

On the whole life expectancy at various ages did not improve until the period 1845-81 (Table 6.32), although the data is not adequate enough to allow a more precise dating of the upswing. Indeed prior to 1845 there may well have been a marginal deterioration particularly at birth and at age ten years. The most impressive improvement has been in life expectancy at birth, particularly in the second half of the nineteenth century. In contrast only negligible gains were made at ages fifty and seventy, except perhaps for the post-1930 period. The life expectancy of women was consistently higher than for men, and the gap between the two sexes has remained remarkably constant over time. Furthermore the differences in life expectancy in 1832 and between 1891 and 1900 confirm the earlier impression that mortality was lower in rural areas than in the towns. On a regional basis life expectancy at birth in the Flemish provinces at the turn of the century was well below the national average. By the period 1959-61, however, this position had been taken over by the Walloon provinces.

The earliest life table was constructed by Quetelet and Smits for 1827-9. For the purpose of this analysis separate tables for the male and female population have been used, although the two earliest tables do not unfortunately contain such data. This is to some extent compensated by a breakdown of the two sexes according to urban and rural areas. It is clear from the life tables for 1827-9 and 1841-5 (Table 6.33) that the number of surviving women between the ages of 0 and 15 was higher in rural areas than in the urban centres. From age twenty onwards, however, the survival rate was higher in the cities. The male survival rate in rural areas was consistently higher in both periods. In urban districts, however, the female survival rate was always higher, while life expectancy for men was greater in rural areas from the ages of 40-45 onwards.

Between 1847-56 and 1891-1900 the rate of survival at age one hardly changed for either sex, although a considerable improvement did take place in the numbers surviving at ages five and ten, particularly in relation to females at age ten. For the ages fifteen and over there was a progressive improvement for both sexes, although this was more noticeable for women from age forty-five and over. However, in the period between 1891-1900 and 1946-9 there were equal improvements for both sexes, thus maintaining the original gap. The smallest improvements are in the survival rate at age one. On a comparative basis the rate of change between the second half of the nineteenth century and the first fifty years of the present century was roughly similar for men up until age fifty, although there was a significantly greater increase in the number of survivors in the older age groups in the later period. A similar situation existed in relation to women, with significant improvements in the survival rate occurring after age fifty-five. The life tables for 1841-5 reveal that the lowest survival rates existed in Brabant, and West and East Flanders for all ages. By 1891 to 1900, however, the lowest rates from age one up to fifty are recorded in Antwerp, Brabant, both parts of Flanders and Limburg, which reinforced the comparatively disadvantageous position of Flanders as a whole. From age fifty onwards, however, the difference between Flanders and Wallony is not as severe or clear-cut.

Data on infant mortality in Belgium, on the other hand, is only available from 1841 and a distinction between endogenous and exogenous rates was only made from the turn of the century onwards. Earlier estimates of endogenous mortality almost certainly underestimated its significance.[38] The national rates (Table 6.34) indicate almost no change in infant mortality between 1841 and 1910 and even an increase between 1871 and 1895. Infant mortality only falls sharply after World War I, as a result of a decline in exogenous mortality, which was reinforced by a similar process after World War II. The endogenous rate changed little until after 1940 when a slight increase was reported. The fall in infant mortality in the post-1918/19 period has benefited females more than males. Male infant mortality rates between 1870 and 1885 were between 16 and 19 per cent higher than the female rates, and since World War I the difference has grown to about 25 per cent (Table 6.35). Although endogenous mortality did rise in the 1940s, there was a decline in still-births for both sexes, probably as a result of improved pre-natal facilities. This in turn may have caused a postponement of still-births into the endogenous age bracket. Between 1940 and 1949 the male still-birth rate fell from 31.6 to 26.7 per 1,000, and the equivalent rates for girls declined from 25.8 to 21.9. The highest infant mortality rates according to province (Table 6.36) in the period 1898-1900 were found in the Flemish regions (East and West Flanders, Antwerp and Limburg). Indeed over time an *arrondissement* in West Flanders has consistently recorded the highest infant death rate in the whole of the country. Although the Flemish rates fell faster than in Wallony, the provinces of Flanders still registered the highest figures in 1950, with Hainaut having also joined this specific high mortality group.

In the case of the Netherlands the crude death rate fell almost without interruption for both sexes between 1840 and 1950, although there was a slight increase in 1941-5 as a result of the famine in the last months of the Second World War. The rates for women were consistently lower than for men, although the rate of decrease was identical for both sexes (Table 6.37). Regional information on mortality is unfortunately comparatively rare, although the highest rates in 1955-65 were found in Groningen, Friesland, Utrecht, Noordholland and Zeeland.[39] However, the crude death rate in smaller communities (less than 20,000 inhabitants) between 1880 and 1899 was generally lower than in larger settlements, although this was being gradually eroded. In the twentieth century lower rates have been largely recorded in the more substantial communities (over 20,000 inhabitants).[40]

Life expectancy at birth and at ages 10, 50 and 70 also increased continuously and for both sexes between 1880 and 1949. The improvement seems to have been slightly greater for men than for women, with the highest increase in life expectancy at birth, particularly in the first half of the twentieth century (Table 6.38). Life expectancy for women at all ages was generally higher than for men. Data on life expectancy according to region is only available for the period 1840-51. Rural life expectancy at birth was considerably higher than in urban centres and the difference between the sexes is uniformally higher in urban areas than in rural districts. The highest difference between men and women in urban centres is recorded in the provinces of Noord- and Zuidholland, which were also the areas of extensive urban population growth. It is also worth noting that over time the life expectancy of married individuals had increased more significantly than that of single persons.[41]

If mortality trends are examined on the basis of existing life tables (Table 6.39) it is clear that the survival rate of women was consistently higher than that of men. Furthermore for all ages and both sexes there was a continuous increase. However, in 1840 the survival rates for both men and women in Belgium were noticeably higher than in the Netherlands; by the turn of the century this position had been reversed and the Netherlands was to improve its relative position during the first half of the twentieth century. The least improvement for both sexes was in the survival rate at age one. For all other ages a considerable improvement was registered with men benefiting disproportionally during the second half of the nineteenth century in comparison with subsequent periods. In the first half of the twentieth century the gains, specifically for women, were in the fifty years and above bracket. As a result of the considerable increase in male survival rates, the original gap between the two sexes has been narrowed, although the highest difference at sixty years and over continued to remain.

An analysis of infant mortality trends, on the other hand, is complicated by the absence of data between 1855 and 1880. However, between 1821 and 1855 there was a significant increase, particularly in female mortality (Table 6.40). In the period 1880-1949 there was a continuous fall in this rate, with only a slight increase during World War II. Male mortality which was initially higher actually declined at a slower pace between 1826 and 1949 than the female rate, which aggravated the gap between the two sexes. Furthermore the increase in mortality between 1821 and 1855 was also accompanied by a rise in the still-birth rate from 65.7 to 71.2 per 1,000 for boys and 51.5 to 59.0 for girls.[42] On a provincial basis there was a general decline between 1880 and 1930 except for Limburg, where there was a relative rise between 1880 and 1904. In 1880 the highest rates were recorded in the western part of the country (Utrecht, Noordholland, Zuidholland, Zeeland and Noordbrabant), although by 1930 Noordbrabant and Limburg headed the table, with the lowest rates in Friesland, Noordholland, Zuidholland and Utrecht. The highest decrease over time had been in the last three provinces, which can be attributed to the considerable fall in infant mortality in cities with over 50,000 inhabitants. Between 1880 and 1930 infant mortality in urban centres (100,000 inhabitants+) fell from 219 to 37.6 per 1,000, whereas the corresponding decline for towns with a population between 50,000 and 100,000 was from 195 to 45, and for rural communities of less than 5,000 inhabitants from 187 to 57 per 1,000.

Infant mortality also fluctuated according to occupational status and income level. In 1946/50, for example, the highest rates in Amsterdam were found among the children of artisans, small shopkeepers and workers.[43] A similar difference existed in 1937-40.[44] Furthermore although the

death rate of children aged five years and less rose with a progressive
fall in family income, the differences were also more marked in urban
centres than in rural areas.[45] However, between 1897 and 1927 the
fall in mortality was greater in the cities than in the countryside. In
1897 the urban rate stood at 248 per 1,000 as against 165 in rural
areas and by 1927 the rate for both areas was 93 pro mille.

Conclusion

An effective comparison of the demographic development of Belgium
and the Netherlands is inevitably complicated by differences in
measurements and in data. Moreover if the Netherlands was
characterised by relative homogeneity with regional differences in the
basic indices failing to produce a consistent pattern, cultural differences
were clearly evident in Belgium, where differences between Flanders
and Wallony, with Brabant caught in the middle, occur continuously
during this period. This pattern was emphasised by the slow pace of
demographic change in Wallony, which eventually led to the loss of its
numerical hegemony in the country as a whole. On the other hand some
of the underlying problems in Flanders, such as a high rate of infant
mortality, which were evident in the nineteenth century have not yet
completely disappeared. Over time population grew faster in the
Netherlands than in Belgium. The age structure of the population was
much younger, both at the base and the top of the population pyramid,
than in Belgium, with a particularly small number of women aged
sixty-five years and over. However, the incidence of single women aged
fifty which had been significantly higher in Belgium in the mid-
nineteenth century had fallen below the Dutch percentage by 1947.
In terms of average age at first marriage, women tended to marry later
in Belgium until 1866, when the national roles were reversed. The
largest differences between the two countries, however, are to be
found in relation to mortality. All the indices for mortality reflect a
better situation in the Netherlands than in Belgium. Life expectancy at
birth in 1840 was already higher in the former case, and although the
gap had narrowed by 1947, life expectancy for both sexes was still
higher in the Netherlands. If the survival rates for the Belgian
population in 1840 were consistently higher than for the Dutch
population, this situation had been radically altered from 1900
onwards. Finally although Belgian infant mortality rates were initially
lower, from 1900 onwards the Dutch rates clearly had the edge.

   The present contribution can only mark the beginning of research
into many of these fundamental aspects of the demographic history of

the Low Countries. It is hoped that we have been relatively successful in bringing together a reasonable quantity of empirical data which may serve as a basis for further analysis. Many of the factors which determined the specific development of the two countries have also been touched upon and it can only be hoped that this will serve as a stimulus to a continuing examination of the fundamental interaction of population growth, economic development and social change.

Notes

1. 'Le vieillissement des populations et ses conséquences économiques et sociales', United Nations, Demographic Studies, no.26, p.12.
2. E. Smits, *Statistique Nationale. Développement des trente et un tableaux publiés par la Commission de Statistique*, Brussels, 1827, Table 1.
3. H. Damas, 'Population de la Belgique: Les migrations intérieures', *Population et Famille*, no.4, December 1964, pp.31-62.
4. C. Mertens, 'Repartition territoriale de la population belge. Modifications survenues entre 1930 et 1947', *Proceedings of the World Population Conference*, Rome, 1954, vol.4, pp.587-95.
5. J.M.J. Leclerc, 'Table de Mortalité 1890-1900', *Bulletin de la Commission Centrale de Statistique*, vol.19, pp.76-81.
6. R. André and J. Pereira-Roque, 'Le rôle des migrations dans l'évolution de la structure des âges des provinces belges au course de la dernière decennie due XIXe siècle', *Revue de l'Institut de Sociologie*, Brussels, 1972, no.1, pp.138-58.
7. G. Kurgan-Van Hentenryck, 'Aspects de l'émigration belge (1830-1844)', *Bulletin de l'Académie royale des Sciences d'Outre-Mer de Belgique*, 1964, no.6, pp.1306-36.
8. *Recensement de la Population*, 1846, p.XXXVI.
9. R. André and J. Pereira-Roque, *La démographie de la Belgique au XIXe siècle*, Brussels, 1974, p.185.
10. G. Kurgan-Van Hentenryck, op.cit., p.1315.
11. I. Ferenczi, 'International Migrations', *National Bureau of Economic Research*, New York, 1929, vol.I, pp.604-7.
12. *Annuaire Statistique de la Belgique*, various years.
13. R. André and J. Pereira-Roque, op.cit., p.178.
14. I. Ferenczi, op.cit., pp.608-11.
15. J. Morsa, 'L'immigration en Belgique (1890-1954)', *Population et Famille*, nos. 9-10, December 1966, p.44.
16. E. Smits, op.cit., Table 1.
17. 12e Volkstelling, 31.5.1947, *Belangrijkste uitkomsten der eigenlijke volkstelling*, The Hague, 1954, pp.44, 47.
18. Inleiding tot de uitkomsten van de 10e Algemene Volkstelling, p.67.
19. A.J. Coale, 'Factors associated with the development of low fertility: a historic summary', *World Population Conference*, Beograd, 1965, vol.2, p.206.
20. J. Duchêne and R. Lesthaeghe, 'Essai de reconstitution de la population belge sous le régime français: quelques caractéristiques démographiques de la population feminine', *Population et Famille*, no.36, 1975, p.44.
21. R. Lesthaeghe, 'Vruchtbaarheidscontrole, nuptialiteit en social-econommische veranderingen in België 1846-1910', *Bevolking en Gezin*,

1972, vol.2, pp.251-305; E. Van Hyfte, 'De invloed van de taalgrens op de evolutie van de vruchtbaarheid in Belgie vanaf 1846', *Bevolking en Gezin*, 1976, vol.2, pp.167-81.

22. J.D. Buissink, *De analyse van regionale verschillen in de huwelijksvruchtbaarheid*, Delft, 1970, pp.28-9.

23. J.D. Buissink, ibid., p.22.

24. E.W. Hofstee, *Enkele opmerkingen over de ontwikkeling van de huwelijksvruchtbaarheid in Nederland*, Nederlands Interuniversitair Demografisch Instituut, Serie Overdrukken 3, pp.46-7. Originally published, but covering a shorter period, in E.W. Hofstee, *De Groei van de Nederlandse Bevolking in Drift en Koers*, Assen, 1962, pp.22-3.

25. J.D. Buissink, op.cit., p.86 and ibid., 'Regional Differences in Marital Fertility in the Netherlands in the Second half of the Nineteenth Century', *Population Studies*, vol.25, no.3, 1971, p.367.

26. H.W. Methorst and M.J. Stirks, *Het Bevolkingsvraagstuk*, Amsterdam, 1948, p.42.

27. J.D. Buissink, op.cit. (1971), p.366.

28. E.W. Hofstee, op.cit. (1962), p.26.

29. Ibid., pp.23-7.

30. J.D. Buissink, op.cit. (1970), *passim.*

31. F. Van Heek, *Het geboorteniveau der Nederlandse Rooms-Katholieken*, Leiden, 1954, *passim.* A good summary of the discussion can be found in F.W.A. Van Poppel, 'De differentiele vruchtbaarheid in Nederland in historisch perspectief: de invloed van de religie', *Bevolking en Gezin*, 1974, vol.3, pp.329-47.

32. E.W. Hofstee, op.cit., pp.66-7.

33. F.W.A. Van Poppel, op.cit., pp.336-41.

34. H.W. Methorst, 'Differential Fertility in the Netherlands', *Population*, vol.1, Special Memoir, 1935, pp.10-11.

35. H. Damas, 'Le mouvement naturel de la population belge. Son évolution de 1846 à 1960', *Population et Famille*, 1964, vol.2, pp.88-9.

36. Ibid., p.88.

37. E. Smits, op.cit., Table 1; A. Quetelet, 'Sur l'appréciation des documents statistiques', *Bulletin de la Commission Centrale de Statistique*, vol.2, Brussels, 1845, p.212.

38. R. André and J. Pereira-Roque, op.cit., p.117.

39. E.W. Hofstee, 'Regionale Sterfteverschillen', in *Differentiele Sterfte. Vereniging voor Demografie*, The Hague, 1958, p.9.

40. *Statistiek van de Sterfte naar den Leeftijd en de oorzaken van den dood voor het jaar 1930*, The Hague, 1931, pp.vii and ix; E.W. Hofstee, op.cit. (1958), p.11.

41. F.A.M. Kerckhaert and F.W.A. Van Poppel, 'Het verloop van de sterfte naar leeftijd, geslacht en burgerlijke staat in Nederland: periode 1850-1970', *Bevolking en Gezin*, 1975, vol.1, pp.78-82.

42. *Statistiek van de Sterfte naar den Leeftijd en de oorzaken van den dood voor het jaar 1930*, The Hague, 1931, p.xii.

43. P. de Wolff and J. Meerdink, *Infant Mortality by Social Groups in Amsterdam*, 28th Meeting of the International Statistical Institute, Rome, 1953, p.93.

44. J. Meerdink, 'Differentiele sterfte naar sociale groepen', in *Differentiele Sterfte. Vereniging voor Demografie*, The Hague, 1958, p.37.

45. H.W. Methorst, op.cit., pp.32-4.

APPENDIX

Table 6.1: The Population of Belgium and the Netherlands

Year	Belgium			The Netherlands		
	Total population	Index	Density sq.km.	Total population	Index	Density sq.km.
1784	2,417,975[a]	100	82			
1795				2,078,541	100	62
1815	3,246,734[b]	135	110	2,177,768	105	64
1829	3,747,154[c]	155	127			
1830				2,613,298	126	77
1840				2,860,559	138	85
1846	4,337,196[d]	179	147			
1849				3,056,879	147	90
1856	4,529,560	187	154			
1859				3,309,128	159	98
1866	4,827,833	200	163			
1869				3,579,529	172	106
1876	5,336,185	221	181			
1879				4,012,693	193	119
1880	5,520,009	228	187			
1889				4,511,415	217	134
1890	6,069,321	251	206			
1900	6,693,548	277	227	5,162,593	247	152
1909				5,858,175	282	173
1910	7,423,784	307	252			
1920	7,401,353[e]	306	251	6,865,314	330	203
1930	8,092,004[f]		265	7,935,565	382	235
1940				8,923,245	429	264
1947	8,512,195		279	9,625,499	463	285

Sources and Notes: Belgium. a. H. Van Werveke, 'La densité de la population belge au cours des ages', *Studi in Onore di Armando Sapori*, pp.1428-9. The census deals with the part of Belgium under Austrian rule which means that the old principality of Liège was not included; we have attempted to adjust the figure on the basis of the present-day territory, but one should still allow for a margin of error; b. E. Smits, *Statistique Nationale*, Table 1; c. H. Van Werveke, p.1427; d. Ibid., p.1426; note also valid of all following years; e. The figures including the area Eupen-Malmedy are 7,465,782 inhabitants with a density of 244 persons per sq.km.; f. For 1930 and 1947 the population figures relate to the expanded territory; if related to the pre-1920 area the densities would have been 274 and 289 for 1930 and 1947 respectively. Sources: The Netherlands. *Bevolking van Nederland naar geslacht, leeftijd en burgerlijke staat, 1830-1969*, The Hague, 1970, pp.24-5, except for 1795: A.M. Van der Woude, *Het Noorderkwartier*, vol.1, A.A.G. Bijdragen 16, Wageningen, 1972, p.101; 1815: E. Smits, *Statistique Nationale, Développement des trente et un tableaux publiés par la Commission de Statistique*, Brussels, 1827, Table 1.

Table 6.2: Growth of the Population of Belgium by Province (1813 = 100)

Province	1801	1806	1811	1813	1816	1829ᵃ	1846	1866	1890	1910	1930	1947
Antwerp	246,436 (84)	284,584 (98)	281,801 (97)	291,696 (100)	293,723	354,974 (122)	406,354 (139)	465,607 (160)	699,919 (240)	968,677 (332)	1,174,367 (403)	1,283,211 (440)
Brabant	243,972 (55)	302,542 (69)		441,649 (100)		556,146 (126)	691,357 (157)	813,552 (184)	1,106,158 (250)	1,469,677 (333)	1,698,828 (385)	1,816,802 (411)
East Flanders	559,989 (91)	602,257 (98)	601,138 (98)	615,689 (100)	519,436	733,938 (119)	793,264 (129)	805,835 (131)	949,526 (154)	1,120,335 (182)	1,150,813 (187)	1,219,384 (198)
West Flanders	459,730 (89)	492,143 (95)		516,324 (100)		601,678 (117)	643,004 (125)	642,217 (124)	738,442 (143)	874,135 (169)	901,177 (175)	996,812 (193)
Hainaut	414,541 (85)	474,497 (97)		488,595 (100)		608,524 (125)	714,708 (146)	845,438 (173)	1,048,546 (215)	1,232,867 (252)	1,265,759 (259)	1,219,314 (250)
Liège		311,191 (97)		358,185 (100)		370,801 (104)	452,828 (126)	557,194 (156)	756,734 (211)	888,341 (248)	965,191 (269)	953,562 (266)
Limburg				148,108 (100)		159,080 (107)	185,913 (126)	195,302 (132)	222,814 (150)	275,691 (186)	365,616 (247)	457,625 (309)
Luxembourg				145,794 (100)		150,371 (103)	186,265 (128)	199,910 (137)	211,711 (145)	231,215 (159)	220,920 (152)	212,084 (145)
Namur				164,400 (100)		212,725 (129)	263,503 (160)	302,778 (184)	335,471 (204)	362,846 (221)	355,044 (216)	356,874 (217)
Flanders				(100)		(118)	(129)	(134)	(166)	(206)	(229)	(252)
Wallony				(100)		(116)	(140)	(165)	(203)	(235)	(243)	(237)
Ratio Flanders/Wallony × 100				100		102	92	81	82	88	94	106

a. Population figures refer to 1830.

Sources: 1801-1816: A. Quetelet, 'Sur les anciens recensements de la population belge', Bulletin de la Commission Centrale de Statistique, vol.3, Bruxelles, 1847, pp.1-34; 1813: Premier Recueil des tableaux de la Commission de Statistique, The Hague, 1826; 1830: A. Quetelet and E. Smits, Recherches sur la reproduction et la mortalité . . . et sur la population de la Belgique, Brussels, 1832, p.5; 1846 and following years: Census of Belgium (recensement de la Population).

Province	1815	1830	1840	1849	1869	1879	1899	1909	1920	1930	1947
Groningen	135,642 (100)	157,504 (116)	174,451 (129)	188,442 (139)	225,510 (166)	253,246 (187)	299,602 (221)	328,058 (242)	363,862 (268)	396,778 (293)	449,862 (332)
Friesland	176,554 (100)	204,909 (116)	228,789 (130)	247,360 (140)	293,521 (166)	329,877 (187)	340,262 (193)	357,349 (202)	384,458 (218)	396,880 (225)	459,361 (260)
Drenthe	46,459 (100)	63,868 (137)	71,496 (154)	82,738 (178)	103,806 (223)	118,845 (256)	148,544 (320)	175,745 (378)	212,825 (458)	222,196 (478)	271,909 (585)
Overijssel	147,229 (100)	178,895 (122)	197,330 (134)	215,763 (147)	254,147 (173)	274,136 (186)	333,338 (226)	380,781 (259)	439,380 (298)	523,747 (356)	638,797 (434)
Gelderland	264,097 (100)	309,793 (117)	346,043 (131)	370,716 (140)	433,123 (164)	466,805 (177)	566,549 (215)	638,541 (242)	727,723 (276)	833,234 (316)	1,028,127 (389)
Utrecht	107,947 (100)	132,359 (123)	145,853 (135)	149,380 (138)	175,397 (162)	191,679 (178)	251,034 (233)	287,051 (266)	343,266 (318)	404,714 (375)	549,566 (509)
Noordholland	375,257 (100)	413,988 (110)	443,278 (118)	477,079 (127)	576,304 (154)	679,990 (181)	968,131 (258)	1,107,195 (295)	1,297,544 (346)	1,507,757 (402)	1,774,273 (473)
Zuidholland	388,505 (100)	479,737 (123)	526,214 (135)	563,425 (145)	687,270 (177)	803,530 (207)	1,144,448 (295)	1,394,245 (359)	1,675,137 (431)	1,960,084 (505)	2,284,080 (588)
Zeeland	111,108 (100)	137,262 (124)	151,573 (136)	160,295 (144)	178,976 (161)	188,635 (170)	216,295 (195)	234,327 (211)	247,151 (222)	246,003 (221)	260,800 (235)
Noordbrabant	294,087 (100)	348,891 (119)	377,501 (128)	396,420 (135)	429,543 (146)	466,497 (159)	553,842 (188)	620,966 (211)	734,588 (250)	896,719 (305)	1,180,133 (401)
Limburg	139,505 (100)	186,281 (133)	197,330 (141)	205,261 (147)	221,931 (159)	239,453 (172)	281,934 (202)	333,916 (239)	439,380 (315)	547,554 (392)	684,105 (490)

Sources: 1815: E. Smits, op.cit., (1827) Table 1; 1830: Uitkomsten der Zesde Tienjarige Volkstelling; 31.12.1879, Algemeen overzicht, The Hague, 1881, p.4; 1840 and 1849: Uitkomsten der Volkstelling van 19.11.1849; 1869 and following: Volkstelling van Nederland (Census of The Netherlands) for each of the respective years.

Table 6.4: Sex Structure of the Belgian Population (1846-1947)

Year (1)	Men[a] (2)	Women[a] (3)	(2)/(3)
1846	2,163	2,173	.995
1856	2,272	2,257	1.006
1866	2,419	2,408	1.004
1880	2,758	2,761	.999
1890	3,026	3,042	.995
1900	3,324	3,368	.987
1910	3,680	3,743	.983
1920	3,641	3,757	.969
1930	4,007	4,084	.981
1947	4,199	4,312	.974

a. In thousands.

Table 6.5: Sex Ratios (M/F) for Flanders, Wallony and Brabant (1846-1947)

Year	Flanders	Wallony	Brabant
1846	.991	1.006	0.985
1866	1.003	1.019	0.976
1880	1.000	1.013	0.965
1890	1.000	1.011	0.949
1910	.987	1.006	0.937
1920	.981	.983	0.919
1930	.988	1.001	0.934
1947	.989	.993	0.914

Table 6.6: Belgium: Age Structure of the Population (in %)
    Male: Female

Year	Age groups							
	0-14		15-44		45-64		65+	
	M.	F.	M.	F.	M.	F.	M.	F.
1846	32.8	31.8	45.7	44.6	15.9	17.4	5.5	6.3
1856	30.4	30.2	46.5	45.3	18.1	18.1	4.9	6.3
1866	31.7	31.6	44.6	43.9	17.7	17.8	5.9	6.8
1880	33.7	33.2	43.2	42.9	16.9	17.0	6.1	6.8
1890	33.0	32.5	44.5	43.7	16.5	16.9	5.9	6.9
1900	32.0	31.4	46.4	45.6	15.8	16.4	5.7	6.6
1910	30.9	30.2	47.0	46.1	16.2	16.9	5.8	6.9
1920	25.5	24.5	49.1	48.5	19.5	19.8	5.8	7.1
1930	23.3	22.6	48.3	47.4	21.4	21.8	6.9	8.2
1947	21.1	20.0	45.3	43.2	23.7	25.1	9.7	11.6

Table 6.7: Belgium: Evolution of Various Age Group Ratios for
    Men and Women

Year	Men		Women	
	0-14 / 65+	65+ / 15-64	0-14 / 65+	65+ / 15-64
1846	5.98	0.09	5.08	0.10
1856	6.14	0.08	4.76	0.10
1866	5.40	0.09	4.66	0.11
1880	5.53	0.10	4.89	0.11
1890	5.52	0.10	4.75	0.11
1900	5.59	0.09	4.74	0.11
1910	5.31	0.09	4.37	0.11
1920	4.41	0.09	4.40	0.12
1930	3.38	0.10	2.73	0.12
1947	2.17	0.14	1.73	0.17

Table 6.8: The Proportion of People in Belgium aged 15 Years and Less, and 65 Years and Over

Year	Flanders		Wallony		Brabant	
	−15	65+	−15	65+	−15	65+
1846	31.3	5.7	33.5	6.1	32.4	5.5
1866	30.8	6.7	32.4	6.2	32.3	5.8
1880	33.8	7.0	33.0	6.2	33.9	5.5
1890	34.0	7.0	31.3	6.2	33.0	5.5
1910	34.0		27.4		28.7	
1920	28.1	6.1	22.3	7.2	22.9	6.1
1930	25.9	6.9	20.8	8.6	20.4	7.4
1947	23.9	9.4	17.6	12.3	17.9	11.2

Table 6.9: Belgium: Age Group Ratios for the Three Main Regions

Year	$\frac{0\text{-}14}{65+}$			$\frac{65+}{15\text{-}64}$		
	Flanders	Wallony	Brabant	Flanders	Wallony	Brabant
1846	5.45	5.46	5.91	0.09	0.10	0.09
1866	4.60	5.27	5.58	0.11	0.10	0.09
1880	4.83	5.32	6.16	0.12	0.10	0.09
1890	4.89	5.03	5.95	0.12	0.10	0.09
1920	4.61	3.10	3.75	0.09	0.10	0.09
1930	3.75	2.42	2.76	0.10	0.12	0.10
1947	2.54	1.43	1.60	0.14	0.18	0.16

Appendix 265

Table 6.10: The Netherlands: Evolution of Sex Structure (1830-1950)

Year (1)	Men[a] (2)	Women[a] (3)	(2)/(3)
1830	1,278	1,335	.96
1849	1,498	1,558	.96
1859	1,628	1,679	.97
1869	1,763	1,814	.97
1879	1,983	2,030	.98
1889	2,228	2,283	.98
1899	2,520	2,583	.98
1900	2,535	2,598	.98
1909	2,899	2,959	.98
1920	3,410	3,455	.99
1930	3,943	3,993	.99
1940	4,454	4,469	.99
1947	4,791	4,834	.99

a. In thousands.

Table 6.11: The Netherlands: Male/Female Ratio per Province

	1830	1849	1869	1889	1909	1920	1930	1947
Groningen	.97	.96	.97	.97	.98	.99	.99	.99
Friesland	.97	.97	.98	.99	1.01	1.00	1.00	1.01
Drenthe	1.04	1.04	1.07	1.11	1.08	1.06	1.07	1.07
Overijssel	1.02	1.01	1.04	1.04	1.03	1.03	1.02	1.02
Gelderland	1.01	1.01	1.02	1.02	1.02	1.01	1.01	1.01
Utrecht	.96	.95	.96	.98	.96	.97	.96	.96
Noordholland	.88	.91	.92	.93	.94	.96	.95	.96
Zuidholland	.91	.91	.92	.93	.95	.96	.96	.96
Zeeland	.96	.97	.96	.97	.99	.99	1.00	1.01
Noordbrabant	.99	.99	1.00	1.01	1.00	1.01	1.01	1.02
Limburg	.99	1.02	1.03	1.03	1.03	1.04	1.04	1.02

Table 6.12: The Netherlands: Changes in the Proportional Age Structure of the Population (in %) Male:Female

Year	Men		Women	
	$\dfrac{0\text{-}14}{65+}$	$\dfrac{65+}{15\text{-}64}$	$\dfrac{0\text{-}14}{65+}$	$\dfrac{65+}{15\text{-}64}$
1830	7.26	0.09	6.25	0.10
1849	7.98	0.07	6.23	0.08
1859	7.72	0.07	5.87	0.09
1869	6.82	0.08	5.45	0.10
1879	7.12	0.08	5.86	0.10
1889	6.51	0.09	5.41	0.11
1899	6.34	0.10	5.33	0.11
1900	6.32	0.10	5.33	0.11
1909	6.19	0.10	5.20	0.11
1920	5.95	0.09	5.15	0.10
1930	5.32	0.09	4.60	0.10
1940	4.25	0.10	3.73	0.11
1947	4.43	0.11	3.85	0.12

Table 6.13: The Netherlands: Evolution of Various Age Group Ratios for Men and Women

Year	Age groups							
	0-14		15-44		45-64		65+	
	M	F	M	F	M	F	M	F
1830	38.5	35.6	41.7	42.9	14.5	15.3	5.3	5.7
1849	34.3	32.4	45.7	45.4	15.6	17.0	4.3	5.2
1859	33.2	31.7	46.7	46.3	15.7	16.6	4.3	5.4
1869	34.1	32.7	44.3	44.3	16.5	17.0	5.0	6.0
1879	35.6	34.6	42.8	42.6	16.5	17.0	5.0	5.9
1889	35.8	34.6	42.3	42.2	16.3	16.7	5.5	6.4
1899	35.5	34.1	43.4	43.6	15.5	15.9	5.6	6.4
1900	35.4	34.1	43.4	43.8	15.5	15.8	5.6	6.4
1909	35.3	33.8	43.9	44.3	15.0	15.3	5.7	6.5
1920	33.3	31.9	45.3	45.5	15.9	16.4	5.6	6.2
1930	31.4	29.9	45.8	46.3	16.9	17.3	5.9	6.5
1940	28.5	27.2	46.8	46.9	17.9	18.6	6.7	7.3
1947	30.1	28.5	44.9	45.2	18.2	18.9	6.8	7.4

Table 6.14: Origin of Inhabitants (in Percentage of Total Provincial Polulation): Belgium

	% originating from another community (same province)			% originating from another province		
	1846	1866	1890	1846	1866	1890
Antwerp	21.7	28.5	32.8	6.5	4.5	4.1
Brabant	21.9	33.7	38.8	9.6	2.9	3.3
West Flanders	26.7	29.7	31.5	2.7	1.2	1.7
East Flanders	22.6	26.0	26.7	4.6	0.8	1.2
Hainaut	20.5	27.3	31.8	4.1	1.7	2.5
Liège	25.8	31.7	35.0	4.6	4.4	5.0
Limburg	19.2	23.9	24.4	5.0	2.7	2.1
Luxembourg	15.5	19.4	21.2	2.9	3.7	3.9
Namur	18.6	25.2	30.1	6.7	0.9	1.5

Table 6.15: Origin of Inhabitants in Percentage of Total Population: The Netherlands

Year	Originating from another community (same province)		Originating from another province	
	M	F	M	F
1849	19.1	21.6	8.3	8.0
1869	19.7	22.6	8.6	8.9
1889	20.2	23.1	10.7	11.4
1909	20.0	22.7	12.4	13.6
1920	19.9	22.6	13.8	14.8
1935	27.3	34.0	18.8	20.5
1951-52	19.7	23.0	21.5	20.7

Sources: 1849-1920: 'Inleiding tot de uitkomsten van de 10e Algemene Volkstelling, 31 December 1920', *Statistiek van Nederland*, no.378, The Hague, 1924, pp.67-8; 1935-1952: E.W. Hofstee, 'Some preliminary conclusions concerning internal migration of families and individual males and individual females in the Netherlands based on new statistical data', *World Population Conference*, Rome, 1954, vol.2, pp.545-54.

Table 6.16: Net Migration Rates per Province (1840-1947): The Netherlands (per 1,000 population)

	1840-1869	1869-1909	1909-1940	1940-1947
Groningen	− 2.0	− 6.5	− 4.6	− 6.8
Friesland	− 2.7	− 9.5	− 6.9	− 8.6
Drenthe	+ 3.9	− 3.1	− 7.1	− 6.1
Overijssel	+ 0.2	− 2.5	− 0.4	− 1.5
Gelderland	− 2.5	− 3.5	− 1.0	− 2.4
Utrecht	− 1.4	− 1.0	+ 5.9	+ 3.7
Noordholland	+ 2.1	+ 3.3	+ 4.0	+ 4.1
Zuidholland	+ 0.4	+ 3.1	+ 1.6	+ 1.9
Zeeland	− 4.7	− 10.0	− 8.4	− 10.0
Noordbrabant	− 2.7	− 2.6	+ 0.0	− 1.8
Limburg	− 4.0	− 2.5	+ 2.6	− 1.3

Source: *Belangrijkste uitkomsten der eigenlijke Volkstelling,* 31 May 1947, p.16.

Table 6.17: Total Number of Emigrants and Percentage Breakdown According to Destination: The Netherlands

Period	Total number of emigrants	Colonies (in percentages)	Foreign countries (in percentages)
1865-74	111,898	8.7	91.3
1875-84	127,916	14.3	85.7
1885-94	194,353	18.5	81.5
1895-1904	247,713	15.8	84.2
1905-14	351,262	13.8	86.2
1915-24	284,651	18.7	81.3
1925-34	447,342	21.9	78.1
1935-44	485,585	28.7	71.3
1945-54	600,969	25.3	74.7

Sources: 1865-1924: I. Ferenczi, op.cit., pp.743-5; 1925 and following: *Zeventig jaren statistiek in tijdreeksen 1899-1969*, The Hague, 1970, p.21.

Table 6.18: Percentage of Persons Never Married at Age 50: Belgium

Year	Men	Women
1829	15.0	23.5
1846	15.3	17.7
1856	19.5	19.2
1866	19.4	18.2
1880	18.1	18.9
1890	17.3	17.5
1900	15.9	16.8
1910	14.5	16.4
1920	13.0	15.4
1930	10.5	13.3
1947	9.1	10.4

Sources: 1829-1930: E. Van de Walle, 'La nuptialité en Belgique de 1846 à 1930 et sa relation avec le déclin de la fecondité', *Population et Famille*, nos.6-7, December 1965, p.51; 1947: G. Wunsch-C. Wattelar, 'La situation démographique de la Belgique', *Dossiers de l'action sociale catholique*, October 1967, p.5.

Table 6.19: Evolution of the Percentage of Single Women for Various Age Groups (1829-1947): Belgium

Age group	1829	1846	1856	1900	1910	1920	1930	1947
15-19	—	99.5	99.2	97.5	97.4	97.8	95.9	95.4
20-24	86.5	87.1	87.1	71.4	68.8	69.5	59.5	56.3
25-29	61.6	60.0	61.8	40.8	37.0	39.7	27.0	24.5
30-34	43.1	37.9	40.5	26.8	24.2	24.6	17.1	14.5
35-39	32.7	26.0	29.3	21.1	19.1	18.0	15.0	11.6
40-44	26.4	21.6	23.0	18.2	17.3	16.1	14.1	10.6
45-49	24.3	18.0	19.7	17.1	16.6	15.3	13.3	10.4

Sources: 1829-1856: E. Van de Walle, op.cit., pp.44 and 45; 1900-1947: C. Wattelar, 'Evolution et comparaison de la nuptialité en Belgique', *Recherches Economiques de Louvain*, September 1966, p.437.

Table 6.20: Percentage of Single Women Aged 50 (per Province): Belgium

	1866	1900	1930
Antwerp	17.7	16.0	12.3
Brabant	16.6	16.5	14.0
West Flanders	22.6	21.1	17.2
East Flanders	25.0	22.5	16.4
Hainaut	15.0	11.2	8.4
Liège	14.8	16.0	12.8
Limburg	18.8	18.2	15.2
Luxembourg	13.4	15.8	15.8
Namur	12.6	15.2	12.6

Source: E. Van de Walle, op.cit., p.52.

Table 6.21: Evolution of the I_m — Index per Province: Belgium

	1829	1846	1866	1900	1930
Antwerp		36.5	39.4	48.2	60.5
Brabant		38.4	40.9	47.0	60.2
West Flanders		34.7	37.8	43.7	55.1
East Flanders		34.5	36.1	43.9	56.1
Hainaut		41.1	46.5	57.2	69.9
Liège		40.4	40.0	46.8	60.5
Limburg		35.9	37.0	41.1	52.9
Luxembourg		42.1	39.8	43.2	52.4
Namur		41.5	43.3	49.7	62.1
Belgium	35.5	37.5	40.4	47.9	60.1

Source: 1866-1930: E. Van de Walle, op.cit., p.40; 1829: J. Duchêne and
R. Lesthaeghe, 'Essai de reconstitution de la population belge sous le régime
français: quelques caractéristiques démographiques de la population féminine',
Population et Famille, 36, 1975, p.44.

Table 6.22: Average Age at First Marriage by Sex (Hajnal Method)
(in Years and Tenths of Years): Belgium

Period	Men	Women
1852-1856	30.5	28.6
1862-1866	30.0	28.0
1886-1890	28.6	26.7
1896-1900	27.6	25.7
1906-1910	27.3	25.2
1916-1920	27.5	25.6
1926-1930	26.6	24.2
1947	26.3	23.4

Sources: 1852-1930: E. Van de Walle, op.cit., p.46; 1947: C. Wattelar, op.cit., p.419.

Table 6.23: Regional Evolution of the Average Age at Marriage
(Hajnal Method) (in Years and Tenths of Years): Belgium

	1862-1866	1896-1900	1926-1930
Antwerp	28.8	25.3	24.1
Brabant	28.7	25.8	24.2
West Flanders	28.5	26.4	24.8
East Flanders	29.1	26.2	24.8
Hainaut	26.6	24.3	22.6
Liège	27.6	26.1	24.3
Limburg	28.7	27.0	25.2
Luxembourg	28.2	26.9	25.5
Namur	27.9	25.6	23.9

Source: E. Van de Walle, op.cit., p.47.

Table 6.24: Index of Fertility of Married Women (I_g): Belgium

	1800-12	1829	1846	1866	1880	1900	1930	1961
Antwerp	73.8		78.6	87.0	83.7	65.8	30.4	53.7
Brabant	78.8		73.7	78.9	71.0	50.8	22.0	44.6
West Flanders	87.7		81.0	93.8	91.8	83.6	38.5	52.1
East Flanders	83.7		79.3	93.8	92.1	71.0	33.5	50.5
Hainaut	80.3		71.7	69.2	57.7	38.6	20.1	52.1
Liège	80.1		76.5	79.1	70.4	48.0	22.3	48.0
Limburg	—		77.3	86.6	88.1	88.1	58.3	69.0
Luxembourg	85.4		77.4	77.9	73.3	62.1	37.1	57.3
Namur	76.7		74.3	72.2	61.8	45.9	27.1	55.4
Belgium	81.5	87.3	75.1	81.4	75.1	57.8	28.1	51.6

Sources: 1800-1846: Duchêne-Lesthaeghe, op.cit., p.45; 1866-1930: E. Van de Walle, op.cit., p.40; 1961: Based on Louis Jadin, 'Aspects régionaux de la fécondité en Belgique depuis 1930', *Recherches économiques de Louvain*, September, 1967, pp.373-4.

Table 6.25: Percentage of Never Married Persons for Various Age Groups: The Netherlands

Year	Men				Women			
	20-24	30-34	40-44	50-54	20-24	30-34	40-44	50-54
1830	89.4	31.2	14.4	—	80.9	29.4	16.2	—
1840	90.3	32.4	14.6	—	81.8	29.6	16.5	—
1849	93.6	37.3	15.2	10.6	86.6	32.5	16.5	13.6
1859	93.6	35.6	16.6	11.3	85.4	31.1	16.9	13.2
1869	92.6	33.8	15.7	12.3	83.2	29.2	16.4	13.7
1879	90.1	29.7	15.6	11.6	78.3	25.9	15.8	13.1
1889	89.6	30.1	15.5	12.3	78.5	26.2	16.1	13.2
1899	89.0	28.5	15.7	12.2	78.6	26.6	16.7	13.7
1909	88.7	27.0	14.4	12.2	77.5	25.8	17.1	14.2
1920	87.7	24.4	13.7	11.5	74.8	24.4	16.9	14.8
1930	89.6	21.2	11.3	10.7	75.5	21.7	16.2	14.6
1947	86.3	21.6	10.9	8.0	69.2	18.7	14.7	13.1

Source: *Bevolking van Nederland naar geslacht, leeftijd en burgerlijke staat, 1830-1969*, The Hague, 1970, pp.82-93.

Table 6.26: Evolution of the Percentage of Never Married Women in Age Groups 20-24 and 50-54 (per Province): The Netherlands

	20-24 years				50-54 years			
	1849	1879	1899	1947	1849	1879	1899	1947
Groningen	86.2	75.9	76.7	65.6	9.9	9.0	10.0	10.7
Friesland	83.1	75.0	78.7	66.9	9.2	9.1	8.9	11.8
Drenthe	86.6	75.7	73.0	62.3	8.8	7.8	7.4	7.8
Overijssel	86.4	78.8	77.9	73.9	12.0	12.9	11.6	11.3
Gelderland	89.8	82.0	80.6	71.3	11.1	12.1	14.5	13.0
Utrecht	87.4	79.7	79.5	70.9	14.8	14.6	14.8	15.4
Noordholland	84.9	75.5	77.3	66.9	15.0	12.8	13.1	12.7
Zuidholland	83.4	74.6	75.7	65.9	14.5	12.4	13.8	13.4
Zeeland	84.7	78.2	76.3	66.1	10.2	10.5	10.6	13.9
Noordbrabant	92.5	86.2	84.8	77.1	18.3	19.8	19.8	14.9
Limburg	89.0	86.6	86.0	71.9	14.7	16.8	17.6	15.1

Table 6.27: Evolution of the Average Age at Marriage of Women: The Netherlands

Period	Age
1851-55	27.8
1856-60	27.4
1861-65	27.0
1866-70	26.7
1871-75	26.3
1876-80	26.0
1881-85	26.3
1886-90	26.6
1891-95	26.6
1896-1900	26.6
1926-30	25.7

Sources: 1851-1900: J.D. Buissink, op.cit., p.40; 1926-1930: E. Van de Walle, op.cit., p.52.

Table 6.28: Number of Legitimate Live Births per 1,000 Married Women Aged 50 Years and Less (per Province): The Netherlands 1850-1914

	1850/54	1855/59	1860/64	1865/69	1870/74	1875/79	1880/84	1885/89	1890/94	1895/99	1900/04	1905/09	1910/11
Groningen	285.7	275.7	272.0	279.2	285.5	294.2	270.3	266.4	263.5	258.8	252.2	236.0	212.9
Friesland	276.4	266.4	267.6	282.5	281.3	278.9	249.9	249.0	241.6	233.3	226.9	209.6	193.5
Drenthe	273.7	274.8	273.9	269.0	275.0	282.7	270.3	277.7	285.5	286.5	286.6	275.0	258.2
Overijssel	285.2	276.5	281.7	284.2	284.5	290.8	281.8	286.6	284.7	285.0	278.0	256.2	229.8
Gelderland	289.5	286.9	293.3	294.3	289.1	301.8	301.7	299.5	292.9	294.7	284.6	270.9	246.9
Utrecht	323.8	306.7	310.5	311.7	310.0	322.7	317.9	321.4	307.8	299.7	269.2	237.6	231.8
Noordholland	301.1	277.7	284.7	284.3	280.1	295.2	289.3	282.0	261.4	243.5	226.4	202.3	181.1
Zuidholland	343.6	314.6	319.7	322.6	324.7	330.1	321.6	314.3	296.1	283.8	273.2	250.0	223.7
Zeeland	339.6	313.0	328.0	332.2	339.0	331.0	304.2	303.4	296.5	288.5	226.4	202.3	212.0
Noordbrabant	307.0	287.4	304.6	317.8	324.8	336.1	330.8	330.0	329.6	337.9	346.0	328.5	308.5
Limburg	285.6	289.3	295.9	305.8	314.5	330.7	320.3	319.4	322.9	334.8	341.4	328.8	314.3
Netherlands	304.2	289.8	296.1	300.6	302.7	310.2	299.5	296.9	286.6	280.2	271.1	250.5	228.5

Source: J.D. Buissink, *Regional Differences...*, p.367.

Table 6.29: General Fertility Rates per Province: The Netherlands 1831-1950 (Hofstee data)

Province	1831/5	1836/40	1841/5	1846/50	1851/5	1855/60	1861/5	1901/5	1906/10	1916/20	1926/30	1936/40	1946/50
Groningen	322.7	342.3	349.8	326.3	335.7	327.0	341.7	296.7	276.2	237.7	188.6	154.5	184.9
Friesland	314.2	332.8	330.5	307.7	320.1	304.5	326.3	265.9	239.7	219.7	199.4	176.7	209.6
Drenthe	300.9	321.1	324.3	313.6	318.5	330.7	327.1	326.0	309.4	290.7	237.0	185.8	213.0
Overijssel	309.4	349.9	339.2	320.4	336.1	329.9	333.8	314.2	287.5	246.6	216.9	177.9	216.8
Gelderland	335.9	376.6	370.2	342.1	354.0	352.8	359.4	332.7	310.8	265.9	230.3	186.8	226.9
Utrecht	353.6	394.6	390.4	368.8	390.0	378.0	389.9	333.1	296.0	244.8	202.4	172.4	218.3
Noordholland	326.3	384.2	360.9	341.8	359.4	329.1	353.1	265.1	233.1	195.7	158.4	141.2	189.1
Zuidholland	351.7	374.0	389.4	375.5	397.4	379.0	392.1	317.2	286.6	226.7	180.4	151.2	196.5
Zeeland	384.2	420.4	397.6	382.0	392.1	379.3	401.8	309.7	274.3	227.8	176.4	151.4	182.9
Noordbrabant	373.0	395.1	376.3	342.8	351.9	361.5	378.2	404.4	377.1	332.7	297.8	243.4	268.5
Limburg			370.0	339.4	361.3	367.5	369.7	398.9	378.1	319.0	273.9	218.1	245.2
Netherlands			367.0	344.5	356.4	346.0	359.5	315.1	287.5	242.9	204.2	173.5	215.1

Source: E.W. Hofstee, *Enkele opmerkingen. . .*, p.46.

Table 6.30: Evolution of the Crude Death Rate per Thousand: Belgium

Year	Rate
1815	25.6
1820	24.9
1825	22.9
1831-35	26.1
1841-45	23.2
1851-55	22.3
1861-65	22.6
1871-75	23.2
1881-85	20.6
1891-95	20.1
1901-05	16.9
1911-15	14.6
1921-25	13.4
1931-35	12.9
1941-45	14.7
1946-50	12.8

Source: 1815-1825: J. Jacquart, 'Mouvement de l'état civil et de la population Belgique', *Bulletin de la Commission Centrale de Statistique*, vol.19, p.317; 1831-1950: J. Gabriel, *Evolution et Tendances actuelles de la mortalité en Belgique*, World Population Conference, Roma 1954, vol.1, p.99.

Table 6.31: Belgium: Crude Death Rate per Province per Thousand

	1815-24	1845-47	1879-81	1909-11	1935-37	1959-61
Antwerp	23.1	22.9	22.2	14.5	10.5	10.3
Brabant	25.6	25.1	22.1	14.6	11.9	11.9
West Flanders	26.3	32.5	23.6	18.8	11.9	10.4
East Flanders	25.2	28.7	22.6	17.3	12.1	11.6
Hainaut	23.2	21.9	18.8	14.4	14.3	13.7
Liège	23.6	22.7	20.6	13.9	13.2	13.7
Limburg	23.3[a]	22.4	21.6	15.5	10.4	7.7
Luxembourg	23.1[b]	19.2	17.8	14.9	13.2	12.6
Namur	19.3	18.7	16.6	15.1	14.2	13.6

a. Includes present-day Dutch Limburg; b. Includes present-day Grand Duchy of Luxembourg.

Sources: 1815-24: E. Smits, op.cit., Table 1; 1845-1961: H. Damas, *Le mouvement naturel...*, p.109.

Table 6.32: Evolution of Life Expectancy at Various Ages (in Years): Belgium

Period	At birth M	At birth F	Age 10 M	Age 10 F	Age 50 M	Age 50 F	Age 70 M	Age 70 F
1. 1827 urban pop.	22.4		44.8		18.9		7.5	
2. 1832 urban pop.	20.6		45.6		18.0		7.4	
3. 1832 total pop.	25.0		47.7		19.7		7.5	
4. 1841-47 total pop.	24.9		45.8		20.7		7.5	
5. 1841-45 total pop.	22.9		45.9		20.1		7.5	
6. 1881-90 total pop.	43.6	46.7	49.6	51.7	19.9	21.9	8.2	8.8
7. 1891-1900 total pop.	45.4	48.8						
8. 1891-1900								
1. communities with less than 20,000 inhabitants	47.2	49.8						
2. communities with more than 20,000 inhabitants	40.3	45.5						
9. 1928-32 total pop.	56.0	59.8	54.9	57.2	21.6	23.5	8.7	9.6
10. 1946-49 total pop.	62.0	67.3	57.3	61.7	22.5	25.5	9.5	10.6

Sources: Rows 1-5: A. Quetelet, 'Nouvelles tables de Mortalité pour la Belgique', *Bulletin de la Commission Centrale de Statistique*, vol.4, Brussels, 1854, p.12; Row 6: J.M.J. Leclerc, 'Tables de Mortalité de 1880-1890', *Bulletin de la Commission Centrale de Statistique*, vol.17, pp.59-62; Rows 7-8: J.M.J. Leclerc, 'Table de Mortalité 1890-1900', *Bulletin de la Commission Centrale de Statistique*, vol.19, p.106; Rows 9-10: *Bulletin de l'Institut de Statistique de Belgique*, December 1967.

Table 6.33: Belgium: Life Tables for Men and Women (1827-1949)

Age	1827/29 Urban		Rural		1841/45 Urban		Rural		1847/56		1880/90		1891/1900		1928/32		1946/49	
	M	F	M	F	M	F	M	F	M	F	M	F	M	F	M	F	M	F
0	10,000	10,000	10,000	10,000	10,000	10,000	10,000	10,000	1,000	1,000	10,000	10,000	10,000	10,000	10,000	10,000	10,000	10,000
1	7,426	7,932	7,575	8,001	7,588	8,148	7,708	8,231	864	838	8,274	8,545	8,311	8,580	8,993	9,215	9,360	9,507
5	5,738	6,295	6,169	6,528	5,772	6,383	6,102	6,619	741	720	7,445	7,706	7,630	7,904	8,710	8,962	9,249	9,412
10	5,384	5,916	5,734	6,082	5,399	5,971	5,647	6,095	699	684	7,252	7,495	7,466	7,727	8,609	8,869	9,155	9,369
15	5,241	5,732	5,502	5,796	5,238	5,734	5,404	5,751	681	666	7,146	7,361	7,374	7,619	8,541	8,799	9,152	9,333
20	5,038	5,500	5,242	5,484	4,963	5,399	5,109	5,367	650	640	6,974	7,166	7,221	7,465	8,409	8,669	9,077	9,275
25	4,662	5,201	4,881	5,153	4,487	5,024	4,731	5,025	607	604	6,720	6,924	7,003	7,248	8,237	8,503	8,950	9,191
30	4,335	4,881	4,572	4,812	4,163	4,682	4,451	4,712	576	566	6,492	6,686	6,782	7,017	8,066	8,335	8,816	9,092
35	4,034	4,558	4,337	4,474	3,846	4,351	4,201	4,384	539	525	6,250	6,436	6,538	6,775	7,881	8,161	8,763	8,985
40	3,744	4,208	4,134	4,112	3,529	4,011	3,950	4,037	499	484	5,974	6,173	6,247	6,506	7,666	7,970	8,488	8,864
45	3,411	3,907	3,887	3,761	3,167	3,650	3,653	3,673	459	443	5,644	5,887	5,889	6,222	7,395	7,746	8,242	8,706
50	3,115	3,592	3,588	3,458	2,804	3,339	3,367	3,370	415	403	5,263	5,593	5,484	5,920	7,043	7,468	7,887	8,487
55	2,739	3,225	3,194	3,118	2,478	2,999	3,079	3,046	373	366	4,815	5,243	4,963	5,532	6,582	7,100	7,389	8,168
60	2,329	2,862	2,767	2,762	2,116	2,636	2,737	2,687	337	319	4,272	4,795	4,353	5,028	5,965	6,598	6,730	7,717
65	1,859	2,397	2,277	2,310	1,710	2,214	2,258	2,222	290	250	3,577	4,168	3,624	4,369	5,142	5,874	5,872	7,041
70	1,372	1,864	1,713	1,758	1,275	1,726	1,713	1,710	221	179	2,785	3,368	2,759	3,494	4,094	4,879	4,803	6,074
75	891	1,261	1,114	1,182	822	1,166	1,126	1,148	137	111	1,879	2,384	1,786	2,407	2,841	3,588	3,494	4,721

Sources: 1827-29: A. Quetelet and E. Smits, *Recherches sur la reproduction et la mortalité de l'homme et sur la population de la Belgique*, Brussels, 1832, pp.36-9; 1841-45: A. Quetelet, 'Nouvelles tables de mortalité pour la Belgique', *Bulletin de la Commission Centrale de Statistique*, vol.4, pp.20-21; 1847-56: A. Quetelet, 'Tables de Mortalité d'après le recensement de 1856', *Bulletin de la Commission Centrale de Statistique*, vol.17, pp.475-6; 1880-90: J.M.J. Leclerc, 'Tables de Mortalité. . .dressées au moyen de statistiques officielles de 1880 à 1890', *Bulletin de la Commission Centrale de Statistique*, vol.17, pp.46-7; 1891-1900: J.M.J. Leclerc, 'Tables de Mortalité 1890-1900', *Bulletin de la Commission Centrale de Statistique*, vol.19, pp.91-2; 1928-32: *Tables de Mortalité de la Population Belge 1928-32*, Census of 31 December 1930, vol.7, p.48; 1946-49: *Tables de Mortalité 1946-49*, Brussels, n.d., p.41.

Table 6.34: Evolution of the Infant Mortality Rates in Belgium

Period	Endogenous	Exogenous	Total
1841-50			150.0
1851-60			155.3
1861-70			153.3
1871-80			138.9
1881-85			155.8
1891-95			164.0
1896-1900			157.9
1901-05	19.2	134.9	154.1
1906	18.4	129.5	147.9
1911-20	missing		
1921-25	19.4	87.5	106.9
1926-30	16.9	84.3	101.2
1931-35	18.3	70.3	88.6
1936-39	19.7	63.4	83.1
1940-45	22.3	65.2	87.5
1946-50	22.7	39.7	62.4

Source: 1840-80: *Statistique de Belgique 1885-1905*, p.302; From 1881 on: André-Gysselings, op.cit., p.8.

Table 6.35: Infant Mortality Rates by Sex (per 1,000 Live Births of Each Sex): Belgium

Year	Male	Female
1870	157.4	132.8
1875	172.0	144.0
1880	199.8	172.6
1922-24	113.8	90.9
1925-29	113.3	88.6
1930-34	102.8	79.8
1935-39	93.8	72.4
1940-44	94.7	74.1
1945-49	79.7	62.2

Source: 1870-80: *Bulletin de la Commission Centrale de Statistique*, vol. 15, pp.426 and 444; 1922-49: *Annuaire Statistique de la Belgique*, tome 87, 1966, p.82.

Table 6.36: Evolution, per Province of Infant Mortality Rates: Belgium (per 1,000 Live Births)

	1881-85	1898-1900	1921-25	1936-39	1946-50
Antwerp	166.9	169.6	103.9	76.9	62.3
Brabant	155.1	154.1	94.1	70.4	54.7
West Flanders	187.8	229.7	125.8	80.4	68.8
East Flanders	188.1	199.2	113.1	81.6	69.7
Hainaut	115.9	131.1	81.1	68.1	70.3
Liège	149.2	132.0	86.2	68.4	55.3
Limburg	133.0	145.5	105.0	77.6	58.4
Luxembourg	117.7	125.0	76.7	65.7	54.4
Namur	118.9	117.3	81.4	65.7	55.3

Sources: 1881-85: C. Jacquart, 'Mouvement de l'état civil et de la population en Belgique pendant les années 1876 à 1900', *Bulletin de la Commission Centrale de Statistique*, vol.19, pp.295-424; 1898-1900: C. Jacquart, *La mortalité infantile dans les Flandres*, Brussels, 1907, p.7; 1921-50: André-Gysselings, op.cit., p.17.

Table 6.37: Evolution of the Crude Death Rate (per 1,000): The Netherlands

Period	Men	Women	Total
1840-49	27.7	25.7	26.6
1850-59	26.2	24.9	25.5
1860-69	25.4	24.2	24.8
1870-79	25.3	23.6	24.5
1880-89	22.2	20.4	21.3
1890-99	19.4	17.9	18.7
1900-09	16.2	15.0	15.7
1910-19	13.7	13.1	13.4
1920-23	11.3	10.9	11.1
1924-28	9.9	9.7	9.8
1931-35	9.0	8.8	8.9
1941-45	12.4	10.2	11.3
1946-50	8.2	7.6	7.9

Sources: 1840-1928: *Statistiek van de Sterfte naar den Leeftijd en de oorzaken van den dood voor het jaar 1930*, The Hague, 1931, pp.vii and ix; 1931-35: *De Sterfte in Nederland naar geslacht, leeftijd en doodsoorzaken 1921-1955*, The Hague, 1957, p.35.

Appendix 281

Table 6.38: Evolution of Life Expectancy at Various Ages: The
Netherlands

Period	At birth		Age 10		Age 50		Age 70	
	M	F	M	F	M	F	M	F
1840-51	36.2	38.5	44.4	46.1	18.0	19.3	7.2	7.6
1850-59	36.4	38.2	45.6	46.3	18.3	19.5	7.8	8.0
1860-69	37.2	39.1	46.7	47.4	19.2	20.4	8.1	8.4
1870-79	38.4	40.7	48.0	48.7	19.6	21.0	8.2	8.4
1880-89	42.5	45.0	50.4	51.5	20.5	21.9	8.5	9.0
1890-99	46.2	49.0	51.7	53.0	20.7	22.2	8.6	9.0
1900-09	51.0	53.4	54.3	55.4	21.8	22.9	8.9	9.4
1910-20	55.1	57.1	55.4	56.0	22.4	23.4	9.1	9.6
1921-30	61.9	63.5	58.7	58.9	23.5	24.1	9.6	10.0
1931-40	65.7	67.2	60.3	60.8	24.1	24.7	9.8	10.2
1947-49	69.4	71.5	62.7	64.1	25.6	26.6	10.7	11.1

Source: *Sterftetafels voor Nederland, afgeleid uit waarnemingen voor de perioden 1951-55 and 1953-55*, The Hague, 1957, p.33.

Table 6.39: Life Tables for Men and Women: the Netherlands (1840-1955)

Age	1840/51 M	1840/51 F	1850/59 M	1850/59 F	1860/69 M	1860/69 F	1900/09 M	1900/09 F	1910/20 M	1910/20 F	1921/30 M	1921/30 F	1951/55 M	1951/55 F
0	10,000	10,000	10,000	10,000	10,000	10,000	10,000	10,000	10,000	10,000	10,000	10,000	10,000	10,000
1	6,890	7,446	7,902	8,180	7,882	8,175	8,595	8,823	8,982	9,174	9,347	9,494	9,751	9,805
5	5,505	5,991	6,772	7,023	6,791	7,051	8,024	8,269	8,519	8,727	9,086	9,263	9,691	9,754
10	5,184	5,650	6,448	6,684	6,454	6,704	7,885	8,131	8,394	8,607	9,001	9,191	9,657	9,732
15	5,033	5,480	6,291	6,495	6,282	6,506	7,801	8,034	8,312	8,509	8,942	9,133	9,632	9,715
20	4,842	5,289	6,090	6,279	6,090	6,300	7,661	7,894	8,165	8,358	8,842	9,034	9,598	9,696
25	4,524	5,066	5,794	6,033	5,788	6,059	7,468	7,733	7,976	8,188	8,713	8,914	9,551	9,670
30	4,237	4,823	5,507	5,724	5,514	5,766	7,291	7,550	7,792	7,995	8,591	8,780	9,499	9,637
35	3,947	4,541	5,211	5,362	5,260	5,446	7,116	7,343	7,609	7,786	8,467	8,631	9,441	9,589
40	3,632	4,220	4,898	4,993	4,967	5,088	6,809	7,111	7,414	7,556	8,322	8,450	9,365	9,521
45	3,265	3,887	4,542	4,634	4,629	4,729	6,653	6,856	7,184	7,308	8,145	8,238	9,248	9,425
50	2,893	3,574	4,149	4,310	4,256	4,414	6,327	6,573	6,889	7,021	7,896	7,972	9,056	9,276
55	2,500	3,217	3,656	3,906	3,825	4,047	5,911	6,209	6,484	6,660	7,533	7,608	8,743	9,044
60	2,074	2,792	3,117	3,441	3,336	3,625	5,355	5,730	5,926	6,176	6,998	7,102	8,262	8,693
65	1,632	2,318	2,525	2,857	2,711	3,033	4,629	5,047	5,166	5,491	6,226	6,375	7,566	8,143
70	1,115	1,685	1,832	2,124	2,028	2,341	3,687	4,124	4,174	4,534	5,151	5,344	6,567	7,249
75	625	1,045	1,155	1,364	1,331	1,549	2,580	2,977	2,966	3,322	3,781	3,990	5,193	5,890

Sources: 1840-51, 1850-59, 1860-69: 'Sterftetafelen 1840-51, 1850-59 en 1860-69: *Bijdragen tot de Algemene Statistiek van Nederland*, The Hague, 1878, pp.28-33;
1900-1909: A.J. Van Pesch, 'Tables de mortalité déduites des données de la période 1900-1909, Annexe au 9e recensement général des Pays-Bas (31 December 1909)',
The Hague, 1912, pp.40-41; 1910-1920: J.J.A. Muller, 'Sterftetafels voor de periode 1910-1920', *Statistiek van Nederland*, no.367, Volkstelling van 31 December 1920,
pp.31-2; 1921-1930: J.J.A. Muller, 'Sterftetafels voor Nederland afgeleid uit de waarnemingen over de periode 1921-1930': Volkstelling, 31 December 1930, vol.6,
The Hague, 1934, pp.54-5; 1951-1955: 'Sterftetafels voor Nederland afgeleid uit de waarnemingen voor de perioden 1951-1955 en 1953-1955', The Hague, 1957, pp.26-7.

Table 6.40: Evolution of Infant Mortality Rates: The Netherlands
(per 1,000 births)

Period	Male	Female	Total
1821-26 and 1830	220.3	188.9	205.0
1831-40	232.1	193.9	213.5
1841-50	241.6	206.0	224.3
1851-55	240.0	215.2	227.9
1880-84			190.9
1885-89			174.7
1890-94			166.1
1895-99			153.1
1900-04			141.2
1905-09			118.8
1910-14			103.4
1915-19			87.1
1920-24			74.4
1925-29			57.9
1930-34	51.4	39.5	46.7
1935-39	42.0	32.5	37.4
1940-44	46.8	36.6	41.8
1945-49	45.1	35.3	40.4

Sources: 1821-1855: *Bevolkingstafelen...*, p.xxxvii; 1880-1914: *Statistiek van de Sterfte...1930*, p.xii; 1915-1949: *Foetal, Infant and early Childhood Mortality*, vol.1, United Nations, Population Studies 13, New York, 1954, p.84.

7 NORWAY

Michael Drake

Between 1760 and 1960, the population of Norway rose five-fold:
from around 700,000 to 3,591,000. Although the absolute figures are
small, the significance of the rise is considerable, for in that period
Norway experienced each phase of the demographic transition. In the
1760s her crude birth rate was in the low thirties, her death rate in the
twenties (except in 1763 when a crisis pushed it to at least 35 per
1,000). By the 1960s both rates had about halved. So although the
rate of natural increase in the two periods was broadly similar, the
demographic mechanisms sustaining those rates had altered out of all
recognition.

The change briefly outlined above is unremarkable, being parallelled
in most Western countries. However, the Norwegian experience is
especially worthy of examination because we have reasonably accurate
statistics, by which we can chart the change for the period as a whole.
Indeed, few countries can boast of a national census taken as early as
1769, let alone a vital registration system dating back even further, to
1735. A second feature of interest is that because Norway industrialised
relatively late — crudely put we might say her industrial revolution
occurred about a century after England's — we are able to examine the
socio-economic relationships of a pre-industrial population, with the
precision that only numbers can bring, over a much longer period than
is usually the case. Finally, we are aided in this task by the
quantitatively and historically minded pioneer sociologist, Eilert Sundt
(1817-75) who wrote numerous demographic studies in the 1850s and
1860s. Although Sundt's work was not pursued after his death, there
has in recent years been a major surge of interest among Norwegian
scholars in the population history of their country, particularly in that
of the eighteenth and early nineteenth centuries. In a short chapter it
is not possible to examine all of the myriad relationships that exist
between demographic and social or economic factors. Even if space
permitted, we would be constrained by the paucity of sources, both
primary and secondary, in some areas. I propose, therefore, to examine
four main problems. These have been chosen largely because they cover
topics of general interest to historical demographers. In brief they are,
first, the causes of population growth in the late eighteenth and early

nineteenth centuries; second, the determinants of the age at marriage
in pre-industrial Norway; third, illegitimate fertility from the eighteenth
to the twentieth centuries, and fourth, the nature of migration and
emigration in pre-industrial and industrialising Norway. Finally, in a
postscript I shall endeavour to point up some of the demographic
changes of the post-1960 period. Before dealing with these various
topics, I will attempt to give a brief review of the growth and
distribution of Norway's population and of the changes in nuptiality,
fertility, mortality and migration that have occurred over the past two
hundred years. Sketchy though this must be, it is needed to provide
the context for the later discussion.

Norway, excluding Svalbard and Jan Mayen, has an area of 317,000
sq.km. It is thus a little larger than Italy, or Great Britain and the
Republic of Ireland combined. It is also a very long country; 1,700 km.
in a straight line from its most northerly to its most southerly tip.
Pivot it on the latter and its most northerly point would reach the
Pyrenees. In the south, the country stretches about 400 km. from east
to west, narrowing to about 100 km. in the north. These measurements
do not take account of the massive indentations made by the fjords,
which in one place bring the Swedish frontier to within 8 km. of the
coast. Climatically Norway endures long, cold winters, partly because
of its northerly position (it extends from $57° 59'N$ to $71° 7'N$) and its
mountainous terrain. The climate is tempered, however, by the Gulf
Stream which sweeps along its west coast. The summers are short,
though often quite hot and dry in the east. The growing season is longer
than might be supposed because of long hours of daylight in the summer
months, arising from the country's polar position. Agriculture is,
however, cruelly restricted by the paucity of cultivable soil, only about
3 per cent of the land area.

These physical features have played an important role in Norway's
demographic history. The movement of people and goods, for instance,
has until recent years been much easier by water than by land. Even in
the interior, travel on snow and ice was better than on the bare earth.
Taken together with the mountainous character of many areas away
from the coasts, this has encouraged Norwegians to settle near the sea
and to look outwards for economic gain.

It will be apparent from Table 7.1 that the country was and is very
lightly populated by European standards. Table 7.1 also shows that
until recently this density statistic was not wholly illusory in that the
population has not been concentrated in urban areas. Indeed, it will be
noted that even after the tremendous surge in population growth in the

period 1815-65, some 80 per cent of the population lived in rural areas which, given that Norway had relatively few nucleated villages, meant a widely dispersed population. Looking at the rate of growth of population it will be seen that the heroic age was the period 1815-65, when the population almost doubled. This rate was sharply higher than that of the previous period and would appear to be the product of a fall in mortality combined with a maintained level of fertility. From 1865 the growth of population fell back to more moderate levels, though still higher than those of the late eighteenth century. The main reason for this fall was the sharp rise in emigration, as there was comparatively little change in birth and death rates (see Table 7.3). The moderate rate of increase was maintained into the twentieth century due to a realignment of the population variables. Overseas migration, at a rate which had been second only to that of Ireland in the late nineteenth century, fell away to almost nothing by the 1930s. But from the beginning of the twentieth century the birth rate began to fall sharply, after being comparatively constant since the early eighteenth century (see Table 7.3). The death rate too went into sharp decline, for the first time in a hundred years.

What effect did this growth of population and the accompanying changes in vital rates have on the distribution of population across the country as a whole? Table 7.2 gives at least part of the answer. Apart from the area of the capital, Oslo, and its immediate neighbourhood it will be seen that few counties increased or lost their share of the country's population to any dramatic extent. This was certainly the case for the period 1769-1875. The major changes occurred in the southeast of the country, with the increasingly urbanised Oslo and Akershus counties raising their share of the nation's population from 4.7 per cent in 1769, to 10.6 per cent in 1875 and 19.8 per cent in 1960. Conversely the largely rural counties in the interior to the north and west of Oslo, namely Oppland, Hedmark and Buskerud, saw their collective share of the population fall from 25.9 per cent in 1769, to 18.6 per cent in 1875 and 14.2 per cent in 1960. Distribution by county is only a rough and ready indicator of the population realignment. More significant is the extent of the shift into towns. An attempt to show this is made in Figure 7.1. It will be noticed that whereas only the massive shift to Oslo shows up at the county level (Table 7.2), intra-county movements elsewhere were towards the towns and, since most towns were on the coasts, out of the core of the country and towards its periphery.

To sum up so far; we have seen first, that over the period 1769-1960

Figure 7.1: Percentage Rural and Urban Population in Norwegian Counties, together with Principal Towns in 1769 and 1950

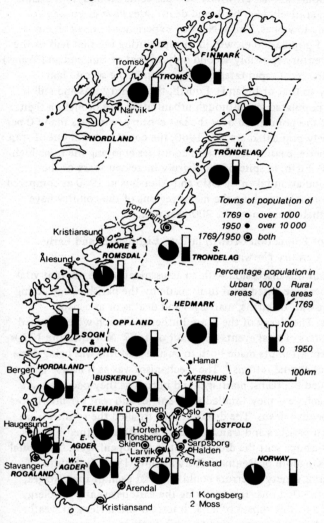

Note: The urban areas in 1769 are taken to be the market towns (Kjøbstedene) listed in the Census of Norway, 15 August 1769 (manuscript copy in the Statistisk Sentralbyrå, Oslo). In 1950 all built up areas are included in the urban population, as given in *Norges Offisielle Statistikk*, xii 87 (1962), *Statistisk Årbok for Norge 1962*.

Source: Statistisk Sentralbyrå, Oslo, Table 8, p.12.

Norway's population has grown by 500 per cent. Second, in the same period, comparatively high birth and death rates have given way to comparatively low ones. Third, Norway experienced one of the most rapid rates of population growth in Europe during the first half of the nineteenth century (possibly second only to that of England and Wales) and one of the most rapid rates of emigration in the second half (second only to that of Ireland). Fourth, the country was and still is very lightly populated and although urbanisation has brought a tighter clustering of the population over the last century, with less than 60 per cent in densely populated areas in 1960, the country is still out of step with the experience of most Western countries enjoying the same high level of GNP. Fifth, in spite of the sharply increased share of the country's population taken by Oslo and Akershus in 1960 as compared with 1769, broadly speaking the major regions of the country have maintained their shares over the 200-year period.

The Causes of Population Growth in Late Eighteenth- and Early Nineteenth- Century Norway

We must begin this discussion with an assessment of the relevant vital statistics. These are based on returns made by the parish clergy acting either as registrars of births, marriages and deaths or as census enumerators. The clergy of the State Lutheran Church were enjoined to keep registers of vital events by an act of 1687. Not until the 1730s, however, were attempts made both to ensure that this was being done and to collect annual returns.[1] The mechanism was as follows. The clergy recorded baptisms, marriages and burials as they occurred. At the end of each year they totalled their entries and sent off the figures to their respective deans. The deans in turn totalled the returns from the individual parishes and transmitted these figures to their bishops. Finally the bishops sent the diocesan totals to Copenhagen, the capital of the dual Kingdom of Denmark-Norway until 1814. It is quite apparent that a variety of errors could occur at each of these stages, particularly the first one. In registering the various events, the clergy had to overcome the impact of a harsh terrain and inclement weather, both of which might be expected to inhibit religious observances. They had also to contend with vast distances. On the other hand they had little trouble with dissenters or rapidly expanding urban populations — as had their counterparts in England at this time. In recent years greater doubt than hitherto has been cast upon the Norwegian clergy's vital registration work. Herstad, in a detailed study of the Bergen diocesan deanery in the years 1770-75, suggests there may have been a 10 per cent under-registration of births. This was made up of still-births (about 4 per cent) which were not registered as births but were registered as deaths, and a 6 per cent under-registration of live births, consisting partly of children who were unbaptised, and partly of those who were baptised at home.[2] On the basis of scattered evidence from the diocese of Bergen Herstad believes that some 100,000 births (presumably live births, though the point is not made clear) may not have been recorded in the *national* totals during the period 1735-1814. This figure consisted of 70,000-85,000 missed out of the registers and a further 15,000-30,000 which were in the registers but through the maladministration of parish clergy, deans and bishops never reached Copenhagen.[3] Dyrvik, working on the parish of Etne (also in the Bergen diocese) believes that the under-registration of births amounted to 2 per cent, that of deaths 6 per cent. Slips in elementary arithmetic also appear to have been legion; the result being that in this parish an horrendous 19 per cent of births and 16 per cent of deaths were not reported to the dean. Dyrvik writes: 'on the assumption that the local studies described [these are Herstad on Bergen, Oldervoll on Os and himself on Etne] are representative of the country as a whole, the excess of births in the diocesan lists must be increased by 15-20 per cent'.[4] In a more recent review of the registration system as a whole, Herstad also highlights serious shortcomings, particularly before the 1760s and in the most northerly diocese, Troundheim.[5]

These strictures are serious, but one needs to set them in context. First of all, as the Norwegian historical demographers are the first to admit, one should not read too much into the experiences of individual, and by no means randomly selected, parishes. Indeed in one of the most recent studies,[6] the clergy of the Akershus diocese in the period 1769-1801 put up a much better showing than do their brothers across the watershed in Bergen. Arithmetical errors are minimal and those that occur often cancel each other out. This is reassuring, especially as the Akershus diocese contained over 40 per cent of the country's population at this time. A second point to note is that although Herstad's estimate of 100,000 births missing from the returns is a large one, it has to be set against over 1,800,000 births that did manage to cross all the hurdles and appear in the national totals. It is also apparent that whilst some clergy made the error of putting still-births with the deaths, they also included unbaptised children there *and* in the birth register too. In other words, some registers are closer to being a record of actual births, marriages and deaths than of baptisms, marriages and burials. Thirdly, one must bear in mind that for the questions one is

likely to ask of it, the data is robust enough. For in the eighteenth and
early nineteenth centuries, one is dealing with a demographic regimen
not remarkable for subtle changes. Death rates fluctuated sharply; birth
rates were more stable, but even they were subject to movements, over
the short term, of quite a gross character. Even Herstad, the most
knowledgeable critic of the registration system, admits that the existing
figures are sufficiently accurate to show the main lines of demographic
development both over time and between one part of the country and
another.[7]

Let us assume then that the statistics are adequate for our purpose.
Table 7.3 indicates that the crude birth rate was relatively stable at
around 30 per 1,000 from the 1740s to the 1890s. A more age-specific
measure of fertility (as in Table 7.4) suggests that in this instance the
crude rate was not too misleading. In the face of this stability one must
look for changes in mortality to explain the sharp increase in population
growth indicated in Table 7.3. In Figure 7.2 the crude death rate is
shown for the country as a whole, and for each of its four constituent
dioceses. For the location of these, see Figure 7.5. If one focuses on the
bottom graph on the page, the one representing the crude death rate
for the country as a whole, the distinction between the pre- and
post-1815 period is sharp. From 1815 the death rate dipped below
20 per 1,000 and oscillated within one or two points of this for the
next twenty five years. Prior to 1815 fluctuations in the crude death
rate were of a much wider amplitude, and by almost any standards
reached what must be described as high levels on a number of occasions.
Thus in 1748, 1763, 1785, 1789 and 1809, the rate topped 30 per
1,000, whilst in 1741, 1742 and 1773 it was above 40. Undoubtedly
the collection and processing of the raw data was better after 1815 than
before,[8] yet it would seem inherently unlikely that this could seriously
have altered the marked contrast in the size and movement of the death
rate in the two periods.

Turning to the graph for the Akershus diocese, we note that the
general mortality profile was the same, in almost every detail, as the
national one we have just examined; the major difference being that
the movement was more violent and the peaks were higher (over 60 per
1,000 in 1742 and 1773 and over 50 per 1,000 in 1809). As Akershus
contained about 42 per cent of the country's population at this time
(Kristiansand had 15 per cent, Bergen 17 per cent and Trondheim 25
per cent), this similarity is not surprising. It is when we turn to the
other graphs, notably the one for Bergen and the one for Kristiansand,
that differences emerge. These differences occur in the middle of the

and Kingdom of Norway, 1740-1840

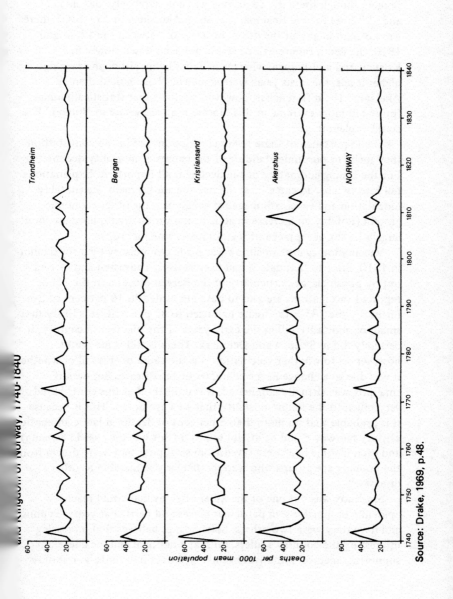

Trondheim

Bergen

Kristiansand

Akershus

NORWAY

Deaths per 1000 mean population

1740   1750   1760   1770   1780   1790   1800   1810   1820   1830   1840

Source: Drake, 1969, p.48.

period from about 1770 to 1815. Before and after those dates all four
dioceses have very much the same mortality profile. One notes,
however, that the 1773 crisis which hit Akershus very hard and also
Trondheim, was muted in Kristiansand and did not show itself in
Bergen, though there the death rate was comparatively high in 1771
and 1772. As for the final major crisis in Akershus, that of 1809, there
was no echo in any of the other dioceses. In between the 1770s and
1810, the death rate remained stable or edged down slowly in
Kristiansand and Bergen, whereas in Trondheim, although reaching
higher levels, the crisis years were somewhat less marked than in
Akershus. The difference is, however, so slight that statistical failings
(probably more extreme in this diocese than elsewhere in Norway[9])
could explain it.

The importance of these regional variations lies in the contribution
they make to our understanding of the causes of mortality decline.
For the timing and nature of the decline is all important. Explanations
fall into two broad categories; the one preventive medicine (notably
inoculation and vaccination against smallpox); the other economic
growth (notably an increase in agricultural productivity, brought about
largely by the acceptance of the potato as a major crop).

Vaccination against smallpox was made compulsory by a royal edict
in 1810. Prior to that date it had been actively canvassed and carried
out by parish clergy particularly in the Bergen diocese. In the 1800s
reported vaccinations are said to have amounted to 16 per cent of live
births; by the 1850s the figure had risen to 82 per cent. It is likely that
smallpox mortality fell in the early years of the nineteenth century; it
certainly did in Sweden and Denmark. There is still some doubt,
however, as to whether vaccination was the cause of this fall or whether
it was due to a change in the character of the disease. But even if
smallpox was virtually eliminated, it is unlikely that this contributed
very much to the fall in mortality that we have noted. This is because
it is probable that no more than 8 per cent of deaths in late eighteenth-
century Norway could be attributed to it (this was the case in Sweden),
and even if some lives were saved from smallpox, they were drawn from
the younger age groups who were particularly vulnerable to other
diseases.[10]

Smallpox was but one of the killer diseases that could reach
epidemic proportions, in particular places and particular years. Typhus
and dysentery were two others. Sølvi Sogner believes that increasing
interest by the country's rulers, both at a national and local level, in
supporting medical initiatives against typhus and dysentery, not only

came earlier than similar moves against smallpox, but also had a considerable effect in keeping them at bay.[11] There is no doubt that her evidence shows increased medical activity, particularly in the 1790s, but as she admits it is impossible to quantify its impact. Evidence from other countries, notably England, suggests one must view the activities of the medical profession at this time with some scepticism.[12]

The potato appears to have reached Norway in the 1750s. As with vaccination, and before that inoculation, the parish clergy seem to have been active in encouraging its adoption.[13] Not until the 1800s does the crop appear to have got much of a foothold, except possibly in the southwestern parts of the country. By the 1830s, however, it was undoubtedly a major crop, being used both as a food and drink; farmers and cottars being permitted to distill spirit freely after 1816. Various factors seem to have encouraged this growth in cultivation. One was the failure of grain harvests; another the blockade of the coasts which both prevented the import of food and the export of timber (a major source of foreign exchange) during a part of the Napoleonic War period. Failure of the fishing in certain western areas and, after 1815, the rapid growth of population itself are also likely to have pointed people in the direction of a comparatively cheap alternative foodstuff.

As in the case of vaccination against smallpox, so with the potato, we are tantalised on the one hand by the fact that advances seem to have come first in areas which witnessed the earliest significant fall in death rates, namely in the dioceses of Bergen and Kristiansand; and on the other by the fact that our quantitative evidence is so sketchy. A most ingenious attempt to treat the problem statistically has, however, been made recently by Kåre Lunden who puts forward the hypothesis that the fall in mortality after 1815 came about because potatoes met the energy, protein and Vitamin C requirements of the population more adequately than had the alternative foodstuffs available in earlier years.[14] Drawing on various censuses or quasi-censuses of agriculture in the period 1723-1865, he comes to the following conclusions. First, that the calorific value of the average Norwegian's daily diet rose from 1,400 in 1723 to 1,800 in 1809, 2,250 in 1835 and 3,300 in 1855-65. Since the minimum requirement for the average man is 2,000 calories per day, it is at once apparent that although the position improved between 1723 and 1809, it was still not satisfactory even by the latter date. A second point made by Lunden is that potatoes made no contribution in 1723 to energy provision and 'in a normal year' around 1809 only 4 per cent of the total. By 1835 this had risen to 28 per cent,

but fell back to 26 per cent by 1865. These figures take account both
of Norwegian agricultural production and corn imports. Third, the
potato made its biggest contribution to energy requirements in the
period 1809-35: 45 per cent of the net increase in the energy output
of Norwegian agriculture coming from this one source.[15] Fourth –
a counter-factual point, this – the increase in the amount of energy
resulting from planting potatoes rather than growing corn in the period
1809-35 amounted to 34 per cent; but over the period 1809-65, only
18 per cent. Fifth, if one postulated that *all* the fall in mortality
between 1809 and 1865 resulted from the increase in calories of the
average Norwegian diet, then 40 per cent of the fall must be attributed
to the increase in corn output, 27 per cent to the increased production
of animals, 18 per cent to growing potatoes rather than using the land
for barley and 15 per cent to the unspecified effects of increased
acreage. Finally if one assumes that vaccination against smallpox may
have reduced mortality by as much as 30 per cent (a most unlikely
figure since as I noted earlier a high proportion of the age group being
saved from death by smallpox would be likely to succumb to other
diseases), and all the rest of the fall was due to an increased calorie
intake, then the contribution of the potato to the overall reduction
would amount to only 13 per cent. How are the mighty fallen!

Although the burden of Lunden's argument is to diminish the
importance of the potato in reducing mortality, he does enter several
caveats. For instance, he notes that it provided all the necessary
Vitamin C by 1835, that in the 'take-off' to lower mortality it played
a dominant role; that having two field crops (i.e. potatoes and corn)
providing sizeable portions of the average diet, which did not make the
same demands on soil or weather, or suffer from the same diseases, was
an insurance against harvest failure.[16] One must note, too, as Lunden
does, that the statistics on which he is working are fallible. Indeed, one
might suggest they are more likely to err than the vital and census data
which has come under such fire recently.

Lunden's article has soon drawn critical fire and has been challenged
on two counts. First, the yield of the potato has been underestimated
by some 15 per cent for several reasons, including the use of an
inaccurate measure.[17] Land planted with potatoes would otherwise
have been cultivated with oats and not barley, although the energy
content of the former was 75 per cent lower than the latter. Finally
potatoes were a much safer crop in the north and in the more
mountainous parts of the south than grain. On this basis the increase
in the amount of energy derived from planting potatoes between 1809

and 1835 rather than corn was 75 per cent and not 34 per cent. For the period 1809-65 the increase was 37 per cent, not 18 per cent.[18] Aggregate figures do not emphasise sufficiently the fact that it was the poorest members of the community, with little or no land, who derived the biggest benefit from potatoes.[19]

Apart from quantifying the role of the potato in Norwegian demographic history, the articles by Lunden and Teigen also make a contribution to the debate on whether mortality peaks in seventeenth- and eighteenth-century Western Europe were a product of food shortages, or of epidemic diseases operating independently of the food position.[20] The figures on the average daily intake of calories in eighteenth century Norway suggest that many people must have been close to starvation and therefore prone to disease. But they show an improvement between 1723 and 1809 which might help explain the tendency, albeit slight, towards falling mortality in the country as a whole, particularly in the dioceses of Kristiansand and Bergen. The potato's role was minimal in the eighteenth century — certainly at the national level — but there is evidence that other agricultural improvements were taking place which might account for the increase in productivity. For example, in a painstaking study of farm inventories, Fartein Valen-Sendstad has shown a marked rise in the amount of equipment on Norwegian farms. Thus in a representative sample of farms in Eastern Norway, he found that 44.8 per cent had wheeled equipment in the 1770s, as against 68.3 per cent in the 1800s, 93.5 per cent in the 1830s and 95.7 per cent in the 1850s. The number with harrows rose from 77.2 per cent in the 1770s to 84.2 per cent in the 1800s, 95 per cent in the 1830s, though it fell slightly to 93.5 per cent in the 1850s. It should be noted, however, that between the 1830s and the 1850s the total *number* of harrows on these farms rose by 44.1 per cent.[21] The shift from primitive tools (the spade, rake and sledge) to more advanced ones (the plough, the harrow and the wagon) was particularly noticeable in western areas of the country.

To sum up: it would appear that though there is little doubt that a fall in mortality propelled Norway's population into one of the fastest growth rates in Europe,[22] the cause or causes of that fall remain obscure. The situation is complicated by the differential timing of the fall; by the competing claims of medical aids, agricultural advances, administrative changes (the development of corn magazines from the 1770s or the ending of the Danish monopoly of corn imports)[23] and inevitably by the inadequacy of the statistics upon which all arguments must be based.

The Determinants of the Age at Marriage in Pre-industrial Norway

The mean age of brides and bridegrooms at first marriage changed little between the 1840s and the 1950s, being around 28 to 29 years for men and 25 to 27 years for women.[24] What changes there were could easily be explained in terms of shifts in the age structure of the population in the marrying age groups. What patchy evidence we have suggests that the mean age at marriage was little different in the mid-eighteenth century.[25]

If anything the proportion remaining unmarried at each age group rose during the nineteenth and early twentieth centuries. The relative stability of the national averages, however, masks considerable variations between different parts of the country and different socio-economic groups. It is impossible to describe, let alone acount for all this diversity. By focusing our attention on differences in the age at marriage of farmers and farm labourers, we shall, however, get some insight into a great deal of it. This is because until Norway began to industrialise in the late nineteenth century, these two groups formed the overwhelming bulk of the workforce. Although the size of both groups increased as the population of the country grew, the number of farm labourers grew at a faster rate than did the number of farmers. The labourers were divided into two categories. On the one hand there were farm servants; young men and women almost invariably unmarried and living in the household of their employer. If they were the sons or daughters of farmers (especially if they were the eldest sons or daughters) they might look forward to becoming farmers or farmers' wives. If on the other hand they were the sons or daughters of farm labourers, then their likely fate on marriage was to become a farm labourer or labourer's wife. Ceasing to live in their employer's household, they would occupy a croft belonging to the farmer for whom they worked. Often this had some land attached to it, but increasingly as the nineteenth century wore on, the proportion of 'crofters without land' increased. The croft, the land or various 'rights' that went with it, e.g. cutting firing, grazing stock, was often a substantial part of a farm labourer's payment.

The approach to marriage of these two groups was very different, especially in those areas where the social boundaries between them was marked. We can for ease of exposition posit two models; the one for the farmer, the other for the crofter. Farmers' sons usually married farmers' daughters. In the mid-1850s, according to Sundt, about 76 per cent did so, the range being from 60 per cent to 82 per cent.[26] Similarly farmers' daughters rarely married the sons of crofters; only about 18 per cent in

Norway 297

fact, though the range varied across the country from only 8 per cent
to 40 per cent in the fifteen regional areas utilised by Sundt for this
analysis. The goal of both sons and daughters was a farm. Inheritance
did not necessarily involve waiting upon the death of the incumbent,
as a system of allowances on retirement was widespread. Not
surprisingly, however, a farmer (or his widow) was unlikely to give up
his farm until he was in his sixties, unless ill health forced him to do so.
This, together with the fact that a farmer's son was unlikely to marry
until he got a farm (few other ways of supporting a wife and children
being open to him), and since it was the *eldest* son who was the one
likely to inherit as legally he had the first claim, the mean age at
marriage was inevitably high. Several factors might, however, affect
this outcome. First, a farmer's son might marry the widow of a farmer.
If she were providing the means of livelihood then the bridegroom
could well be comparatively young. In certain western areas of the
country, according to the 1801 census, some 14 to 15 per cent of
farmers, who were themselves in their first marriage, were married to
widows.[27] A second way in which a relatively young man might get
hold of a farm was if he took part in a 'home exchange'. This meant
that he married a woman from a family which in turn supplied a
bridegroom for a member of his family. The purpose of this
arrangement was to ensure that one family did not gain at the expense
of the other. Frequently such an exchange appears to have occurred
between neighbouring farms, perhaps with the intention of reducing
the risk of disputes between neighbours over property rights.[28] The
extent of such arrangements could be quite startling. For instance in
a recent study of 3,103 marriages contracted by the eldest sons or heirs
to 463 farms in the two mountain parishes of Vang and Slidre during
the years 1600-1850, it was found that in 74 per cent of marriages the
partners lived no more than 8 km. from each other.[29] Even this figure
hides the degree of spatial propinquity evidenced by the origins of the
marriage partners, as the farms were situated in clusters on both sides
of a river, hemmed in by high mountains. The actual frequency of
marriages taking place between partners drawn from the same cluster
of farms was thirteen times greater than one would expect had the
partners been chosen at random. With adjoining clusters the number
of marriages was six times greater than expected. A third of the
marriages were contracted within a distance of two clusters or less,
though some fifteen clusters of farms were within 7 km. of each other.
   We began this discussion by looking at the factors determining the
age at marriage of farmers. But what of their brides? Usually they were

younger than their husbands: Sundt found that in southern Norway in
1851-2, the mean age at marriage of farmers was 29.5 years, that of
their brides 26.0 years.[30] In a study of some 2,978 marriages (neither
partner previously married) from a wide area of southern Norway in
1801, in which the husband was a farmer, as many as 65.5 per cent
of the men were older than their wives.[31] Sundt's explanation for this
was that the 'expectations' of a farmer's daughter were known long
before she reached marriageable age, for according to Norwegian law,
the proportion of an inheritance going to a son or daughter was fixed,
and as it usually consisted of land or stock the amount could be
estimated fairly easily. Hence as a girl's prospects were not particularly
enhanced with age, she could well marry relatively early, though in
actual practice this was rarely before the early twenties. As with the
sons, so with the daughters of farmers, arranged marriages based on
propinquity of land or blood could well disturb factors bringing about
the age at marriage pattern just described.

When we turn to the crofters we find a wholly different set of
determinants. A crofter was likely to have started life as the son of a
crofter or, increasingly, the son of a small farmer. In his teens he would
become a living-in farm servant. Marriage for him depended upon
obtaining a croft. He might 'take over' his father's . More likely
however he would either clear one himself, or be offered an existing
one, other than that on which he was raised. In offering such a croft,
a farmer would be looking for a reliable worker, fit and skilled enough
to perform the duties required of him. Fitness was likely to be a
characteristic of young men, whilst the necessary skills were such as to
be acquired by the early twenties. Hence crofters were normally
younger than farmers at marriage. In first marriages in the early 1850s
Sundt found the mean age of crofter bridegrooms to be a couple of
years lower than farmer bridegrooms at 27.25 years. The wives of
crofters, unlike the wives of farmers, were usually almost the same age
as their husband, at about 26.75 years. Quite frequently such wives
were older than their husbands. In an 1801 survey of some 2,593
crofter marriages in which neither partner had been previously married,
almost 40 per cent of the wives were in this position. Sometimes the
age difference was quite large, with 20.9 per cent of wives in 1801 at
least five years older than their husbands.[32] Sundt argued that a farm
servant aspiring to a croft would find considerable attractions in a
mature woman. She would be experienced in farm work and would be
able to look after the croft whilst he was at work on his master's farm.
If she had been in service long, she may well have accumulated a modest

but important, collection of clothing, bed linen, pots and pans and possibly even a cow. Were she particularly well favoured by her master she may even be the source of a croft for a potential suitor, since just as a farmer would hold onto a good male servant by offering a croft, so he might do the same with a good female servant.

The evidence presented so far as to the determinants of the age at marriage in pre-industrial Norway suggests a strong link between economic circumstances and the choice of marriage partner. This link between marriage and economic opportunity is, of course, frequently remarked upon, though usually the discussion focuses almost exclusively on the age at marriage of men. The assumption seems to be that if economic circumstances predicate early marriage for men, then early marriage for women follows. The discussion above shows some of the dangers of such a line of reasoning.

The link between economic circumstances and the number of marriages can also be demonstrated from Norwegian experience. For instance the rise in the number of marriages from the 1830s to the 1840s was greater in two coastal deaneries (Stavanger and Karmsund in the southwestern county of Rogaland) than in any other deanery in the country, 49 and 51 per cent respectively. In the neighbouring deanery of Lista in the county of Vest-Agder to the south of Rogaland, there was a fall of 7 per cent in the number of marriages between these two decades. The explanation of these changes appears to be the arrival of herring shoals off Rogaland which led to rich catches in the 1840s, and with them general prosperity. The herring appear to have migrated from Vest-Agder, hence the decline there both of economic opportunity and of marriages.[33] Figure 7.3 shows another example of the link between the number of marriages and 'good and bad times'.

Illegitimate Fertility, 1760-1960

Traditionally interest in illegitimate fertility has been the preserve of moralists. In recent years, however, a number of practitioners of the 'new social history' have begun to focus upon it.[34] For them, illegitimacy has an important place in a much broader spectrum of interests which embrace marriage, the formation of the family, household structure, the history of childhood and attitudes towards sexual relationships. As with socio-demographic subjects, Norway offers the student of non-marital fertility two valuable assets: first, a long run of statistical material, exceptionally long for a pre-industrial Western society, and second, several works by Eilert Sundt which are social-scientific both in the questions posed and the methods used.

Figure 7.3: Relationship between Annual Number of Marriages per 1,000 Mean Population and Annual Rate of Increase of Gross National Product, 1866-1940

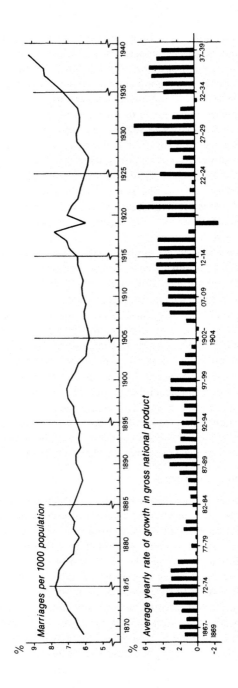

Source: Backer, 1965, pp.30-31.

The analysis of illegitimate fertility in the past is particularly difficult as it is almost impossible to get hold of the two basic measurements: namely, the *number* of illegitimate births *classified* by age group of the unmarried women who produced them. Lacking this, scholars have usually had to adopt the *illegitimacy ratio*, i.e. the number of births out of wedlock per 100 births. Unfortunately this can be highly misleading, partly because a change in the ratio could just as well be the product of a change in legitimate as illegitimate fertility, and partly because the bulk of legitimate births are produced by older women than those producing illegitimate births. Unmarried women are naturally much more numerous at the younger age groups, as entry into marriage takes them out of the population at risk. Tables 7.5 and 7.6 illustrate these points.

Between 1890 and 1930 the number of illegitimate births per 1,000 women fell sharply in every age group but one and there the rise was tiny in absolute terms. Yet over this same period there was barely any change in the illegitimacy ratio, a fall in fact of less than 2 per cent. From 1930 to 1960 there was a rise in four age groups, a fall in one, with one remaining the same. Yet over this period the illegitimacy ratio fell by as much as 47 per cent. Table 7.6 covers an earlier period. It was compiled by Sundt to show that as illegitimate births were produced by women in different age groups than those producing legitimate births, one should not relate the one to the other — as the illegitimacy ratio does. Thus, Sundt argues, the apparent fall in illegitimacy from 1816-20 to 1831-5 was an illusion, being largely a product of a changing age structure. From 1825-35 the population in the age group most at risk (aged 20-29) actually fell by 1.8 per cent.[35] In the following decade (1835-45) it rose by a startling 38.8 per cent. During this latter period the illegitimacy ratio also rose by 22 per cent. Sundt argued that, failing precise information on the number of illegitimate births by age group of mother, one could get an approximate measure by relating illegitimate births to marriages. In this way, Sundt was relating the couples who were, from a sexual point of view, married *de facto*, with those who were married *de jure*.[36]

Sundt had a further, more pragmatic reason for choosing this form of measurement. Wishing to compare the experience of illegitimacy among both the propertied and propertyless classes (in effect the farmers and the crofters respectively), he conducted a nationwide survey. For this he depended upon the parish clergy abstracting information from their registers, recognising that it would be much less difficult for priests to get from their registers the class or occupation

of married couples and of the parents of illegitimate children, than it
would for the parents of *each* legitimate child.[37] His judgement paid
off, for he had an over 80 per cent return to his questionnaire.

The graph in Figure 7.4 shows the changes in non-marital fertility
in Norway from the 1730s to the 1960s, using Sundt's method of
measurement and the more conventional illegitimacy ratio. Although
data for the country as a whole has not yet been compiled for the
eighteenth century, that for the major diocese of Akershus is available.
Since movements in the Akershus figures match closely the national
ones in the period where they overlap (1771-85 and 1801-55), it seems
reasonable to suppose that they did so in the earlier period. The general
configuration is of a comparatively low and stable non-marital fertility
in the years 1731-71: a more or less continuous rise from 1771 which
lasted for a century, followed by a fall of sizeable proportions, unbroken
except for the Second World War period, down to the 1950s. Recently,
twentieth century data has been subject to a series of ingenious
calculations which take into account all the demographic variables
which affect the 'level of illegitimacy', i.e. age structure, level of marital
fertility, level of nuptiality and so give a much more sensitive index
than either the ratio or the rate. Kumar has produced an index showing
the 'probability of occurrence of an illegitimate birth to a specified
female',[38] which has been superimposed on Figure 7.4. Interestingly,
Sundt's illegitimate birth/marriage ratio more nearly reflects Kumar's
index than does the conventional illegitimacy ratio. When one goes
behind this aggregate data, considerable variation is exposed. Here I
will report briefly on Sundt's work which, though it was carried out in
the 1850s and 1860s, went back in part to the mid-eighteenth century.

Sundt looked at the number of illegitimate births per 100 marriages
in each of Norway's 53 deaneries for the years 1831-40, 1841-50 and
1851-60. The ratio varied enormously from one part of the country to
another. At one end of the spectrum the deanery of Lister in the
southwest of the country had only 4.8 illegitimate live births per 100
marriages per year in the decade 1831-40, whereas the diocesan deanery
of Trondheim had 69.1.[39] This latter deanery was an urban one and in
common with the other major towns, had a consistently high ratio over
the period studied. Ignoring such deaneries, however, one notes ratios
of 54.3 and 53.3 in Nordmøre and Indre Sogn respectively (both in the
west of the country) and ratios of 52.5 and 49.0 in Østerdalen and
Gudbrandsdalen respectively (both in the east of the country). Althoug
the ratio changed over time, the ranking of the 53 deaneries one to
another remained very stable (Spearman 0.9). For the fifteen rather

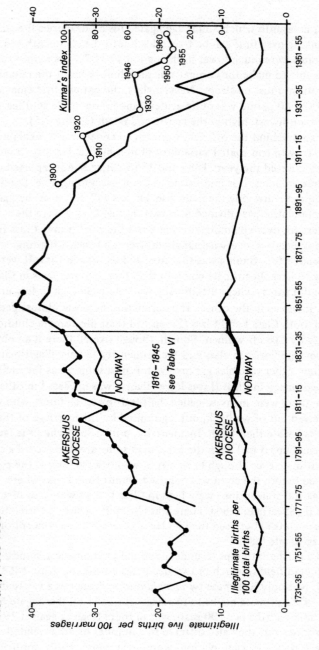

Figure 7.4: Illegitimate Live Births per 100 Marriages and per 100 Total Births in Norway, 1801-1965 and in the Akerhus Diocese, 1731-1860, together with an Index of the 'Illegitimacy Level' in Norway, 1900-1960

Source: Sundt, 1866, p.126; Norges Offisielle Statistikk, XII, 245, 1969, pp.44-7; Kumar, 1969, p.100.

larger areas into which Sundt aggregated his 53 deaneries the stability
of ranking over time can be traced back into the eighteenth century.
The rates were much lower in the period 1762-71, the period for which
I was able to make the comparison, and doubts about the reliability of
the returns must be strong. Nevertheless, the pattern that emerges in
the 1830-60 period was quite evident; moderate in the southeast, low
in the southwest, high in the centre and north (Figure 7.5).

To get behind the official returns in an endeavour to explain the
level, growth and spatial variability of non-marital fertility, Sundt's
survey covered the years 1855 and 1856. Since Sundt reported on this
in three volumes, it is impossible to cover everything here. Some
attempt at conveying the main conclusions will, however, be made.
The population was divided into two classes: Class I were the
propertied, overwhelmingly farmers and their offspring; Class II were
the propertyless, overwhelmingly crofters and their offspring.

Sundt's first finding was that men and women in Class II were more
likely to have illegitimate children than their counterparts in Class I.
Second, in areas where illegitimacy was relatively high or low in one
class, it was so in the other. The correlation here was almost perfect.
Third, both Class I and Class II men had their illegitimate children
mostly by Class II women. Fourth, though overall there is an obvious
relationship between class and the propensity to have illegitimate
children, other variables are involved. For in some areas the incidence
of illegitimacy in Class II was lower than it was in Class I in other areas.
Fifth, there were many so-called 'half-legitimate' children, who were
conceived out of wedlock, but legitimised by the marriage of their
parents before their birth. Incidentally, until 1851 (when the law was
tightened up) it had been the custom in some areas to record a child
as legitimate even though born out of wedlock, so long as the parents
married before the child was baptised. Sundt found that where
pre-marital conceptions were high in Class I, they were also high in
Class II (Spearman 0.86). There was also quite a strong correlation
(Spearman 0.7) between the incidence of pre-marital conceptions and
of illegitimate births.

In a further attempt to understand the phenomenon, Sundt
conducted field research in two deaneries during the years 1864 and
1865. Not only had these two *neighbouring* deaneries a vastly different
ratio of illegitimate births to marriages (in 1851-60 there were 69.3
illegitimate births per 100 marriages in Indre Sogn as against 19.8 in
Søndfjord), but they also differed in a number of other related
characteristics. Sexual relations were much more tightly controlled

Figure 7.5: Illegitimate Births per 100 Marriages in Groupings of Norwegian Deaneries

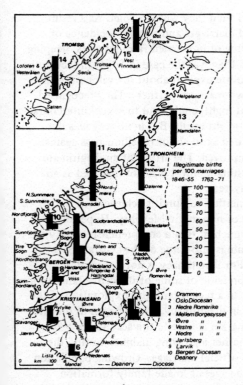

1 Nedre, Mellem, Vestre and Øvre Borgesyssel, Nedre Romerike.

2 Øvre Romerike, Østerdalen, Hedemarken, Gudbrandsdalen.

3 Toten, Valdres, Hadeland, Ringerike and Hallingdal, Kongsberg.

4 Drammen, Jarlsberg, Larvik, Nedre Telemark.

5 Øvre Telemark, Østre and Vestre Nedenes, Råbygdelaget.

6 Mandal, Lista, Dalerne.

7 Jaeren, Stavanger, Karmsund, Ryfylke.

8 Hardanger and Voss, Sunnhordland, Nordhordland.

9 Ytre and Indre Sogn.

10 Sunnfjord, Nordfjord, Søndre and Nordre Sunnmøre.

11 Romsdal, Nordmøre, Fosen.

12 Dalerne.

13 Innherad, Namdalen.

14 Helgeland, Salten, Lofoten, Vesterålen.

15 Tromsø, Vest and Øst Finnmark. Note: The 'major' urban concentrations in the Bergen and Trondheim diocesan deaneries omitted.

Source: (1762-71) Bishops Lists, Statsarkiv, Oslo; (1846-55) Sundt, 1864, p.27.

by one's parents in Søndfjord than they were in Sogn. As a result Søndfjord had more arranged marriages and a lower incidence of night-courtship and the locating of unmarried farm servants' sleeping quarters in byres and stables, than was the case in Sogn. In fact in the latter deanery, parents were quite explicit about the value of letting their children choose their own marriage partners. They recognised that meeting, unsupervised, at night, could lead to sexual intercourse and that an illegitimate child might result. But in no way was the behaviour of the young regarded as an act of rebelliousness against the parents. It was socially approved. The arrival of an illegitimate child was undoubtedly unfortunate, but it was not regarded as an indictment of the courtship system.

This account does justice neither to Sundt's achievement nor to the data available for a study of non-marital fertility. Hopefully, however, it will have given some hint that a comprehensive study of illegitimacy offers many openings into some of the central concerns of the new social historians. For illegitimacy is not a marginal experience but instead an expression of some of the central institutions of the society. Indeed Sogner in a recent tentative exploration of the subject, suggests that the rise in illegitimacy, which began in the late eighteenth century, did not mark a change in the acceptability of pre-marital cohabitation but rather a growing inability to find the economic wherewithal for an official marriage. 'Growing population and inadequate resources', she suggests 'made family formation increasingly difficult. The arrival of a child which used to lead to the establishment of a family household, tends at first to lead to a delayed marriage, then, more often than before, to no marriage at all'.[40] Eventually because of the misery caused by the rise in illegitimate births, pre-marital cohabitation becomes socially unacceptable and from the 1890s illegitimacy declines.

The Nature of Migration and Emigration in Pre-industrial and Industrialising Norway

Studies of internal migration in Norway are beginning to show that the population was much more mobile at a much earlier date than had been thought.[41] In this, Norway's pre-industrial society is proving similar to that of other Western communities. Herstad, for instance, reckons that the deaneries of the Bergen diocese each lost 35 to 55 per cent of their natural increase by migration in the period 1769-1815; there being two exceptions to this, one the Bergen diocesan deanery which was a net gainer of population through migration, and Sunnmøre where the loss through migration might have been as high as 90 per cent.[42] Whilst Bergen depended upon immigrants to maintain its population up to 1815, after that date this was no longer the case. The town shared this characteristic with other major centres (Drammen, Kongsberg, Kristiania, Kristiansand and Trondheim). More attention should therefore be focused on the towns, although small by international standards, in seeking an explanation of the post-1815 fall in mortality.[43] This is also a good example of how a study of one aspect of demographic development (migration) can throw some light on the study of another (mortality changes).

In the middle decades of the nineteenth century, Sundt drew attention to the incidence of internal migration, which he said was increasing.[44] For the period 1836-45, the general pattern was one of out-migration from the central areas, in-migration to the coastal areas. Urban areas on the coast were particularly noticeable as gainers by migration. Thus Kristiania grew by 25.7 per cent in this decade as a result of migration alone (its total increase including the excess of births over deaths was 31.7 per cent). Trondheim grew by 7.2 per cent through migration, Bergen by 1.7 per cent. Kristiansand, on the other hand, gained only 0.4 per cent from this source. Two other areas notable for the extent of in-migration were, on the one hand Karmsund and Stavanger, neighbouring deaneries in the southwest of the country with increases in population through migration (1836-45) of 8.2 and 14.5 per cent respectively; and on the other hand, East and West Finmark, with increases of 16.8 and 13.1 per cent.[45] The increases in Karmsund and Stavanger seem to have been the result of the sudden appearance off the coasts of vast herring shoals which produced a boom in employment. East and West Finmark were 'colonial areas' in nineteenth-century Norway, with much new land being taken into cultivation.

This considerable amount of internal migration in eighteenth- and nineteenth-century Norway had no counterpart in migration overseas until the second half of the nineteenth century. But then, from 1866-1930, a massive migration occurred, almost all of it to the United States (see Figure 7.6). Both before and after those dates, overseas migration was negligible.[46] Up to the 1890s the main areas to lose population overseas were those which had a long tradition of out-migration, notably the counties of Oppland, Hedmark, Buskerud and Telemark. From the 1890s this leading role was taken over by the southwestern counties of Rogaland, East Agder and West Agder.[47]

The explanation of this overseas migration has been given a great

boost recently by Thorvald Moe's study which noted that by 1890
some 90 per cent of Norwegian-born immigrants to the USA were
settled in the North Central Region (i.e. the states of Illinois, Wisconsin,
Minnesota, Iowa, North and South Dakota): 90 per cent of emigrants
up to 1900 were in the 15-49 year group; females accounted for
between 26 and 36 per cent of the total; 60 per cent of emigrants were
landless labourers (the crofters discussed above), the bulk of the rest
being handicraft workers and people employed in water transport;
between one third and one quarter travelled on tickets supplied from
the United States.[48] *No single variable* accounts for the extent or timing
of migration. Moe takes issue on this point with Easterlin who has
argued that both the long swings and the shorter-term cyclical
fluctuations in migration to the United States were dominated by
conditions in that country. On the contrary, the determinants were
partly demographic, namely the size of the pool of young people in
the emigrant age group; and partly economic, namely the relative
attraction of Norwegian cities as against the United States in terms of
income possibilities.[49] Moe's study demonstrates once again the
inter-relation of demographic phenomena. For instance, his discussion
of the importance of the size of the pool of potential migrants as a
determinant of the extent of migration is reminiscent of Sundt's
discussion of the same pool, though in his case in terms of the number
of newly marrieds.[50] The links between local migrations, both in terms
of area and personnel and long-distance migration is also related to
factors determining fertility and nuptiality levels. It is interesting to
note, for instance, differences in the extent of emigration from the
deaneries of Sogn and Søndfjord in connection with the arguments
about the causes of variations in the amount of non-marital fertility.

Postscript

Broadly speaking, an attempt has been made in this chapter to examine
some of the major socio-demographic features of Norway over the two
centuries from the mid-eighteenth to the mid-twentieth centuries.
Long-run stability and unidirectional change has been noted both for
legitimate fertility and mortality. By contrast, non-marital fertility
and overseas migration has shown both a marked rise and a marked fall
over the period. Behind the national aggregates, however, some
evidence of sizeable variations in experience has been shown. One
feature is, however, common to all the phenomena so far discussed,
and that is their comparative stability. This is, of course, not to say that
there were no short-term fluctuations. Figure 7.2, showing mortality

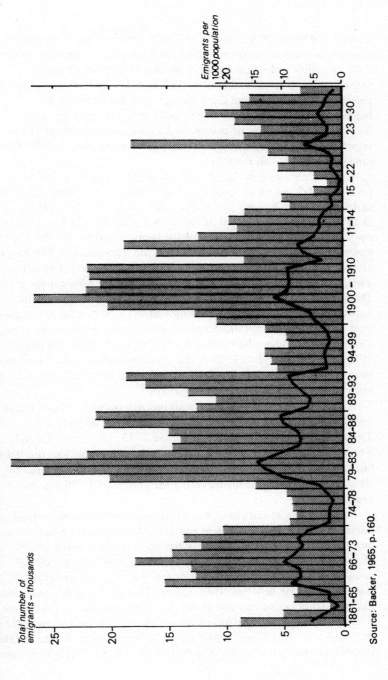

Figure 7.8. Overseas Emigration from Norway, 1861-1930

Total number of emigrants – thousands

Emigrants per 1000 population

Source: Backer, 1965, p.160.

crises in the eighteenth century, or Figure 7.6, showing sharp annual changes in overseas emigration, are both examples of this. Nevertheless, both mortality and migration were set in a pattern which itself extended over a considerable period of time. By contrast, the post-1960 period has witnessed some sharp changes in socio-demographic behaviour which appear to mark a significant break with the past. Such a judgement may, of course, be no more than a product of the inevitable foreshortened view of recent phenomena, but they do deserve some discussion in this context.

The first change is in the age and incidence of marriage. In the period 1951-5 the mean age at marriage of previously unmarried men and women was 28.5 and 25.5 years respectively. Neither figure is at all exceptional in the light of the known position over the previous century, and the likely position for the century before that. By 1961-5, however, the two ages had fallen to 26.0 and 22.9 years.[51] These figures are not mere expressions of a change in the age structure, but reflect a major change in the probability of marriage in the younger age groups. Thus, to take but a couple of examples: in the period 1959-62 the expectation of marriage per 1,000 men aged 15-20 was 36, as compared with eight in the years 1945-8 and a previous peak of ten in the years 1909-12. For women the comparable figures were 178 in the years 1959-62, 74 in the years 1945-8, the previous highest being 49 in the years 1909-12. These tendencies continued into the 1960s but were reversed in the late 1960s and early 1970s.[52]

A striking break with earlier trends has also occurred in non-married fertility. From a low of 3.9 illegitimate births per 100 births, the illegitimacy ratio rose to a startling 9.1 in 1973. This was not simply a reflection of changes in age structure, legitimate fertility or nuptiality, but marked a rise in the likelihood of bearing an illegitimate child for all women except in the higher fertile age groups of 35-39 and 40-44 years.[53]

On migration, studies of recent developments have shown a final break with the earlier settlement pattern. Although Norwegians have been a mobile people, this mobility has not led to the development of many major urban areas. Norway remained a sparsely populated country with a comparatively high proportion of its people in rural areas. Since 1950, however, the number of people living in rural areas has been falling at an ever-increasing rate. Thus whereas in 1950 some 67.8 per cent of the population lived in 'rural communities', by 1972 the proportion had fallen to 44.8 per cent, 'the greatest change to take place in any comparable period in Norway's history'.[54] This movement has not, however, reinforced the greatest concentration of urban population around the Oslo fjord, but rather benefited regional centres close to the original settlements of migrants.

In these three ways, then, Norwegian demographic experience appears to break the pattern of earlier decades. For some of them, such as new settlement patterns resulting from migration, there would seem little likelihood of a return to an earlier form. For others, such a conclusion would be risky indeed. To understand any of them, however, it would seem wise to examine their historical roots if only to get some measure of their novelty.

Notes

1. S.B. Sogner, *Folkevekst og flytting: en historisk-demografisk studie i 1700-årene Øst Norge*, University of Oslo Ph.D. thesis, 2 vols. (in the press), vol.1, pp.17-21 (for details of registration in Akershus diocese): J. Herstad, 'Bispelistene som Kilde til eldre norsk befolkningsstatistikk', *Heimen*, XV, 1975, pp.609-28, 689-704 (for the country as a whole).

2. J. Herstad, 'Folkemengdens bevegelser i Bergen stift, 1735-1820. Tall og fakta', *Bergens Historiske Forenings Skrifter*, no.69/70, 1970, pp.126-7.

3. Ibid., pp.137-8.

4. S. Dyrvik, 'Historical Demography in Norway 1660-1801: a short survey', *Scandinavian Economic History Review*, vol.XX, no.1, 1972, pp.31-2.

5. J. Herstad, op.cit. (1975).

6. S.B. Sogner, op.cit., vol.1, pp.22-9.

7. J. Herstad, op.cit. (1975), pp.393-4.

8. Ibid. (1970), p.140.

9. Ibid. (1975).

10. M. Drake, *Population and Society in Norway 1735-1865*, Cambridge, 1969, pp.50-4.

11. S.B. Sogner, op.cit., vol.1, pp.113-20.

12. T. Mckeown and R.G. Brown, 'Medical evidence related to English population changes in the 18th century', *Population Studies*, vol.9, 1955/56, pp.119-41; T. Mckeown and R.G. Record, 'Reasons for the decline in mortality in England and Wales during the 19th century', *Population Studies*, vol.16, 1962, pp.94-122.

13. M. Drake, op.cit., pp.54-65, for details of the dissemination of the potato.

14. K. Lunden, 'Potetdyrkinga og den raskare folketalsvoksteren in Noreg fra 1815', *Historisk Tidsskrift*, vol.55, 1976, p.285 (English summary).

15. Ibid., p.294.

16. Ibid., p.298.

17. H. Teigen, 'Poteta og Folkeveksten i Noreg 1815-1865', *Historisk Tidsskrift*, vol.56, 1976, pp.438-51. A measure of 139.4 litres per 'ton' was used rather than 160.

18. Ibid., p.445.

19. Ibid., pp.446-9.

20. G. Utterström, 'Some population problems in pre-industrial Sweden', *Scandinavian Economic History Review*, vol.2, 2, 1954, pp.103-65; P. Goubert,

Beauvais et le Beauvaisis de 1600 à 1730, 2 vols, Paris, 1960; A. Lassen, *Fald og Fremgang: Traek af Befolkningsudviklingen i Danmark 1645-1960*, Universitetsforlaget, Aarhus, 1965; J.D. Chambers, *Population, Economy and Society in Pre-industrial England*, Oxford, 1972; A.B. Appleby, 'Disease or famine? Mortality in Cumberland and Westmoreland 1580-1640', *Economic History Review*, 2nd Series, vol.26, no.3, 1973, pp.403-32.

21. F. Valen-Sendstad, *Norske landbruks-redskaper, 1800-1850 arene*, Lillehammer, 1964, pp.151, 174.

22. C.J. O'Neill, 'A fresh look at Norway's pre-industrial population growth using stable population theory', unpublished paper presented at the General Conference of the International Union for the Scientific Study of Population. Liège, August 1973. This presents an opposite view.

23. K. Lunden, op.cit., p.299.

24. M. Drake, op.cit., p.78; J.E. Backer, 'Ekteskap, fødsler og vandring i Norge 1856-1960', *Samfunnsøkonomiske studier, No.13*, Statistisk Sentralbyrå, Oslo, 1965, p.47 (English summary).

25. S. Dyrvik, op.cit. (1972), p.43.

26. E. Sundt, *Fortsatte Bidrag angaaende Saedeligheds-Tilstanden i Norge*, Christiania, 1864, pp.14-5, 31-2: cited in detail in M. Drake, op.cit., Table 6.1, p.135.

27. M. Drake, op.cit., pp.136, 224.

28. L.P. Saugstad and Ø. Ødegård, 'Naboskap og ekteskap: giftermålsmønsteret i en norsk fjellbygd 1600-1850', *Norveg. Folkelivsgransking*, 19, 1976, p.113.

29. Ibid., pp.105-7.

30. E. Sundt, *Om Giftermaal i Norge*, Christiania, 1855, p.197.

31. Drake, op.cit., pp.131, 225.

32. Ibid., p.132.

33. E. Sundt, op.cit. (1855), p.166.

34. J. Knodel, 'Law, marriage and illegitimacy in 19th century Germany', *Population Studies*, vol.20, no.3, 1967, pp.279-94; P. Laslett and K. Oosterveen, 'Long-term trends in bastardy in England: a study of the illegitimacy figures in the Pari Registers and in the reports of the Registrar General 1561-1960', *Population Studies*, vol.27, no.2, 1973, pp.255-84; P. Laslett, *Family Life and Illicit Love in Earlier Generations: Essays in Historical Sociology*, Cambridge, 1977; E. Shorter, 'Illegitimacy, sexual revolution and social change in modern Europe', *Journal of Interdisciplinary History*, vol.2, no.2, 1971, pp.237-72; Ibid., *The Making of the Modern Family*, London, 1976; T.C. Smout, 'Aspects of sexual behaviour in 19th century Scotland', in A.A. Maclaren (ed.), *Social Class in Scotland: Past and Present*, Edinburgh, 1976; E. Van de Walle, E. Shorter and J. Knodel, 'The decline of non-marital fertility in Europe 1880-1940', *Population Studies*, vol.25, no.3, 1971, pp.375-93.

35. M. Drake, op.cit., p.45.

36. E. Sundt, *Om Saedeligheds-tilstanden i Norge*, Christiania, 1857, p.8.

37. Ibid., p.311.

38. J. Kumar, 'Demographic analysis of data on illegitimate births', *Social Biology*, vol.16, no.2, 1969, p.95.

39. E. Sundt, op.cit. (1864), pp.8, 92.

40. S.B. Sogner, Illegitimacy in the old rural society: some reflections on the problem arising from two Norwegian family reconstitution studies, MS, 1977.

41. S.B. Sogner, op.cit. (1975), vol.1, pp.81-95.

42. J. Herstad, op.cit. (1970), pp.129-31.

43. Ibid., pp.140-1.

44. E. Sundt, *Om Dødeligheden i Norge*, Christiania, 1855, p.126.

45. Ibid., pp.128-9.

Norway					313

46. J.E. Backer, op.cit. (1965), pp.158-60.
47. Ibid., pp.164-5.
48. T. Moe, *Demographic developments and economic growth in Norway 1740-1940: an econometric study*, Arno Press, New York, 1977, pp.133-69.
49. Ibid., p.176.
50. M. Drake, op.cit., pp.43-5; for a discussion of this.
51. *Norges Offisielle Statistikk XII*, 245, p.49.
52. S. Dyrvik and C.J. O'Neill (eds.), *Norges Befolkning*, Oslo, 1975, pp.21, 43-8.
53. Ibid., p.50.
54. Ibid., pp.80-1.

General Bibliography

T.C. Blegen,*Norwegian Migration to America*, 2 vols., Northfield Minnesota, 1931/40.
T. Christiansen, *Befolkningsutviklingen og endringer i samfunnstrukturen i Overhalla prestegjeld 1664-1801*, Historisk Institutt, Bergen (duplicated).
S. Dyrvik, 'Om giftarmål og sosiale normer. Ein studie av Etne 1715-1801', *Tidsskrift for samfunnsforskning*, vol.11, 1970, pp.285-300.
S. Dyrvik, *Befolkningsutvikling og sociale tilhøve i Etne prestegjeld 1665-1801*, Historisk Institutt, Bergen, 1971 (duplicated).
S. Dyrvik, 'Infant Mortality about 1800 – a Preliminary Exploration into Norwegian Local Material', *Yearbook of Population Research in Finland*, XIII, 1974, pp.125-34.
S. Dyrvik, K. Mykland and J. Oldervoll, 'The demographic crises in Norway in the 17th and 18th centuries: some data and interpretations', Dept. of History, University of Bergen, n.d.
A. Engen, *Oppbrott og omlegging. Utvandring og økonomisk omlegging i Dovre på 1800-tallett*, Historisk Institutt, Oslo, 1973 (duplicated).
O.K. Finnøy, 'Gudbrandsdøler som flytta til Romsdal i 17-1800 åra', *Årbok for Gudbrandsdalen*, 1974, pp.82-9.
T. Gedde-Dahl Jr., 'Population structure in Norway: inbreeding, distance and kinship', *Hereditas*, vol.73, pt.2, 1973, pp.211-32.
H. Gille, 'The demographic history of the Northern European countries in the 18th century', *Population Studies*, III, 1949/50, pp.3-65.
B. Gjerdåker, *Geografisk og sosial mobilitet i Ullensaker på 1800 talet*, Historisk Institutt, Oslo, 1974 (duplicated).
S.F. Hartley, *Illegitimacy*, Berkeley, 1975.
A. Hattestad, 'Skjukdomsar i Fåberg på 1700-talet', *Årbok for Gudbrandsdalen*, XXXV, 1967, pp.50-61.
L. Henry, 'La population de la Norvège depuis deux siècles', *Population*, 25, no.3, 1970, pp.543-57.
H. Hyldbakk, 'Utvandring av husmenn fra Gudbrandsdalen til Nordmøre', *Årbok for Gudbrandsdalen*, XLI, 1973, pp.52-9.
H. Hyldbakk, 'Utvandrarar frå Surnadal 1857-1914', *Årsskrift for Nordmøre historielag*, 1974, pp.32-44.
L. Juhasz, 'Demografiske kriser', *Heimen*, vol.XV, 1971, pp.397-417.
L. Juhasz, 'Den selvregulerende mekanisme hos befolkningen i eldre tid', *Heimen*, vol.XVIII, 1974, pp.255-8.
L.G. Koppang, *Befolkningsutvikling og yrkesstruktur i Stord prestegjeld 1666-1801*, Historisk Institutt, Bergen, 1974 (duplicated).

314   Norway

A. Lanes, *Befolkningsutvikling og yrkesstruktur i Lyngen prestegjeld 1660-1801*, Historisk Institutt, Bergen, 1973 (duplicated).

S. Langholm, 'Short-distance migration, circles and flows: movement to and from Ullensaker according to population census lists of 1865', *Scandinavian Economic History Review*, XXIII, no. 1, 1975, pp.36-62.

S. Lieberman, 'Norwegian population growth in the 19th century', *Economy and History*, vol.11, 1968.

S. Lieberman, 'The industrialization of Norway 1800-1920', *Scandia Books*, no.8, Oslo, 1970.

O. Løfgren, 'Family and household among Scandinavian peasants: an exploratory essay', *Ethnologia Scandinavica*, 1974, pp.17-52.

P. Mathiesen, 'Lokalmigrasjon eller tømmernomadisme i Nordøy 1769-1865', *Heiman*, XIV, no.3, 1967, pp.102-11.

T. Moe, 'Some economic aspects of Norwegian population movements 1740-1940: an econometric study', *Journal of Economic History*, vol.30, no.1, 1970, pp.267-70.

M. Naevvdal, *Emigrasjonen fra Søndre Bergenhus amt til USA og Canada i perioden 1895-1905*, Historisk Institutt, Bergen, 1971 (duplicated).

E. Niemi, *Migrasjonen fra Nord-Finnland og Nord-Sverige til Vadsø by og landdistrikt 1845-1885*, Historisk Institutt, Oslo, 1972 (duplicated).

J. Oldervoll, *Befolkningsutviklingen i Os prestegjeld ca.1660-1801*, Historisk Institutt, Bergen, 1970 (duplicated).

S. Ordahl, *Befolkningstilhøve, naeringsgrunnlag og sosiale tilhøve i Spind 1800-1865*, Historisk Institutt, Oslo, 1972 (duplicated).

I. Semmingsen, *Veien mot Vest*, 2 vols., Oslo, 1941/1950.

I. Semmingsen, 'Emigration from Scandinavia', *The Scandinavian Economic History Review*, vol.XX, no.1, 1972, pp.45-60.

K.E. Skaaren, *Utvandringen til Amerika fra Brønnoy og Vik 1867-1899*, Historisk Institutt, Trondheim, 1971 (duplicated).

B. Skorgen, *Befolkningsutviklingen og yrkesstructuren i Nesset prestegjeld 1665-1801*, Historisk Institutt, Bergen, 1973 (duplicated).

S. Sogner, 'Freeholder and cottar: property relationships and the social structure in the peasant community in Norway during the 18th century', *Scandinavian Journal of History*, vol.1, no.3/4, 1976, pp.181-99.

R. Sunde, *Ei undersøking av utvandringa til Amerika fra Vik i Sogn 1839-1915*, Historisk Institutt, Trondheim, 1974 (duplicated).

E. Sundt, *Om Saedeligheds-Tilstanden i Norge: Tredie Beretning*, Kristiania, 1866.

E. Sundt, 'Harham: et exempel fra fiskeri distrikterne', *Folkevennen*, no.7, 1858, pp.329-424.

F. Suorza, *Befolkningsutviklingen i Sør Varanger 1900-1920*, Historisk Institutt, Bergen, 1973 (duplicated).

A.A. Svalestuen, *Tinns emigrasjonshistorie 1837-1907*, Universitetsforlaget, Oslo, 1972.

R.F. Tomasson, 'Premarital sexual permissiveness and illegitimacy in the Nordic countries', *Comparative Studies in Society and History*, vol.18, no.2, 1976, pp.252-70.

H.O. Tveiten, *En utvandring blusser opp og slakner*, Historisk Institutt, Oslo, 1974 (duplicated).

APPENDIX

Table 7.1: Population of Norway 1769-1960

Year	Total pop.	Pop. per sq.km.	Females per 1,000 males[b]	% living in densely pop'd areas[c]	Inter-censal pop. growth per annum	%
1769	739,180[a]	2.3	1,108	8.9[d]		
1815	904,777[a]	2.9	1,089	9.8[d]	1769-1815	0.4
1865	1,701,756[b]	5.4	1,036	19.6	1815-1865	1.3
1910	2,391,782[b]	7.6	1,076	38.5	1865-1910	0.8
1960	3,591,234[b]	11.3	1,007	57.4	1910-1960	0.8

a. M. Drake, 'A revision of census totals', *Population and Society in Norway, 1735-1865*, Cambridge, 1969, pp.165-6; b. *Norges Offisielle Statistikk XII*, 245, 1969, p.33; c. Defined as a collection of houses numbering at least 20 and containing at least 100 people: J.E. Backer, 'Dødeligheten og dens årsaker i Norge, 1856-1965', *Samfunnsøkonomiske Studier*, no.10, Statistisk Sentralbyrå, Oslo, 1961, p.27 (English summary); d, These figures are below the true figures, being only the population living in urban municipalities.

Table 7.2: Resident Population by County in Norway 1769-1960

	1769[a]		1875[c]		1960[c]	
	Total	% share	Total	% share	Total	% share
1. Østfold	38,904	5.4	107,562	5.9	202,641	5.6
2. Oslo and Akershus	33,755	4.7	191,733	10.6	709,309	19.8
3. Hedmark	63,544	8.8	119,449	6.6	177,195	4.9
4. Oppland	48,847	6.8	115,522	6.4	166,109	4.6
5. Buskerud	74,770	10.3	101,712	5.6	168,328	4.7
6. Vestfold	30,879	4.3	89,344	4.9	174,362	4.9
7. Telemark	38,064	5.3	83,570	4.6	149,828	4.2
8. Aust-Agder	28,595	4.0	75,609	4.2	77,061	2.2
9. Vest-Agder	30,567	4.2	77,059	4.2	108,876	3.0
10. Rogaland	40,233	5.6	113,675	6.3	238,662	6.6
11. Bergen and Hordaland	67,588	9.3	155,672	8.6	340,985	9.5
12. Sogn and Fjordane	40,673	5.6	86,108	4.8	99,844	2.8
13. Møre and Romsdal	49,331	6.8	116,781	6.4	213,027	5.9
14. Sør-Trøndelag	44,722	6.2	116,722	6.4	211,648	5.9
15. Nord-Trøndelag	33,276	4.6	81,421	4.5	116,635	3.2
16. Nordland	40,886	5.7	103,369	5.7	237,193	6.6
17. Troms	⎰18,579	2.6	53,931	3.0	127,549	3.6
18. Finmark	⎱		24,185	1.3	71,982	2.0
Norway	723,213[b]		1,818,853		3,591,234	
Regions						
North[d]	137,463	19.0	379,628	20.9	765,007	21.3
West[e]	197,825	27.4	472,236	26.0	892,518	24.9
South[f]	97,226	13.4	236,238	13.0	335,765	9.3
Southeast[g]	290,699	40.2	725,322	40.0	1,597,944	44.5

a. The 1769 census was based on ecclesiastical rather than civil divisions. In order to arrive at areas comparable with the counties used in the 1875 and 1960 censuses I have grouped together deaneries. The differences are not great. For details see M. Drake, op.cit., p.230; b. This is the official figure and, in my view, is lower than the actual population total, for which see Table 7.1. It is used here for convenience; c. *Norges Offisielle Statistikk XII*, 245, 1969, p.3‹ The total for 1875 includes 5,429 people who were not allocated to a particu county; d. Counties 14-18; e. Counties 10-13; f. Counties 7-9; g. Counties ‹

Table 7.3: Births, Marriages, Deaths, Emigrants per 1,000 Mean
Population in Norway 1741-1960[a]

Period	Marriages	Rates per 1,000 mean population						
		Total births	Total deaths	Illegit. births[c]	Deaths under 1 year[c]	Emigrants	Natural increase	Net increase[f]
1741-1750		29.6	29.0				0.6	
1751-1760		33.4	24.2				9.2	
1761-1770		31.7	25.4				6.3	
1771-1780	7.6	29.8	25.9	41.7			3.9	
1781-1790		30.0	25.1	47.5[d]			4.9	
1791-1800	8.0[b]	32.7	22.6				10.1	
1801-1810	7.3	27.9	25.4	63.0			2.5	
1811-1820	8.5	30.2	21.4	73.5			8.8	
1821-1830	8.2	33.4	18.9	72.2			14.5	
1831-1840	7.0	29.9	20.4	68.4	140.0	0.2[e]	9.5	9.5
1841-1850	7.8	30.7	18.2	81.7	115.0	1.3	12.5	12.4
1851-1860	7.7	32.9	17.1	87.7	103.5	2.4	15.8	14.3
1861-1870	6.7	30.9	18.0	81.4	110.0	5.8	12.9	7.9
1871-1880	7.2	30.9	17.1	86.9	104.0	4.7	13.8	9.7
1881-1890	6.5	30.7	17.1	77.8	97.6	9.6	13.6	4.1
1891-1900	6.6	30.1	16.3	72.8	96.8	4.5	13.8	11.3
1901-1910	6.0	27.5	14.2	68.2	74.6	8.2	13.3	6.4
1911-1920	6.6	24.8	13.8	69.9	64.1	2.5	11.0	10.4
1921-1930	6.2	20.1	11.3	69.2	50.6	3.2	8.8	5.9
1931-1940	7.5	15.3	10.3	65.9	42.1	1.9	5.0	5.8
1941-1950	8.5	19.5	9.8	60.9	34.2	0.3	9.7	9.4
1951-1960	7.4	18.2	8.7	36.6	21.3	0.7	9.5	9.1

a. For marriages, births and deaths 1741-1860 see M. Drake, op.cit., pp.163-98.
All other figures from *Norges Offisielle Statistikk XII*, 245, 1969, pp44-7;
b. 1795-99 only; c. Per 1,000 live births; d. 1781-83 only; e. 1836-40 only;
f. Derived from J.E. Backer, op.cit., p.25 and ibid., Ekteskap, fødsler og
vandring i Norge, 1856-1960, Samfunnsøkonomiske studier. No.13, Statistisk
Sentralbyrå, Oslo, 1965, p.192 (English summary). Immigration figures
arrived at by calculation. It is generally reckoned that before the 1840s
migration had little impact on population growth rates.

318   *Appendix*

Table 7.4: Births per 100 Women 21-50 (at Various Dates) in Norway, 1769-1900[a]

Census	Women 21-50	Births in 5 years preceding census	Births in 5 years preceding census per 100 women 21-50
1769	147,687	113,336	77
1801	187,294	138,156	74
1835	232,914	181,363	78
1865	340,766	262,738	77
1900	438,789	325,710	74

a. Sources: 1769-1865, M. Drake, op.cit., p.76: for 1900 derived from *Norges Offisielle Statistikk XII*, 245, 1969, pp.35 and 46.

Table 7.5: Non-marital Fertility by Age of Mother in Norway, 1889-1962[a]

Period	Annual births per 1,000 unmarried women aged						Illegitimate births per 100 live births
	15-19	20-24	25-29	30-34	35-39	40-44	
circa							
1890	3	24	33	26	19	8	7.1
1930	4	14	11	9	6	3	7.0
1960	6	17	16	11	6	2	3.7

a. S. Dyrvik and C.J. O'Neill (eds.), *Norges Befolkning*, Oslo, 1975, p.50.

Table 7.6: Illegitimate Live Births per 100 Live Births and per 100 Marriages[a]

Period	Illegitimate live births per 100	
	Live births	Marriages
1816-20	8.5	29.2
1821-25	8.0	28.7
1826-30	7.5	29.6
1831-35	7.2	28.7
1836-40	7.5	29.5
1841-45	8.8	31.1

a. E. Sundt, *Fortsatte Bidrag angaaende Saedeligheds-Tilstanden i Norge*, Christiania, 1864, p.5.

8 PORTUGAL

Nuno Alves Morgado

Basic Determinants and Trends of Population Growth

Population growth in Portugal followed a similar pattern to that of other Western European countries. After a period of slow growth, determined by high levels of morbidity and constant peaks of mortality as a result of wars, epidemics and famines, an abrupt fall in mortality took place in the mid-nineteenth century and initiated what is generally known as the first 'demographic revolution'. If 330 years had been needed for the population to reach a figure of 3½ million (Table 8.1), only a further century was needed before this passed 8 million. The average annual increment in the two periods was 0.6 per cent and 1.3 per cent respectively. However, within the first of these two periods, from 1527 to 1854, two further sub-periods can be identified. Between 1527 and 1636 the population grew very slowly indeed, but in the two centuries following the regaining of national independence in 1640 an increase of 2½ million was recorded. However, the annual growth rate was still only 1 per cent, which was significantly lower than the rate achieved after 1864.

This process of population development was essentially a result of consistently high levels of both fertility and mortality, until the gradual fall in the latter index towards the end of the nineteenth century. However, the absence of adequate statistical data for most of this early period precludes any quantification of the factors which determined the overall process of natural growth. It is only with the compilation of the first census of 1864 and particularly after the improvements in the collection of population statistics in 1890 that a satisfactory data base can be said to exist for an examination of the major factors influencing the process of natural population growth.

Information of natality, however, is provided by the 1801 enumeration of both population and households[1] and this can be supplemented by a survey of 1819, which covered 24 of the 44 comarcas, or approximately 53 per cent of the total population.[2] Discontinuous data is also available from various sources for 1843, 1849, 1864, 1871-75, 1878, 1886 and 1892,[3] which provide a rough picture of the level and trends of the birth rate during the nineteenth century. Between 1801 and 1929 this remained relatively stable within the range of 30-33 per 1,000. Despite a short-term rise in the years immediately following the conclusion of the First World War, there is a progressive decline to lower levels from 1929 onwards. The birth rate fell from 33 per 1,000 (1920-24), to 24 per 1,000 (1950-54), and although the colonial wars and emigration after 1965 do impinge on the birth rate, this slowly levels off at 20 per 1,000. In the post-1945 period the birth rate has been substantially affected by the decline in the average size of the family in Portugal. Between 1960 and 1970, for example, 56 per cent of all families had no children or only 1; 39 per cent between 2 and 5, and only 4.6 per cent 6 children or more. At the same time, however, the average age at first marriage has also fallen gradually from 25.4 to 23.3 years in the period 1950 to 1973.

Statistical information on mortality, however, is even less abundant for the nineteenth century than in the case of fertility.[4] Indeed the only reliable figure would seem to indicate a death rate of 30.7 per 1,000 in 1801. Despite the scarcity of data, it is clear that mortality declined fairly spectacularly in the course of the nineteenth century from a level of approximately 30 per 1,000 to 22 per 1,000 (Table 8.2). From then on, until 1924, mortality remained stable at this level following the secular decline of the late nineteenth century. Exceptionally high rates, however, were recorded in 1917 and 1918, as a result of the influenza epidemic, but after 1924 there is a further steady decline which effectively brought Portuguese mortality levels down to the European level of 9-10 per 1,000 by 1960.

In this context it is interesting to note that although mortality tended to vary on a regional basis, with the more economically developed parts of the country, such as the South and the coastal regions, enjoying more favourable mortality conditions, the original North-South axis in this trend tends to weaken over time, whereas the divergence in mortality rates between the coastal and interior regions becomes more pronounced. This particular aspect, however, will be examined at a later stage in more detail.

The general economic progress of the country is most clearly evident in the case of infant mortality, which is susceptible among other factors to relative income levels. Although infant mortality rates did decline spectacularly from a level of 75 per 1,000 in 1960 to 43 per 1,000 in 1974, they are still significantly higher than in other European states. A similar trend, however, is also evident in relation to foetal mortality, which fell from 32 to 18.4 per 1,000 during the same period. Regional variations are also very strong in the case of these indices, which effectively reflect the marked asymmetry of the socio-economic pattern of development.

The overall growth rate of the Portuguese population during this period, however, would have been much greater than the census data indicate, were it not for the role of extensive overseas emigration. Although this was a permanent feature in Portugal's development, it was also subject to short-term variations in both intensity and direction. Between 1891 and 1970, however, 48 per cent of the natural growth of population was lost through emigration, which reached particularly high levels during the period 1912 to 1920, and from 1961 to 1970 (Table 8.3). Significant changes in the direction of emigration also took place during this period. At the beginning of the century Brazil was the main destination for emigrants, but by the 1960s attention had been switched to Western Europe (Table 8.4). It must be borne in mind, however, that in addition to legal emigration, there was also a strong flow of illegal emigrants in the later period, particularly in the direction of France, which as a proportion of total migration rose from only 1.26 per cent in 1960 to a peak of 66.66 per cent by 1971. As far as the sex ratio of migrants was concerned, it is clear that men predominated in the early periods of this century (Table 8.5), although with increasing migration to Western Europe there was a tendency for a more equitable balance to emerge between the sexes. At the same time the occupational structure of emigrants has changed and the original predominance of individuals from the primary sector has been reduced by an increasing number of migrants from manufacturing industry and service occupations. Migrants from the secondary sector, for example, increased from a total of 16,067 (1960-64), to 37, 161 (1965-9), and from trade and services from 9,127 to 11,187 during the same period. Migration to Portugal's overseas territories, however, has never reached any significant proportions, and population flows between Portugal and the colonies never reached comparable levels to emigration figures to other foreign countries. The total number of Portuguese nationals in the colonies in Africa and Asia only amounted to approximately 60,000 in 1940 and 100,000 in 1950. Migration to colonial territories never exceeded 2,000-3,000 each year until 1947, although there was something of an expansion to over 10,000 after 1947. This trend, however, was occasionally disrupted and reversals did occur as a result of contemporary political and economic developments. As a whole, therefore, this migratory flow was never comparable to the pattern of Portuguese emigration to other foreign countries.

The age and sex structure of the population faithfully reflected the

basic determinants of natural growth and the heavy toll of emigration.
The preponderance of women within the population has remained
fairly constant at approximately 52 per cent, but the decline in the
birth rate from the end of the nineteenth century has produced a
gradual ageing of the population, until it has assumed an age structure
common to most areas of Western Europe. The age groups 0-9 and
10-19, which constituted 43 per cent of the total population in the
early part of the century, have declined to only 36 per cent by 1970.
The corresponding increase in the proportion of those inhabitants of
sixty years or more has been from 9.4 per cent (1920) to 14.5 per cent
of the total population (Table 8.6).

However, the population of Portugal is not distributed evenly
throughout the whole country. Average density per square kilometre
in 1970 stood at 72 inhabitants, but this was exceeded substantially
in the Azores and Madeira (122 and 317 respectively), as well as in the
coastal and northern areas of the mainland. Although physical,
geographical and climatic factors have influenced spatial distribution,
it has also been conditioned by the historical process of settlement.
This pattern has been reinforced by the increasing urbanisation of the
population, which in turn has reflected the essential divivision of the
country by hydrographic basins which make communications on a
north-south axis particularly difficult. The separate ports at the mouth
of the major rivers served as focal points for each separate geographic
zone. Furthermore the distribution of population has been influenced
by the process of recolonisation after the expulsion of the Arab
invaders, with the initial phase of settlement and consolidation taking
place in the North. As a result this part of the country has been
characterised by *minifundia* and a comparatively high population
density level. In contrast the open spaces and poorer soils in the area
south of the Tagus encouraged the emergence of *latifundia* on a
semi-feudal basis and with low population densities. However, with the
expansion of external trade the litoral zone became the focus for
internal migration movements, with the result that the basic traits of
the spatial distribution pattern of population were already obvious in
the sixteenth century (Table 8.7). The litoral areas, even at this
comparatively early date, had a population density double that of the
interior zones, and the northern coastal area boasted a figure three time
the national average. However, this pattern was only reinforced in the
following centuries, with the result that by 1970, 72 per cent of the
population was concentrated in the litoral area, although this only
constituted 34 per cent of the total surface area of the country. The

relative population density of this area was then five times the figure for the interior zones.

The capital of Lisbon had contributed significantly to this process of unbalanced development. Even in 1864 Lisbon and its immediate surrounding area constituted 11.4 per cent of the total population, and by 1970 this had risen to 25 per cent. Indeed the changes in the spatial distribution of population were closely linked with the trend towards urbanisation, particularly in the early decades of the nineteenth century (Table 8.8). By 1970, 17 per cent of the Portuguese population lived in towns which acted as administrative centres for particular districts, although their population could vary from little more than 6,000 to 760,000 in the municipal area of Lisbon. A further 9 per cent lived in other towns and urban centres.

Economic Development and Population Growth

At the turn of the nineteenth century the Portuguese economy was still on the basis of Rostow's terminology in the transition phase prior to the creation of the conditions necessary for a take-off into self-sustained economic growth. Modern industrial development did not begin in Portugal until the consolidation of the liberal regime in 1840, and the process of modernisation was not substantially speeded up until the 1880s. It is important to note, however, that the extent of development in the nineteenth century was very limited. Large-scale manufacturing units were not created, and the nascent industrial scene was still dominated by small family-type enterprises.

However, significant changes did take place in the structure of the primary sector, including the compulsory sale of Church estates and the abolition of the *morgadios* (entailed land traditionally inherited as a whole by the eldest son). Furthermore the termination of all tithe and feudal obligations, and the modernisation of the system of land taxation gave a significant impulse to agricultural development. Land which had previously remained unused was now put to better use and the fact that many areas had remained fallow for a considerable time gave rise to an initially high level of yield. As a result of these improvements wheat imports fell and Portugal even managed to become a net exporter of this commodity between 1838 and 1855. New crops were also introduced and developed, such as potatoes and rice, and viticulture and horticulture were expanded. However, because of a limited application of artificial fertilisers, grain yields tended to fall after the initial period of expansion and with the natural increase in the indigenous population wheat production became insufficient to satisfy the continuous growth in consumption. Bread remained the staple foodstuff throughout Portugal, and wheat imports inevitably increased to 31,000 tons in 1856-7, 67,000 tons in 1865-88 and finally to 134,000 tons at the turn of the century. Indeed in the second half of the nineteenth century agricultural production ceased to expand and even began to stagnate as far as the technological side was concerned and also in relation to the area of tillage. By 1900 less than half of the 7 million hectares of arable land was in cultivation and this to some extent was the result of the development of a land market which had seen the transference of property rights from peasant producers to the emergent middle class of businessmen, financiers and members of the professional elites in general. Commerce, however, maintained its traditional role and with a widespread network of retail outlets, based primarily on family stores, effectively met the marketing requirements of rural communities and at the same time provided them with their limited demand for industrial goods. Larger commercial firms only existed in the urban areas and were basically involved in the import-export business, with a certain element of specialisation in a few trades such as the export of port wine.

This pattern, in turn, is reflected in the census data. In 1900, 64.2 per cent of an active population of 2,350,280, or 1,507,600 individuals, were employed in the primary sector. Only 435,000 (or 19.4 per cent) worked in the secondary sector; 6 per cent in commerce, 8 per cent in transportation and 3.7 per cent in the service industries. The continued prominence of agriculture was particularly marked, specifically in relation to the contemporary occupational distribution of such countries as the United Kingdom and France.

The basic features of the Portuguese economy, however, were not to alter until after 1945. The long period of political instability that preceded and followed the fall of the Monarchy in 1910, and the unfavourable development of the international economy in the late 1920s and early 1930s, did not provide the conditions necessary for an effective reorganisation of the economy. Modernisation of the productive sectors was therefore impeded and there was little improvement in the general standard of living. Agriculture, despite its crucial role within the economy and its employment of 60 per cent of the active work force, actually declined. Between 1910 and 1925 less than 100,000 hectares of unused land was actually cultivated, or about 10 per cent of the corresponding figure for the period 1873-1903. Over 1,300,000 hectares of arable land remained uncultivated. Although wheat and wine production did increase between 1901-03 and 1923-5 by 13 per cent and cork production by 29.5 per cent, total output from the primary sector either declined or remained relatively stable. Traditional exports of primary produce, such as wine, cork, wool and raisins were increasingly incapable of balancing the growth in imports, in which foodstuffs were assuming a growing role. If exports had constituted 115 per cent of imports in 1805, this proportion had fallen continuously to 81 per cent (1894), 51 per cent (1900) and to less than 20 per cent in 1920. The prerequisites for the development of a fully capitalist economy were still lacking. An insufficiently developed banking mechanism, for example, was unable to stimulate domestic savings or to mobilise financial resources on a scale necessary for the promotion of dynamic economic growth.

The military *coup* of 1926, however, and the establishment of the authoritarian regime of Salazar inaugurated a long period of financial orthodoxy, accompanied by a rigorous balancing of the government budget and a stabilisation of both prices and wages at a generally low level. Although such policies might well have led to a general stagnation within the economy, one of the positive results was the creation of the basic conditions necessary for the growth of entrepreneurial initiative which had previously been lacking in the Portuguese economy. The close control of labour, enforced through a corporative structure of labour unions, low wage levels and an effective ban on strike action facilitated the development of industrial production, untroubled by labour problems and with the advantage of low labour costs. At the same time the government was active in fostering the development of large-scale corporations to replace the traditional family enterprises. This produced immediate results in the building trades, which had previously suffered from the lack of firms with adequate capital resources. In the manufacturing industries, the new system of economic control, known as the *condicionamento industrial*, provided new industries with effective protection from competition and the possibility of earning high profits which would reinforce the process of self-financed growth. The disadvantages of such a system were not to emerge until later. The Portuguese economy, therefore, was pushed along the path of capitalist development, although it still had not lost its traditional parochial character.

This model of economic growth, however, was only possible because of the contemporary pattern of population development, with its high natural growth rate and constant surplus of population. Indeed this factor was reinforced by the continued backwardness of the primary sector. By failing to provide an adequate standard of living for the majority of the population, it effectively aggravated the underlying problem of relative overpopulation. The factors that determined the constant surplus in total population were essentially demographic, and were linked primarily with the fall in mortality at a time when the birth rate remained relatively stable. The reduction in overseas emigration, through the introduction of stricter admission regulations in Brazil, Venezuela, Canada and the USA only served to aggravate the situation. It is clear, therefore, that economic development in Portugal was strongly determined by demographic factors, which created a position of underemployment, low wages and financial and price stability.

However, from the late 1930s significant changes were taking place in the economy. Between 1938 and 1956 GNP, at 1966 prices, rose by 3.9 per cent annually, or at 3.2 per cent if the rate is adjusted for population growth. The structure of national expenditure retained its traditional pattern, with investment running at 12-13 per cent and public consumption at 10 per cent, but a gradual shift in the structure of the economy was clearly taking place. The proportion of GNP generated by the secondary sector rose from 37 per cent in 1949 to 40 per cent in 1956, with a corresponding reduction in the importance of agriculture. Nevertheless this change was achieved through a programme of austerity, social injustice and a restriction on private consumption, which in the long term would generate considerable political unrest, and lead to the eventual undermining of the economic system.

These structural changes, however, did not impinge on the structure of the population. The proportion of active population remained practically constant between 1900 and 1970, at approximately 60 per cent for men and 16 per cent for women (Table 8.9). The number of non-active to active inhabitants, which had reached 1.82 in 1932, had also stabilised at 1.6. The sectoral distribution of the population only changed gradually over time. Partly because of a reduction in the rate of emigration in the 1930s and 1940s, as a result of the international economic crisis and World War II, there was an increase of 160,000 active individuals in the primary sector, although its importance as an employer of labour continued to decline (Table 8.10). The secondary sector, which declined in importance during the 1930s, was able to maintain until 1950 the position which it had already achieved at the turn of the century.

The resumption of emigration after the end of World War II, first to Brazil and Venezuela in the 1950s and then to the EEC and particularly to France and Germany, was by far the most important factor in the further development of the Portuguese economy. At the same time, however, multinational enterprises were increasingly attracted to Portugal by its large reserves of unused manpower, and particularly by the cheap reserves of female labour within the economy. In 1960, for example, only 13 per cent of those women in the active age groups of the population were in fact employed in the labour force. These two factors led to an increasing scarcity of labour in relation to earlier conditions and undermined the continued maintenance of artificially low wages which had been an important cornerstone of the Portuguese economy. Furthermore the increased inflow of invisibles, including earnings from tourism and the remittances from emigrants, exceeded the absorptive capacity of the economy and contributed to a quickening of the overall pace of economic growth. This would have had beneficial results for Portugal whose economy was still one of the most retarded in Western Europe, if it had not been for the creation of a climate of artificial speculation which bore no relationship to the actual growth in GNP as a result of high productivity levels and a breakthrough in the spheres of research and technology.

An additional dimension was given to the Portuguese economy by its colonial empire, which provided sheltered markets for its products and a supply of raw materials under conditions which were more favourable than those obtainable in world markets. Apart from offering employment possibilities to the professional classes, the colonies also allowed transport firms to operate on a larger scale than would normally have been warranted on the basis of the domestic market.

All these factors affected the pattern of population development. The 1970 census showed for the first time a significant reduction in the level of employment in the primary sector. The proportion of the active population dependent on agriculture fell from 43.9 per cent in 1960 to 32.6 per cent in 1970, and the secondary sector grew by 8 per cent to 24 per cent of the total. However, as a function of unbalanced growth, the relative importance of the tertiary sector, which increased its share of employment from 33 per cent (1960) to 45 per cent (1970), clearly exceeded the actual requirements of the Portuguese economy.

The Portuguese economy has therefore been dominated through its various stages of development from the early nineteenth century onwards by the demographic variable. The situation of relative overpopulation and low levels of emigration in the inter-war period created the conditions favourable for the policies of the Salazar regime, of stability, austerity and financial conservatism. In the post-1945 period, on the other hand, the revival of extensive emigration to other Western European countries was the primary cause of the gradual breaking down of the earlier social and economic isolation of Portugal. If the new economic order of the post-Salazar era does not prove capable of employing the human resources at its disposal, there is a great danger that demographic determinism will come to the fore.

Population Growth and Social Change

The process of social change during this period was closely tied to the pace of economic development, although it was strongly influenced by the population factor. Indeed the evolution of social and behaviour patterns, particularly from the late nineteenth century onwards, has been strongly conditioned, if not retarded, by the changes in population. At the beginning of this period Portuguese society was essentially traditional and profoundly rural in nature. Even in 1900 more than 85 per cent of the population lived in rural areas and over 65 per cent of the active population were still employed in the primary sector. Furthermore workers in the other sectors of the economy still retained their original rural character and were still essentially part of rural society. Rural family life in many instances provided a welcome refuge for proletarian workers in urban centres, where the process of social integration had not really begun to function at all. The continuing importance of rural ties can be found in the choice of holiday periods by urban dwellers which invariably coincided with peak periods in the agricultural year, such as the harvest, grape gathering, and the beginning of the partridge hunting season. Seasonal migration back to the village community *a sua aldeia* was essentially a ritual recognition of the significance of a rural origin.

This social pattern was reinforced by the influence of the Catholic religion and its dependent hierarchy. Census returns show that well into the present century the majority of the people were officially Roman Catholic (Table 8.11). Of equal importance was the continuing low level of literacy in Portuguese society. In the first decade of the present century over 70 per cent of the population were still illiterate and by 1920 this still stood at 66.2 per cent. The situation was aggravated by a low rate of school attendance and a generally low level of cultural activity, apart from in the three major urban centres. Society was also characterised by a highly stratified and complex network of local influence groups, whose power was frequently based on aristocratic positions, but primarily on economic power, such as landed property, investment capital or extensive holdings of government bonds. It was essentially a paternalistic, rather than a semi-feudal structure. Despite the influence of the Church, however, it was not sufficient to prevent the secular decline in fertility from the end of the nineteenth century onwards.

However, the proclamation of the Republic in 1910 was accompanied by a new wave of anti-clericalism, as the Church hierarchy had been traditionally associated with the monarchy. As a result Church and State were officially separated, a civil registration system for births, deaths and marriages was instituted, divorce was accepted and a prohibition placed on religious instruction in schools. The effect of this legislation on Portuguese society, however, was very limited. Indeed the evolution of an electoral system based on *caciquism* reinforced not only the role of local dignitaries, but also indirectly the position of the Church. Statistical data do not indicate any significant changes in the pattern of social behaviour. The proportion of marriages in each quinquennial period later subject to divorces remained relatively stable, rising from 1.78 per cent (1921-5), to 1.82 per cent (1936-40) and finally to only 2.27 per cent (1941-50). Although civil marriage was now officially recognised, the majority of people were still married in a Catholic Church. The proportion of Catholic marriages actually rose from 76.9 per cent (1931-5), to 79.7 per cent (1936-40), 84.3 per cent (1941-5), and to 88.4 per cent (1946-50). From a demographic point of view social stability was also accompanied by the absence of significant changes in nuptiality. Both the marriage rate and the average age at marriage remained stable throughout this period, as did the illegitimacy rate (Table 8.12).[5] Indeed the establishment of an authoritarian regime in 1926 effectively marked a return to social traditionalism, which in any case had not been severely disrupted during the republican period. Although there were a few underlying symptoms of change, the traditional structure of Portuguese society was visibly reinforced through the policy of financial stability and the growing isolationism of Portugal from the outside world. All the political factors which might have stimulated social change were effectively neutralised by the new regime, at least until the outbreak of World War II.

It was only in the mid-1950s, however, that the social structure of Portugal began to change significantly, and this was largely the result of the mass emigration of labour to other Western European countries, which produced an assimilation of new attitudes on the part of individuals involved in this migration process. The colonial wars, by extending the scope of compulsory military service, also had a long-term impact on social attitudes, which were widened by an extension of economic contacts with other world markets as a result of the increasing role of multinationals, and the different perspectives brought to the indigenous population through tourism. These forces culminated in the final disappearance of the authoritarian regime in April 1974.

Notes

1. A. Balbi, *Essai statistique sur le Royaume de Portugal et d'Algarve comparé aux autres états de l'Europe, suivi d'un coup d'oeil sur l'état actuel des sciences, des lettres et des beaux arts parmi les Portugais des deux hémisphères*, Paris, 1822.
2. Ibid., final table. The coverage of this survey varies according to the individual part of the country, fluctuating from 36 per cent in the case of the Beiras provinces (central litoral area), to 100 per cent in the Algarve. Its quality is also difficult to evaluate. However, the sex ratio at birth (1.06) is normal and the percentage of foundlings is the same as the proportion of illegitimate births at the end of the century. Regional variations in the birth rate were also apparent, ranging from 35.2 in the North and 43.3 in the South (per 1,000).
3. Data for the following years are draw from different sources: 1843, 1849-51: A. Oliveira Marreca, *Parecer e memória sobre um projecto de estatística*, n.d.; 1864, 1871-75: G. Pery, *Statistique du Portugal et des Colonies*, Lisbon, 1878; 1866 and following years: official sources.
4. A. Balbi, op.cit., p.211, '. . .the Portuguese lists [of vital events] are very inexact and offer only very approximate data, especially as far as the deaths in the larger cities are concerned'.
5. Illegitimate birth rates in Portugal have been higher than in Spain and Italy and close to the high levels of Northern European countries. After the Republic, religious practices were abandoned in many villages, particularly in the South and West. Civil marriage was avoided because it cost 180 escudos, although alienation from the Church also precluded a marriage in Church. Cf. Descamps, *Le Portugal*, Paris, 1935 and Montalvão Machado, *Alguns aspectos na natalidade*, RCED, no.10.

Bibliography

1. Historical Demography

Maria Eurídice da Costa Ramos Ascenso, *A freguesia da Sé de Lisboa no. 1º quartel do século XVIII*, Lisboa, 1960 (unpublished).

Mario Marques Machado da Costa Carvalho, *A freguesia de S. Martinho de Gandara no século XVIII*.

Antonio Artur Valente de Abreu Freire, *A freguesia de Santa Marinha de Avanca de 1700 a 1724*, Coimbra, 1970.

Carlota Maria Borges Landeiro, *A vila de Penamocor no 1º quartel de século XVIII*, INE, 1965.

Maria Lucilia de Sousa Pinheiro Marques, *A freguesia de S. Martinho de Arrifiana*, CED, Lisboa, 1974.

Maria de Lourdes Arola da Cunha e Silva Neto, *A freguesia de Nossa Senhora das Mercês de Lisboa no 1º quartel do século XVIII*, INE, Lisboa, 1967; *A freguesia de Santa Catarina de Lisboa no 1º quartel do século XVIII*, INE, Lisboa, 1959.
Carlos Manuel Assunção Rodrigues, *A freguesia da Se de Coimbra no 1º quartel do seculo XVIII*, Coimbra, 1970.

2. Fertility

Maximo Livi Bacci, *A Century of Portuguese Fertility*, Princeton, 1971.
A. de Almeida Garrett, *Os problemas da natalidade*, RCED, nos. 2, 3 and 5, Lisboa.
J.J. Montalvão, *Como nascem e morrem os portugueses*, Lisboa, 1957.
——, *Alguns aspectos da natalidade*, RCED, no.10, Lisboa.

3. Nuptiality

J.J. Pais Morais, *Tabuas de extinção de solteiros para 1940 e 1950*, RCED, no.9.

4. Emigration

J. de Souza Bettencourt, 'El fenómeno de la emigración portuguesa', *Rev. Int. de Sociologia*, no.68, 1959.
Affonso Costa, *O problema da emigração*, Lisboa, 1911.
Oliveira Martins, *Fomento rural e emigração*, Lisboa, 1956.

5. General Demographic Studies

(a) Nineteenth Century

A. Balbi, *Compendio di geographia*, Turin, 1840.
Soares de Barros, *Sobre a causa de diferentes populações em diversos tempos da Monarchia*, Lisboa, 1788.
A. Rebelo da Costa, *Descripção topográphica e histórica da cidade do Porto*, Porto, 1788.
Ricardo Jorge, *Demografia e hygiene da cidade do Porto*, Porto, 1899.
G. Pery, *Statistique du Portugal et des Colonies*, Lisboa, 1878; *Subsídios para a história da estatística em Portugal*, vol.II. *Táboas topográficas e estatísticas, 1801*, Lisboa, 1948; *Variétés politico-statistiques sur la monarchie portugaise*, Paris, 1822.

(b) Twentieth Century

Alberto de Alarcão and J.J. Pais Morais, 'A população de Portugal, *(Ano Mundial da População) CED Caderno*, no.2, Lisboa, 1976.
J. Pais Morais, 'Portugal, a Country Profile', Lisboa, 1976 (unpublished).

332 *Portugal*

6. Social and Economic History

Armando de Castro, *A economia portuguesa no seculo XX*, Lisboa, 1970.
——, *Estudos de História Socio-económica de Portugal*, Lisboa, 1971.
Azevedo Gomes, Henrique de Barros, Eugenio Castro Caldas, 'Traços principais da evolução de agricultura portuguesa entre as duas Guerras Mundiais', *RCED*, no.1, Lisboa, 1945.
N.H. de Oliveria Marques, *História de Portugal*, Lisboa, 1976 (2nd edition).
História da 1a República Portuguesa, Lisboa, 1973.
Manuel Jacinto Nures, Francisco Pereira de Moura and Luis Maria Teixeira Pinto, 'Estrutura da Economia Portuguesa', *RCEE*, no.14, 1954.
Maria Belmira Martins, *Sociedades e Grupos em Portugal*, Lisboa, 1973.
Moura, Francisco Pereira de, Luis Maria Teixeira Pinto, *Problemas do Crescimento economico português*, Lisboa, 1958.
A.G. Franco Nogueira, *Salazar*, vol.I, Lisboa, 1975.
J. Nogueira Pinto, *Portugal. Os anos do fim*, Lisboa, 1977.
Relatório Geral Preparatório – IV Plano de Fomento, Lisboa, 1973.

APPENDIX

Table 8.1: The Population of Portugal (the Mainland and Atlantic
Islands), 1527-1976 (in Thousands)

Year	Total	Mainland	Atlantic Islands
1527[a]		1,120	
1636[a]		1,100	
1732[b]		2,143	
1768[b]		2,410	
1801[c]		2,932	
1821[d]		3,026	
1835[d]		3,062	
1838[d]		3,224	
1841[d]	3,737	3,397	340
1854[d]	3,844	3,499	345
1858[d]	3,923	3,549	339
1861[d]	4,035	3,693	342
1864[e]		3,830	
1900[e]	5,423	5,016	407
1910[e]	5,960	5,548	412
1920[e]	6,033	5,622	411
1930[e]	6,826	6,360	466
1940[e]	7,722	7,185	537
1950[e]	8,441	7,857	584
1960[e]	8,851	8,255	596
1970[e]	8,863	8,123	540
1975[f]	9,449	8,891	558

a. Numerical counts; b. Estimates; c. Poll counts; d. Estimates; e. General
censuses; f. Intercensal estimated (excluding *retornados* — those returning from
the former Portuguese colonies) for the mid-year period.

333

Table 8.2: Birth, Death and Natural Growth Rates in Portugal, 1801-1976 (per 1,000)

Period	Birth rate	Death rate	Natural growth
1801	33.9	30.7	3.2
1811	33.2		
1815-19	36.5		
1843	31.2		
1849-51	32.5		
1864	33.6		
1871-75	32.7		
1878	33.8		
1886-92	33.9	21.98	11.9
1890-99	30.77	21.73	9.04
1900-09	31.32	20.09	11.23
1910-19	32.26	23.23	9.03
1920-29	32.40	19.67	12.73
1930-39	28.23	16.43	11.80
1940-49	25.04	14.94	10.10
1950-59	24.13	13.63	10.50
1960-69	22.68	10.58	12.10
1970	20.17	10.68	9.49
1971	21.29	11.09	10.20
1972	20.49	10.60	9.89
1973	20.30	11.07	9.23
1974	19.93	11.05	8.88
1975	19.01	10.36	8.65
1976	18.36	10.09	8.27

Note: Death rates in the years marked by the influenza epidemic stood at 41.4 (1918), 25.4 (1919) and 23.7 (1920). By 1921 the death rate, at 20.8, had returned to its normal level. Birth rates in the two years following World War I stood at 32.6 and 33.5 respectively.

Table 8.3: Natural Growth and Emigration Balances for Intercensal
Periods (in Thousands)

Intercensal periods	Natural growth balance (1)	Emigration balance (2)	$\frac{(2)}{(1)} \times 100$	Total (1)—(2)
1891-1900	488.2	270.0	55.3	218.2
1901-1911	749.4	385.9	51.5	363.5
1912-1920	424.5	366.1	86.2	58.4
1921-1930	810.4	324.7	40.1	485.7
1931-1940	828.7	109.2	13.2	719.5
1941-1950	847.8	90.4	10.7	757.4
1951-1960	1,090.8	353.4	32.4	737.4
1961-1970	1,072.6	1,000.3	93.2	72.3
1970-1975	408.3	619.8	152.0	−214.5

Source: J.J. Pais Morais, 'Portugal. Population Country Profile', unpublished M.S.,
Lisbon, 1975.

Table 8.4: Emigration from Portugal by Country of Destination

Period	South America		USA	Europe	Total
	Brazil	Other countries		France	
1891-1900	203,662	267	231		2,484
1901-1911	277,186	3,956	5,016		1,892
1912-1920	238,803	3,897	35,590		23,157
1921-1930	200,315	1,821	8,047		64,965
1931-1940	86,116	—	—		—
1941-1950	53,190	9,379	1,885	749	—
1951-1960	207,393	27,091	11,993	17,851	—
1961-1965	43,662	8,722	12,005	118,806	164,956
1966-1970	13,596	19,509	93,624	228,545	290,812
1971	1,200	3,559	16,000	10,023	28,438
1972	1,158	3,600	14,577	17,800	33,962

Table 8.5: Emigration by Sex

Period	Male (1)	Female (2)	Total (3)	$\frac{(2)}{(3)} \times 100$	$\frac{(2)}{(1)} \times 100$
1920-1929	28,147	8,487	36,634	23.2	30.2
1930-1939	8,122	3,800	11,922	31.9	46.8
1940-1949	5,402	2,769	8,171	33.9	51.2
1950-1954	23,786	12,868	36,654	35.1	54.1
1955-1959	19,228	12,703	31,931	39.8	66.1
1960-1964	24,134	14,776	38,910	38.0	61.2
1965-1969	51,482	39,002	90,484	43.1	75.8
1970-1974	177,159	116,599	293,758	39.7	65.8
1970	43,332	23,028	66,360	34.7	53.1
1971	29,225	21,175	50,400	42.0	72.4
1972	30,585	23,499	54,084	43.4	76.8
1973	51,660	27,857	79,517	35.0	53.9
1974	22,357	21,040	43,397	48.5	94.9

Table 8.6: The Population of Portugal by Sex and Major Age Groups, 1920-1970

Census year	Total population (in thousands)	Age groups %				Sex %	
		0-9	10-19	20-59	60+	M	F
1920	6,001	21.3	21.8	47.5	9.4	47.3	52.7
1930	6,814	22.4	19.5	48.4	9.5	47.6	52.4
1940	7,698	21.6	20.1	48.4	9.1	48.0	52.0
1950	8,441	20.0	19.0	50.5	10.5	48.1	51.9
1960	8,889	19.7	17.8	50.7	11.8	47.8	52.2
1970	8,611	19.0	17.9	48.6	14.5	47.4	52.6

(Compiled from official sources.)

Table 8.7: Population by Regions in 1535 (Estimate), 1864 and 1970

	1535			1864			1970		
	Litoral	Interior	Total	Litoral	Interior	Total	Litoral	Interior	Total
	in % of total population								
North	23.3	7.4	30.7	23.9	9.7	33.6	26.9	5.6	32.5
Centre	8.5	12.7	21.2	17.8	18.9	36.7	16.3	10.9	27.2
Lisbon	15.7	7.6	23.3	11.4	5.2	16.6	25.3	5.3	30.6
South	5.3	19.5	24.8	4.5	8.6	13.1	3.3	6.5	9.8
Total	52.8	47.2	100.0	57.6	42.4	100.0	71.8	28.2	100.0
	density per sq.km.								
North	47.6	10	25	182.6	34.5	71.9	306.6	40.9	146.5
Centre	12.3	10.7	11.3	67.0	42.0	51.3	130.7	50.8	80.3
Lisbon	26.1	16.2	23.2	55.6	29.0	43.3	260.2	64.3	171.4
South	15.5	12.0	12.5	34.0	13.9	17.4	53.0	22.1	27.5
Total	25.4	11.8	16.4	73.0	27.7	43.2	192.9	38.8	91.9

Source: J.J. Pais Morais, 'Portugal. Population Country Profile', unpublished MS, Lisbon, 1975.

Table 8.8: Urban Population in Portugal (as a Proportion of Total Population), 1911-1970

Census year	Proportion
1911	15.7
1920	17.8
1930	19.1
1940	19.8
1950	20.0
1960	23.1
1970	26.4

Table 8.9: The Active Population of Portugal (in Thousands), 1900-1970

Census year	Total population		Active population		% active		Ratio of inactive to active
	M	F	M	F	M	F	
1900	2,591.6	2,831.5	1,714.2	636.1	66.1	22.5	1.31
1910	2,288.7	3,131.5	1,818.2	656.0	64.3	22.5	1.28
1920	2,855.8	3,177.2					
1930	3,255.9	3,570.0	1,923.4	483.2	59.4	13.5	1.82
1940	3,711.7	4,010.4	2,270.1	650.2	61.2	16.2	1.64
1950	4,120.2	4,390.1	2,471.8	724.6	60.0	16.5	1.66
1960	4,254.4	4,635.0	2,713.0	602.6	63.7	13.0	1.68
1970	4,089.2	4,521.9	2,344.4	829.5	57.1	18.3	

Table 8.10: Active Population in Agriculture and Industry (in Thousands and as a Proportion of the Total Active Population)

Census year	Agriculture		Industry	
	Total	%	Total	%
1900	1,507.6	64.2	455.3	19.4
1930	1,247.9	54.2	468.8	20.4
1940	1,419.1	51.1	439.0	15.8
1950	1,519.8	47.6	592.8	18.6
1960	1,445.0	43.9	690.9	21.0
1970	987.4	32.6	731.3	24.2

Table 8.11: The Distribution of Population According to Religious
Denomination

Year	Catholic	Other Christian religions	Other religions
1940	5,929,655	51,123	4,660
1950	6,701,475	n.a.	n.a.
1960	6,979,272	37,988	n.a.

Table 8.12: The Illegitimacy Rate in Portugal, 1815/19-1946/50

Period	Illegitimacy rate (as a % of total births)
1815-19	8.9
1886-90	13.3
1891-95	12.2
1896-00	12.3
1900-05	11.6
1906-09	10.2
1910-15	12.7
1916-20	13.0
1921-25	12.6
1926-30	14.3
1931-35	14.9
1936-40	15.7
1941-46	13.6
1946-50	12.6

9 SWEDEN

Gunnar Fridlizius

This chapter will attempt to discuss various aspects of the relationship between demographic changes and the economic and social structure of Sweden during the period 1750 to 1930. Our point of departure will be a systematic disaggregation at both county and parish level, which will also take into consideration geographical, economic and social factors.[1] Three clear periods can be delineated within the theory of the demographic transition; 1750-1800, 1810-1880 and 1890-1930. Population growth during these periods was 5.5 per cent p.a., 8.6 per cent p.a., and 6.3 per cent p.a. respectively.[2] Unfortunately there are no systematic regional studies available, either at the county or parish level. One of the major reasons for this could be the fact that data in this area are very difficult to master. To quote Professor Utterström:

> In principle, it is desirable that many studies of local scope should be made for various parts of the Scandinavian countries. However, it is not difficult to explain why the method is seldom used quite apart from the fact that the results reached only have a limited range. For Sweden, part of the explanation lies in the difficulties of mastering the source material; the unreliability of the existing statistics relating to small ecclesiastical units being only one of the obstacles to be overcome.[3]

This collection of data from the unpublished population registers must be seen against this background. Obvious errors in the material have been corrected, although inevitably further minor corrections could be made, particularly in relation to the age-specific series. However, irrespective of this problem, the demographic variables are not affected in any substantial way.

The Period 1750-1800

Our interpretation of demographic developments on a regional basis during this period is still influenced by Gustaf Sundbärg's initial division

* The author is deeply indebted to Dr Rolf Ohlsson for statistical advice and valuable comments

of the country into three major areas; North, East and West Sweden.[4] East Sweden was characterised by a high marriage frequency, early marriages, low marital fertility, high mortality and a relatively low rate of natural increase. West Sweden, on the other hand, was noted for a low marriage frequency, late marriages, high marital fertility, low mortality and a large natural increase. By contrast North Sweden had a high marriage frequency, high marital fertility and a large natural increase. Furthermore this distinctive pattern was evident for a long period prior to the great wave of emigration, with primary differences being evident in marital fertility, and secondary differences in the marriage rate, illegitimate births and mortality. Indeed these regional differences '. . .show up clearly in the statistics even during the first part of the nineteenth century and, probably date from very early times'.[5]

An attempt has been made to assess the validity of this regional division using *Tabell Kommissionen's* material (Table I). However, the census returns upon which this is based, do not record population distribution by age and marital status, although 'this distribution would have been of paramount importance to the future generation since it would have revealed the very contents of our population statistics'.[6] This is probably one of the most serious deficiencies in the census returns. As a result direct calculations of marital fertility and the rate of marriage cannot be made. We have sought to bypass this critical point by means of the following construction:

$$F = Fe \, M$$

where F is the general fertility rate based on empirical data, Fe the marital fertility rate based on a birth-marriage construction and M the marital rate as a function of the other two variables.[7] However, the model is only a tentative one and cannot be expected to give more than a first approximation. The conclusions on the age at marriage are based on a construction involving a manipulation of age-specific fertility.[8]

The analysis largely verifies Sundbärg's original regional divisions, as far as demographic differences were concerned. It is also clear that further disaggregation on the basis of geographical and socio-economic criteria would reveal a well-structured pattern in the levels of different demographic variables. The manorial regions of the Southern plain, for example, exhibit a totally different pattern to that of other peasant and manorial regions, which were themselves essentially dissimilar. Furthermore this pattern was markedly stable over time and constituted

Table I: Average Figures for Various Demographic Variables, 1751-1800 (per Thousand)

	The whole country	DR	GR	LR	MR	RR	SR	ACR	A	MR 1	MR 2	LR 1	LR 2
Crude marriage rate	8.5	8.5	8.0	7.8	8.9	8.3	8.3	7.8	10.2	9.7	9.6	7.1	8.0
Specific marriage rate	39.4	40.5	37.8	36.5	43.6	38.6	39.0	37.5	–	50.8	48.7	32.4	36.0
Crude birth rate	33.6	32.5	34.0	32.7	35.6	33.4	33.5	36.9	33.5	32.0	37.6	31.0	32.2
Illegitimacy birth rate	3.4	3.2	2.3	3.0	3.2	2.4	3.5	2.0	18.9	2.5	2.7	4.0	2.7
Total fertility rate[a]	436	417	451	414	498	427	434	486	297	499	560	365	392
Marital fertility rate[b]	285	271	304	302	293	289	289	333	–	258	289	291	309
Marital rate[b]	480	491	464	434	522	471	467	453	–	569	602	436	382
Crude death rate	27.4	25.6	25.9	24.9	27.0	26.6	26.3	25.0	43.9	23.8	30.9	22.5	26.2
Infant death rate[c]	204	183	197	204	232	184	179	250	364	189	268	190	209
Death rate 1-4 years	40.8	34.7	32.9	30.3	35.1	39.7	40.4	34.5	81.2	30.6	46.0	25.4	34.6
Death rate 5-9 years	13.2	11.8	12.4	9.9	10.1	13.7	13.8	9.4	22.0	10.5	12.2	9.7	12.1
Death rate 10-24 years	7.3	6.9	7.1	5.2	5.5	7.2	7.1	5.1	11.5	5.0	5.9	4.7	6.0
Death rate 25-49 years	13.3	12.8	10.3	10.1	10.9	11.6	12.0	8.6	25.6	10.5	12.0	9.6	10.1
Males death rate 25-49 years	14.1	13.7	10.2	10.2	10.4	11.9	12.6	8.8	30.2	9.7	11.3	9.4	10.2
Females death rate 25-49 years	12.6	11.9	10.4	9.9	11.5	11.2 ·	11.4	8.4	21.4	11.4	12.8	9.6	10.1

a. 1775-1800; b. 1765-1795; c. Per 1,000 live births.

Sources: See Tables 9.1-9.26.

Sweden   343

an equilibrium upon which later growth would build. The underlying causes of this pattern, however, are not known. In the case of East Sweden, Sundbärg attributed the high marriage rate, low age at marriage and low marital fertility to racial characteristics,[9] whereas Utterström has argued for a predominance of socio-economic factors.[10] First, there was a large number of cities in the region close to Stockholm, which resulted in a particular mortality pattern and also influenced fertility. Secondly, the area had a peculiar social structure, linked with the distribution of land and the relative size of the upper class. However, a closer study of the manorial areas would be highly profitable within the context of this analysis, as certain features of these regions may well have acted as obstacles to population growth, at least in comparison with peasant regions, where the growth rate was perceptively higher. Significantly, apart from the movement of farm hands and maid servants, the only distinct form of internal migration during this period was between manorial and peasant areas.[11] However, the overall rate of growth did not differ substantially in the different regions, except for the 'new colonisation' county of Västerbotten (Table II). As inter-county migration was slight, these growth rates also reflect the natural increase in population.

Table II: County-wide Population Growth 1750-1805 and 1805-1860. Annual Growth (per cent)

	1750-1805[a]	1805-1860
Sodermanland	0.43	0.41
Kronoberg	0.55	0.98
Mristianstad	0.52	1.03
Malmohus	0.64	1.10
Skaraborg[b]	0.62	0.88
Varmland[c]	0.61	1.10
Vasterbotten[d]	1.25	1.54

Source: *Historisk statistik for Sverige. Del 1 Befolkning 1720-1967* (Historical Statistics of Sweden. Part 1. Population), pp.49-52.

a. 1750-1805 rural areas + cities: 1805-1860 only rural areas. For the period 1805-1860, the population for 1805 is an average of the rural population for 1800 and 1810; b. The population of the county of Skaraborg for 1750 has been approximated; c. 1750-1805 Varmland + Orebro; d. 2750-1805 Vasterbotten + Norrbotten.

The short-term development was characterised by very strong annual fluctuations, especially within the mortality series, with considerable differences in mortality rates occurring between different regions. The dispersion, however, as reflected in the variation coefficient, is considerably less for infant mortality than for other groups. This was probably because infants were immune for some time after birth to infectious diseases which accounted for large variations in other groups. However, both infant mortality and mortality in other age groups show a very high co-variation in the short run. It is debatable whether this also implies a co-variation beyond regional boundaries, so that the changes at the national level would be a reflection of these fluctuations. Significantly there is a surprising conformity in grain price variations during this period, indicating a well-integrated national economy. By means of spectral analysis of short-term demographic changes at the national level, an attempt has been made to show that there was a similar homogeneity in the different demographic series.[12] The correlation coefficients, however, for the different regions hardly confirm such a marked homogeneity.

Another short-run aspect is the connection between economic conditions and short-term demographic changes. Indeed this relationship has been the point of departure for many interpretations of the socio-economic structure of pre-industrial Sweden. Heckscher observed a clear connection between harvests and mortality. In a society close to the subsistence level poor harvests were immediately reflected in higher mortality, because poor nutrition reduced resistance to a number of different diseases. Epidemic diseases only played a secondary role. 'They were the instruments which caused a decline in the population but not the principal cause of this decline'. Recent Swedish research, however, has been critical of this essentially Malthusian viewpoint,[13] and Utterström has stressed the multifarious pattern of causation. 'Lack of food was seldom the sole cause of increases in mortality and far from always the principal cause. Epidemics, whether connected or not with wars and famine, also played a large part. Climate, the standard of housing and hygiene were all of importance'.[14] Nevertheless the possibility that the late eighteenth century was characterised by a Malthusian poverty[15] has not been excluded and no attempt has been made to grade systematically the different causative 'factors' in time and space.

The relationship between economic and demographic fluctuations can be elucidated in a more methodical way by means of regression analysis.[16] Changes in economic variables have been correlated with changes in demographic variables in different models, and the demographic variables have been correlated with each other, both on a national and regional level. If prices are treated as an independent variable, and the crude death rate as a dependent variable, no significant correlation emerges for a one-year lag, which would seem to minimise the importance of harvests in influencing mortality. On the other hand a significant correlation emerges for current year in most regions during the earlier part of this period. The factors which influence the outcome of the harvest but not the harvest itself also determine changes in mortality. Weather conditions contributing to poor harvests also caused endemic diseases such as tuberculosis and influenza to be prevalent and thereby raised overall mortality. This would appear to be a plausible explanation and can be further tested if the crude death rate in the model is substituted by disease-specific mortality of common endemic diseases including influenza, tuberculosis and infirmities of old age.[17] In none of these cases was there a significant correlation for a one-year lag, but a significant correlation emerged for current year. On the other hand mortality from epidemic diseases including smallpox, measles, typhus and dysentery, shows no correlation either for current year or for any of the 'lags', which would indicate that the spread of epidemic disease was not connected with the outcome of the harvest or climatic conditions (further information on disease-specific mortality can be found in Tables 9.27-9.29). Although there may have been a connection between harvests and mortality during an extended series of crop failures, particularly in relation to the mortality-sensitive groups of children and the aged,[18] this does not provide any support for a Malthusian interpretation. Irrespective of regional nutrition levels, such a pattern was necessarily implicit in a pre-industrial society with an undeveloped transport network and inadequate grain storage facilities. However, in the short run the co-variation between harvests and various demographic variables is less marked than initially anticipated.

It is commonly held that crop failures or generally hard years would have an adverse effect on both the rate of marriage and marital fertility. A significant fall in grain prices, on the other hand, inevitably meant that 'boys and girls were ready for the bridal bed and for married couples love began to burn more vigorously'.[19] By employing a similar analytical model, however, with the marriage rate as a dependent variable, such a hypothesis can be accurately tested. In fact the anticipated correlation for a one-year lag is consistently absent, although a tendency to correlate can be discerned. However, for certain regions a significant correlation emerges for a one-year lag between the

crude birth rate (independent variable) and the marriage rate
(dependent) during the earlier part of the period, but not in the later
part. This could be interpreted in such a way that during the earlier
years changes in the availability of homesteads, as a consequence of
mortality changes, also influenced to a large extent variations in the
frequency of marriage. However, the strong growth of the lower classes
changed this pattern, as their marriage decisions were not primarily
influenced by property considerations.

Utterström, however, also argued for a direct relationship between
harvests and marital fertility.[20] Indeed this is not contradicted by a
model with prices as an independent variable and the crude birth rate
as a dependent variable,[21] and for the latter part of this period there is
a significant correlation for a one-year lag. On this basis good harvests
increased marital fertility and poor harvests had the reverse effect.
Utterström has postulated that this is evidence of a planned birth
control, at least in Eastern Sweden.[22] However, it is equally plausible
that factors influencing harvests and mortality may well have
occasioned changes in fecundity. A decline in marital fertility can be
seen not only as a conscious decision to have fewer children, but also
as a biological response to a poorer state of health.

A Malthusian context is also absent within the long-term process
of development. Although little is known concerning the growth in
production during this period, economic development not only meant
increased pauperisation, but also a real deterioration for the masses.
Furthermore if Jörberg's calculations of real wage levels can be taken
as symptomatic of underlying socio-economic conditions, then the
decline in living standards would have already begun in the late 1770s.[23]
However, this trend did not produce a response in the different fertility
variables, which would seem to indicate the operation of preventive
checks, in the form of a lower marriage frequency, higher age at
marriage or lower marital fertility. The increase in poverty, however,
was not due to a shrinking potential of food resources, and may well
have been just as widespread even if population growth had been
significantly lower.

Indeed the relationship between economic and demographic
variables points to totally different factors as 'obstacles'. The crucial
problem was not whether food resources were adequate, but the
non-utilisation of the existing potential. Further studies may well
illuminate institutional factors as important 'obstacles', together with
the nature of the market economy, attitudes to work and other forms
of habit and custom. The implementation of enclosures in Southern

Sweden has also been ascribed to the impact of rapid population growth, which led to a greater pressure on food resources. However, this would seem to be debatable, as enclosures were probably more a response to increased market integration, which brought about rationalisation within the primary sector. It is also important to note that as a consequence of the enclosure movement, land was not given to those who most needed it, but to those who could cultivate it most effectively.[24]

The Period 1810-1890

The period around 1810 can be considered as a turning point in Swedish demographic development. Population growth began to accelerate and although this occurred after the emergence of new regional patterns, it was also accompanied by a new relationship between demographic and economic variables, in both the long- and short-term processes.

A. Mortality

Without doubt the decline in mortality was the most important factor in determining population growth. Nationally the crude death rate fell from c.26 (per 1,000) at the beginning of the period to c.17 (per 1,000) at the end (Table 9.19), with the decline having more or less the same general magnitude in the different geographic regions. Three important patterns of this decline emerge from a closer analysis of age-specific mortality series on a national and regional basis (Tables 9.20-9.26).

1. The decline occurred in the course of a marked regional conformity for all, the mortality series and the relationship between different regions remained unaltered.

2. The decline occurred in the course of a distinct conformity between the different age-specific mortality series.

However, it should be noted that the decline in mortality of different age groups did produce a different pattern of change. The mortality decline of the age group 1-4 years was more rapid than for other groups, while the initial decline in the age group 25-49 years was significantly lower. In spite of this, an approximately similar index level was reached by 1870, largely because of a sudden increase in mortality in the age group 1-4 years during the 1850s, and also because the subsequent decline occurred from a higher mortality level than earlier. This is also related to the accelerated decline in mortality of the age group 25-49 during the same period. In this respect the pattern of decline for infant mortality clearly deviates from that of other age groups, precisely because of its regular and continuous nature in all the geographic regions.

3. The decline seems to begin with a time-lag between infant and child mortality on the one hand, and mortality for the remaining groups on the other. The onset of the decline in the case of the former group can be roughly dated to 1790, with a certain lag in the fall in child mortality in the central Swedish counties. The decline in the case of the latter group, however, did not start until about 1810. However, any generalisations on the basis of these rather uncertain dates must be viewed with caution, as the special conditions of the first decade of the nineteenth century, as a result of war, may have temporarily delayed the mortality decline of higher age groups. In any case a secular decline with marked regional uniformity for the different age groups clearly began towards the end of the eighteenth and beginning of the nineteenth centuries.

This pattern of change is also apparent at a further level of disaggregation. In Scania, for example, the pattern was present not only in manorial and peasant regions of the plains, but also in forest districts irrespective of the different initial levels. It would also have been valuable to have examined mortality decline according to different social groups, in order to assess whether there was a similar homogeneity between different socio-economic groups as there was in the case of geographic regions, or whether there was a tendency towards different lags for different regions. However, the statistical data does not facilitate such an analysis and the few local studies based on church registers do not yet enable one to make effective generalisations. Winberg, however, in his study of Dala, has found that peasant mortality was not significantly lower than that of the poor (*obesuttna*).[25]

The cause of the secular decline in mortality has been widely discussed among Swedish researchers, but no satisfactory answer has yet emerged. For Heckscher, with his Malthusian view, the answer was clear. The decline in mortality was the result of an improved level of nutrition, as the increase in production from the early nineteenth century onwards was more rapid than the growth in population.[26] Other researchers have pinpointed a number of concurring factors: change in climate, in food supply, in the immunological balance, improvements in medicine especially vaccination and the rapid spread of potato cultivation. Surprisingly enough Mckeown has recently accepted Heckscher's original viewpoint, arguing that population growth before the twentieth century was essentially due 'to a decline in

mortality which resulted from improvement in diet. . .through a large
increase of food supply'.[27] An attempt will now be made to examine
the relevance of the different 'factors', particularly in relation to the
contemporary social and economic structure and the established
pattern of the mortality decline.

The Nutrition Factor   It is not enough to note an increase in total
production, as the per capita level was clearly more significant.
Furthermore any per capita increase should not have occurred under a
lopsided income distribution which would reduce the average to a
statistical fiction. Finally the extent of the increase should be such
that it can be reasonably associated with an extensive mortality decline.
As yet these criteria have not been adequately examined. Although total
production clearly rose at a faster pace than previous epochs, was it in
fact more rapid than the rate of population growth? Utterström's view,
despite a certain element of quantification in relation to price and wage
movements, is extremely ambivalent.

> Probably the development in the decades prior to 1850, characterised
> by growing underemployment, resulted in a lower standard of
> foodstuffs, and thereafter an improvement. However, it should be
> noted that potato cultivation resulted in a more even supply of food
> since the population was now less dependent upon the outcome of
> grain harvests. A large increase in the production of spirits does not
> point to a better foodstuffs situation during the 19th century
> compared to the 18th century.[28]

Furthermore Jörberg's studies, based on extensive data, confirm a
smaller decline in national aggregates between 1820 and 1850.[29] On a
regional level the pattern was varied, with a general rise in real wages in
the Western districts, and a downward trend in the East, particularly in
Malmöhus county. If these trends are contrasted with the established
pattern of mortality decline an important contradiction emerges. There
was a slower fall in mortality in regions with rising real wages and vice
versa. If there was an extensive improvement in real wages this would
not have resulted in a declining mortality.
    In the case of the potato, dissemination was rapid. Between 1800-10
and 1820-30 potato output rose six-fold, constituting a per capita
increase from 32 to 174 kgs. Indeed the resultant improvement in the
quality of the average diet meant that changes in real wages were no
longer an effective indicator of shifts in the nutrition level.[30] Two

factors have been particularly emphasised. Firstly, potato cultivation led to a more even supply of food, where the consequences of crop failure were no longer so severe. Secondly, there was a qualitative improvement in diet through the addition of a large quantity of 'protective' food, particularly in the form of vitamin C, which resulted in an improved state of health and greater resistance to infectious diseases and thereby a lower mortality. However, these conclusions cannot be taken for granted. It has yet to be shown that the outcome of the potato and grain harvests did not coincide and there is an equal lack of corroborative evidence to show that an improvement in health does really make the body more resistant to invading micro-organisms. Indeed the protagonists of the potato hypothesis assume the existence of a Malthusian situation in relation to mortality, which was not the case during this period and the breakthrough in potato cultivation occurred some three decades after the downward trend in mortality had set in. Furthermore some time must have elapsed before the 'protective' qualities of the potato could have had an effect on the organisms and thereby on the level of mortality.

b. The Hygiene Factor   Although improvements in personal hygiene, particularly the increased use of soap and cotton underwear, probably contributed to the downward trend in mortality, this factor was not relevant before the mid-nineteenth century.

c. The Medical Factor   Except for smallpox vaccination there were few developments in this sphere which would have influenced the decline in mortality before the end of the century. Nor should the role of vaccination be exaggerated. Although smallpox mortality could be high in occasional years, its average share in total mortality was slight (Tables 9.27-9.29). However, the rapid mortality decline in the smallpox-sensitive age group (1-4 years) after 1810 was probably a consequence of vaccination.

By a process of elimination it can be argued that the long-term fall in mortality during the earlier part of this period was connected with a long-term change in immunological composition, and a new balance between infective micro-organisms and the human host. Indeed the immunological factor is the only one that can be easily associated with the observed homogeneity in the decline in Swedish mortality, which was a secular fall similar to that which can be observed in earlier epoch in the history of Western society. To this extent the beginning of Phase Two characterises more the end of something old, rather than the beginning of something new. It was probably only in the mid-1800s, or perhaps somewhat earlier, that new factors entered the picture and prevented a rise in mortality which in earlier periods had been invariably unavoidable.[31]

B. Fertility (Tables 9.9-9.14)

The rapid growth in population during the earlier part of this period was also connected with a rise in fertility. A rough estimate of the changes which took place is provided by the crude birth rate (Diagram 9.1; Table 9.7). However, this rate is a poor measure of fertility, which can be more effectively studied by reference to the total fertility rate (Table 9.15), where the influence of age structure is clearly less prominent. As far as national figures are concerned, the rise in fertility reached a maximum in the 1820s and 1830s. This was followed by a slight fall in fertility to the 1880s, when a very pronounced decline set in. The table also shows that the national figures incorporate two different patterns of growth: one for East Sweden, with a growth below the national average; and one for other regions, with a growth considerably above the average figure. After the Great Emigration of the 1880s, however, it is important to note that this difference is eliminated and the secular decline in fertility continued on the whole homogeneously for the different regions of Sweden. Noticeable changes also occurred within these two broad patterns influenced by regional factors.

The changes in total fertility are reflected, on the whole, in the changes in the marriage rate (Table 9.1) and thereby also in the marriage frequency. The marital rates observed for the different regions during the 1820s are the highest for the whole period between 1750 and 1930 (Table III). In relation to the decline, it can be noted that it does not come to a standstill when the earlier level is once again reached, but continues to a considerably lower level. Thus the marriage frequency in 1870, measured as the crude marriage rate for the different regions, is about 25-30 per cent below the eighteenth-century level, and continues to fall until the end of the century. However, the crude marriage rate is not a good indicator in this particular context, as it is influenced by changes in age structure. It nevertheless reveals an indisputable tendency, confirmed by an analysis of the specific marriage rate (Table 9.2), which is even more remarkable given the clear rise in real wages from the end of the 1850s onwards.[32] This phenomenon has a complex background and can be seen as a problem of social transformation where increasingly fewer marriages were contracted on

352 *Sweden*

Diagram 9.1: Crude Birth Rate for the Whole Country (A), Skaraborg, (B) and Sodermanland (C) 1750-1880 (5-Year Moving Averages)

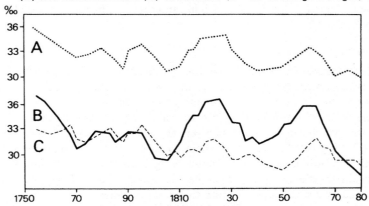

Note: Crude birth rate also includes illegitimate children.

Sources: A. *Historisk Statistik for Sverige. Del 1. Befolkning 1720-1967* (Historical Statistics of Sweden. Part 1. Population 1720-1967), 1969, Table 28, p.88; B. Tabellkommissionen, Folkmangds- och Mortalitetstabeller (Census- and Mortality tables), unpublished; C. Tabelkommissionen, Folkmangds- och Mortalitetstabeller (Census- and Mortality tables), unpublished.

Table III: Marital Rate. Proportion of Persons Married Among Women 15-44 Years

	The whole country[a]	DR	CR	LR	MR	RR	SR	ACR	MR 1	MR 2	LR 1	LR 2
1765-95[b]	480	491	464	434	522	471	467	453	557	602	382	435
1810-35	480	488	492	482	524	511	502	499	562	561	413	479
1835-55	450	462	432	429	461	448	442	440	476	474	359	437
1870	391	477	429	392	403	419	394	409				
1880	399	485	410	392	425	384	340	436				
1900	411	510	402	395	440	379	377	451				
1910	406	485	394	411	443	366	397	458				
1930	424	505	415	441	459	412	434	451				

a. The whole country according to Sundbarg, op.cit., 1909; b. 1765-1855 according Bmr-model.

Source: See Table 9.1.

the basis of the original determining factor behind marriage in a rural society, namely the availability of land.

C. Illegitimacy

In this context the problem of illegitimate births must also be considered (Table 9.8). Illegitimacy increased during the whole period and this has been generally attributed to changing moral values generated by the emergence of a new industrial society. It is perhaps more correct to relate it to the marriage patterns of the old society. In a large number of marriages the child was born before the wedding, and this practice was sanctioned by the Church. 'People did not get married when the child was expected but had a child when they wanted to get married.'[33] The declining marriage frequency after 1830 indicates that there were fewer marriages than before, although it is highly improbable that the old habit of living together in the hope of getting married was given up. The confrontation between old habits and new marriage conditions produced the rise in the number of illegitimate births, not because of a new 'immorality', but because of the continued adherence to the old morality. Significantly the average age of unmarried mothers was roughly the same as that for women at first marriage. Regression analysis also shows that the changes in the crude birth rate exhibit a high covariation with illegitimate births.[34]

D. Age at Marriage (Tables 9.3-9.6)

The problem in this context is to determine to what extent the various marriage rate levels and the changes in these levels reflected (1) changes in the average age at marriage, or (2) changes in the marriage frequency within the traditional age groups, or (3) the effect of both these factors combined. Changes in the age at marriage have generally been taken as a natural starting point for an analysis of the causes behind changes in general fertility, which cannot be attributed to changes in marital fertility, or to structural age factors. This assumption is possibly correct, as Wrigley's study of Colyton has shown large and rapid changes in the age at marriage in a pre-industrial society. On the other hand, it is not clear whether conspicuous changes in the marriage age could really have had any consequences for population growth as some researchers have claimed. It is quite possible, for example, that child bearing at an early age also leads to an earlier termination of fertility.[35]

The second possibility, namely that an increased marriage frequency produced a rise in general fertility, is seldom discussed. This is remarkable, since the number of married women in relation to the total number of women was generally very low during this period. According to one estimate only 30-40 per cent of women of fertile age were married around 1800.[36] Theoretically this would almost certainly allow for a rise in marriage frequency, without producing a fall in the average marriage age. It is perhaps interesting to note that investigations into later periods focus on the second and third possibilities, since the data permit a better specification of the underlying variables in general fertility. Hofstee, for example, has shown that the increase in the Dutch birth rate between 1850 and 1875 was a result of a lower marriage age and an increased marriage frequency within the different age groups.[37]

Using national figures, Sundbärg argued that there was no change in the marriage age for females, although there was a clear rise in the case of men (Table 9.5). Furthermore the observed changes were largely due to shifts in age distribution.[38] How valid is this result on the regional level, where the picture is slightly more composite because of a more pronounced pattern of change in many regions? However, deficiencies in the statistical data before 1830 mean that the present conclusions derived through certain manipulations of age-specific fertility rates can only be regarded as tentative (see note 8). The small changes observed hardly point to any significant change in the long term. Indeed a similar conclusion emerges from an examination of contracted marriages divided according to age groups (Table 9.4),[39] and the same result can be obtained from the table giving an arithmetically calculated marriage age for the latter part of this period (Table 9.6). There were no significant deviations from the eighteenth-century pattern, except for the fact that development was less dispersed between the regions.

By manipulating the age-specific components, a similar result is obtained for the disaggregated Scanian study, where it is possible to test the reliability of the earlier method with data from marriage registers, at least from 1830 onwards. Table IV provides information on the average age at first marriage for the ten-year periods, 1831-40, 1841-50, 1851-60 in the various regions,[40] and shows that there was little regional variation at all. Changes in the age structure pattern have not been considered, as they were similar in all regions. Nevertheless the average age at first marriage rose continuously from 1831 onwards in all the regions investigated and it is quite possible that this reflected significant changes in the age structure of the Swedish population as a whole during this period.

Both these conclusions therefore confirm the results obtained by

Table IV: Mean and Median Age for Brides and Bridegrooms, Where
Neither Partner was Previously Married, in 1830s, 1840s and 1850s
(in Different Regions)

		Number	Mean age Bridegrooms	Brides	Median age Bridegrooms	Brides
MR:1	a	130	27.3	25.0	27	24
	b	222	28.2	26.0	27	25
	c	213	28.9	26.5	28	26
MR:2	a	297	27.4	25.2	27	24
	b	353	28.0	26.1	27	25
	c	403	29.1	26.3	29	26
LR:1	a	143	28.2	26.1	28	25
	b	274	28.3	26.3	27	26
	c	237	29.5	27.0	29	26
LR:2	a	140	28.5	26.8	28	26
	b	186	28.3	26.8	27	26
	c	169	28.1	26.6	27	26
MT	a	258	29.6	26.8	28	26
	b	413	29.5	27.1	28	26
	c	569	31.1	28.2	30	27

Note: a. 1830s; b. 1840s; c. 1850s.
Sources: Vigselböcker (Marriage registers).

the earlier method of calculation and it can be said that the positions
are approximately the same in both series. If this structuring in the
marriage age level is compared with the one obtained earlier for the
marriage rate, the impression is strengthened that there were only very
small variations in the average marriage age both over time and between
regions. Although the marriage rate in the southern regions was
consistently 40-60 per cent higher than that recorded in the peasant
districts of the northern areas, the marriage age was approximately the
same. The higher marriage rate in the former regions was therefore
entirely due to an increased marriage frequency within the earlier age
groups.

It is also possible that the average age at marriage masks significant
variations between different social groups. Winberg, for example, has

shown that higher social groups invariably showed a lower marriage age for the female.[41] Although access to marriage registers is possible from 1830 onwards, the occupational terminology in these registers precludes any meaningful classification. However, by using a much simpler method we have been able to obtain some preliminary results. On the basis of *mantalslangderna* (population registers) married women of fertile age have been classified according to age (in five-year groups) and according to social class. By using sufficient data and by spacing the years of investigation over a period of time, we should be able to say something concerning the marriage age of different groups by comparing the number of married women aged 25-30 years with the total number of married women between 15 and 45 years. If a group had a higher figure relative to another group, this would indicate a lower average marriage age. Although these results are only preliminary, they do show that the average marriage age for peasant women in the southern plains was lower than that for the lower social groups. Furthermore the difference in marriage age for these two categories was only evident in the plain regions. Since we have assumed a constant marriage age for the whole period, our analysis must lead to the conclusion that the female marriage age for the peasant group should have decreased during this period since this group grew more slowly in relation to the lower strata with a higher age at marriage.

E. Marital Fertility (Table 9.16)

The rise in general fertility may have also been conditioned by a rise in marital fertility, although this was clearly not the case in East Sweden where the figures indicate a relative stagnation or even a decline or indeed for the national average. This in turn would have accentuated the regional differences in marital fertility which had already existed in the eighteenth century. However, towards the end of the 1800s marital fertility began to decline generally in Sweden. This trend set in approximately at the same time in all the different counties, irrespective of the existing level of marital fertility. Furthermore the level at which this trend began represented a sort of equilibrium, which had prevailed over a long period of time in the past.[42] If our fertility models are correct, then the origin of this equilibrium could be traced back to the early eighteenth century, having developed from an earlier and generally lower equilibrium with small differences between the various counties. However, disaggregation on a county basis fails to cast any significant light on the changing level of marital fertility, although on a more local basis there would seem to have been considerable differences in the fertility pattern between different subregions. Indeed the Scanian study also points in this direction, with the lowest marital fertility recorded in the peasant districts of the Southern Plain (Table V).

The question then remains as to whether family planning was generally practised, or restricted to certain social groups.[43] The peasant is generally assumed to have practised family limitation in some areas to prevent a far-reaching segmentation of the homestead, and a Dutch author has recently claimed that 'the achievement of and dependence from property whether agrarian or urban, and the social status connected with property created a different style of life which made it meaningful to restrict the number of children'.[44] Krause, on the other hand, has argued that 'most of the evidence suggests that poverty was a major cause of family limitation and that it was the poor who often restricted the size of their families'.[45] However, as far as the Southern Plain was concerned, it would appear that the freehold peasants had a slightly lower marital fertility than the lower classes,[46] and individual studies at the parish level have also shown that some form of birth control was practised, particularly among freehold peasants in certain parts of Sweden.[47] It is too early, however, to make any effective generalisations.

Table V: Marital Fertility Rate (Legitimate Live Births per 1,000 Married Women)

	The whole country[a]	DR	CR	LR	MR	RR	SR	ACR	MR 1	MR 2	LR 1	LR 2
1765-55	285	271	304	302	293	289	333	264	264	289	309	292
1810-35	290	260	321	301	307	298	303	363	283	303	315	280
1835-55	286	264	336	308	304	300	304	346	284	302	348	297
1870-80	302	270	327	304	298	319	318	362				
1881-90	293	263	321	291	281	308	294	356				

Note: a. The whole country according Sundbärg, op.cit., 1907; b. 1765-1865 according Bmr-model.

Source: See Table 9.1.

The Causes of the New Pattern of Fertility (Tables 9.17, 9.18)

What then were the causes of this marked change in regional fertility patterns, and in particular what factors explain the failure of Ostsverige to experience the 'lift' shown in the general fertility of other areas after 1810?[48] The age-specific fertility curves for Södermanland county are almost identical for the four different periods, which clearly emphasises the static position characteristic of this area. The comparative curves for Kristianstad, on the other hand, demonstrate the shift in fertility levels for counties outside Eastern Sweden. The curves for the first periods are almost identical in the same way as the curves for the two last periods are at a different level (Diagrams 9.2 and 9.3). Although it is difficult to generalise on this basis, it is significant that the rapid rise in general fertility in all counties except Södermanland occurred in areas dominated by peasants,[49] whereas Södermanland itself had a marked manorial character. It is also important to note that the increase came about before the start of the enclosure movement.[50] This could have been partly due to the increased marriage frequency, which occurs traditionally after years of war, but this does not explain why the rise was so protracted especially as the harvests were not very favourable. Nor was the age distribution of the population particularly favourable to a high marriage rate. On the other hand the increase could possibly be attributed to the improved feasibility of raising new families as a result of increased potato cultivation, which gave bigger returns per unit of area than other crops. Potatoes grew well on sandy and inferior soil and could be cultivated on recently reclaimed land. It was also well suited for growing on small-holdings and gardens. The crucial point, however, was that agricultural productivity could be raised substantially without resorting to enclosure. The manorial economy was not an institutional barrier to the introduction of the new crop and potato cultivation was as extensive in Söderland as in other areas. The institutional obstacle lay in the fact that the manorial economy did not permit the full realisation of the potential for intensified family raising which potato cultivation facilitated.

Utterström has put forward similar lines of thought. 'Population pressure was strongest in the plains in Eastern Sweden, not because of the inadequacy of food resources there, but because of the difficulties of young people in acquiring houses, farms or other means of gaining an independent livelihood.'[51] Furthermore the steps taken by estate owners in the plains of Central Sweden to introduce wage labour and at the same time to incorporate tenant small-holdings into the demesne 'counteracted any further great increase in population there' particularly after 1820.[52] In relation to the surrounding peasant parishes, the Scanian manorial parishes show the same growth patterns

Diagram 9.2: Södermanland
County. Age-specific Fertility
Rate for the Periods 1780-95,
1800-10, 1815-30 and 1835-50
(per thousand)

Diagram 9.3: Kristianstad
County. Age-specific Fertility
Rate for the Periods 1780-95,
1800-10, 1815-30 and 1835-50
(per thousand)

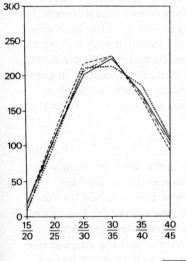
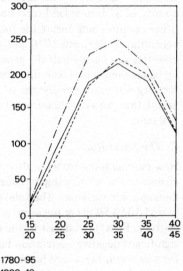

————— 1780-95
----------- 1800-10
— — — 1815-30
················ 1835-50

Note 1: Also includes illegitimate
children.
Note 2: The age group 40-45 years
includes childbearing women
over 45 years.
Sources: Tabellkommissionen,
Folkmangds- och
Mortalitetstabeller (Census- and
Mortality tables), unpublished.

Note 1: Also includes illegitimate
children.
Note 2: The age group 40-45 years
includes childbearing women
over 45 years.
Sources: Tabellkommissionen,
Folkmands- och
Mortalitetstabeller (Census- and
Mortality tables), unpublished.

s the manorial county of Södermanland relative to 'peasant' counties.[53]
urthermore as the institutional framework changed, population growth
ecame more rapid and it is quite possible that these institutional
actors played a central role in the different developments in marital
ertility.

However, it is more difficult to explain the rise in marital fertility in areas outside the Eastern region, where an increase was recorded despite a declining infant mortality rate. This rise possibly reflects a process of social redistribution, with more fertile groups achieving greater predominance (Table 9.31). It was also possibly a consequence of vaccination, which may have resulted in a declining sterility among women.[54] Already by the second half of the eighteenth century the county of Södermanland recorded a lower rate of annual growth than other counties and during the following period the differences were accentuated. Between 1810 and 1865 the annual growth in these two counties was hardly half the general rate. Although other demographic variables should be taken into consideration, the stagnation in general fertility was undoubtedly one of the crucial reasons for the slow population growth rate during this period in the counties around Mälaren.

G. The Short Run

New demographic patterns also emerge in the short run, signifying a change in the relationship between economic fluctuations and demographic variables. The following results are obtained for the period 1810-59 using the same model as was applied for the eighteenth century. First, in contrast to the eighteenth century there was a significant negative correlation between prices and the marriage rate for a one-year lag. Good harvest years generated sufficient income to enable a large number of lower-class workers to marry. However, since a large number of marriages were contracted when the child was under way, it could also mean an increased number of conceptions during the harvest year which were legitimised through marriage in the following year. The reasons here would be the same as those which caused an increase in marital fertility during the harvest year (see below). Secondly, there was no correlation between mortality and marriage. This could not be anticipated through the unchanged mortality structure, but mainly the new social stratum where the peasants were between the crude birth rate and contemporary price levels, indicating greater co-variation between changes in marital fertility and changes in the harvests than had been evident earlier. Here again it is questionable whether this was an expression of changes in fecundity, or a form of conscious birth control, although Carlsson using national data and more sophisticated methods has claimed that it was due to the latter factor.[55] It is therefore only during this half century that a distinct correlation between harvests and demographic changes finally becomes evident, although it was to be cancelled out again by the later emergence of the new industrial society.

The Period 1890-1913

The third phase of the transition model is characterised by a strong decline in the birth rate mainly due to a decline in marital fertility. The initial onset of this trend can be placed in the 1890s (Tables 9.16-9.18). In examining the causal factors behind this trend, some important conclusions can be drawn from the tables. First, the decline must have begun more or less simultaneously in the different regions, both in rural and urban areas. As regional differences existed in the level of marital fertility in the 1890s, it is clear that the decline occurred from an earlier differentiated regional equilibrium. We can therefore reject a number of 'lag' theories which have been prominent in past research on the demographic transition, including the metropolitan factor, the urban-rural factor and the regional factor. None of these were relevant to Swedish experience. Secondly, there was a marked regional conformity in the decline in fertility. The relative positions at the initial stage were still prevalent at the end of the period under examination. Once the decline was well under way, it was much more rapid in the cities than in other regions, although it is remarkable that there was hardly any difference between Stockholm and the smaller cities. However, this was only the case until 1920 when a clear structural break emerges in the fertility decline in rural areas, thereby implying that the decline was as rapid as in the cities. Disaggregation beyond the county level, however, produces in the initial stage a rather heterogeneous picture, with different patterns of lag between individual sub-regions. This in turn rapidly disappears after 1910. Perhaps fertility decline

> was part of a more general process which 'ironed out' many of the formerly existing local and regional differences, and which first hit the purely local differences, the 'parochial' variation. For a time this levelling effect makes the differences between remote parts of the country rather more visible than before. In this sense we have passed to a regional pattern, which is finally followed by a pattern in which national fertility standards prevail.[56]

Thirdly, there are clear differences in the pattern of change in age-specific fertility between rural and urban areas, although development in both regions is very homogeneous. A clear lag can be observed in rural areas, with the decline beginning in the highest of the two age groups 35-39, 40-44 and subsequently continuing downwards. Only during the final decade of this period did all age groups exhibit a similar pace. The pattern was also different in cities. Except for a certain lag in the lowest age group (15-19), the downward trend was continuous in all age groups. We do not know, however, whether a social class factor is concealed behind this homogeneous decline, nor are there sufficient local studies to permit any generalisations.

The changes which took place around 1900, however, were not confined to the fertility variable, and there were clear structural changes within a large number of different demographic components. The mortality series, for example, show a considerably more rapid decline from 1890 onwards. The marriage rate after a long decline from the 1830s also now exhibited an upward trend and changes in marriage frequency can be linked for the first time to changes in the average age at marriage, which now begins to decline. Similarly there is a clear downward shift in the series for illegitimate births in the average age for unmarried mothers, towards a more 'modern' pattern. We can also observe at this stage a clear connection between high real wages and a large increase in population.

The period around 1900 can be considered with the early 1800s as a turning point in Swedish demographic development. However, the pattern of change to phase three in the transition model appears to have been the result of socio-economic factors to a far greater extent than was the case during the first two phases. A number of possible delay mechanisms, including customs, habits and continuing links to the traditional agrarian way of life, were now simultaneously released as the Swedish economy entered a stage of more rapid growth.

The demographic mechanism has been viewed increasingly as an important explanation of long swings in economic growth. The drastic changes in age structure in Australia in the 1850s, for example, following a big wave of immigration, had direct consequences for subsequent economic growth.[57] It is equally clear that the pattern of demographic change in Sweden after 1810 had a similar 'shock' effect (Table VI). The age group 20-24 increased by roughly 50 per cent within fifteen years and this was probably the most drastic change ever as far as Sweden was concerned.[58] This pattern of change in age structure created a special dynamics of growth and must be taken into account when analysing economic and social developments during the nineteenth century. It can partly be related to a cyclical generation process transferred over from the eighteenth century. High birth rates during the 1720s were also reflected in high birth rates during the early

Figure 9.1: The Division of Sweden into Counties

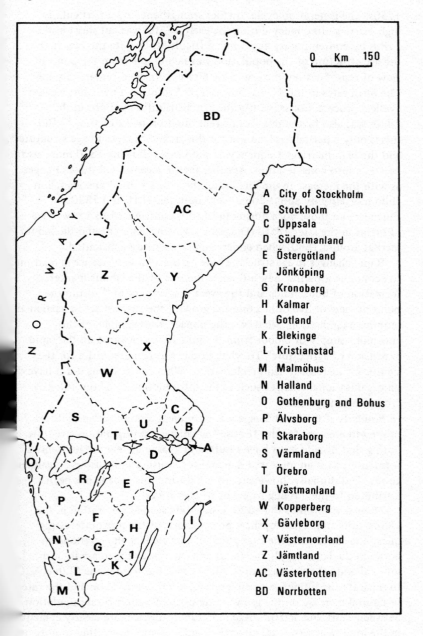

A   City of Stockholm
B   Stockholm
C   Uppsala
D   Södermanland
E   Östergötland
F   Jönköping
G   Kronoberg
H   Kalmar
I   Gotland
K   Blekinge
L   Kristianstad
M   Malmöhus
N   Halland
O   Gothenburg and Bohus
P   Älvsborg
R   Skaraborg
S   Värmland
T   Örebro
U   Västmanland
W   Kopperberg
X   Gävleborg
Y   Västernorrland
Z   Jämtland
AC Västerbotten
BD Norrbotten

1750s. The generation cycle, further strengthened by a particularly
high marriage frequency during the early 1750s, was cut short in the
1780s by contemporary economic difficulties. Despite the fact that
the age structure of the population was favourable from the point of
view of reproduction, the crude birth rates remained remarkably low.
The birth rates in the 1790s, however, did result in a new, but weaker
cyclical process. Consequently the age distribution pattern in the
1820s was also favourable from a reproduction point of view.[59] But
this is only a partial explanation for the drastic changes in age structure
and the high marriage frequency of the years following 1810 must also
be taken into consideration. Another factor accentuated these changes,
as with the increase in the birth rate, there was a simultaneous fall in
child mortality by about 20 per cent between 1810 and 1830.
Furthermore those born during the 1820s contributed to a new wave
of births in the later 1850s (Diagram 9.4), who later entered the labour
market around 1880, when emigration was already substantial.

Rapid changes in age structure have a particular significance in relation
to economic growth: they influence the size of the labour market,
formation of households and the average savings ratio.[60] From the
point of view of Swedish economic growth, the first aspect in particular
requires examination. What was the impact, for example, of the
enormous supply of labour from the mid-1830s onwards on the rapid
expansion of agriculture? To what extent was it prerequisite for the
significant increase in land reclamation? What implications did it have
on organisational changes such as the introduction of labour-intensive
crop rotation systems?

Similarly if the second aspect is examined, a more varied picture
of growth emerges for the 1850s. The changes in population structure
during that decade must have resulted in a large increase in household
formation, with an increased demand for housing and various consumer
goods. Traditionally, however, growth during this decade has been
attributed to the 'driving force' of foreign trade.

The baby boom of the 1820s created its second generation in the
1850s, initiating a new cyclical process. One of the most interesting
questions concerning the first phase of this cycle is the relationship
between the large supply of labour and the marked increase in both
internal and external migration. An attempt has been made (Table 9.30
to separate the influence of emigration, internal migration and the rate
of natural increase on the growth rate of the Swedish rural population
between 1861 and 1910.[61] Age structure influences are clearly evident
in the long swings of total migration and it is also interesting to note

Table VI: Age Group 20-24 Years. Changes between Different Counties.
Index.

	1830 Index 1815 = 100	1845 Index 1830 = 100	1860 Index 1845 = 100
Sodermanland	97	125	95
Kronoberg	106	147	111
Kristianstad	106	145	102
Malmohus	111	140	106
Skaraborg	86	164	97
Varmland	86	184	90
For the whole country	98	148	97

Sources: For the counties see Table 9.1. For the whole country see G. Sundbärg,
Bevölkerungsstatistik Scwedens 1750-1900. (Swedish Population Statistics
1750-1900), 1970, Table 5, p.84.

Diagram 9.4: Percentage Share of Different Age Groups in the Total
Population 1750-1880. The Figures are for Every Fifth Year
Beginning 1750

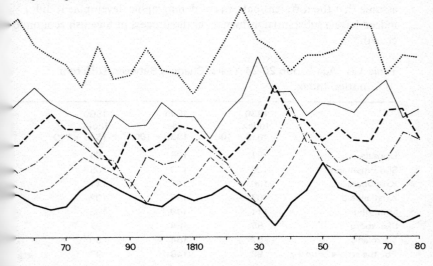

Age group 0-5 years; 2 = 5-10 years; 3 = 10-15 years; 4 = 15-20 years;
5 = 20-25 years; 6 = 25-30 years.

Source: G. Sundbärg, *Bevölkerungsstatistik Scwedens 1750-1900* (Swedish
Population Statistics 1750-1900), 1970, Table 5, p.84.

that the long swings in the 1880s show a distinct co-variation between internal and external migration. However, it cannot be taken for granted that total migration included a large migration to urban areas during years of weak external migration and vice versa.

This analysis has been based on national series and regional differentiations have not been attempted. However, the regional pattern of change observed in the case of the fertility rate after 1810 should have resulted in different prerequisites for the beginning of a process of generation cycle. In areas which experienced a large 'lift' in general fertility, the prerequisites for the development of a cyclical generation process must have been considerably greater than in areas where this did not occur (Table VII). Between the years 1830 and 1845, for example, the age group 20-24 years grew twice as fast in Malmöhus county and three times as fast in Skaraborg county as in Södermanland.

These large differences are also clearly indicated in Diagram 9.5 where a curve has been drawn over the age group 20-24 years for Sweden as a whole, and the counties of Södermanland and Skaraborg. Only a detailed regional analysis, however, can provide an answer as to what extent these different development patterns would have influenced regional economic growth. Nevertheless, we can safely assume that the different patterns of demographic development did indeed have a substantial influence on the process of Swedish economic growth.

Table VII: Age Group 20-24 Years. Changes Between Different Counties. Index.

	1830 Index 1815 = 100	1845 Index 1830 = 100	1860 Index 1845 = 100
Uppsala	91	126	95
Södermanland	106	126	105
Kronoberg	106	147	111
Kristianstad	107	145	102
Malmöhus	111	140	106
Skaraborg	85	164	97
Värmland	87	184	90
For the whole country	98	148	97

Sources: For the whole country see G. Sundbärg, Bevölkerungsstatistik Schwedens 1750-1900 (Swedish Population Statistics 1750-1900), 1970, Table 5, p.84.

Diagram 9.5: The Age Group 20-24 Years 1750-1890 for the Whole
Country (A) Skaraborg (B) and Södermanland (C)

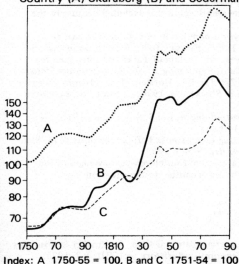

Index: A 1750-55 = 100, B and C 1751-54 = 100

Note: For A the figure is every fifth year beginning 1750; for B and C the
figures are for every third year 1751-72 and for every fifth year 1775-1890.

Sources: A. G. Sundbärg, *Bevölkerungsstatistik Schwedens 1750-1900* (Swedish
Population Statistics 1750-1900), 1970, Table 5, p.84. B. Tabellkommissionen,
Folkmängdstabeller (Census-tables), unpublished. C. Tabellkommissionen,
Folkmängdstabeller (Census-tables), unpublished.

In conclusion it can be argued that one of the most striking features
in the pattern of the demographic transition in Sweden has been the
marked homogeneity between the different regions. Except perhaps
for an accentuated difference between high and low fertility areas
within the period 1810 to 1880, the relationship between the different
counties as far as the different demographic variables were concerned
was surprisingly similar at the beginning of the 1900s, to what it had
been in the latter part of the eighteenth century. The large decline in
both mortality and fertility had acted in an 'epidemic' fashion, in
relation to the pattern of regional dispersion. However, the causes and
the course of the decline in both mortality and fertility are far from
clear. In the case of Sweden, research into this phenomenon is still in
its infancy, and the series we have presented, as well as the conclusions
which have been drawn, must therefore be considered preliminary.

Notes

1. See Table I and following tables.
2. The first decade of the nineteenth century is excluded because of the Napoleonic Wars.
3. G. Utterström, 'Two essays on population in Eighteenth Century Scandinavia', in D.V. Glass and D.E.C. Evarsley (eds), *Population in History*, London, 1965, p.531. For a survey of the data of Tabellkommissionen see *Historisk Statistik för Sverige*, del.I, *Befolkning 1720-1967/Historical Statistics of Sweden*, Part I, *Population 1720-1967*; E. Hofsten, H. Lundström, *Swedish Population History in Urval*, no.8, Stockholm, 1976; G. Fridlizius, *Economy and History*, vol.XVIII, 1, 1975.
4. G. Sundbärg, *Emigrationsutredningen*, Bol.5, Stockholm, 1910, p.4.
5. G. Utterström, op.cit., p.130.
6. G. Sundbärg, 'Fortsatt bidrag till en svensk befolkningsstatistik för åren 1750-1910, I-IV', *Statistisk tidskrift*, 1906, p.226.
7. Birth-marriage rate is the average of four eleven-year averages of the marriage rate related to the birth rate according to the equation

$$\text{Bmr} = \frac{Bt}{\frac{1}{4}(M + M_{t-2} + M_{t-5} + M_{t-10})}$$

where: B is birth rate; M is marriage rate; t is time. See further G. Fridizius, 'Swedish population growth', *Economy and History*, vol.XIII, 1-2, 1975.
8. With the age group 25-30 as the base, the index for every region is calculated from the figures obtained for each period and for each age group. The index number thus obtained for the age group 20-25 years should give a rough idea of the levels in marriage age for different periods and regions. Thus, a high index number should indicate a low marriage age. Similarly a low index number would indicate a high marriage age.
9. G. Sundbärg, op.cit., 1910, pp.4, 9.
10. G. Utterström, *Jordbrukets arbetare*, I, Stockholm, 1957, pp.60-63.
11. L. Herlits, *Jordegendom och ränta*, Lund, 1974, pp.188-90, 361-6; G. Fridlizius in *Economy and History*, vol.XXI, 2, 1978.
12. T. Bengtsson and R. Ohlsson, forthcoming publication.
13. E. Heckscher, *Svenskt arbete och liv*, Stockholm, 1957, p.15d.
14. G. Utterström, 'Some Population Problems in Pre-industrial Sweden', *Scandinavian Economic History Review*, vol.II, 1954, pp.107-65.
15. G. Utterström, 'Sakkunnig utlåtande i samband med tillsättningen av professur i Umeå 1957', unpublished, p.12.
16. Linear regression by means of the least squares method was carried out. Because we were interested in the short-run variations around the trend, this was eliminated in such a way that only the changes from one year to the next were taken into account $(X_t - X_{t-1})$. It should be pointed out that the variables used in the regressions show marked yearly fluctuations around the trend, i.e. there are no positive or negative deviations from the trend that last for more than a couple of years ('sawtooth-pattern').

We also hypothesised that there were lagged relationships between the dependent and independent variables according to the following:

$$Y_{t-1} - Y_{t-1} = f(X_t - X_{t-1}; X_{t-1} - X_{t-2}; X_{t-2} - X_{t-3}).$$

The independent variables (X) were gradually eliminated when they gave no further explanation of the variations in the dependent variable (Y) i.e. the R^2-value remained largely unchanged when a further variable was included. The t statistics have been used to test if the regressions-coefficients were significant at the 0.05 level or not.

The following regressions were run for eight different regions in Sweden and for nine different periods of time:
Harvest = f (prices); infant mortality rate = f (mortality rate age groups 1-5, 25-50, 50 years); prices = f (crude death rate); prices = f (infant mortality rate); prices = f (mortality rate age groups 1-5, 25-50, 50- years); crude death rate = f (marriage rate); mortality rate age group 25-50 = f; (marriage rate); prices = f (crude birth rate); crude birth rate = f (illegitimate birth rate); marriage rate = f (crude birth rate); prices = f (mortality rate smallpox); prices = f (mortality rate measles); prices = f (mortality rate dysentery and typhus); prices = f (mortality rate endemic diseases); prices = (mortality rate infirmities of old age). The prices were fixed in October/November when the harvest result could be taken into consideration. A more detailed account of the methods used and of the results of the calculations will be presented in a forthcoming article.

17. In Table 9.27 we have systematised the mortality due to different diseases. See also A.E. Imhof and I. Lindskog, 'Dödsorsalerna Sydsverige', *Sydsvenska Medicinnistoriska Sällskapet Årsksrift*, 1973, pp.120-43; L. Widén, 'Mortality and causes of death in Sweden during the 18th century', *Statistisk tidskrift*, 1975, 2; A.E. Imhof, *Aspekte der Bevölkerungsentwicklung in den nordischen Ländern 1720-1750*, vol.I, Bern, 1976, pp.489-590. In the statistics, infirmities of old age is a collective name for causes of death in the higher age groups. These must have been largely endemic in character.

18. Although an interesting question, no residual analysis is attempted here to throw light on this problem.

19. Swedish Population Commission 1761, quoted in M.W. Flinn, *British Population Growth 1700-1850*, London, 1970, p.33.

20. G. Utterström, op.cit., 1954, p.158.

21. We consider that changes in the crude birth rate also reflect changes in marital fertility. The number of births following new marriages is too small to have really influenced the changes in the total number of births.

22. G. Utterström, op.cit., 1954, p.158.

23. L. Jörberg, *A History of Prices in Sweden 1732-1914*, 1-2, Lund, 1972, vol.2, pp.334-49.

24. G. Fridlizius, op.cit., 1978, forthcoming.

25. Ch. Winberg, *Folkökning och proletarisering*, Göteborg, 1975, p.263.

26. E. Heckscher, op.cit., 1957.

27. T. McKeown, R.G. Brown and R.G. Record, 'An interpretation of the modern rise of population in Europe', *Population Studies*, 1972, no.3.

28. G. Utterström, op.cit., p.216, §§ 695-6, 708; O. Lundsjö, *Fattigdomen å den svenska landsbygden under 1800-talet*, Stockholm, 1975, p.168.

29. L. Jörberg, op.cit., pp.334-49.

30. *Emigrationsutredningen*, Betänkande, 1913, p.69. The figures are of course very unreliable.

31. G. Fridlizius, op.cit., 1975, 2, p.150.

32. L. Jörberg, op.cit., pp.334-49.

33. A.S. Kälvemark, 'Att vanta barn när man gifter sig', *Historisk tidskrift*, 1977, vol.2, p.195.

34. The different methods of measurement used to determine the 'illegitimate' fertility rate could also have made it difficult to interpret the process. If the illegitimate births are related to the total number of births, we obtain a continuously rising trend for the whole period. If, instead, they are related to

370 *Sweden*

the total number of unmarried females in the fertile age – which is a better
indicator of the changes in the frequency – then the growth decreases from the
1870s and completely stagnates from the 1880s.

35. E.A. Wrigley, 'Family Limitation in Pre-industrial England', in M.D. Drake
(ed.), *Population in Industrialization*, London, 1969, pp.162-5.
36. E. van de Walle, 'Marriage and Marital Fertility', *Daedalus*, Spring 1968,
p.488.
37. E. van de Walle, ibid., p.490.
38. G. Sundbärg, 'Fortsatta bidrag till en svensk befolkningsstatistik for
åren 1750-1900, V-VII', *Statistisk tidskrift*, 1907, pp.206-9.
39. The marriages from this period are divided into four age groups: 25 years,
25-30 years, 35-50 years and over 50 years. On the basis of one-year groups
started in 1860, we can calculate the average marriage age. The lowest age group
is probably too high since the tables include the ages 25-26 years as well. This
has been corrected.
40. Since several marriage series are either lacking or incomplete, our regional
series are based on a smaller number of parishes than for the rest of the
investigation.
41. Ch. Winberg, op.cit., pp.215-17.
42. G. Carlsson, 'The decline of fertility: Innovation or adjustment process',
Lund, 1965, mimeographed.
43. A. Montgomery, *Industrialismens genombrott*, 1947, p.57.
44. W. Fischer, op.cit., *Comparative Studies in Society and History*, p.167.
45. J.T. Krause, 'Neglected Factors in English Industrial Revolution', in
M. Drake (ed.), *Population in Industrialization*, London, 1969, p.106. However,
it must be noted that many of the authors referred to by Krause discuss a
short-term process, namely, changes in fertility in connection with high grain
prices. In such a situation it is not unlikely that the changes should mainly be
attributed to the poorer classes. However, this must, for many reasons, be
separated from the long-term process, namely, family limitation as a normal
habit.
46. G. Fridlizius, op.cit., 1975:II, pp.140-42.
47. Ch. Winberg, op.cit., pp.225-4.
48. G. Utterström, *Befolkningsutveckling och näringsliv efter mitten av
1700-talet in En bok om Mälarlandskapen*, 1953.
49. One exception here is the county of Malmohus which had a rather
special character.
50. Prior to the introduction of the Enclosure Act in 1827, only some parts
of Scania and Skaraborg had been subjected to enclosure.
51. G. Utterström, op.cit., 1954, p.158.
52. G. Utterström, 'Population and Agriculture in Sweden, circa 1700-1830',
Scandinavian Economic History Review, vol.IX, p.194.
53. G. Fridlizius, op.cit., 1978:1.
54. In the developing countries of today, it has been observed that there is
a certain risk of sterility for those who have recovered from smallpox. Thus,
vaccination against smallpox could explain the rise in the marital fertility.
55. G. Carlsson, 'Nineteenth Century Fertility Oscillations', *Population
Sstudies*, vol.24, no.3, 1970, pp.413-22.
56. G. Carlsson, op.cit., 1965, p.18.
57. A.C. Kelley, 'Demographic Cycles and Economic Growth: The Long
Swing Reconsidered', *The Journal of Economic History*, no.4, 1969, pp.633-56.
58. It has been recently stated that the changes in the age structure during
the 1950s have been the most revolutionary changes in Sweden. 'Not even the
large waves of emigration during the 1800s and the beginning of the 1900s have

constituted similar demographic shocks.' This statement should be modified to some extent. It seems as though the early nineteenth century shock was at least as big and had considerably broader effects. C.-A. Nilsson and R. Ohlsson, *Ekonomisk debatt*, 1973:2.

59. On the basis of the national figures, this process of generation cycle has been pointed out by both Sundbärg — 'Emigrationsutredningen', *Betänkande* and G. Utterström, 'Some Population Problems in Pre-industrial Sweden', *The Scandinavian Economic History Review*, 1954. See also L. Jörberg, 'Svensk ekonomi under 100 år', in Bo Söderstrom (ed.), *Svensk ekonomi*, Stockholm, 1970.

60. A.C. Kelley, op.cit.,

61. See G. Fridlizius, *Sydsvensk migration* (forthcoming). This table effectively separates the influence of emigration, internal migration and the rate of natural increase on the Swedish rural population during the period 1861-1910. Here also we have separated the different factors which determine the growth of population on county levels, separating towns and rural areas.

APPENDIX 1

The Sampled Regions

On County Levels

Södermanland: Manorial area in Eastern plains. DR

Kronoberg: Peasant area in forest region. GR.

Kristianstad: Peasant and manorial area in different geographical
regions. LR.

Malmöhus: Peasant and manorial area in different geographical
regions. MR.

Skaraborg: Peasant/dominant/and manorial area in the Western plains,
RR.

Värmland: Peasant area in a forest region. SR. (Up to 1774 Värmland
covered also the county of Närke.)

Västerbotten: Peasant area in the north. ACR. (Up to 1810
Västerbotten covered also the county of Norrbotten.)

Stockholm: A.

DR is included in Eastern Sweden, ACR in the Northern and the rest
of the rural counties in Western Sweden.

Note that for the period 1774-94 the figures are based on a diocese
somewhat larger than a county.

R refers to rural areas and T to the towns. For the period 1751-1810
the towns are included in R. However, for this early period it is of no
importance.

On Parish Levels

This stratified sample is from a larger investigation based on twelve
parish and one town strata in the county of Kristianstad and Malmöhus,
Scanian study.

The sample for each of these strata is comprised of five to nine parishes
and the urban sample four towns.

Here we are restricted to a part of the regions sampled.

The peasant area in the southern plains. 'The southern peasant parishes
MR:1.

The manorial area in the same geographical area. 'The southern manorial parishes.' MR:2.

The peasant area in the northern forest area. 'The northern peasant parishes.' LR:1.

The manorial area in the northern border area. 'The northern manorial parishes.' LR:2.

The towns. MT. Malmö, the biggest of the towns, had 5,000 inhabitants in 1805, 13,000 in 1850 and 61,000 in 1900.

MR:1 and MR:2 were neighbouring regions as were LR:1 and LR:2. The distance between the former and the latter regions was about 100 kilometers.

See further G. Fridlizius, *Economy and History*, vol.XVIII, nos. 1 and 2, 1975. A more thorough investigation of the Swedish population material will be presented in G. Fridlizius-R. Ohlsson, *Regional Population Growth in Sweden 1750-1970* (forthcoming), where also annual figures are given.

Table 9.1: Crude Marriage Rate (per thousand)

	The whole country	DR	GR	LR	MR	RR	SR	ACR	A	MT	MR 1	MR 2	LR 1	LR 2
1751-60	9.0	8.9	–	8.2	9.2	9.1	8.8	8.5	–	–	–	9.1	7.8	8.7
1761-70	8.5	9.1	8.0	7.9	9.1	8.0	8.2	7.6	12.7	–	10.2	9.7	8.0	7.9
1771-80	8.5	8.9	8.2	7.7	9.0	8.4	8.6	7.4	9.2	–	9.8	9.0	6.5	8.2
1781-90	7.9	8.2	7.8	6.6	7.8	7.7	7.8	7.6	7.2	7.6	7.7	9.5	6.2	7.2
1791-1800	8.6	9.1	8.0	7.4	8.9	8.4	8.2	8.1	8.8	9.7	9.7	10.7	6.8	8.0
1801-10	8.3	8.4	8.2	8.0	8.8	8.7	7.7	7.9	8.2	8.1	11.8	9.4	7.2	7.8
1811-20	8.7	8.3	8.2	8.4	8.9	9.5	8.7	7.7	9.1	9.2	9.9	9.4	7.4	8.9
1821-30	8.3	8.5	7.9	7.9	8.7	8.1	8.3	7.9	8.6	7.8	8.6	8.3	7.3	7.7
1831-40	7.1	7.6	6.8	7.0	7.4	7.0	6.4	6.1	7.8	7.2	7.7	7.9	6.1	6.9
1841-50	7.3	7.2	6.8	7.0	7.2	7.5	6.8	7.1	7.3	6.9	8.6	7.5	5.4	7.1
1851-60	7.6	7.7	7.0	6.8	7.0	7.8	7.2	7.4	9.2	5.5	7.3	8.0	6.0.	7.6
1861-70	6.5	7.2	6.3	6.1	6.6	6.5	5.8	6.3	8.1	7.1				
1871-80	6.8	6.9	6.1	6.2	6.9	6.2	5.8	7.2	9.3	8.2				
1881-90	6.3	6.4	5.3	5.6	6.0	5.5	5.1	7.1	8.9	7.4				
1891-1900	5.9	6.1	5.0	5.2	6.0	5.2	5.1	6.7	7.8	7.4				
1901-10	6.0	5.8	5.2	5.5	5.9	5.2	5.4	6.2	8.7	7.6				
1911-20	6.3	6.1	5.4	5.6	5.5	5.6	5.6	6.7	9.1	6.8				
1921-30	6.5	5.8	5.8	5.8	5.9	5.6	6.0	6.7	9.7	7.6				

Note: The figures for the whole country are taken from *Historisk statistik för Sverige*, op.cit., p.89.

Sources: For the period 1751-1859, the figures are derived from *Tabellkommissionen*, Folkmangds- och Mortalitetstabeller (Census- and Mortality tables), unpublished; for the period 1860-1930 from *Bidrag till Sveriges Officiella statistik* and *Sveriges Officiella statistik*. The figures for the counties MR and LR, 1751-1800 are taken from the Scanian sample. Because diocese figures for 1774-94 cover both countries, compared with the figures for the countries between 1751-1773 and partly between

Table 9.2: Specific Marriage Rate (per thousand)[a]

	The whole country	DR	GR	LR	MR	RR	SR	ACR	A	MT	MR 1	MR 2	LR 1	LR 2
1751-60	42.4	41.1	41.2	39.3	47.2	42.5	41.9	39.7	–	–	–	45.6	36.0	40.1
1761-70	40.1	41.3	38.7	37.7	46.3	39.4	40.1	37.2	–	–	54.4	49.9	37.7	35.1
1771-80	39.0	40.8	37.1	35.6	44.8	38.4	39.2	35.3	!	–	50.0	46.1	29.3	37.3
1781-90	35.8	37.8	35.7	30.8	38.4	35.1	35.4	36.1	–	31.4	42.0	47.4	27.9	32.0
1791-1800	39.5	41.5	36.3	32.9	44.3	37.7	38.4	39.4	–	38.0	49.7	54.7	30.9	35.7
1801-10	37.9	40.0	39.0	36.8	41.7	39.5	36.1	38.7	–	33.2	57.2	45.9	32.8	35.8
1811-20	40.9	39.5	40.0	39.6	47.7	44.2	43.2	39.8	–	37.5	51.4	48.8	33.6	42.0
1821-30	39.4	41.4	40.2	40.0	43.7	38.5	42.7	41.4	–	33.6	47.5	44.8	34.5	38.2
1831-40	35.2	38.0	35.7	35.1	38.5	36.1	34.7	33.8	–	30.4	41.5	41.8	29.8	34.5
1841-50	34.4	35.5	33.1	33.9	35.9	36.8	35.6	36.3	–	31.5	41.2	38.1	26.8	34.8
1851-60	35.3	36.7	33.6	31.7	34.7	36.5	35.5	39.1	–	34.2	34.5	39.6	29.4	36.5
1861-70	35.6	35.6	31.7	29.8	33.4	31.8	28.8	32.6	–					

a. Specific marriage rate = (Number of marriages) / (Total number of females 20-50 years) × 1000.

Source: See Table 9.1.

Table 9.3: Age-specific Fertility Rate 20-24 Years in Relation to the Age-specific Fertility Rate 25-29 Years

	The whole country	DR	GR	LR	MR	RR	SR	ACR	A	MT	MR 1	MR 2	LR 1	LR 2
1781-90	58	58	65	50	50	55	62	49	61	–	45	45	69	35
1791-1800	57	57	61	47	54	53	63	51	69	38	39	55	44	42
1801-10	56	56	62	51	50	51	58	54	86	56	52	53	46	43
1811-20	56	54	66	54	54	52	53	48	77	61	45	60	69	45
1821-30	56	55	67	57	49	52	57	55	71	58	54	46	62	50
1831-40	51	53	59	52	52	45	49	47	70	52	45	44	56	42
1841-50	47	51	55	49	54	39	45	45	65	53	39	47	55	45

Source: See Table 9.1.

Table 9.4: First Married Women under 25 Years (per 100)

	The whole country	R	DR	GR	LR	MR	RR	SR	ACR	T	A	DT	MT	OTª	RT
1831-35	54	55	58	66	52	48	43	56	52	37	20	42	36	33	34
1841-45	52	54	56	62	47	53	52	54	53	36	31	45	38	36	31
1851-55	44	46	48	52	44	44	42	45	48	31	28	33	30	31	29
1861-65	41	43	47	47	40	40	37	40	49	32	28	37	37	29	30
1871-75	42	44	51	44	40	39	40	41	46	34	28	37	39	31	29
1881-90	46	48	54	45	39	43	40	42	51	38	35				
1891-1900	46	48	54	43	42	48	39	43	53	40	33				
1901-10	50	52	58	43	48	53	43	47	52	45	39				
1911-20	49	51	59	44	50	53	44	50	52	43	38	51	46	43	37
1921-30	48	51	57	45	51	55	45	51	53	43	36	48	46	42	43

a. OT = the towns in the county of Göteborg and Bohuslän.

Source: See Table 9.1.

Table 9.5: First Married Men under 25 Years (per 100)

	The whole country	R	DR	GR	LR	MR	RR	SR	ACR	T	A	DT	MT	OT[a]	RT
1831-35	40	41	46	54	37	27	40	44	44	28	21	31	26	33	29
1841-45	38	40	40	47	33	30	38	43	39	28	22	28	24	37	32
1851-55	30	31	33	36	24	24	30	31	36	21	17	25	19	20	24

a. OT = the towns in the county of Göteborg and Bohuslän.

Source: See Table 9.1

Table 9.6: Average First Marriage Age for Females, 1861, 70 and 90

	The whole country	DR	GR	LR	MR	RR	SR	ACR	A	MT	RT
1861	27.5	26.4	27.3	27.7	27.7	27.8	27.8	26.5	30.2	27.7	29.6
1870	27.4	26.6	27.4	27.8	27.7	28.1	27.9	27.7	29.9	28.0	29.3
1890	26.9	25.7	27.5	27.6	27.2	27.9	27.1	26.4	28.0	26.1	27.8

Source: See Table 9.1.

Table 9.7: Crude Birth Rate (per thousand)

	The whole country	DR	GR	LR	MR	RR	SR	ACR	A	MT	MR 1	MR 2	LR 1	LR 2
1751-60	35.7	32.2	36.4	36.1	37.4	36.9	36.2	39.0	40.5	—	—	37.2	34.3	35.6
1761-70	34.2	33.2	34.0	34.0	36.1	33.7	34.3	41.8	36.5	—	32.5	36.6	33.8	34.3
1771-80	33.0	32.3	33.8	32.5	36.1	32.3	31.1	32.9	28.6	—	32.9	39.0	30.0	34.0
1781-90	32.0	32.1	32.2	30.5	32.8	32.2	33.0	32.5	28.7	37.3	31.9	36.5	27.2	29.6
1791-1800	33.3	32.8	33.4	30.3	35.4	31.7	32.9	38.3	33.1	34.5	30.8	38.6	29.6	27.7
1801-10	30.9	31.4	32.6	30.1	33.3	29.1	31.0	37.9	32.4	30.3	32.5	34.6	28.2	27.1
1811-20	33.3	30.1	35.2	33.2	36.0	34.6	35.0	39.1	34.2	32.5	37.5	37.3	31.8	31.5
1821-30	34.6	32.1	37.0	34.5	36.9	36.1	35.6	44.2	33.0	31.8	36.3	37.0	33.5	32.3
1831-40	31.5	30.3	34.3	32.7	34.7	31.9	31.4	36.0	32.2	30.4	35.0	34.3	32.3	32.3
1841-50	31.1	28.9	33.3	32.9	33.7	32.1	31.9	35.2	32.3	32.5	34.2	34.9	31.0	31.0
1851-60	32.8	29.9	34.2	32.7	33.2	34.8	34.0	36.2	35.5	36.2	31.6	34.7	29.8	32.0
1861-70	31.4	30.9	31.9	30.8	30.8	32.7	31.9	34.4	34.6	34.0				
1871-80	30.5	29.3	30.7	29.1	29.6	28.7	28.9	35.5	32.4	30.7				
1881-90	29.1	28.3	27.9	26.9	27.5	26.3	25.2	35.6	32.4	33.1				
1891-1900	27.1	27.0	25.9	24.5	26.2	23.8	24.2	34.5	26.3	28.4				
1901-10	25.8	24.8	23.9	24.2	25.4	21.1	23.4	32.1	24.1	28.7				
1911-20	22.1	22.0	21.2	23.0	21.8	19.7	20.4	28.9	17.8	22.0				
1921-30	17.5	17.5	17.8	19.2	18.6	17.1	17.6	25.0	12.1	15.3				

Note: See note, Table 1.
Source: See Table 9.1.

Table 9.8: Illegitimate Births (per 100 Live Births)

The whole country	DR	GR	LR	MR	RR	SR	ACR	A	MT	MR 1	MR 2	LR 1	LR 2
1751-60 — 2.4	2.2	1.9	2.1	2.7	1.9	2.4	1.4	10.7	–	3.3	1.3	2.7	1.7
1761-70 — 2.6	2.1	2.0	2.1	2.8	2.0	2.7	1.3	13.3	–	3.4	2.6	2.8	2.0
1771-80 — 2.9	2.7	1.9	2.8	2.9	2.1	3.2	1.9	15.6	–	1.7	2.9	4.1	2.0
1781-90 — 3.9	3.8	2.6	3.5	3.2	2.8	3.9	2.4	20.9	10.1	1.5	2.8	4.8	4.1
1791-1800 — 5.0	5.0	3.3	4.3	4.5	3.2	5.1	3.1	34.0	9.5	2.4	4.0	5.6	3.8
1801-10 — 6.1	5.3	4.0	4.7	5.0	3.5	5.7	4.3	38.7	12.2	2.2	3.5	6.3	4.1
1811-20 — 6.8	6.2	4.3	5.5	5.0	3.8	7.1	4.0	36.3	12.9	2.6	3.6	6.6	5.6
1821-30 — 6.6	6.4	3.6	5.9	5.3	3.5	6.9	4.1	38.0	16.5	3.0	4.9	7.4	6.9
1831-40 — 6.7	5.4	3.9	6.8	5.5	3.5	6.4	3.5	41.4	16.7	3.3	7.1	7.8	6.4
1841-50 — 8.6	7.2	5.3	8.8	7.2	4.9	9.4	4.8	44.3	19.4	4.8	8.1	11.6	10.1
1851-60 — 9.0	8.0	6.4	8.7	6.9	5.4	10.4	4.6	43.9	16.5	5.3	7.1	11.3	9.0
1861-70 — 9.6	8.1	6.6	9.6	8.1	5.2	9.4	5.0	40.2	15.7				
1871-80 — 10.4	8.7	6.9	10.3	8.6	6.1	11.0	5.8	35.6	15.4				
1881-90 — 10.2	8.1	6.2	10.2	8.3	6.5	10.8	4.6	29.0	13.1				
1891-1900 — 10.9	8.8	6.0	10.7	9.3	6.8	10.9	5.1	29.6	15.6				
1901-10 — 12.7	10.3	6.3	11.2	11.0	8.1	12.0	5.3	33.6	18.5				
1911-20 — 15.0	13.2	7.2	13.7	13.7	9.4	13.8	6.7	32.5	21.4				
1921-30 — 15.4	13.2	9.0	14.0	15.6	9.9	15.3	8.8	27.0	20.9				

Note: See note, Table 9.1.
Source: See Table 9.1.

Table 9.9: Age-specific Fertility Rates (per thousand). Age of Mother 15-19 Years.

	The whole country	DR	GR	LR	MR	RR	SR	ACR	A	MT	MR 1	MR 2	LR 1	LR 2
1781-90	21.5	17.3	37.4	9.9	13.9	18.1	29.2	13.2	25.4	–	6.6	17.1	15.4	5.3
1791-1800	19.6	17.2	32.3	10.7	17.0	16.3	34.2	17.0	26.5	16.8	7.6	16.9	12.9	9.1
1801-10	16.2	18.0	25.4	13.6	15.5	10.7	19.3	17.5	39.0	25.5	17.0	16.5	10.9	5.8
1811-20	16.1	13.3	28.6	15.6	21.1	13.6	17.6	13.2	30.1	21.0	17.7	21.4	14.8	5.5
1821-30	15.5	11.3	26.7	17.4	15.8	12.6	19.4	14.2	23.5	11.3	11.8	12.7	7.0	8.8
1831-40	10.5	9.2	19.6	11.0	11.8	5.9	10.6	8.9	14.5	7.3	9.2	7.1	11.7	9.1
1841-50	8.1	6.0	14.2	8.8	8.5	5.2	8.2	6.6	11.5	10.0	5.2	7.7	6.6	5.0
1851-60	7.8	5.8	10.7	8.0	6.9	5.4	7.1	6.7	14.2	8.3	1.9	4.8	6.4	4.8
1869-72	8.9	12.1	7.3	5.9	6.8	5.0	5.4	5.7	15.8					
1879-82	10.2	13.0	7.2	6.5	9.2	5.0	5.7	9.3	14.2					
1889-92	11.2	16.9	5.3	7.7	10.8	5.7	6.9	11.1	16.3					
1899-1902	15.3	23.8	7.5	12.8	18.2	7.8	12.4	11.6	18.3					
1909-12	19.2	25.9	9.5	19.7	24.2	13.1	16.8	11.7	24.2					
1919-22	17.4	22.4	10.8	18.6	19.0	15.2	20.7	14.4	16.8					
1929-32	17.8	20.6	13.2	21.0	20.4	16.2	21.4	16.7	13.5					

Note: 1781/84-1929/32 figures for the whole country and 1869/72-1929/32 figures for the counties and A, are taken from
Hofsten-Lundström, op.cit., Tables 2.1 and 6.3-6.9.

Source: See Table 9.1.

Table 9.10: Age-specific Fertility Rate (per thousand). Age of Mother 20-24.

	The whole country	DR	GR	LR	MR	RR	SR	ACR	A	MT	MR 1	MR 2	LR 1	LR 2
1781-90	115	118	142	89	110	103	120	101	87	–	97	117	101	59
1791-1800	123	115	156	84	122	103	134	122	111	72	93	154	81	67
1801-10	114	123	137	93	116	99	118	143	148	90	114	124	82	67
1811-20	118	117	146	113	133	114	124	122	144	116	130	155	130	93
1821-30	129	118	176	135	146	120	140	157	135	115	134	140	130	115
1831-40	114	120	158	119	132	103	115	121	125	96	110	119	121	89
1841-50	98	105	124	108	112	86	108	114	114	95	94	111	109	90
1851-60	98	95	118	100	99	85	104	113	118	98	74	100	90	87
1861-72	102	111	102	85	87	80	86	96	120					
1879-82	106	133	94	89	103	79	83	110	105					
1889-92	108	129	88	89	102	74	87	131	100					
1899-1902	118	144	90	105	125	84	100	135	99					
1909-12	118	147	97	119	129	92	115	113	101					
1919-22	101	124	90	114	108	96	113	125	68					
1929-32	80	86	78	98	80	82	85	102	46					

Note: See note, Table 9.9.

Source: See Table 9.1.

Table 9.11: Age-Specific Fertility Rate (per thousand). Age of Mother 25-29.

	The whole country	DR	GR	LR	MR	RR	SR	ACR	A	MT	MR 1	MR 2	LR 1	LR 2
1781-90	200	202	219	179	222	187	194	207	142	188	215	262	147	167
1791-1800	216	203	254	179	228	196	212	241	160	189	240	280	186	160
1801-10	204	219	221	183	233	195	204	265	172	162	220	232	178	157
1811-20	212	217	220	210	247	219	234	255	186	190	289	260	189	208
1823-30	229	216	263	235	298	233	244	288	190	198	248	302	210	232
1831-40	223	225	270	228	255	228	234	255	178	185	246	271	216	210
1841-50	207	207	225	220	209	248	242	254	176	179	218	238	198	201
1851-60	202	207	214	215	214	205	237	243	176	202	178	237	184	204
1869-72	201	205	202	187	188	191	185	220	172					
1879-82	206	214	215	187	195	190	184	236	175					
1889-92	196	215	198	182	184	167	169	247	153					
1899-1902	194	207	195	187	193	169	176	256	135					
1909-12	175	183	176	187	171	158	171	223	189					
1919-22	141	156	155	172	143	148	152	210	140					
1929-32	100	98	116	127	92	108	101	150	92					

Note: See note, Table 9.9.

Source: See Table 9.1.

Table 9.12: Age-specific Fertility Rate (per thousand). Age of Mother 30-34.

	The whole country	DR	GR	LR	MR	RR	SR	ACR	A	MT	MR 1	MR 2	LR 1	LR 2
1781-90	214	217	229	220	269	228	205	239	154	254	287	277	179	216
1791-1800	234	224	254	226	267	225	220	292	169	231	242	354	209	206
1801-10	218	230	198	205	262	223	212	308	172	164	247	325	187	205
1811-20	229	227	219	234	275	240	244	297	177	170	331	294	205	215
1821-30	246	235	262	253	295	267	259	331	161	201	350	294	231	244
1831-40	240	223	266	257	282	259	248	304	165	195	309	282	227	285
1841-50	236	215	262	255	271	257	266	298	161	196	248	276	240	251
1851-60	235	227	255	251	259	259	258	293	175	216	248	261	223	251
1869-72	226	228	228	225	221	240	216	263	164					
1879-82	229	230	251	233	228	225	214	268	170					
1889-92	214	214	232	205	199	200	196	274	148					
1899-1902	198	189	235	200	187	184	194	277	120					
1909-12	172	127	183	150	118	149	164	247	164					
1919-22	130	126	162	154	122	145	137	217	120					
1929-32	88	79	112	108	77	99	86	143	78					

Note: See note, Table 9.9.

Source: See Table 9.1.

Table 9.13: Age-specific Fertility Rate (per thousand). Age of Mother 35-39.

	The whole country	DR	GR	LR	MR	RR	SR	ACR	A	MT	MR 1	MR 2	LR 1	LR 2
1781-90	168	169	157	196	230	183	167	211	114	157	252	237	159	204
1791-1800	178	177	173	201	209	176	175	237	122	163	227	239	165	177
1801-10	172	169	146	182	210	178	157	273	109	146	200	253	175	182
1811-20	185	159	169	210	224	202	197	256	117	159	214	256	184	207
1821-30	199	184	206	213	235	240	218	274	114	149	257	251	211	207
1831-40	196	190	208	215	228	221	223	254	119	150	229	253	212	234
1841-50	199	186	218	215	228	228	233	253	111	159	238	248	209	215
1851-60	203	182	215	213	222	240	227	258	120	187	243	245	221	212
1869-72	198	188	212	204	200	226	202	240	124					
1879-82	200	187	228	200	195	214	201	246	126					
1889-92	185	175	215	174	167	190	184	256	118					
1899-1902	166	152	204	169	150	170	170	250	89					
1909-12	140	127	183	150	118	149	140	223	124					
1919-22	102	98	136	120	89	113	109	184	87					
1929-32	64	54	84	78	53	73	67	116	52					

Note: See note, Table 9.9.
Source: See Table 9.1.

Table 9.14: Age-specific Fertility Rate (per thousand). Age of mother 40-44.

	The whole country	DR	GR	LR	MR	RR	SR	ACR	A	MT	MR 1	MR 2	LR 1	LR 2
1781-90	130	100	81	118	135	128	120	132	52	107	149	160	105	118
1791-1800	134	107	107	126	123	115	119	173	51	107	140	114	109	108
1801-10	129	88	108	119	131	112	109	195	53	87	128	124	105	101
1811-20	153	90	110	135	133	112	130	151	45	99	137	142	111	137
1821-30	147	106	139	134	147	143	152	152	49	87	152	166	124	130
1831-40	142	109	135	127	136	146	150	147	47	79	132	138	120	135
1841-50	143	112	149	132	141	154	157	153	53	81	143	138	143	136
1851-60	151	113	148	133	137	165	156	162	55	92	137	144	145	121
1869-72	150	114	146	123	117	160	149	164	66					
1879-82	150	114	161	128	116	157	156	186	109					
1889-92	135	109	151	114	99	131	131	175	93					
1899-1902	115	91	137	100	82	114	116	164	87					
1909-12	91	71	114	86	62	170	91	141	70					
1919-22	66	55	87	66	45	65	63	118	45					
1929-32	34	29	46	39	25	39	34	76	23					

Note 1: See note, Table 9.9.   Note 2: Includes childbearing women over 44 years.

Source: See Table 9.1.

Table 9.15: Total Fertility Rate (per hundred)

	The whole country	DR	GR	LR	MR	RR	SR	ACR	A	MT	MR 1	MR 2	LR 1	LR 2
1775-84	453	419	432	423	520	441	437	464	284	–	519	566	361	428
1781-90	413	411	433	406	490	424	418	452	287	353	504	535	352	385
1791-1800	443	422	488	414	483	416	447	541	320	390	475	579	382	364
1801-10	417	424	418	398	484	409	410	601	347	338	463	538	369	359
1811-20	440	412	447	459	517	451	474	547	350	378	560	584	417	433
1821-30	465	435	537	494	569	508	516	608	337	381	577	583	457	469
1831-40	454	438	529	479	523	482	496	545	325	356	518	535	473	481
1841-50	438	416	496	470	485	474	507	540	314	380	473	509	453	449
1851-60	440	415	481	460	469	480	495	538	329	402	441	496	435	440
1869-72	435	428	448	415	410	451	421	495	330					
1879-82	442	445	478	421	424	435	421	528	324					
1889-92	417	429	444	384	382	384	386	547	296					
1899-1902	398	403	434	386	377	364	384	547	250					
1909-12	353	357	389	372	327	333	348	479	220					
1919-22	271	290	319	321	261	290	296	434	139					
1929-32	192	181	223	234	172	207	196	300	95					

Note: See note, Table 9.9.
Source: See Table 9.1.

Table 9.16: The Whole Country, Marital Fertility Rates (Legitimate Live Births per 1,000 Married Women)

Years	Age of mother						Total
	20-24	25-29	30-34	35-39	40-44	45-59	20-44
1751-60	467	402	339	236	128	31	306.0
1761-70	448	381	334	232	124	31	291.3
1771-80	450	359	318	229	127	32	286.1
1781-90	459	362	306	214	116	28	276.5
1791-1800	469	397	337	229	220	29	289.7
1801-10	456	374	307	220	118	27	276.1
1811-20	459	378	319	235	127	26	288.9
1821-30	461	384	325	245	137	27	295.8
1831-40	448	368	310	237	133	24	280.2
1841-50	457	371	317	245	137	23	288.6
1851-60	470	378	327	258	148	25	296.2
1861-70	457	376	321	258	153	25	289.5
1871-80	475	390	333	266	156	25	301.0
1881-90	447	374	322	256	146	23	191.9
1891-1900	462	367	302	239	133	19	276.1

Source: Sundbärg, op.cit., 1907, p.272.

Table 9.17: Age-specific Marital Fertility Rates for the Rural Areas, 1890/91-1930/31

Age	Period	DR	GR	LR	MR	RR	SR	ACR	Total
15-19	1890/91	529	474	648	625	485	514	443	515
	1900/01	539	654	650	512	729	630	569	603
	1910/11	504	640	636	569	654	657	740	609
	1920/11	438	712	529	629	708	642	673	625
	1930/31	632	593	518	448	526	536	588	531
20-24	1890/91	412	448	451	450	475	470	482	446
	1900/01	439	500	494	465	489	467	511	470
	1910/11	394	463	456	423	450	420	488	432
	1920/21	380	489	463	435	449	408	481	423
	1930/31	301	351	329	305	355	310	371	313
25-29	1890/91	330	403	393	371	385	373	454	377
	1900/01	322	417	392	358	383	363	449	378
	1910/11	295	372	358	311	360	326	406	335
	1920/21	196	342	330	308	338	301	390	309
	1930/31	177	247	231	193	240	190	273	210
30-34	1890/91	270	347	314	298	330	320	393	316
	1900/01	255	357	318	283	309	320	384	309
	1910/11	222	329	279	231	280	248	343	268
	1920/21	133	262	248	224	256	226	321	239
	1930/31	121	180	161	139	165	131	197	149
35-39	1890/91	213	294	247	225	274	276	330	256
	1900/01	186	285	242	220	250	250	323	246
	1910/11	166	250	212	174	229	200	285	211
	1920/21	97	209	179	156	187	168	260	180
	1930/31	81	120	103	95	114	109	154	106
40-44	1890/91	120	180	137	123	163	160	195	147
	1900/01	101	168	121	109	142	150	177	135
	1910/11	89	134	109	85	115	112	155	110
	1920/21	50	119	89	71	98	89	150	94
	1930/31	40	58	49	42	56	47	88	52
15-44	1890/91	257	317	277	263	297	296	367	290
	1900/01	240	315	276	262	276	284	358	283
	1910/11	216	287	262	226	255	242	326	254
	1920/21	137	251	234	210	240	247	310	229
	1930/31	124	166	156	137	158	136	201	147

Source: See Table 9.1.

Table 9.18: Age-specific Rates of Marital Fertility for the Towns,
1890/91-1930/31

Age	Period	A	DT	MT	RT	ACT	Total
15-19	1890/91	444	368	591	–	–	469
	1900/01	441	531	660	625	–	586
	1910/11	482	444	585	421	–	585
	1920/21	505	500	584	630	–	612
	1930/31	538	560	480	370	643	535
20-24	1890/91	413	471	432	405	519	430
	1900/01	405	395	455	405	451	444
	1910/11	356	358	420	460	444	401
	1920/21	297	315	394	350	431	364
	1930/31	205	235	242	317	317	249
25-29	1890/91	336	344	361	387	367	362
	1900/01	299	311	345	350	418	340
	1910/11	241	251	281	302	334	282
	1920/21	183	225	244	273	297	236
	1930/31	124	133	148	191	189	147
30-34	1890/91	252	277	294	318	320	284
	1900/01	210	214	256	273	290	252
	1910/11	164	150	203	240	281	204
	1920/21	113	138	165	189	258	159
	1930/31	71	87	93	112	116	92
35-39	1890/91	192	240	251	246	267	220
	1900/01	141	162	183	213	177	182
	1910/11	107	122	139	185	186	143
	1920/21	72	96	104	129	158	107
	1930/31	36	43	54	74	71	53
40-44	1890/91	89	100	111	134	–	113
	1900/01	62	97	74	102	112	87
	1910/11	44	60	64	77	69	67
	1920/21	27	43	48	65	72	47
	1930/31	12	21	22	30	39	21
15-44	1890/91	234	270	266	281	289	262
	1900/01	190	218	245	240	251	235
	1910/11	168	172	207	234	251	202
	1920/21	112	145	159	181	227	157
	1930/31	70	82	95	116	129	92

Source: See Table 9.

Table 9.18. Crude Death Rate (per thousand)

	The whole country	DR	GR	LR	MR	RR	SR	ACR	A	MT	MR 1	MR 2	LR 1	LR 2
1751-60	27.2	23.8	24.4	27.2	28.9	25.1	25.9	24.6	50.0	—	23.5	29.7	24.9	27.8
1761-70	27.6	25.2	25.6	25.6	27.2	27.5	26.8	29.5	47.3	—	22.8	29.1	22.8	28.1
1771-80	28.9	28.0	26.5	26.6	27.3	29.7	29.3	21.3	40.9	—	25.9	32.5	24.3	28.5
1781-90	27.9	26.5	29.9	24.4	26.2	25.4	26.0	24.0	41.7	34.2	23.5	31.5	21.3	24.2
1791-1800	25.4	24.3	23.2	20.9	25.6	25.4	23.3	25.4	39.4	21.9	23.1	31.6	19.3	22.5
1801-10	28.2	25.3	27.3	25.2	25.9	27.9	28.1	29.2	49.6	24.7	23.3	28.5	23.2	23.0
1811-20	25.8	24.3	25.5	23.5	23.3	27.0	23.7	21.3	43.9	23.7	19.9	26.5	22.6	23.9
1821-30	23.6	23.1	23.2	23.9	23.2	23.3	21.1	20.5	44.4	24.4	21.2	28.1	21.9	24.1
1831-40	22.8	21.0	21.4	22.0	23.6	22.5	18.3	20.0	46.1	24.0	20.9	27.3	19.0	21.7
1841-50	20.6	20.8	19.7	19.2	19.2	20.7	17.8	14.3	38.1	24.6	18.1	22.0	17.1	18.4
1851-60	21.7	20.2	19.1	20.2	18.9	22.2	20.4	17.5	41.5	24.2	17.9	20.7	16.8	20.5
1861-70	20.2	20.7	19.8	18.6	18.4	18.5	18.7	20.2	32.0	21.1				
1871-80	18.3	18.8	15.7	17.5	17.6	15.4	15.9	15.6	30.8	20.2				
1881-90	16.9	16.4	16.0	17.1	17.0	14.5	14.1	16.9	22.6	19.3				
1891-1900	16.4	15.5	16.0	17.5	16.6	14.9	15.3	16.5	19.1	16.4				
1901-10	14.9	14.3	15.1	15.8	14.9	14.5	15.3	11.1	15.7	14.1				
1911-20	14.3	13.8	14.6	14.7	14.2	15.0	15.2	14.6	13.9	12.5				
1921-30	12.1	12.2	12.9	12.5	12.1	13.4	13.1	12.1	11.6	10.2				

Note: See note, Table 9.1.
Source: See Table 9.1.

Table 9.20: Infant Death (0-1 Years) per 1,000 Live Births, 1751/60-1929/32

	The whole country	DR	GR	LR	MR	RR	SR	ACR	A	MT	MR 1	MR 2	LR 1	LR 2
1751-60	205	165	190	225	230	162	175	221	395	—	209	271	211	229
1761-70	216	188	225	204	245	197	192	296	374	—	176	275	184	225
1771-80	202	206	198	216	247	209	197	235	382	—	190	293	202	207
1781-90	200	188	189	202	223	177	174	243	354	—	191	266	187	203
1791-1800	196	167	183	173	216	175	158	254	314	198	181	233	164	182
1801-10	199	163	208	181	205	178	162	273	353	181	132	195	167	181
1811-20	183	154	196	166	163	169	151	237	316	153	137	182	136	188
1821-30	167	144	189	161	156	152	125	202	295	152	162	178	146	157
1831-40	167	134	182	155	153	173	131	178	330	187	135	163	143	147
1841-50	153	133	170	138	129	162	122	131	315	169	119	136	124	139
1851-60	146	123	169	135	125	148	119	121	322	141	112	137	123	153
1870-71	139	117	116	103	119	112	89	117	260	116				
1881-82	113	97	117	107	107	100	87	112	178	175				
1889-92	106	100	96	92	98	75	76	116	175	137				
1899-1902	99	91	84	90	93	78	74	108	156	114				
1909-12	72	63	57	74	75	57	55	80	95	95				
1919-22	58	51	51	60	64	51	45	77	53	75				
1929-32	54	50	44	56	44	46	45	69	56	57				

Note 1: Figures for the whole country 1751/60-1851/60 are taken from *Historisk statistik*, op.cit., p.89. Note 2: Data for the whole country, DR, GR, LR, RR, SR, ACR and A, 1889/92-1929/32 are taken from Hofsten-Lundström, op.cit, Tables 7.4-7.8. In these figures the towns are included. However, for these counties it is of no importance.

Table 9.21: Death Rate 1-4 Years, 1751/60-1929/32 (per thousand)

	The whole country	DR	GR	LR	MR	RR	SR	ACR	A	MT	MR 1	MR 2	LR 1	LR 2
1751-60	38.8	28.0	34.5	34.3	40.1	39.2	39.0	35.8	99.8	—	35.6	35.0	30.4	35.9
1761-70	40.0	31.5	30.7	29.2	35.7	39.7	41.5	45.7	83.4	—	28.1	33.2	20.5	34.4
1771-80	46.9	44.5	39.8	33.2	32.3	44.1	49.8	25.1	76.2	—	35.7	51.8	34.7	39.4
1781-90	43.0	37.8	34.5	28.9	34.2	42.1	39.3	29.8	75.9	—	28.1	56.3	23.1	32.6
1791-1800	35.2	31.8	24.9	26.1	33.0	33.3	32.6	32.8	70.8	41.6	25.4	54.1	18.5	30.5
1801-10	37.0	31.0	38.4	31.6	30.7	48.1	41.0	33.8	66.2	28.8	28.9	44.9	29.7	25.8
1811-20	35.1	28.9	32.3	27.5	29.5	48.4	39.6	20.4	59.4	31.7	26.5	38.2	28.6	25.3
1821-30	26.8	26.7	24.6	28.7	29.6	29.7	23.9	18.7	54.6	29.2	27.5	39.8	25.3	23.8
1831-40	25.1	25.7	22.7	25.1	27.6	26.6	19.8	23.1	62.9	32.4	21.2	43.6	18.7	25.3
1841-50	24.0	28.5	20.5	21.4	22.1	23.6	25.0	15.6	59.6	34.3	21.6	30.4	16.2	19.1
1851-60	30.1	21.8	26.1	29.5	33.0	31.0	32.0	27.2	74.7	45.6	28.7	40.4	21.5	26.5
1870-71	22.0	16.6	20.8	16.7	16.6	22.5	18.6	19.4	52.4	22.6				
1881-82	24.9	20.8	19.7	21.2	19.9	20.2	18.7	23.0	44.8	35.6				
1889-92	19.5	17.4	20.4	19.9	23.3	15.5	14.6	17.9	39.8	30.1				
1899-1902	16.3	16.5	13.6	13.7	14.2	11.0	12.1	18.2	28.2	21.4				
1909-12	9.2	7.9	6.4	9.0	8.4	7.4	6.6	8.4	16.4	11.4				
1919-22	7.8	7.3	6.8	7.6	6.3	6.5	3.7	10.0	9.0	6.7				
1929-32	4.1	3.6	3.7	3.4	3.7	3.5	3.4	5.4	4.6	4.0				

Note 1: See note 2, Table 9.20. Note 2: The whole country 1751/60-1851/60 from G. Sundbärg, *Statistisk tidskrift 1905 and 1908*, pp.133-7 and 199-204.

Source: See Table 9.1.

Table 9.22: Death Rate 5-9 Years (per thousand)

	The whole country	DR	GR	LR	MR	RR	SR	ACR	A	MT	MR 1	MR 2	LR 1	LR 2
1751-60	12.6	9.0	13.4	11.7	12.7	12.0	11.7	10.0	24.4	–	10.5	11.1	11.7	14.0
1761-70	13.2	12.0	12.6	10.7	9.3	13.5	12.4	11.7	23.9	–	8.9	9.0	9.6	14.5
1771-80	15.7	14.5	12.7	11.3	9.4	18.7	19.3	7.1	23.0	–	12.0	13.3	12.0	11.8
1781-90	14.0	12.7	11.5	9.8	9.9	14.2	15.6	8.3	20.7	12.9	10.3	17.7	9.7	10.8
1791-1800	10.4	10.9	7.4	6.0	9.1	10.0	11.5	9.1	17.8	13.2	10.8	9.8	5.5	9.2
1801-10	12.1	10.2	8.3	9.8	10.0	14.7	15.8	11.4	17.2	9.2	10.6	11.1	10.8	9.9
1811-20	9.7	9.3	8.3	8.5	8.5	12.5	11.7	4.8	15.0	11.0	11.6	10.1	10.6	8.8
1821-30	7.6	8.0	5.2	8.0	8.6	8.3	7.2	3.8	13.6	11.0	10.7	11.8	6.0	7.1
1831-40	7.5	9.6	4.7	8.0	9.1	7.2	5.7	4.7	15.7	11.9	10.0	14.0	7.4	8.0
1841-50	7.8	9.7	5.6	7.5	9.4	7.3	8.3	3.5	14.0	11.9	10.3	12.2	5.3	6.5
1851-60	10.9	9.6	7.5	10.4	11.0	12.4	13.5	10.2	17.4	11.8	10.2	12.1	6.4	8.6
1870-71	9.1	4.8	6.2	6.6	6.6	6.5	6.2	5.2	11.0	8.2				
1881-82	8.9	9.7	5.2	7.2	8.3	7.2	6.4	9.5	12.2	12.2				
1889-92	6.5	5.5	6.7	7.4	8.1	5.8	4.6	7.0	10.4	7.5				
1899-1902	5.4	5.5	4.5	4.8	5.6	3.6	4.2	7.2	5.6	4.8				
1909-12	3.5	3.0	2.7	3.0	2.7	2.8	2.8	3.0	4.5	2.9				
1919-22	3.0	3.1	2.8	2.6	2.4	2.5	2.6	3.8	3.5	2.0				
1929-32	1.7	1.5	1.5	1.3	1.3	1.4	1.7	2.0	2.0	1.7				

Note 1: See note 2, Table 9.1. Note 2: See note 2, Table 9.21.
Source: See Table 9.1.

Table 9.20. Death rate 10-24 Years (per thousand)

	The whole country	DR	GR	LR	MR	RR	SR	ACR	A	MT	MR 1	MR 2	LR 1	LR 2
1751-60	6.9	6.3	7.7	5.4	6.0	6.2	6.6	7.3	11.9	–	5.3	6.4	5.5	5.6
1761-70	7.0	6.7	6.5	4.3	4.4	6.8	6.2	4.9	12.8	–	3.2	4.9	3.5	5.0
1771-80	8.8	7.8	8.4	7.1	5.5	11.8	10.3	3.5	11.6	–	5.9	5.3	6.1	8.8
1781-90	8.1	7.2	7.8	5.3	6.3	5.6	6.8	5.0	10.8	6.1	5.6	6.1	4.6	5.7
1791-1800	5.8	6.7	5.2	3.9	5.3	5.3	5.8	4.6	10.3	5.4	5.0	7.0	3.7	4.7
1801-10	8.0	7.6	7.2	6.6	7.2	8.0	9.3	7.6	15.5	7.8	6.6	7.7	6.2	5.0
1811-20	6.7	6.6	7.0	5.9	6.2	7.3	6.7	3.9	12.3	5.8	3.9	7.0	5.6	5.2
1821-30	5.5	5.8	5.3	5.3	5.4	5.2	5.1	3.6	11.0	5.5	5.2	6.2	5.4	6.2
1831-40	5.5	5.5	4.4	4.7	5.6	4.8	5.1	3.8	12.2	5.6	6.2	6.3	4.3	4.3
1841-50	5.1	5.9	4.3	4.8	5.3	4.8	4.9	3.5	9.1	6.2	5.0	5.2	3.5	5.3
1851-60	5.9	3.8	4.8	5.3	4.5	6.6	6.0	4.9	9.3	6.1	4.8	4.8	4.1	4.3
1870-71	4.5	4.0	4.1	4.5	4.2	3.6	3.7	3.6	7.8	4.9				
1881-82	4.4	4.2	3.7	4.5	4.5	3.5	3.8	3.9	5.3	5.6				
1889-92	4.1.	4.3	3.6	4.2	4.5	3.1	3.7	4.5	4.4	4.3				
1899-1902	4.4	4.3	4.1	4.2	4.3	3.3	4.1	5.5	4.2	4.1				
1909-12	3.5	3.0	3.1	3.0	2.8	3.0	3.3	4.7	3.6	2.6				
1819-22	3.3	2.8	3.0	2.6	2.2	3.1	3.0	4.7	3.3	2.1				
1829-32	2.3	1.8	2.4	1.7	1.8	2.0	2.5	3.1	2.4	1.6				

Note 1: See note 2, Table 9.20. Note 2: 1881/82-1929/32 death rate 10-19 years. Note 3: See note 2, Table 9.21.
Source: See Table 9.1.

Table 9.24: Death Rate 25-49 Years (per thousand)

The whole country	DR	GR	LR	MR	RR	SR	ACR	A	MT	MR 1	MR 2	LR 1	LR 2
1751-60	13.7	12.1	10.3	10.1	11.9	10.1	11.8	10.2	26.6	–	13.5	12.5	10.6	9.0
1761-70	13.0	12.7	9.6	10.6	10.1	12.5	11.7	8.0	29.4	–	10.0	11.4	9.8	11.6
1771-80	14.4	13.1	10.4	11.6	11.6	13.5	15.1	7.9	24.2	–	10.6	12.0	11.4	11.9
1781-90	13.8	14.4	12.2	11.0	11.3	10.5	11.4	9.1	25.9	–	10.2	13.0	9.4	9.4
1791-1800	11.6	11.7	8.9	7.1	9.4	11.3	10.2	8.0	22.0	12.3	8.2	11.3	6.6	8.3
1801-10	13.9	12.8	10.5	11.7	12.1	13.0	14.6	12.7	32.8	11.8	12.8	13.8	10.3	9.1
1811-20	12.9	13.3	9.8	9.9	10.8	11.9	13.1	8.5	25.8	12.0	7.8	10.7	10.5	9.8
1821-30	12.3	11.3	9.9	9.9	10.0	9.8	12.0	8.8	35.6	13.5	9.1	11.5	9.1	10.9
1831-40	12.9	11.2	9.4	10.9	11.9	11.7	11.1	8.5	35.4	14.2	12.1	14.3	8.3	9.8
1841-50	10.8	10.3	8.4	8.3	9.1	10.1	9.6	7.4	24.3	14.0	8.6	10.4	6.6	7.6
1851-60	10.8	10.3	7.5	8.2	8.4	10.1	9.9	7.5	26.7	13.1	9.1	9.2	6.4	7.6
1870-71	9.5	6.4	7.6	8.0	8.8	7.1	8.2	7.8	19.0	10.4				
1881-82	7.3	6.5	6.5	7.2	7.1	5.8	5.9	6.8	13.2	12.2				
1889-92	7.1	7.4	6.3	5.8	6.0	5.7	6.4	6.9	9.6	8.2				
1899-1902	7.0	6.3	6.3	6.5	5.2	5.7	7.2	8.1	8.9	7.7				
1909-12	6.0	5.2	6.0	5.6	4.8	5.2	5.9	6.5	8.1	6.2				
1919-22	5.6	5.2	5.7	5.2	4.7	5.5	5.5	7.4	6.4	5.1				
1929-32	4.3	3.5	4.5	4.0	3.0	4.0	4.9	5.6	4.4	3.7				

Note1: See note 2, Table 9.20. Note 2: 1881/82-1929/32 death rate 30-39 years. Note 3: See note 2, Table 9.21.
Source: See Table 9.1.

Table 9.25: Death Rate (25-49 Years), Males (per thousand)

	The whole country	DR	GR	LR	MR	RR	SR	ACR	A	MT	MR 1	MR 2	LR 1	LR 2
1751-60	13.5	12.9	10.7	10.1	11.7	10.1	13.0	11.0	31.5	–	11.9	12.0	9.4	9.3
1761-70	14.0	13.5	9.2	11.2	9.1	13.1	12.8	8.0	35.4	–	8.6	10.5	10.8	11.4
1771-80	15.1	13.5	10.0	11.7	11.2	13.7	15.4	7.5	28.6	–	11.2	9.2	11.8	11.7
1781-90	15.5	16.4	12.2	11.3	11.5	10.6	11.6	9.7	30.3	–	10.1	13.1	9.1	10.0
1791-1800	12.2	12.2	8.7	6.5	8.4	11.9	10.4	8.0	25.3	14.4	6.8	11.8	6.1	8.4
1801-10	14.9	13.4	9.9	12.2	12.0	13.9	15.2	12.8	42.8	14.3	14.4	12.0	10.0	8.3
1811-20	14.1	14.6	9.5	10.1	10.8	12.6	13.5	8.4	29.4	14.3	8.5	9.4	10.1	9.6
1821-30	14.2	12.5	9.9	10.1	9.6	10.3	13.2	8.2	50.5	18.7	8.7	11.1	9.6	11.0
1831-40	14.8	12.5	9.2	11.1	11.6	12.8	12.5	8.4	47.3	18.9	11.3	14.3	8.0	10.1
1841-50	12.4	11.5	8.4	8.4	9.2	10.9	10.2	7.6	32.5	17.8	7.6	11.3	7.2	7.6
1851-60	12.0	10.9	7.4	8.3	8.3	10.5	10.9	7.5	35.9	16.0	8.9	8.1	6.3	7.8
1870-71	10.4	8.6	6.0	7.5	8.8	7.4	8.9	7.8	25.0	12.2				

Note: See note 2, Table 9.21.
Source: See Table 9.1.

Table 9.26: Death Rate 25-49 Years, Females (per thousand)

	The whole country	DR	GR	LR	MR	RR	SR	ACR	A	MT	MR 1	MR 2	LR 1	LR 2
1751-60	13.8	11.3	9.9	10.1	12.1	10.0	10.6	9.6	22.4	–	15.5	13.1	11.6	8.7
1761-70	12.1	11.9	9.9	10.0	11.1	11.9	10.7	8.1	23.7	–	11.5	12.4	8.8	11.8
1771-80	13.8	12.8	10.8	11.6	11.8	13.3	14.7	8.2	20.4	–	9.9	14.8	11.1	12.0
1781-90	12.3	12.3	12.2	10.4	11.6	10.4	11.1	8.4	22.1	–	10.3	12.9	9.7	9.7
1791-1800	11.0	11.2	9.1	7.6	10.8	10.7	10.0	7.9	18.5	10.2	9.6	10.7	7.0	8.3
1801-10	12.9	12.3	11.1	11.7	12.1	12.4	14.1	12.5	24.4	9.7	11.1	15.5	10.6	9.8
1811-20	11.7	12.3	10.0	9.7	10.8	11.1	12.7	8.7	21.6	9.9	7.1	12.0	10.9	10.0
1821-30	10.5	9.7	9.8	9.6	10.4	9.3	10.8	8.2	21.7	9.0	9.6	12.0	8.6	10.8
1831-40	11.2	9.9	9.5	10.6	12.1	10.6	9.6	8.5	24.7	10.3	12.9	14.3	8.6	9.5
1841-50	9.3	9.0	8.3	8.2	8.9	9.9	8.7	7.2	17.1	10.8	9.6	9.4	5.9	7.6
1851-60	9.7	9.2	7.5	8.0	8.4	9.6	8.9	7.5	19.0	10.6	9.3	10.3	6.5	7.4
1870-71	8.7	4.1	9.3	8.5	8.8	6.8	7.5	7.9	14.0	8.6				

Note: See note 2, Table 9.21.

Source: See Table 9.1.

Table 9.27: The County of Malmöhus: Crude Death Rate and Mortality from Different Diseases, 1751-1800 (per thousand)

		1	2	3	4	5	6	7	8	9	10	11	12	13
1751	32.4	2.6		0.8	6.7	3.2	1.7	4.3	1.2	0.2	0.5	5.3	5.9	3.0
1752	25.7	0.7		0.3	8.0	2.6	0.9	3.5	0.7	0.9	0.2	3.2	4.7	2.1
1753	26.0	2.4		0.4	5.7	2.8	0.9	3.0	0.8	0.1	0.3	3.7	5.9	2.2
1754	31.4	7.6		0.3	6.9	2.2	0.8	3.0	1.0	0.2	0.5	4.5	4.4	2.3
1755	38.5	7.7		3.5	7.6	3.1	0.8	3.7	0.9	0.2	0.1	5.5	5.4	2.4
1756	33.2	5.8		1.7	7.2	2.9	1.3	3.3	0.7	0.2	0.2	5.0	4.9	2.0
1757	29.5	1.3		0.4	7.8	2.8	1.1	4.2	0.7	0.6	0.2	4.5	5.9	2.6
1758	34.0	4.2		0.2	7.6	2.5	1.1	3.5	0.7	2.8	0.5	5.9	5.0	2.1
1759	26.5	5.1		0.2	5.9	2.4	0.8	2.6	0.6	0.6	0.6	3.7	4.0	1.8
1760	24.6	2.5		0.0	6.5	2.7	0.8	2.1	0.7	0.2	0.7	3.7	4.7	1.7
1761	29.6	5.0		2.2	7.6	2.1	0.5	2.3	0.6	0.3	0.4	3.0	4.7	1.6
1762	31.1	4.4		1.5	8.0	2.5	0.6	3.1	0.7	0.1	0.3	4.8	5.1	1.9
1763	27.3	3.2		0.4	7.2	2.3	0.7	2.9	0.7	0.0	0.2	4.7	5.0	1.9
1764	27.2	2.9		0.6	6.7	2.5	0.7	2.4	0.8	0.0	0.4	4.7	5.5	1.9
1765	28.7	4.5		0.5	6.4	2.5	0.6	3.1	0.8	0.0	0.2	4.8	5.3	2.1
1766	26.4	4.4		0.6	6.2	2.3	0.6	3.0	1.0	0.0	0.2	4.4	3.7	2.3
1767	26.5	4.3		0.4	6.3	2.3	0.5	2.9	0.6	0.1	0.2	4.6	4.3	2.0
1768	29.7	5.7		0.4	7.1	2.1	0.5	4.3	0.5	0.1	0.2	5.3	3.5	2.3
1769	28.9	5.4		0.3	7.2	2.3	0.6	4.4	0.6	0.1	0.1	5.0	2.9	2.3
1770	31.6	7.5		0.3	6.1	3.6	0.6	4.1	0.4	0.2	0.2	6.0	2.6	2.1

Table 9.27 *(contd.)*

		1	2	3	4	5	6	7	8	9	10	11	12	13
1771	35.2	7.6		0.1	5.9	4.5	0.3	4.4	0.2	0.2	1.2	8.6	2.2	2.0
1772	44.9	7.5		0.6	6.3	7.8	0.1	2.4	0.3	1.5	9.2	8.1	1.1	1.4
1773	28.0	3.4		0.3	4.2	4.4	0.1	1.7	0.1	1.3	5.7	5.1	1.7	0.8
1774	21.2	2.8	0.6	0.4	2.1	2.7	1.0	0.2	0.2	2.4	0.9	3.4	4.5	0.4
1775	28.5	2.8	0.4	0.6	4.0	3.1	1.3	0.3	0.4	2.5	1.9	4.7	6.5	0.8
1776	26.2	2.9	0.4	0.3	3.6	3.0	1.3	0.3	0.2	1.4	1.7	5.0	6.1	0.6
1777	28.0	2.7	0.4	0.2	3.4	2.8	1.4	0.4	0.3	1.4	1.9	5.6	7.5	0.8
1778	32.7	3.2	0.6	0.3	5.0	3.1	1.5	0.5	0.3	1.5	2.1	6.0	8.6	0.9
1779	25.6	2.6	0.5	0.2	3.8	2.4	1.4	0.5	0.2	1.1	1.7	4.4	6.8	0.8
1780	22.9	1.8	0.2	0.1	2.5	1.9	1.1	0.5	0.1	0.5	0.9	7.4	5.9	0.7
1781	23.2	1.8	0.1	0.1	3.1	1.5	1.2	0.6	0.1	0.5	0.9	6.7	6.6	0.8
1782	27.3	2.2	0.1	0.2	4.4	1.3	0.9	1.0	0.1	0.6	1.0	6.9	8.6	1.2
1783	21.5	1.9	0.1	0.1	4.0	1.2	0.6	0.6	0.1	0.4	0.3	1.8	7.4	0.7
1784	36.5	4.4	0.1	0.4	5.8	3.0	0.5	0.5	0.1	3.2	1.7	5.8	11.0	0.6
1785	32.0	3.1	0.4	0.2	5.9	1.1	0.8	0.2	0.1	2.1	1.6	7.0	9.5	0.5
1786	29.0	0.1	0.1	1.2	5.2	2.6	3.0	1.0	1.1	1.1	2.1	4.8	6.7	2.2
1787	22.5	1.3	0.1	0.2	4.2	1.9	2.3	0.8	0.9	0.2	1.1	3.6	5.9	1.8
1788	23.2	1.6	0.1	0.2	4.5	1.5	2.2	0.8	0.9	1.4	0.8	3.2	6.0	1.8
1789	28.9	1.1	0.3	0.6	5.4	2.8	3.0	0.9	1.0	0.9	1.9	3.9	7.1	2.1
1790	28.0	1.7	0.2	2.8	5.0	2.2	2.4	1.0	0.8	0.1	1.0	3.8	7.0	2.0

		1	2	3	4	5	6	7	8	9	10	11	12	13
1791	23.9	1.6	0.5	0.4	4.6	1.9	2.2	0.8	0.8	0.4	0.5	3.7	6.5	1.7
1792	24.8	2.0	1.6	0.3	5.1	1.3	2.1	0.8	0.7	0.2	0.4	3.7	6.6	1.6
1793	23.4	1.7	1.3	0.2	4.4	2.0	2.1	0.7	0.7	0.1	0.4	3.2	6.6	1.5
1794	23.9	2.2	0.3	0.2	4.3	2.0	2.3	0.8	0.8	0.9	0.7	3.9	5.5	1.7
1795	25.6	1.9	0.7	0.2	4.2	1.7	3.3	1.1	0.9	0.1	0.5	4.5	6.5	2.0
1796	23.2	0.6	1.5	1.0	5.0	1.0	1.7	1.0	0.9	0.4	0.6	3.7	5.8	2.0
1797	26.9	0.4	0.5	3.0	6.1	1.3	2.3	1.1	0.7	0.1	0.4	4.1	6.9	2.0
1798	24.6	0.5	0.1	0.6	6.7	1.5	2.2	1.3	0.8	0.1	0.3	4.6	5.9	2.2
1799	31.8	6.3	0.1	0.6	6.5	1.6	2.6	1.3	1.1	0.0	0.4	5.1	6.2	2.5
1800	26.5	1.7	0.1	1.3	5.6	1.4	2.7	1.2	0.9	0.1	0.5	5.1	5.9	2.1

Note 1: 1 = smallpox/1751-1773 + measles; 2 = measles; 3 = whooping cough; 4 = unspecified child disease; 5 = fever fits/influenza; 6 = pains in the chest, 1774-1800 + pneumonic disease; 7 = consumption of the lungs, 1751-1773 + pneumonic disease; 8 = signs of consumption/pine-away disease; 9 = dysentery; 10 = putrid and typhus fever; 11 = infirmities of old age; 12 = the rest; 13 = tuberculosis (according to Sundbärg).

Note 2: In 1774, certain changes occurred in the nomenclature; among other things, the continuity in the groups 6 and 7 was broken. By approximating the mortality from consumption of the lungs in group 7 for the period 1751-73 and subsequently adding together the groups 7 and 8 and mortality in haemoptysis, Sundbärg has estimated tuberculosis mortality for the whole country. See G. Sundbärg, 'Dödligheten av Lungtuberkulos i Sverige 1751-1830' (Mortality in Tuberculosis in Sweden), *Statistisk Tidskrift*, 1905.

Column 13 gives the mortality from tuberculosis according to Sundbärg's method of calculation. However, this method would probably give too low a figure for tuberculosis mortality. A part of the mortality from 'pains in the chest' and 'pneumonic disease' is probably tuberculosis mortality. Cf. Imhof and Lindskog, op.cit., and Widén, op.cit. A view of the long-term changes in tuberculosis mortality would, therefore, be obtained by adding the groups 6, 7 and 8. The unpublished population statistics contain information regarding mortality from different diseases up to 1830. However, we have not dealt with this and the causes of mortality in different age groups here.

Note 3: 1774-1795 diocese figures.

Source: See Table 9.1.

Table 9.28: Mortality from Different Diseases during 10-Year Periods,
1751/60-1791/1800 (per thousand)

	1+2	3	4	5	6+7+8	9	10	11	13
1751-60	4.0	0.8	7.0	2.7	5.1	0.6	0.4	4.5	2.1
1761-70	4.7	0.7	6.9	2.5	4.5	0.1	0.2	4.8	1.9
1771-80	4.0	0.3	4.1	3.6	2.3	1.4	2.7	5.8	0.8
1781-90	2.0	0.6	4.8	1.9	3.0	1.1	1.2	5.1	1.3
1791-1800	2.6	0.8	5.3	1.6	4.2	0.2	0.5	4.2	1.8

Note: See note, Table 9.24.
Source: See Table 9.1.

Table 9.29: Share of Different Diseases in Total Mortality during
10-Year Periods, 1751/60-1791/1800 (per hundred)

	1+2	3	4	5	6+7+8	9	10	11	13
1751-60	13.2	2.6	23.2	8.9	16.9	2.0	1.1	14.9	7.0
1761-70	16.4	2.4	24.0	8.7	15.7	0.3	0.7	16.7	6.6
1771-80	13.7	1.0	14.0	12.3	7.8	4.8	9.2	19.8	2.7
1781-90	7.4	2.2	17.6	7.0	11.0	4.0	4.4	18.8	4.7
1791-1800	10.2	3.1	20.8	6.3	16.5	0.8	2.0	16.5	7.1

Note: See note, Table 9.27.
Source: See Table 9.1.

Table 9.30: Different Components in the Population Growth for the
Rural Areas, 1861-1910 (per thousand)

	1	2	3 (−)	4 (−)	5 (−)
1861	12.4	14.8	2.4	0.6	1.8
1862	11.0	12.9	1.9	0.6	1.3
1863	11.4	14.7	3.3	0.8	2.5
1864	9.8	13.9	4.1	1.3	2.8
1865	8.8	14.2	5.4	1.8	3.6
1866	9.8	14.3	4.5	2.0	2.5
1867	6.8	11.6	4.8	2.4	2.4
1868	−2.1	6.9	9.0	7.6	1.4
1869	−6.0	6.4	12.4	11.4	1.0
1870	0.4	9.4	9.0	5.5	3.5
1871	6.6	13.9	7.3	3.9	3.4
1872	7.9	14.7	6.8	3.4	3.4
1873	8.7	14.7	6.0	2.8	3.2
1874	7.0	11.6	4.6	1.3	3.3
1875	7.6	11.8	4.2	1.7	2.5
1876	7.6	11.7	4.1	1.6	2.5
1877	8.3	12.9	4.6	1.2	3.4
1878	7.7	12.0	4.3	1.6	2.7
1879	7.5	13.9	6.4	3.8	2.6
1880	−1.5	11.8	13.3	10.0	3.3
1881	−3.5	10.9	14.4	10.2	4.2
1882	−3.4	12.4	15.8	11.0	4.8
1883	1.3	11.9	10.6	6.4	4.2
1884	3.3	12.6	9.3	4.3	5.0
1885	2.9	11.7	8.8	4.1	4.7
1886	3.6	13.2	9.6	6.2	3.4
1887	0.4	13.8	13.4	10.3	3.1
1888	−1.3	12.8	14.1	10.1	4.0
1889	0.7	11.9	11.2	6.2	5.0
1890	−1.4	10.9	12.3	6.1	6.2
1891	1.2	11.6	10.4	7.7	2.7
1892	−1.4	9.3	10.7	8.4	2.3
1893	1.2	10.8	9.6	7.2	2.4
1894	7.2	11.0	3.8	0.6	3.2
1895	6.2	12.7	6.5	2.2	4.3
1896	4.8	12.0	7.2	2.6	4.6
1897	5.2	11.7	6.5	1.5	5.0
1898	6.3	12.4	6.1	1.3	4.8
1899	1.7	8.9	7.2	1.9	5.3
1900	5.2	10.3	5.1	2.8	2.3

Table 9.30 *(contd.)*

	1	2	3 (−)	4 (−)	5 (−)
1901	5.2	11.3	6.1	3.4	2.7
1902	1.8	11.2	9.4	6.0	3.4
1903	− 0.6	10.6	11.2	6.4	4.8
1904	3.0	10.5	7.5	2.7	4.8
1905	1.8	10.1	8.3	3.3	5.0
1906	− 1.0	11.2	12.2	3.3	9.0
1907	3.5	10.6	7.1	2.9	4.2
1908	7.1	10.4	3.3	0.5	2.8
1909	8.1	11.8	3.7	2.7	1.0
1910	3.4	10.7	7.7	3.7	3.6

Note: 1 = Total growth; 2 = Natural growth; 3 = Total migration;
   4 = External migration; 5 = Internal migration.
Source: See Table 9.1.

Table 9.31: Main Groups within the Agricultural Population, 1754-1890. Male Family Heads (thousand)

	Peasants		Crofters		Cottagers		Farm labourers		Farm hands and farm sons over 15 years	
	The whole country	MR	The whole country	MR	The whole country	MR	The whole country	MR	The whole country	MR
1754	181.9	9.3	28.7	1.5	20.9	2.8	–	–	154.5	10.1
1772	189.8	9.4	33.5	1.6	28.1	4.7	–	–	179.2	11.8
1810	238.5	10.0	63.6	4.1	40.6	5.6	–	–	199.2	13.6
1820	223.9	10.5	76.6	5.4	43.4	5.6	–	–	220.7	15.6
1830	218.8	11.6	86.1	5.9	54.5	6.2	10.4	0.6	220.9	17.3
1840	216.6	12.5	88.4	5.6	65.2	6.3	14.2	0.8	307.9	23.9
1850	221.2	13.0	96.8	5.8	89.2	7.6	17.0	1.1	344.7	25.3
1860	230.9	14.4	99.8	4.9	96.5	–	23.8	–	320.9	24.1
1870	241.9	16.3	95.4	3.4	101.1	9.8	31.2	2.6	287.8	22.7
1880	256.8	17.0	92.6	3.2	84.0	9.0	34.1	3.6	308.2	22.0
1890	264.8	17.0	81.9	2.3	67.2	7.3	33.7	7.0	344.5	21.8

Source: N. Wohlin, 'Den jordbruksidkande befolkningen i Sverige 1751-1900', in *Emigrationsutredningen*, 1909, Part 9, p.26.

NOTES ON CONTRIBUTORS

Heimold Helczmanovszki — Honorary Professor of Demography at the University of Vienna and Director of the Population Section of the Austrian Central Statistical Office.

Otto Andersen — Associate Professor at the Institute of Statistics, Demographic Section, in the University of Copenhagen.

Etienne van de Walle — Professor at the Population Studies Center, University of Pennsylvania.

Robert Lee — Lecturer in Economic History at the University of Liverpool.

Lorenzo del Panta — Lecturer in the Department of Statistics, University of Florence.

Paul Deprez — Professor of Economics, at the University of Manitoba.

Michael Drake — Dean and Director of Studies in Social Sciences, at the Open University, England.

Nuno Alves Morgado — Director General of the Central Planning Office in Portugal (1968-70), and now part of the staff of the Population Department of the UNO.

Gunnar Fridlizius — Professor of Economic History, Ekonomisk-Historiska Institutionen, University of Lund.

INDEX

Aarhus 103
age at marriage: in Belgium 247; in
  Denmark 90, 106; in France 131;
  in Germany 146; in Italy 201;
  in Norway 296, 309; in Oldenburg
  146; in Portugal 320, 329; in Prussia
  146; in Saxony 146; in Sweden
  353-6; in the Netherlands 249
agriculture: in Austria-Hungary 44;
  increase in output 16; in
  Portugal 323
agricultural crisis: in Denmark
  (1818-28) 93
agricultural depression 19; in the
  Netherlands 251
agricultural export quota: in
  Denmark 93
agricultural improvements: in
  Norway 295
Amsterdam 255
Antwerp 243, 246, 247
Aquisgrana, treaties of 196
Armengaud, André 136, 137
Austin, Lionel 27
Austria-Hungary 14; administrative
  regions 31; death, causes of 54;
  demographic transition 49;
  different nationalities 28, 38-9;
  employment, sectoral distribution
  of 44; fertility 48-52; fertility
  decline 53; industrial centres
  37; industrialisation 59;
  infectious diseases 54; life
  expectancy 54-5; mortality
  48-9; mortality, infant 54;
  mortality tables 54-5; physical
  area 27; population, age
  distribution of 52-3; primary
  sector 44; religious denominations
  40-1; self-employed, proportion
  of 46; total population 31-8;
  wars (1859, 1866) 33

baby boom: in Denmark 90; in France
  (Second Empire) 130; in Sweden
  (1820s) 364; in the Netherlands
  (post 1945) 241
Baden: pregnancy wastage 156;
  smallpox inoculation 151

banking mechanism, insufficient
  development in Portugal 325
Bavaria: birth rate 149; Dachsberg
  census 11; death rate 157;
  grain production 153; illegitimacy
  159; marriage controls 148;
  medical assistants 150;
  quarantine measures 152; sexual
  revolution 21; smallpox
  inoculation 151
Beaujeu-Garnier, Jacqueline 139
Belgium: age structure 239;
  economnomic crises (1840s, 1850s)
  243; fertility index (I_g) 247-8;
  immigration 245; internal
  migration 242-3; life expectancy
  252; mortality, infant 253-4;
  mortality decline 251-2; proportion of women married
  (I_m) 246-7; proportion never
  married 246; secession from
  Dutch Crown 10; total population
  236-7
Bergen 306
Berlin 162, 163
birth rate: in Bavaria 149; in Germany
  148; in Italy 199; in Lombardy 199
  in Norway 290; in Tuscany 199
Blayo, Yves 123
Bochum 162
Bologna 200, 211
Bosnia-Hercegovina: agricultural quota
  45; educational reforms 43-4;
  ethnic composition 39; occupation
  of 30; total population 34; war
  losses 57
Brabant 240, 243, 247, 248, 252
Braunschweig 145; illegitimate
  conceptions 165
breast-feeding: in Germany 155
Breslau 157
Brno 61
Brussels 238, 243
Budapest 35, 37, 41, 56, 59;
  population 61
Buissink, J.D. 249, 251
Burgdörfer F. 161

Calabria 204